KAPLAN PUBLISHING

NOW THIS EXAM KIT COMES WITH
FREE ONLINE ACCESS
TO EXTRA RESOURCES AIMED AT HELPING YOU PASS YOUR EXAMS

IN ADDITION TO THE OFFICIAL QUESTIONS AND ANSWERS IN THIS BOOK, GO ONLINE AND EN-gage WITH:

- Fixed Tests
- Interim Assessments
- Exam paper Guides
- Latest Official ACCA exam questions
- Answers updated to include legislation relevant to next exam
- Frequent and varied new additions to these resources – watch this space!

And you can access all of these extra resources anytime, anywhere using your EN-gage account.

How to access your online resources

If you are a Kaplan Financial tuition, full-time or distance learning student	You will already have an EN-gage account and these extra resources will be available to you online. You do not need to register again, as this process was completed when you enrolled. If having problems accessing online materials, please ask your course administrator.
If you purchased through Kaplan Flexible Learning or via the Kaplan Publishing website	You will automatically receive an e-mail invitation to EN-gage online. Please register your details using this e-mail to gain access to your content. If you do not receive the e-mail or book content, please contact Kaplan Flexible Learning.
If you are already a registered EN-gage user	Go to www.EN-gage.co.uk and log in. Select the 'add a book' feature and enter the ISBN number of this book and the unique pass key at the bottom of this card. Then click 'finished' or 'add another book'. You may add as many books as you have purchased from this screen.
If you are a new EN-gage user	Register at www.EN-gage.co.uk and click on the link contained in the e-mail we sent you to activate your account. Then select the 'add a book' feature, enter the ISBN number of this book and the unique pass key at the bottom of this card. Then click 'finished' or 'add another book'.

Your Code and Information

This code can only be used once for the registration of one book online. This registration will expire when the final sittings for the examinations covered by this book have taken place. Please allow one hour from the time you submitted your book details for us to process your request.

FmE7-GboB-D7El-OblO

For technical support, please visit www.EN-gage.co.uk

Paper F9

Financial Management

EXAM KIT

PUBLISHING

British Library Cataloguing-in-Publication Data

A catalogue record for this book is available from the British Library.

Published by:

Kaplan Publishing UK

Unit 2 The Business Centre

Molly Millar's Lane

Wokingham

Berkshire

RG41 2QZ

ISBN: 978-1-84710-776-3

© Kaplan Financial Limited, 2009.

Printed and bound in Great Britain.

Acknowledgements

The past ACCA examination questions are the copyright of the Association of Chartered Certified Accountants. The original answers to the questions from June 1994 onwards were produced by the examiners themselves and have been adapted by Kaplan Publishing.

We are grateful to the Chartered Institute of Management Accountants and the Institute of Chartered Accountants in England and Wales for permission to reproduce past examination questions. The answers have been prepared by Kaplan Publishing.

CONTENTS

	Page
Index to questions and answers	v
Analysis of past exam papers	x
Exam Technique	xii
Paper specific information	xiii
Kaplan's recommended revision approach	xv
Mathematical tables and formulae sheet	xxiii

Section

		Page
1	Practice questions	1
2	Answers to practice questions	67
3	Pilot paper exam questions	287
4	Answers to pilot paper exam questions	293

 New features in this edition

In addition to providing a wide ranging bank of real past exam questions, we have also included in this edition:

- An analysis of all of the recent new syllabus examination papers.

- Paper specific information and advice on exam technique.

- Our recommended approach to make your revision for this particular subject as effective as possible.

  This includes step by step guidance on how best to use our Kaplan material (Complete text, pocket notes and exam kit) at this stage in your studies.

- Enhanced tutorial answers packed with specific key answer tips, technical tutorial notes and exam technique tips from our experienced tutors.

- Complementary online resources including full tutor debriefs and question assistance to point you in the right direction when you get stuck.

December 2009 – Real examination questions with enhanced tutorial answers

The real December 2009 exam questions with enhanced "walk through answers" and full "tutor debriefs" is available on Kaplan EN-gage at:

www.EN-gage.co.uk

You will find a wealth of other resources to help you with your studies on the following sites:

www.EN-gage.co.uk

www.**acca**global.com/students/

INDEX TO QUESTIONS AND ANSWERS

INTRODUCTION

Past exam questions have been modified (sometimes extensively) to reflect the current F9 syllabus.

KEY TO THE INDEX

PAPER ENHANCEMENTS

We have added the following enhancements to the answers in this exam kit:

Key answer tips

All answers include key answer tips to help your understanding of each question.

Tutorial note

Many answers include more tutorial notes to explain some of the technical points in more detail.

Top tutor tips

For selected questions, we "walk through the answer" giving guidance on how to approach the questions with helpful 'tips from a top tutor', together with technical tutor notes.

These answers are indicated with the "footsteps" icon in the index.

ONLINE ENHANCEMENTS

 Timed question with Online tutor debrief

For selected questions, we recommend that they are to be completed in full exam conditions (i.e. properly timed in a closed book environment).

In addition to the examiner's technical answer, enhanced with key answer tips and tutorial notes in this exam kit, online you can find an answer debrief by a top tutor that:

- works through the question in full

- points out how to approach the question

- shows how to ensure that the easy marks are obtained as quickly as possible, and

- emphasises how to tackle exam questions and exam technique.

These questions are indicated with the "clock" icon in the index.

 Online question assistance

Have you ever looked at a question and not known where to start, or got stuck part way through?

For selected questions, we have produced "Online question assistance" offering different levels of guidance, such as:

- ensuring that you understand the question requirements fully, highlighting key terms and the meaning of the verbs used

- how to read the question proactively, with knowledge of the requirements, to identify the topic areas covered

- assessing the detailed content of the question body, pointing out key information and explaining why it is important

- help in devising a plan of attack

With this assistance, you should then be able to attempt your answer confident that you know what is expected of you.

These questions are indicated with the "signpost" icon in the index.

Online question enhancements and answer debriefs will be available from Spring 2010 on Kaplan EN-gage at:

www.EN-gage.co.uk

FINANCIAL MANAGEMENT FUNCTION

BUSINESS VALUATIONS

RISK MANAGEMENT

ANALYSIS OF PAST PAPERS

The table below summarises the key topics that have been tested in the new syllabus examinations to date.

Note that the references are to the number of the question in this edition of the exam kit, but the Pilot Paper is produced in its original form at the end of the kit and therefore these questions have retained their original numbering in the paper itself.

	Pilot 07	Dec 07	Jun 08	Dec 08	Jun 09
Financial management function					
Nature and purpose of financial management					
Financial objectives and corporate strategy					Q5
Stakeholders and their impact on corporate strategy				Q7	
Not for profits					
Financial management environment					
Economic environment					
Financial markets and institutions					
Working capital management					
Elements and importance (including cash operating cycle)		Q13		Q11	
Inventories		Q13	Q12		
Receivables	Q3	Q13	Q12	Q11	
Payables					
Cash	Q3				Q16
Working capital needs and funding strategies	Q3		Q12		Q16
Investment appraisal					
Appraisal process			Q26		Q23
Non-discounted techniques	Q4				Q23
NPV with tax		Q27			
NPV with tax and inflation	Q4		Q26	Q51	Q23
IRR	Q4	Q27	Q26		Q23
Risk and uncertainty		Q27			
Lease or buy					
Asset replacement					
Capital rationing					

	Pilot 07	Dec 07	Jun 08	Dec 08	Jun 09
Business finance					
Sources of short term finance					
Sources of long term finance		Q39		Q7, Q63	Q5
Internal sources and dividend policy		Q39			
Gearing and capital structure	Q1	Q39		Q11	
Small & medium enterprises					
Cost of capital					
Sources and relative costs			Q58		Q47
Estimating cost of equity	Q1		Q48		
CAPM			Q48	Q51	
Cost of debt	Q1		Q48		
Overall cost of capital	Q1		Q48	Q51	Q47
Gearing theories	Q1				Q47
Impact of cost of capital on investments					
Business valuations					
Nature and purpose of valuation					
Models for valuing shares		Q59	Q58		Q47
Valuing debt and other financial assets		Q59		Q63	
Efficient markets hypothesis		Q59			
Risk management					
Foreign exchange risk	Q2			Q63	
Interest rate risk				Q11	
Forward contracts	Q2				
Money market hedge	Q2			Q63	
Futures	Q2				
Hedging for interest rate risk					

EXAM TECHNIQUE

- Use the allocated **15 minutes reading and planning time** at the beginning of the exam:
  - – read the questions and examination requirements carefully, and
  - – begin planning your answers.

  See the Paper Specific Information for advice on how to use this time for this paper.

- **Divide the time** you spend on questions in proportion to the marks on offer:
  - – there are 1.8 minutes available per mark in the examination
  - – within that, try to allow time at the end of each question to review your answer and address any obvious issues

  Whatever happens, always keep your eye on the clock and **do not over run on any part of any question!**

- Spend the last **five minutes** of the examination:
  - – reading through your answers, and
  - – **making any additions or corrections.**

- If you **get completely stuck** with a question:
  - – leave space in your answer book, and
  - – **return to it later.**

- Stick to the question and **tailor your answer** to what you are asked.
  - – pay particular attention to the verbs in the question.

- If you do not understand what a question is asking, **state your assumptions**.

  Even if you do not answer in precisely the way the examiner hoped, you should be given some credit, if your assumptions are reasonable.

- You should do everything you can to make things easy for the marker.

  The marker will find it easier to identify the points you have made if your **answers are legible**.

- **Written elements of questions**:

  Your answer should have a clear structure

  Be concise.

  It is better to write a little about a lot of different points than a great deal about one or two points.

- **Computations**:

  It is essential to include all your workings in your answers.

  Many computational questions require the use of a standard format:

  e.g. net present values, writing down allowances and cash budgets.

  Be sure you know these formats thoroughly before the exam and use the layouts that you see in the answers given in this book and in model answers.

- **Reports, memos and other documents**:

  Some questions ask you to present your answer in the form of a report, a memo, a letter or other document.

  Make sure that you use the correct format – there could be easy marks to gain here.

PAPER SPECIFIC INFORMATION

THE EXAM

FORMAT OF THE EXAM

4 compulsory questions each of 25 marks which will be **a mixture of computations and discussion**:

Total time allowed: 3 hours plus 15 minutes reading and planning time.
Questions will be drawn evenly from across the whole syllabus.

PASS MARK

The pass mark for all ACCA Qualification examination papers is 50%.

READING AND PLANNING TIME

Remember that all three hour paper based examinations have an additional 15 minutes reading and planning time.

ACCA GUIDANCE

ACCA guidance on the use of this time is as follows:

> This additional time is allowed at the beginning of the examination to allow candidates to read the questions and to begin planning their answers before they start to write in their answer books.
>
> This time should be used to ensure that all the information and, in particular, the exam requirements are properly read and understood.
>
> During this time, candidates may only annotate their question paper. They may not write anything in their answer booklets until told to do so by the invigilator.

KAPLAN GUIDANCE

As all questions are compulsory, there are no decisions to be made about choice of questions, other than in which order you would like to tackle them.

Therefore, in relation to F9, we recommend that you take the following approach with your reading and planning time:

- **Skim through the whole paper**, assessing the level of difficulty of each question.

- **Write down** on the question paper next to the mark allocation **the amount of time you should spend on each part.** Do this for each part of every question.

- **Decide the order** in which you think you will attempt each question:

    This is a personal choice and you have time on the revision phase to try out different approaches, for example, if you sit mock exams.

A common approach is to tackle the question you think is the easiest and you are most comfortable with first. Others may prefer to tackle the longest questions first, or conversely leave them to the last.

Psychologists believe that you usually perform at your best on the second and third question you attempt, once you have settled into the exam, so not tackling the hardest question first may be advisable.

It is usual however that student tackle their least favourite topic and/or the most difficult question in their opinion last.

Whatever you approach, you must make sure that you leave enough time to attempt all questions fully and be very strict with yourself in timing each question.

- **For each question** in turn, read the requirements and then the detail of the question carefully.

  Always read the requirement first as this enables you to **focus on the detail of the question with the specific task in mind**.

  For computational questions:

  Highlight key numbers / information and key words in the question, scribble notes to yourself on the question paper to remember key points in your answer.

  Jot down proformas required if applicable.

  For written questions:

  Plan the key areas to be addressed and your use of titles and sub-titles to enhance your answer.

  For all questions:

  Spot the easy marks to be gained in a question and parts which can be performed independently of the rest of the question. For example, laying out basic proformas correctly, entering discount factors or calculating writing down allowances or attempting the more discussional part of the question. Make sure that you do these parts first when you tackle the question.

  Don't go overboard in terms of planning time on any one question – you need a good measure of the whole paper and a plan for all of the questions at the end of the 15 minutes.

  By covering all questions you can often help yourself as you may find that facts in one question may remind you of things you should put into your answer relating to a different question.

- With your plan of attack in mind, **start answering your chosen question** with your plan to hand, as soon as you are allowed to start.

 Always keep your eye on the clock and do not over run on any part of any question!

DETAILED SYLLABUS

The detailed syllabus and study guide written by the ACCA can be found at:

www.accaglobal.com/students/

KAPLAN'S RECOMMENDED REVISION APPROACH

QUESTION PRACTICE IS THE KEY TO SUCCESS

Success in professional examinations relies upon you acquiring a firm grasp of the required knowledge at the tuition phase. In order to be able to do the questions, knowledge is essential.

However, the difference between success and failure often hinges on your exam technique on the day and making the most of the revision phase of your studies.

The **Kaplan complete text** is the starting point, designed to provide the underpinning knowledge to tackle all questions. However, in the revision phase, pouring over text books is not the answer.

Kaplan Online fixed tests help you consolidate your knowledge and understanding and are a useful tool to check whether you can remember key topic areas.

Kaplan pocket notes are designed to help you quickly revise a topic area, however you then need to practise questions. There is a need to progress to full exam standard questions as soon as possible, and to tie your exam technique and technical knowledge together.

The importance of question practice cannot be over-emphasised.

The recommended approach below is designed by expert tutors in the field, in conjunction with their knowledge of the examiner and their recent real exams.

The approach taken for the fundamental papers is to revise by topic area. However, with the professional stage papers, a multi topic approach is required to answer the scenario based questions.

You need to practice as many questions as possible in the time you have left.

OUR AIM

Our aim is to get you to the stage where you can attempt exam standard questions confidently, to time, in a closed book environment, with no supplementary help (i.e. to simulate the real examination experience).

Practising your exam technique on real past examination questions, in timed conditions, is also vitally important for you to assess your progress and identify areas of weakness that may need more attention in the final run up to the examination.

In order to achieve this we recognise that initially you may feel the need to practise some questions with open book help and exceed the required time.

The approach below shows you which questions you should use to build up to coping with exam standard question practice, and references to the sources of information available should you need to revisit a topic area in more detail.

Remember that in the real examination, all you have to do is:

- attempt all questions required by the exam

- only spend the allotted time on each question, and

- get them at least 50% right!

Try and practice this approach on every question you attempt from now to the real exam.

EXAMINER COMMENTS

We have included the examiner's comments to the specific new syllabus examination questions in this kit for you to see the main pitfalls that students fall into with regard to technical content.

However, too many times in the general section of the report, the examiner comments that students had failed due to:

- "misallocation of time"

- "running out of time" and

- showing signs of "spending too much time on an earlier questions and clearly rushing the answer to a subsequent question".

Good exam technique is vital.

THE KAPLAN PAPER F9 REVISION PLAN

Stage 1: Assess areas of strengths and weaknesses

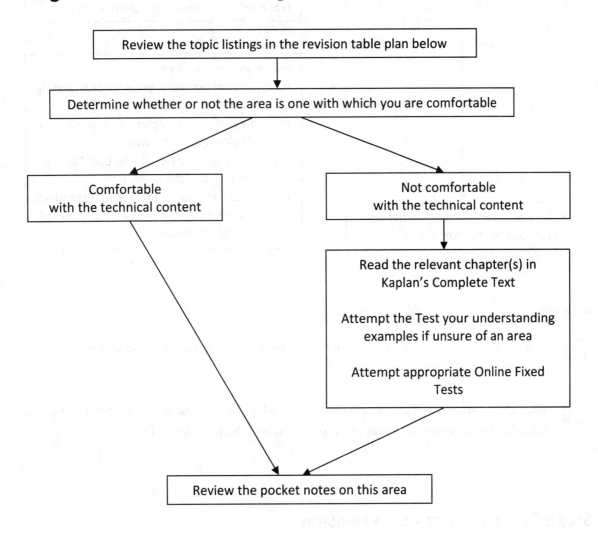

Stage 2: Practice questions

Follow the order of revision of topics as recommended in the revision table plan below and attempt the questions in the order suggested.

Try to avoid referring to text books and notes and the model answer until you have completed your attempt.

Try to answer the question in the allotted time.

Review your attempt with the model answer and assess how much of the answer you achieved in the allocated exam time.

Fill in the self-assessment box below and decide on your best course of action.

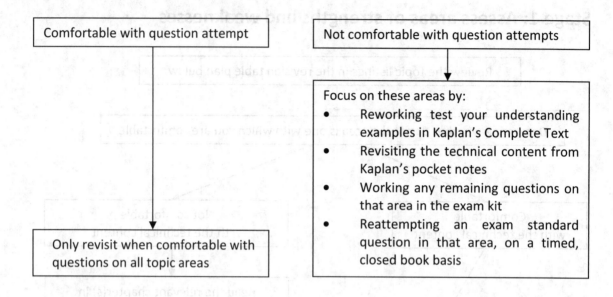

Note that :

 The "footsteps questions" give guidance on exam techniques and how you should have approached the question.

 The "clock questions" have an online debrief where a tutor talks you through the exam technique and approach to that question and works the question in full.

Stage 3:   Final pre-exam revision

We recommend that you **attempt at least one three hour mock examination** containing a set of previously unseen exam standard questions.

It is important that you get a feel for the breadth of coverage of a real exam without advanced knowledge of the topic areas covered – just as you will expect to see on the real exam day.

Ideally this mock should be sat in timed, closed book, real exam conditions and could be:

* a mock examination offered by your tuition provider, and/or

* the pilot paper in the back of this exam kit, and/or

* the last real examination paper (available shortly afterwards on Kaplan EN-gage with "enhanced walk through answers" and a full "tutor debrief").

THE DETAILED REVISION PLAN

Total 34 Questions.

Topic	Complete Text Chapter	Pocket note Chapter	Questions to attempt	Tutor guidance	Date attempted	Self assessment
Investment appraisal	2 & 3	2 & 3	22 23	Start with the basics - remind yourself of the four techniques and ensure you can compare and contrast between them. Start with question 22 before attempting question 23 as an example of a recent past exam question in this area.	7/11/10. Sun.	
– Further aspects of discounted cash flows	4	4	21 28 26 Pilot Q4	A popular exam topic, guaranteed to form part of the exam. There are many questions on this area. Start with questions 21 and 28 which are basic warm up questions covering both inflation and tax. Build up to questions 26 and Q4 from the pilot paper which are more recent past exam questions on this area.		
– Risk and uncertainty	6	6	29 27	This is an aspect that is often examined alongside the more complex areas of discounted cash flow techniques. Question 27 is a good example of how this topic has been examined more recently.		
– Asset investment decisions and capital rationing	5	5	33 35	This is an area that has not been examined in any depth within the recent exam diets. Despite this, it is worth having a quick recap of the techniques using these two questions.		

Topic	Complete Text Chapter	Pocket note Chapter	Questions to attempt	Tutor guidance	Date attempted	Self assessment
Working capital management	7	7	-	Begin by recapping on the key ratio calculations relating to working capital management and the calculation of the cash operating cycle.		
– Receivables and payables	9	9	17	Questions on working capital management will often draw upon several different elements. Question 17 gives a good general introduction to the cash operating cycle before linking in to the management of receivables.		
– Inventory	8	8	13 12	Both of these questions cover many aspects of working capital management and are good illustrations of the way the examiner tends to tackle this topic. You may want to leave part (d) of question 13 until later in your revision.		
– Cash and funding strategies	10	10	Pilot Q3 16	Question 3 from the pilot paper contains good coverage of this chapter. Question 16 covers an area that has not been widely examined under the new syllabus.		
Financial management function	1	1	1	Now is a good point to visit some of the less widely examined areas of the syllabus. Question 1 does not reflect the examiner's style but nevertheless ensures you are able to comment on the current 'hot topics'.		

KAPLAN PUBLISHING

Topic	Complete Text Chapter	Pocket note Chapter	Questions to attempt	Tutor guidance	Date attempted	Self assessment
Sources of finance	14	14	5	Question 5, taken from the June 09 exam, is an excellent illustration of the way the examiner will often pull from more than one syllabus area within his questions.		
Financial ratios	17	17	45 4	Questions involving the calculation and interpretation of financial ratios are very common. You must be able to calculate each of the key ratios as well as appreciate how they interrelate with each other. Both of these questions are good examples.		
The cost of capital	15	15	48 51	This is another popular exam topic. As well as reviewing the complete text and the pocket notes, ensure you download and review the examiner's series of articles relating to CAPM.		
Capital structure	16	16	41 Pilot Q1 50	This is a tricky topic. Be sure to work carefully through the pocket notes, perhaps attempting the test your understandings within the complete text before attempting the exam standard questions.		

Topic	Complete Text Chapter	Pocket note Chapter	Questions to attempt	Tutor guidance	Date attempted	Self assessment
Business valuations and market efficiency	19	19	47 58 7 59	This is another popular exam topic and one which can be easily linked with other areas of the syllabus. You must be able to apply each of the main methods of business valuation and consider the impact that financing may have on a company's valuation.		
Dividend policy	18	18	39	This small topic is often examined alongside business valuations or sources of finance. Question 39 is an excellent illustration.		
Foreign exchange risk	11	11	Pilot Q2 13 (d) 61	Another topic that students often find difficult. Review the illustrations within the complete text but don't neglect the more discussional aspects, which are examined more frequently.		
Interest rate risk	12	12	62 11	This topic has not been extensively tested within the current syllabus exams. Question 11 is a good illustration of the examiner's style.		

Note that not all of the questions are referred to in the programme above. We have recommended an approach to build up from the basic to exam standard questions.

The remaining questions are available in the kit for extra practice for those who require more questions on some areas.

MATHEMATICAL TABLES AND FORMULAE SHEET

Economic order quantity

$$= \sqrt{\frac{2C_oD}{C_H}}$$

Miller-Orr Model

$$\text{Return point} = \text{Lower limit} + (\frac{1}{3} \times \text{spread})$$

$$\text{Spread} = 3 \left(\frac{\frac{3}{4} \times \text{Transaction cost} \times \text{Variance of cash flows}}{\text{Interest rate}} \right)^{\frac{1}{3}}$$

The Capital Asset Pricing Model

$$E(r)_j = R_f + \beta_j (E(r_m) - R_f)$$

The asset beta formula

$$\beta_a = \left(\frac{V_e}{(V_e + V_d(1-T))} \beta_e \right) + \left(\frac{V_d(1-T)}{(V_e + V_d(1-T))} \beta_d \right)$$

The Growth Model

$$P_0 = \frac{Do(1 + g)}{(r_e - g)}$$

Gordon's growth approximation

$$g = br_e$$

The weighted average cost of capital

$$\text{WACC} = \left(\frac{V_e}{V_e + V_d} \right) k_e + \left(\frac{V_d}{V_e + V_d} \right) k_d(1-T)$$

The Fisher formula

$$(1 + i) = (1 + r)(1 + h)$$

Purchasing power parity and interest rate parity

$$S_1 = S_0 \times \frac{(1+h_c)}{(1+h_b)} \qquad F_0 = S_0 \times \frac{(1+i_c)}{(1+i_b)}$$

Present Value Table

Present value of 1 i.e. $(1 + r)^{-n}$

Where   r = discount rate
         n = number of periods until payment

Periods (n)	1%	2%	3%	4%	5%	6%	7%	8%	9%	10%	
1	0.990	0.980	0.971	0.962	0.952	0.943	0.935	0.926	0.917	0.909	1
2	0.980	0.961	0.943	0.925	0.907	0.890	0.873	0.857	0.842	0.826	2
3	0.971	0.942	0.915	0.889	0.864	0.840	0.816	0.794	0.772	0.751	3
4	0.961	0.924	0.888	0.855	0.823	0.792	0.763	0.735	0.708	0.683	4
5	0.951	0.906	0.863	0.822	0.784	0.747	0.713	0.681	0.650	0.621	5
6	0.942	0.888	0.837	0.790	0.746	0.705	0.666	0.630	0.596	0.564	6
7	0.933	0.871	0.813	0.760	0.711	0.665	0.623	0.583	0.547	0.513	7
8	0.923	0.853	0.789	0.731	0.677	0.627	0.582	0.540	0.502	0.467	8
9	0.914	0.837	0.766	0.703	0.645	0.592	0.544	0.500	0.460	0.424	9
10	0.905	0.820	0.744	0.676	0.614	0.558	0.508	0.463	0.422	0.386	10
11	0.896	0.804	0.722	0.650	0.585	0.527	0.475	0.429	0.388	0.350	11
12	0.887	0.788	0.701	0.625	0.557	0.497	0.444	0.397	0.356	0.319	12
13	0.879	0.773	0.681	0.601	0.530	0.469	0.415	0.368	0.326	0.290	13
14	0.870	0.758	0.661	0.577	0.505	0.442	0.388	0.340	0.299	0.263	14
15	0.861	0.743	0.642	0.555	0.481	0.417	0.362	0.315	0.275	0.239	15

(n)	11%	12%	13%	14%	15%	16%	17%	18%	19%	20%	
1	0.901	0.893	0.885	0.877	0.870	0.862	0.855	0.847	0.840	0.833	1
2	0.812	0.797	0.783	0.769	0.756	0.743	0.731	0.718	0.706	0.694	2
3	0.731	0.712	0.693	0.675	0.658	0.641	0.624	0.609	0.593	0.579	3
4	0.659	0.636	0.613	0.592	0.572	0.552	0.534	0.516	0.499	0.482	4
5	0.593	0.567	0.543	0.519	0.497	0.476	0.456	0.437	0.419	0.402	5
6	0.535	0.507	0.480	0.456	0.432	0.410	0.390	0.370	0.352	0.335	6
7	0.482	0.452	0.425	0.400	0.376	0.354	0.333	0.314	0.296	0.279	7
8	0.434	0.404	0.376	0.351	0.327	0.305	0.285	0.266	0.249	0.233	8
9	0.391	0.361	0.333	0.308	0.284	0.263	0.243	0.225	0.209	0.194	9
10	0.352	0.322	0.295	0.270	0.247	0.227	0.208	0.191	0.176	0.162	10
11	0.317	0.287	0.261	0.237	0.215	0.195	0.178	0.162	0.148	0.135	11
12	0.286	0.257	0.231	0.208	0.187	0.168	0.152	0.137	0.124	0.112	12
13	0.258	0.229	0.204	0.182	0.163	0.145	0.130	0.116	0.104	0.093	13
14	0.232	0.205	0.181	0.160	0.141	0.125	0.111	0.099	0.088	0.078	14
15	0.209	0.183	0.160	0.140	0.123	0.108	0.095	0.084	0.074	0.065	15

Annuity Table

Present value of an annuity of 1 i.e. $\dfrac{1-(1+r)^{-n}}{r}$

Where   r = discount rate
           n = number of periods

Periods (n)	1%	2%	3%	4%	5%	6%	7%	8%	9%	10%	
1	0.990	0.980	0.971	0.962	0.952	0.943	0.935	0.926	0.917	0.909	1
2	1.970	1.942	1.913	1.886	1.859	1.833	1.808	1.783	1.759	1.736	2
3	2.941	2.884	2.829	2.775	2.723	2.673	2.624	2.577	2.531	2.487	3
4	3.902	3.808	3.717	3.630	3.546	3.465	3.387	3.312	3.240	3.170	4
5	4.853	4.713	4.580	4.452	4.329	4.212	4.100	3.993	3.890	3.791	5
6	5.795	5.601	5.417	5.242	5.076	4.917	4.767	4.623	4.486	4.355	6
7	6.728	6.472	6.230	6.002	5.786	5.582	5.389	5.206	5.033	4.868	7
8	7.652	7.325	7.020	6.733	6.463	6.210	5.971	5.747	5.535	5.335	8
9	8.566	8.162	7.786	7.435	7.108	6.802	6.515	6.247	5.995	5.759	9
10	9.471	8.983	8.530	8.111	7.722	7.360	7.024	6.710	6.418	6.145	10
11	10.37	9.787	9.253	8.760	8.306	7.887	7.499	7.139	6.805	6.495	11
12	11.26	10.58	9.954	9.385	8.863	8.384	7.943	7.536	7.161	6.814	12
13	12.13	11.35	10.63	9.986	9.394	8.853	8.358	7.904	7.487	7.103	13
14	13.00	12.11	11.30	10.56	9.899	9.295	8.745	8.244	7.786	7.367	14
15	13.87	12.85	11.94	11.12	10.38	9.712	9.108	8.559	8.061	7.606	15

(n)	11%	12%	13%	14%	15%	16%	17%	18%	19%	20%	
1	0.901	0.893	0.885	0.877	0.870	0.862	0.855	0.847	0.840	0.833	1
2	1.713	1.690	1.668	1.647	1.626	1.605	1.585	1.566	1.547	1.528	2
3	2.444	2.402	2.361	2.322	2.283	2.246	2.210	2.174	2.140	2.106	3
4	3.102	3.037	2.974	2.914	2.855	2.798	2.743	2.690	2.639	2.589	4
5	3.696	3.605	3.517	3.433	3.352	3.274	3.199	3.127	3.058	2.991	5
6	4.231	4.111	3.998	3.889	3.784	3.685	3.589	3.498	3.410	3.326	6
7	4.712	4.564	4.423	4.288	4.160	4.039	3.922	3.812	3.706	3.605	7
8	5.146	4.968	4.799	4.639	4.487	4.344	4.207	4.078	3.954	3.837	8
9	5.537	5.328	5.132	4.946	4.772	4.607	4.451	4.303	4.163	4.031	9
10	5.889	5.650	5.426	5.216	5.019	4.833	4.659	4.494	4.339	4.192	10
11	6.207	5.938	5.687	5.453	5.234	5.029	4.836	4.656	4.486	4.327	11
12	6.492	6.194	5.918	5.660	5.421	5.197	4.988	4.793	4.611	4.439	12
13	6.750	6.424	6.122	5.842	5.583	5.342	5.118	4.910	4.715	4.533	13
14	6.982	6.628	6.302	6.002	5.724	5.468	5.229	5.008	4.802	4.611	14
15	7.191	6.811	6.462	6.142	5.847	5.575	5.324	5.092	4.876	4.675	15

Section 1

PRACTICE QUESTIONS

FINANCIAL MANAGEMENT FUNCTION

1 OBJECTIVES
(JUNE 06)

Required:

(a) Discuss, and provide examples of, the types of non-financial, ethical and environmental issues that might influence the objectives of companies. Consider the impact of these non-financial, ethical and environmental issues on the achievement of primary financial objectives such as the maximisation of shareholder wealth **(15 marks)**

(b) Discuss the nature of the financial objectives that may be set in a not-for-profit organisation such as a charity or a hospital. **(10 marks)**

(Total: 25 marks)

2 CCC

(a) CCC is a local government entity. It is financed almost equally by a combination of central government funding and local taxation. The funding from central government is determined largely on a per capita (per head of population) basis, adjusted to reflect the scale of deprivation (or special needs) deemed to exist in CCC's region. A small percentage of its finance comes from the private sector, for example from renting out City Hall for private functions.

CCC's main objectives are:

- to make the region economically prosperous and an attractive place to live and work

- to provide service excellence in health and education for the local community.

DDD is a large listed entity with widespread commercial and geographical interests. For historic reasons, its headquarters are in CCC's region. This is something of an anomaly as most entities of DDD's size would have their HQ in a capital city, or at least a city much larger than where it is.

DDD has one financial objective: To increase shareholder wealth by an average 10% per annum. It also has a series of non-financial objectives that deal with how the entity treats other stakeholders, including the local communities where it operates.

DDD has total net assets of $1.5 billion and a gearing ratio of 45% (debt to debt plus equity), which is typical for its industry. It is currently considering raising a substantial amount of capital to finance an acquisition.

Required:

Discuss the criteria that the two very different entities described above have to consider when setting objectives, recognising the needs of each of their main stakeholder groups. Make some reference in your answer to the consequences of each of them failing to meet its declared objectives. **(13 marks)**

(b) MS is a private entity in a computer-related industry. It has been trading for six years and is managed by its main shareholders, the original founders of the entity. Most of the employees are also shareholders, having been given shares as bonuses. None of the shareholders has attempted to sell shares in the entity, so the problem of placing a value on them has not arisen. Dividends have been paid every year at the rate of 60 cents per share, irrespective of profits. So far, profits have always been sufficient to cover the dividend at least once but never more than twice.

MS is all-equity financed at present although $15 million new finance is likely to be required in the near future to finance expansion. Total net assets as at the last balance sheet date were $45 million.

Required:

Discuss and compare the relationship between dividend policy, investment policy and financing policy in the context of the small entity described above, MS, and DDD, the large listed entity described in part (a). **(12 marks)**

(Total: 25 marks)

3 NEIGHBOURING COUNTRIES

(a) Two neighbouring countries have chosen to organise their electricity supply industries in different ways.

In Country A, electricity supplies are provided by a nationalised industry. In Country B, electricity supplies are provided by a number of private sector companies.

Required:

Explain how the objectives of the nationalised industry in Country A might differ from those of the private sector companies in Country B.

Briefly discuss whether investment planning and appraisal techniques are likely to differ in the nationalised industry and private sector companies. **(10 marks)**

(b) Whilst the financial plans of a business are based on a single objective, it can face a number of constraints that put pressure on the company to address more than one objective simultaneously.

Required:

What types of constraints might a company face when assessing its long-term plans? Specifically refer in your answer to:

(i) **responding to various stakeholder groups, and** **(4 marks)**

(ii)   the difficulties associated with managing organisations with multiple objectives.

(5 marks)

(c)   Financial intermediaries bring together investors and borrowers of funds.

Required:

Explain briefly the role of financial intermediaries.   (6 marks)

(Total: 25 marks)

4   **RZP CO**
    (JUNE 05)

As assistant to the Finance Director of RZP Co, a company that has been listed on the London Stock Market for several years, you are reviewing the draft Annual Report of the company, which contains the following statement made by the chairman:

'This company has consistently delivered above-average performance in fulfilment of our declared objective of creating value for our shareholders. Apart from 20X2, when our overall performance was hampered by a general market downturn, this company has delivered growth in dividends, earnings and ordinary share price. Our shareholders can rest assured that my directors and I will continue to deliver this performance in the future'.

The five-year summary in the draft Annual Report contains the following information:

Year	20X4	20X3	20X2	20X1	20X0
Dividend per share	2.8¢	2.3¢	2.2¢	2.2¢	1.7¢
Earnings per share	19.04¢	14.95¢	11.22¢	15.84¢	13.43¢
Price/earnings ratio	22.0	33.5	25.5	17.2	15.2
General price index	117	113	110	105	100

A recent article in the financial press reported the following information for the last five years for the business sector within which RZP Co operates:

Share price growth	average	increase	per	year	of	20%
Earnings growth	average	increase	per	year	of	10%
Nominal dividend growth	average	increase	per	year	of	10%
Real dividend growth	average increase per year of 9%					

You may assume that the number of shares issued by RZP Co has been constant over the five-year period. All price/earnings ratios are based on end-of-year share prices.

Required:

(a)   **Analyse the information provided and comment on the views expressed by the chairman in terms of:**

(i)   **growth in dividends per share;**

(ii)   **share price growth;**

(iii)   **growth in earnings per share.**

Your analysis should consider both arithmetic mean and equivalent annual growth rates.   (13 marks)

(b)   **Calculate the total shareholder return (dividend yield plus capital growth) for 20X4 and comment on your findings.**   (3 marks)

(c)   Discuss the factors that should be considered when deciding on a management remuneration package that will encourage the directors of RZP Co to maximise the wealth of shareholders, giving examples of management remuneration packages that might be appropriate for RZP Co.   **(9 marks)**

(Total: 25 marks)

5   JJG CO
(JUNE 09)

 Timed question with Online tutor debrief

JJG Co is planning to raise $15 million of new finance for a major expansion of existing business and is considering a rights issue, a placing or an issue of bonds. The corporate objectives of JJG Co, as stated in its Annual Report, are to maximise the wealth of its shareholders and to achieve continuous growth in earnings per share. Recent financial information on JJG Co is as follows

	2008	2007	2006	2005
Turnover ($m)	28.0	24.0	19.1	16.8
Profit before interest and tax ($m)	9.8	8.5	7.5	6.8
Earnings ($m)	5.5	4.7	4.1	3.6
Dividends ($m)	2.2	1.9	1.6	1.6
Ordinary shares ($m)	5.5	5.5	5.5	5.5
Reserves ($m)	13.7	10.4	7.6	5.1
8% Bonds, redeemable 2015 ($m)	20.0	20.0	20.0	20.0
Share price ($)	8.64	5.74	3.35	2.67

The par value of the shares of JJG Co is $1·00 per share. The general level of inflation has averaged 4% per year in the period under consideration. The bonds of JJG Co are currently trading at their par value of $100. The following values for the business sector of JJG Co are available:

Average return on capital employed	25%
Average return on shareholders' funds	20%
Average interest coverage ratio	20 times
Average debt/equity ratio (market value basis)	50%
Return predicted by the capital asset pricing model	14%

Required:

(a)   Evaluate the financial performance of JJG Co, and analyse and discuss the extent to which the company has achieved its stated corporate objectives of:

(i)   Maximising the wealth of its shareholders;

(ii)   Achieving continuous growth in earnings per share.

Note: up to 7 marks are available for financial analysis   **(12 marks)**

(b) **If the new finance is raised via a rights issue at $7.50 per share and the major expansion of business has not yet begun, calculate and comment on the effect of the rights issue on:**

(i) .the share price of JJG Co;

(ii) The earnings per share of the company; and

(iii) The debt/equity ratio

(6 marks)

(c) **Analyse and discuss the relative merits of a rights issue, a placing and an issue of bonds as ways of raising the finance for the expansion** (7 marks)

(Total: 25 marks)

 Calculate your allowed time, allocate the time to the separate parts

---

6 DOE INC
(DEC 03)

Assume that 'now' is December 20X8.

At a recent meeting of the Board of Doe Inc, a supplier of industrial and commercial clothing, it was suggested that the company might be suffering liquidity problems as a result of overtrading, despite encouraging growth in turnover. The Finance Director was instructed to report to the next Board meeting on this matter.

Extracts from the financial statements of Doe Inc for 20X7, and from the forecast financial statements for 20X8, are given below.

Income statement extracts for years ending 31 December

	20X8	20X7
	$000	$000
Sales revenue	8,300	6,638
Cost of sales	4,900	3,720
Gross profit	3,400	2,918
Administration and distribution expenses	2,700	2,318
Operating profit	700	600
Interest	125	100
Profit before tax	575	500

Statement of financial position extracts as at 31 December

	20X8		20X7	
	$000	$000	$000	$000
Non-current assets		1,650		1,500
Current assets				
Inventory	3,200		2,700	
Receivables	2,750		2,000	
		5,950		4,700
Total assets		7,600		6,200

	20X8		20X7	
Equity and liabilities	$000	$000	$000	$000
Ordinary shares	400		400	
Reserves	1,400		1,300	
Total equity		1,800		1,700
Current liabilities				
Trade payables	2,550		1,800	
Bank overdraft	2,750		2,300	
Other liabilities	500		400	
		5,800		4,500
Total equity and liabilities		7,600		6,200

The Finance Director had reported to the recent board meeting that the bank was insisting the company reduce its overdraft as a matter of urgency. Average ratios for the business sector in which Doe Inc operates are as follows:

Inventory days	210 days	Current ratio	1.35
Receivables days	100 days	Quick ratio	0.55
Payables days	120 days		

The Production Director would like to buy a new machine which would cost $365,000 if purchased. The Finance Director is confident this purchase could be financed by a medium-term bank loan at an annual interest cost of 10% before tax.

Alternatively, the machine could be leased for $77,250 per annum, payable annually in advance. The machine has an expected life of five years, at the end of which it would have zero scrap value.

Sales and costs of new machine output

The Finance Director has commissioned research that shows growth in sales of the output produced by the new machine depends on the sales price, as follows:

Sales price	New sales in year 1	Expected annual growth in sales
$70 per unit	10,000 units	20%
$67 per unit	11,000 units	23%

Variable costs of production are $42 per unit and incremental fixed production overheads arising from the use of the machine are expected to be $85,000 per annum. The maximum capacity of the new machine is 20,000 units per annum.

Other information

Doe Inc pays tax one year in arrears at a rate of 30% and can claim annual writing down allowances (tax-allowable depreciation) on a 25% reducing balance basis. The company pays interest on its overdraft at approximately 6% per annum before tax.

Required:

(a) Write a report to the board of Doe Inc that analyses and discusses the suggestion that the company is overtrading. **(12 marks)**

(b) Evaluate whether Doe Inc should buy or lease the new machine, using an after-tax discount rate of 7%.(Assume that payment for the purchase, or the first lease payment, would take place on 1 January 20X9.) **(9 marks)**

(c) Calculate the optimum sales price for the output from the new machine. (Taxation and the time value of money should be ignored.) **(4 marks)**

(Total: 25 marks)

---

7 DARTIG CO *Walk in the footsteps of a top tutor*

(DEC 08)

Dartig Co is a stock-market listed company that manufactures consumer products and it is planning to expand its existing business. The investment cost of $5 million will be met by a 1 for 4 rights issue. The current share price of Dartig Co is $2.50 per share and the rights issue price will be at a 20% discount to this. The finance director of Dartig Co expects that the expansion of existing business will allow the average growth rate of earnings per share over the last four years to be maintained into the foreseeable future.

The earnings per share and dividends paid by Dartig over the last four years are as follows:

	2003	2004	2005	2006	2007
Earnings per share (cents)	27.7	29.0	29.0	30.2	32.4
Dividend per share (cents)	12.8	13.5	13.5	14.5	15.0

Dartig Co has a cost of equity of 10%. The price/earnings ratio of Dartig Co has been approximately constant in recent years. Ignore issue costs.

Required:

(a) Calculate the theoretical ex rights price per share prior to investing in the proposed business expansion. `   (3 marks)

(b) Calculate the expected share price following the proposed business expansion using the price/earnings ratio method.   (3 marks)

(c) Discuss whether the proposed business expansion is an acceptable use of the finance raised by the rights issue, and evaluate the expected effect on the wealth of the shareholders of Dartig Co.   (5 marks)

(d) Using the information provided, calculate the ex div share price predicted by the dividend growth model and discuss briefly why this share price differs from the current market price of Dartig Co.   (6 marks)

(e) At a recent board meeting of Dartig Co, a non-executive director suggested that the company 's remuneration committee should consider scrapping the company 's current share option scheme, since executive directors could be rewarded by the scheme even when they did not perform well. A second non-executive director disagreed, saying the problem was that even when directors acted in ways which decreased the agency problem, they might not be rewarded by the share option scheme if the stock market were in decline.

Required:

Explain the nature of the agency problem and discuss the use of share option schemes as a way of reducing the agency problem in a stock-market listed company such as Dartig Co.   (8 marks)

(Total: 25 marks)

FINANCIAL MANAGEMENT ENVIRONMENT

8   NEWS FOR YOU
(DEC 00)

News For You operates a chain of newsagents and confectioner's shops in the south of a Northern European country, and are considering the possibility of expanding their business across a wider geographical area. The business was started in 20X2 and annual turnover grew to $10 million by the end of 20X6. Between 20X6 and 20X9 turnover grew at an average rate of 2% per year.

The business still remains under family control, but the high cost of expansion via the purchase or building of new outlets would mean that the family would need to raise at least $2 million in equity or debt finance. One of the possible risks of expansion lies in the fact that both tobacco and newspaper sales are falling. New income is being generated by expanding the product range stocked by the stores, to include basic foodstuffs such as bread and milk. News For You purchases all of its products from a large wholesale distributor which is convenient, but the wholesale prices leave News For You with a relatively small gross margin. The key to profit growth for News For You lies in the ability to generate sales growth, but the company recognises that it faces stiff competition from large food retailers in respect of the prices that it charges for several of its products.

In planning its future, News For You was advised to look carefully at a number of external factors which may affect the business, including government economic policy and, in recent months, the following information has been published in respect of key economic data:

(i)   Bank base rate has been reduced from 5% to 4.5%, and the forecast is for a further 0.5% reduction within six months.

(ii)   The annual rate of inflation is now 1.2%, down from 1.3% in the previous quarter, and 1.7% 12 months ago. The rate is now at its lowest for 25 years, and no further falls in the rate are expected over the medium/long term.

(iii) Personal and corporation tax rates are expected to remain unchanged for at least 12 months.

(iv)   Taxes on tobacco have been increased by 10% over the last 12 months, although no further increases are anticipated.

(v)   The government has initiated an investigation into the food retail sector focusing on the problems of 'excessive' profits on certain foodstuffs created by the high prices being charged for these goods by the large retail food stores.

Required:

(a)   Explain the relevance of each of the items of economic data listed above to News For You.   **(13 marks)**

(b)   Explain whether News For You should continue with their expansion plans. Clearly justify your arguments for or against the expansion.   **(12 marks)**

(Total: 25 marks)

9   DISCOURAGING MONOPOLIES
(DEC 03)

Two important elements in the economic and financial management environment of companies are the regulation of markets to discourage monopoly and the availability of finance to fund growth and development.

Required:

(a)   Outline the economic problems caused by monopoly and explain the role of government in maintaining competition between companies.   **(9 marks)**

(b)   Describe the methods of raising new equity finance that can be used by an unlisted company.   **(8 marks)**

(c)   Discuss the factors to be considered by a listed company when choosing between an issue of debt and an issue of equity finance.   **(8 marks)**

(Total: 25 marks)

PAPER F9 : FINANCIAL MANAGEMENT

10   PELLAS CO
(JUNE 98)

Pellas Co is a small manufacturing company which specialises in the production of high quality electronic organisers, which are sold direct to the public by mail order. Summary figures from the Income Statements for the last three years are shown below:

	20X5 $m	20X6 $m	20X7 $m
Sales revenue	1.250	1.500	1.620
Cost of sales	0.650	0.830	0.967
Operating profit	0.600	0.670	0.653

Notes:

(1)   Unit selling price for the electronic organiser has been held fixed by Pellas since 20X5. This is in response to low levels of demand in the domestic consumer electronics market.

(2)   80% of the cost of sales is accounted for by electronic components purchased from a supplier who has increased prices by 10% in each of the last two years.

Government financial statistics for the same period reveal the following:

Consumer price index		Wholesale price index	
December 20X5	150.7	December 20X5	132.4
December 20X6	154.4	December 20X6	134.8
December 20X7	159.5	December 20X7	137.5

Required:

(a)   **Briefly outline the causes of inflation.**   **(5 marks)**

(b)   **Calculate and comment on the annual rate of inflation for 20X5/6 and 20X6/7, as measured by both the consumer and wholesale price indices.**   **(5 marks)**

(c)   **In general terms describe how inflation affects companies.**   **(7 marks)**

(d)   **Write a report for the directors of Pellas, commenting on the way in which they have managed their sales and costs under inflationary conditions.**   **(8 marks)**

(Total: 25 marks)

WORKING CAPITAL MANAGEMENT

11 GORWA CO
(DEC 08)

The following financial information related to Gorwa Co:

	2007	2006
	$000	**$000**
Sales (all on credit)	37,400	26,720
Cost of sales	34,408	23,781
Operating profit	2,992	2,939
Finance costs (interest payments)	355	274
Profit before taxation	2,637	2,665

		2007		2006
	$000	**$000**	**$000**	**$000**
Non-current assets		13,632		12,750
Current assets				
Inventory	4,600		2,400	
Trade receivables	4,600		2,200	
	9,200		4,600	
Current liabilities				
Trade payables	4,750		2,000	
Overdraft	3,225		1,600	
	7,975		3,600	
Net current assets		1,225		1,000
		14,857		13,750
8% Bonds		2,425		2,425
		12,432		11,325
Capital and reserves				
Share capital		6,000		6,000
Reserves		6,432		5,325
		12,432		11,325

The average variable overdraft interest rate in each year was 5%. The 8% bonds are redeemable in ten years' time.

A factor has offered to take over the administration of trade receivables on a non-recourse basis for an annual fee of 3% of credit sales. The factor will maintain a trade receivables collection period of 30 days and Gorwa Co will save $100,000 per year in administration costs and $350,000 per year in bad debts. A condition of the factoring agreement is that the factor would advance 80% of the face value of receivables at an annual interest rate of 7%.

Required:

(a) Discuss, with supporting calculations, the possible effects on Gorwa Co of an increase in interest rates and advise the company of steps it can take to protect itself against interest rate risk. **(7 marks)**

(b) Use the above financial information to discuss, with supporting calculations, whether or not Gorwa Co is overtrading. **(10 marks)**

(c) Evaluate whether the proposal to factor trade receivables is financially acceptable. Assume an average cost of short-term finance in this part of the question only.

(8 marks)

(Total: 25 marks)

12 FLG CO
(JUNE 08)

FLG Co has annual credit sales of $4·2 million and cost of sales of $1·89 million. Current assets consist of inventory and accounts receivable. Current liabilities consist of accounts payable and an overdraft with an average interest rate of 7% per year. The company gives *AR* two months' credit to its customers and is allowed, on average, one month's credit by trade suppliers. It has an operating cycle of three months. *AP*

Other relevant information:

Current ratio of FLG Co $\dfrac{Current\ Assets}{Current\ Liability} = 1·4$
Cost of long-term finance of FLG Co 11%

Required:

(a) Discuss the key factors which determine the level of investment in current assets. **(6 marks)**

(b) Discuss the ways in which factoring and invoice discounting can assist in the management of accounts receivable. **(6 marks)**

(c) Calculate the size of the overdraft of FLG Co, the net working capital of the company and the total cost of financing its current assets. **(6 marks)**

(d) FLG Co wishes to minimise its inventory costs. Annual demand for a raw material costing $12 per unit is 60,000 units per year. Inventory management costs for this raw material are as follows: *D*

Ordering cost: $6 per order
Holding cost: $0·5 per unit per year

The supplier of this raw material has offered a bulk purchase discount of 1% for orders of 10,000 units or more. If bulk purchase orders are made regularly, it is expected that annual holding cost for this raw material will increase to $2 per unit per year.

step 1. Cal. EOQ

step 2. Annual cost using EOQ.

step 3. To get discount. Recal. Annual Cost using X

Required:

(i)   Calculate the total cost of inventory for the raw material when using the economic order quantity.   **(4 marks)**

(ii)   Determine whether accepting the discount offered by the supplier will minimise the total cost of inventory for the raw material.   **(3 marks)**

(Total: 25 marks)

13   **PKA CO**   *Walk in the footsteps of a top tutor*

(DEC 07)

PKA Co is a European company that sells goods solely within Europe. The recently-appointed financial manager of PKA Co has been investigating the working capital management of the company and has gathered the following information:

Inventory management

ROQ

The current policy is to order 100,000 units when the inventory level falls to 35,000 units. Forecast demand to meet production requirements during the next year is 625,000 units. Demand. The cost of placing and processing an order is €250, while the cost of holding a unit in stores is €0.50 per unit per year. Both costs are expected to be constant during the next year. Orders are received two weeks after being placed with the supplier. You should assume a 50-week year and that demand is constant throughout the year.

Accounts receivable management

Domestic customers are allowed 30 days' credit, but the financial statements of PKA Co show that the average accounts receivable period in the last financial year was 75 days. The financial manager also noted that bad debts as a percentage of sales, which are all on credit, increased in the last financial year from 5% to 8%.

Accounts payable management

PKA Co has used a foreign supplier for the first time and must pay $250,000 to the supplier in six months' time. The financial manager is concerned that the cost of these supplies may rise in euro terms and has decided to hedge the currency risk of this account payable. The following information has been provided by the company's bank:

Spot rate ($ per €):   1.998 ± 0.002

Six months forward rate ($ per €):   1.979 ± 0.004

Money market rates available to PKA Co:

	Borrowing	Deposit
One year euro interest rates:	6.1%	5.4%
One year dollar interest rates:	4.0%	3.5%

Assume that it is now 1 December and that PKA Co has no surplus cash at the present time.

Required:

(a)   Identify the objectives of working capital management and discuss the conflict that may arise between them.   **(3 marks)**

(b)   Calculate the cost of the current ordering policy and determine the saving that could be made by using the economic order quantity model.   **(7 marks)**

(c)   Discuss ways in which PKA Co could improve the management of domestic accounts receivable.   **(7 marks)**

(d)   Evaluate whether a money market hedge, a forward market hedge or a lead payment should be used to hedge the foreign account payable.   **(8 marks)**

(Total: 25 marks)

14   VELM
(JUNE 03)

Velm Inc sells stationery and office supplies on a wholesale basis and has an annual turnover of $4,000,000. The company employs four people in its sales ledger and credit control department at an annual salary of $12,000 each. All sales are on 40 days' credit with no discount for early payment. Bad debts represent 3% of turnover and Velm Inc pays annual interest of 9% on its overdraft. The most recent accounts of the company offer the following financial information:

Velm Inc: Statement of financial position as at 31 December 20X2

	$000	$000
Non-current assets		17,500
Current assets		
Inventory	900	
Receivables	550	
Cash	120	
	―――	
		1,570
		―――
Total assets		19,070
		―――
Equity and liabilities		
Ordinary shares	3,500	
Reserves	11,640	
	―――	
Total equity		15,140
Non-current liabilities		
12% loan notes due 20X9		2,400
Current liabilities		
Trade payables	330	
Bank overdraft	1,200	
	―――	
		1,530
		―――
Total equity and liabilities		19,070
		―――

Velm Inc is considering offering a discount of 1% to customers paying within 14 days, which it believes will reduce bad debts to 2.4% of turnover. The company also expects that offering a discount for early payment will reduce the average credit period taken by its customers to 26 days. The consequent reduction in the time spent chasing customers where payments are overdue will allow one member of the credit control team to take early retirement. Two-thirds of customers are expected to take advantage of the discount.

Required:

(a)   **Using the information provided, determine whether a discount for early payment of one per cent will lead to an increase in profitability for Velm Inc.**   **(5 marks)**

(b)   **Discuss the relative merits of short-term and long-term debt sources for the financing of working capital.**   **(6 marks)**

(c)   **Discuss the different policies that may be adopted by a company towards the financing of working capital needs and indicate which policy has been adopted by Velm Inc**
.   **(7 marks)**

(d)   **Outline the advantages to a company of taking steps to improve its working capital management, giving examples of steps that might be taken.**   **(7 marks)**

(Total: 25 marks)

15   FRANTIC CO
(PILOT 01)

Frantic Co is a specialist car manufacturer and is a member of a group of companies that provides a range of automobile products and services. It is currently facing difficulties in the management of its working capital and the financial controller of Frantic Co is to investigate the situation with a view to optimising supplier payments, inventory ordering and receivables discounts to ease projected cash flow problems.

Payables

Payables arise only for engine purchases. Engine suppliers have offered an early settlement discount of 1.5% if invoices are settled within one month of delivery. Frantic has decided to accept its suppliers offer.

Inventory

Frantic has a budgeted production of 800 cars for the year. The most expensive bought-in components for the cars are engines. Other components are either made in-house or are minor items which are bought-in but which do not require special inventory management.

Engine purchase prices are subject to quantity discounts according to the following schedule:

Order quantity	Order quantity
0-49 units	0%
50-249 units	2%
above 249 units	3%

Other details are:

Engine price (before discounts):	$1,300
Inventory holding costs per annum (as a percentage of engine costs):	22%
Delivery costs per order:	$1,200

There is zero lead-time on engine orders.

Receivables

The cars are sold at $42,500 each and unit sales are equal to the units produced in each month. 50% of the cars are made to order and payment is on a 'cash on delivery' basis. The remaining cars are sold to specialist retailers who take two months' credit.

Other factors

A budget forecast is to be prepared for a six-month period. Other variable costs (including the other components) represent 65% of sales value and are payable immediately. Fixed costs are $18,000 per month for the first three months, rising to $22,000 per month thereafter. The first instalment of $3.2 million for a major re-tooling operation will be paid in month three of the budget forecast.

Assume that the opening bank overdraft is $25,000 and that there are payables outstanding to the value of $97,500 which will be paid in the first month of the budget plan. It is expected that receivables payments of $1,062,500 will be received in each of the first two months.

The company uses its bank overdraft rate of 15% as its discount rate. Assume one month comprises 30 days, that no opening inventory of engines is held and that production is evenly spread throughout the year.

Required:

(a) Calculate the optimal ordering policy for engines   (7 marks)

(b) On the basis of your answer to part (a), and the information given above, prepare the cash budget for Frantic for each of the next six months.   (18 marks)

In all your answers clearly state any assumptions you make.   (Total: 25 marks)

16 **HGR CO**

(JUNE 09)

 Timed question with Online tutor debrief

The following financial information relates to HGR Co:

Statement of financial position at the current date (extracts)

	$'000	$'000	$'000
Non-current assets			48,965
Current assets			
Inventory		8,160	
Accounts receivable		8,775	
		16,935	
Current liabilities			
Overdraft	3,800		
Accounts payable	10,200		
		14,000	
Net current assets			2,935
Total assets less current liabilities			51,900

Cash flow forecasts from the current date are as follows:

	Month 1	Month 2	Month 3
Cash operating receipts ($'000)	4,220	4,350	3,808
Cash operating payments ($'000)	3,950	4,100	3,750
Six-monthly interest on traded bonds ($'000)		200	
Capital investment ($'000)			2,000

The finance director has completed a review of accounts receivable management and has proposed staff training and operating procedure improvements, which he believes will reduce accounts receivable days to the average sector value of 53 days. This reduction would take six months to achieve from the current date, with an equal reduction in each month. He has also proposed changes to inventory management methods, which he hopes will reduce inventory days by two days per month each month over a three-month period *6days* from the current date. He does not expect any change in the current level of accounts payable.

HGR Co has an overdraft limit of $4,000,000. Overdraft interest is payable at an annual rate of 6·17% per year, with payments being made each month based on the opening balance at the start of that month. Credit sales for the year to the current date were $49,275,000 and cost of sales was $37,230,000. These levels of credit sales and cost of sales are expected to be maintained in the coming year. Assume that there are 365 working days in each year.

Required:

(a) Discuss the working capital financing strategy of HGR Co. **(7 marks)**

(b) For HGR Co, calculate:

    (i) the bank balance in three months' time if no action is taken; and

    (ii) the bank balance in three months' time if the finance director's proposals are implemented

    Comment on the forecast cash flow position of HGR Co and recommend a suitable course of action. **(10 marks)**

(c) Discuss how risks arising from granting credit to foreign customers can be managed and reduced. **(8 marks)**

(Total: 25 marks)

 Calculate your allowed time, allocate the time to the separate parts

17 ANJO
(DEC 06)

Extracts from the recent financial statements of Anjo Inc are as follows:

Income statements

	20X6 $000	20X5 $000
Sales revenue	15,600	11,100
Cost of sales	9,300	6,600
Gross profit	6,300	4,500
Administration expenses	1,000	750
Profit before interest and tax	5,300	3,750
Interest	100	15
Profit before tax	5,200	3,735

Statements of financial position

	20X6 $000	20X6 $000	20X5 $000	20X5 $000
Non-current assets		5,750		5,400
Current assets				
Inventory	3,000		1,300	
Receivables	3,800		1,850	
Cash	120		900	
		6,920		4,050
Total assets		8,800		7,700

	$000	20X6 $000	$000	20X5 $000
Total equity		4,930		5,950
Current liabilities				
Trade payables	2,870		1,600	
Overdraft	1,000		150	
		3,870		1,750
Total equity and liabilities		8,800		7,700

All sales were on credit. Anjo Inc has no long-term debt. Credit purchases in each year were 95% of cost of sales. Anjo Inc pays interest on its overdraft at an annual rate of 8%. Current sector averages are as follows:

Inventory days: 90 days

Receivables days: 60 days

Payables days: 80 days

Required:

(a)   Calculate the following ratios for each year and comment on your findings.

   (i)   **Inventory days**

   (ii)   **Receivables days**

   (iii)   **Payables days**   **(6 marks)**

(b)   Calculate the length of the cash operating cycle (working capital cycle) for each year and explain its significance.   **(4 marks)**

(c)   Discuss the relationship between working capital management and business solvency, and explain the factors that influence the optimum cash level for a business.   **(7 marks)**

(d)   A factor has offered to take over sales ledger administration and debt collection for an annual fee of 0.5% of credit sales. A condition of the offer is that the factor will advance Anjo Inc 80% of the face value of its receivables at an interest rate 1% above the current overdraft rate. The factor claims that it would reduce outstanding receivables by 30% and reduce administration expenses by 2% per year if its offer were accepted.

Evaluate whether the factor's offer is financially acceptable, basing your answer on the financial information relating to 20X6.   **(8 marks)**

                                                                                    (Total: 25 marks)

18 BLIN
(JUNE 04)

Blin is a company listed on a European stock exchange, with a market capitalisation of €6m, which manufactures household cleaning chemicals. The company has expanded sales quite significantly over the last year and has been following an aggressive approach to working capital financing. As a result, Blin has come to rely heavily on overdraft finance for its short-term needs. On the advice of its finance director, the company intends to take out a long-term bank loan, part of which would be used to repay its overdraft.

Required:

(a) Discuss the factors that will influence the rate of interest charged on the new bank loan, making reference in your answer to the yield curve. **(9 marks)**

(b) Explain and discuss the approaches that Blin could adopt regarding the relative proportions of long- and short-term finance to meet its working capital needs, and comment on the proposed repayment of the overdraft. **(9 marks)**

(c) Explain the meaning of the term 'cash operating cycle' and discuss its significance in determining the level of investment in working capital. Your answer should refer to the working capital needs of different business sectors. **(7 marks)**

(Total: 25 marks)

19 PNP PLC
(JUNE 07)

The following financial information relates to PNP plc, a UK-based firm, for the year just ended.

	£000
Sales revenue	5,242.0
Variable cost of sales	3,145.0
Inventory	603.0
Receivables	744.5
Payables	574.5

Segmental analysis of receivables

	Balance	Average payment period	Discount	Irrecoverable
Class 1	£200,000	30 days	1.0%	None
Class 2	£252,000	60 days	Nil	£12,600
Class 3	£110,000	75 days	Nil	£11,000
Overseas	£182,500	90 days	Nil	£21,900
	£744,500			£45,500

The receivables balances given are before taking account of irrecoverable debts. All sales are on credit. Production and sales take place evenly throughout the year. Current sales for each class of receivables are in proportion to their relative year-end balances before irrecoverable debts. The overseas receivables arise from regular export sales by PNP to the USA. The current spot rate is $1.7348/£ and the three-month forward rate is $1.7367/£.

It has been proposed that the discount for early payment be increased from 1.0% to 1.5% for settlement within 30 days. It is expected that this will lead to 50% of existing Class 2 receivables becoming Class 1 receivables, as well as attracting new business worth £500,000 in turnover. The new business would be divided equally between Class 1 and Class 2 receivables. Fixed costs would not increase as a result of introducing the discount or by attracting new business. PNP finances receivables from an overdraft at an annual interest rate of 8%.

Required:

(a) Calculate the net benefit or cost of increasing the discount for early payment and comment on the acceptability of the proposal. **(9 marks)**

(b) Calculate the current cash operating cycle and the revised cash operating cycle caused by increasing the discount for early payment. **(4 marks)**

(c) Determine the effect of using a forward market hedge to manage the exchange rate risk of the outstanding overseas receivables. **(2 marks)**

(d) Identify and explain the key elements of a receivables management system suitable for PNP plc. **(10 marks)**

(Total: 25 marks)

 Online question assistance

INVESTMENT APPRAISAL

20 ARMCLIFF CO
(JUN 95)

ARR Armcliff Co is a division of Shevin Inc which requires each of its divisions to achieve a rate of return on capital employed of at least 10% pa. For this purpose, capital employed is defined as fixed capital and investment in inventories. This rate of return is also applied as a hurdle rate for new investment projects. Divisions have limited borrowing powers and all capital projects are centrally funded.

The following is an extract from Armcliff's divisional accounts:

Income statement for the year ended 31 December 20X4

	$m
Sales revenue	120
Cost of sales	(100)
Operating profit	20 PBIT

Assets employed as at 31 December 20X4

	$m	$m
Non-current assets (NBV)		75
Current assets (including inventories $25m)	45	
Current liabilities	(32)	
		13
Net capital employed		88

Armcliff's production engineers wish to invest in a new computer-controlled press. The equipment cost is $14m. The residual value is expected to be $2m after four years operation, when the equipment will be shipped to a customer in South America.

The new machine is capable of improving the quality of the existing product and also of producing a higher volume. The firm's marketing team is confident of selling the increased volume by extending the credit period.

The expected additional sales are:

Year 1	2,000,000 units
Year 2	1,800,000 units
Year 3	1,600,000 units
Year 4	1,600,000 units

Sales volume is expected to fall over time due to emerging competitive pressures. Competition will also necessitate a reduction in price by $0.50 each year from the $5 per unit proposed in the first year. Operating costs are expected to be steady at $1 per unit, and allocation of overheads (none of which are affected by the new project) by the central finance department is set at $0.75 per unit. *not relevant*

Higher production levels will require additional investment in inventories of $0.5m, which would be held at this level until the final stages of operation of the project. Customers at present settle accounts after 90 days on average.

Required:

(a) Determine whether the proposed capital investment is attractive to Armcliff, using the average rate of return on capital method, as defined as average profit-to-average capital employed, ignoring receivables and payables.

Note: Ignore taxes. **(10 marks)**

(b) (i) Suggest three problems which arise with the use of the average return method for appraising new investment. *Disadvantages* **(3 marks)**

(ii) In view of the problems associated with the ARR method, why do companies continue to use it in project appraisal? *Advantages* **(3 marks)**

(c) Briefly discuss the dangers of offering more generous credit, and suggest ways of assessing customers' creditworthiness. *4 steps* **(9 marks)**

(Total: 25 marks)

21 HENDIL (PART I)
(DEC 06)

Hendil Inc plans to invest $1 million in a new product range and has forecast the following financial information:

Year	1	2	3	4
Sales volume (units)	70,000	90,000	100,000	75,000
Average selling price ($/unit)	40	45	51	51
Average variable costs ($/unit)	30	28	27	27
Incremental cash fixed costs ($/year)	500,000	500,000	500,000	500,000

The above cost forecasts have been prepared on the basis of current prices and no account has been taken of inflation of 4% per year on variable costs and 3% per year on fixed costs.

Working capital investment accounts for $200,000 of the proposed $1 million investment and machinery for $800,000.

Hendil uses a four-year evaluation period for capital investment purposes, but expects the new product range to continue to sell for several years after the end of this period. Capital investments are expected to pay back within two years on an undiscounted basis, and within three years on a discounted basis.

The company pays tax on profits in the year in which liabilities arise at an annual rate of 30% and claims capital allowances on machinery on a 25% reducing balance basis. Balancing allowances or charges are claimed only on the disposal of assets.

Required:

(a)   Using Hendil Inc's current average cost of capital of 11%, calculate the net present value of the proposed investment. **(15 marks)**

(b)   Calculate, to the nearest month, the payback period and the discounted payback period of the proposed investment. **(4 marks)**

(c)   Discuss the acceptability of the proposed investment and explain ways in which your net present value calculation could be improved. **(6 marks)**

(Total: 25 marks)

22   INVESTMENT APPRAISAL
(JUNE 00)

(a)   **Explain and illustrate (using simple numerical examples) the Accounting Rate of Return and Payback approaches to investment appraisal, paying particular attention to the limitations of each approach.** **(8 marks)**

4' – ARR
4' – Payback

(b)   (i)   **Explain the differences between NPV and IRR as methods of Discounted Cash Flow analysis.** **(7 marks)**

df

(ii)   A company with a cost of capital of 14% is trying to determine the optimal replacement cycle for the laptop computers used by its sales team. The following information is relevant to the decision:

EAC

cost

The cost of each laptop is $2,400. Maintenance costs are payable at the end of *each full year* of ownership, but not in the year of replacement, e.g. if the laptop is owned for two years, then the maintenance cost is payable at the end of year 1.

Interval between replacement (years)	Trade-in value ($)	Maintenance cost
1	1,200	Zero
2	800	$75 (payable at end of Year 1)
3	300	$150 (payable at end of Year 2)

Required:

EAC

Ignoring taxation, calculate the equivalent annual cost of the three different replacement cycles, and recommend which should be adopted. What other factors should the company take into account when determining the optimal cycle? **(10 marks)**

(Total: 25 marks)

23   PV CO
(JUNE 09)

 Timed question with Online tutor debrief

PV Co is evaluating an investment proposal to manufacture Product W33, which has performed well in test marketing trials conducted recently by the company's research and development division. The following information relating to this investment proposal has now been prepared

Initial investment	$2 million
Selling price (current price terms)	$20 per unit
Expected selling price inflation	3% per year
Variable operating costs (current price terms)	$8 per unit
Fixed operating costs (current price terms)	$170,000 per year
Expected operating cost inflation	4% per year

The research and development division has prepared the following demand forecast as a result of its test marketing trials. The forecast reflects expected technological change and its effect on the anticipated life-cycle of Product W33

Year	1	2	3	4
Demand (units)	60,000	70,000	120,000	45,000

It is expected that all units of Product W33 produced will be sold, in line with the company's policy of keeping no inventory of finished goods. No terminal value or machinery scrap value is expected at the end of four years, when production of Product W33 is planned to end. For investment appraisal purposes, PV Co uses a nominal (money) discount rate of 10% per year and a target return on capital employed of 30% per year. Ignore taxation.

Required:

(a)   Identify and explain the key stages in the capital investment decision-making process, and the role of investment appraisal in this process.   **(7 marks)**

(b)   Calculate the following values for the investment proposal:

(i)   net present value;

(ii)   internal rate of return;

(iii)   return on capital employed (accounting rate of return) based on average investment; and.

(iv)   discounted payback period   **(13 marks)**

(c)   Discuss your findings in each section of (b) above and advise whether the investment proposal is financially acceptable.   **(5 marks)**

(Total: 25 marks)

 Calculate your allowed time, allocate the time to the separate parts

24 BFD CO
(DEC 05)

BFD Co is a private company formed three years ago by four brothers who, as directors, retain sole ownership of its ordinary share capital. One quarter of the initial share capital was provided by each brother.

The directors are delighted with the rapid growth of BFD Co and are considering further expansion through buying new premises and machinery to manufacture Product FT7. This new product has only just been developed and patented by BFD Co. Test marketing has indicated considerable demand for the product, as shown by the following research data.

Year of operation	1	2	3	4
Accounting year	20X5/6	20X6/7	20X7/8	20X8/9
Sales volume (units)	100,000	120,000	130,000	140,000

Sales after 20X8/9 (the fourth year of operation) are expected to continue at the 20X8/9 level in perpetuity.

Initial investment of $3,000,000 would be required in new premises and machinery, as well as an additional $200,000 of working capital. The directors have no further financial resources to offer and are considering approaching their bank for a loan to meet their investment needs. Selling price and standard cost data for Product FT7, based on an annual budgeted volume of 100,000 units, are as follows:

	$ per unit
Selling price	18.00
Direct material	7.00
Direct labour	1.50
Fixed production overhead	4.50

The fixed production overhead is incurred exclusively in the production of Product FT7 and excludes depreciation. Selling price and standard unit variable cost data for Product FT7 are expected to remain constant.

BFD Co expects to be able to claim writing down allowances on the initial investment of $3,000,000 on a straight line basis over 10 years. The company pays tax on profit at an annual rate of 25% in the year in which the liability arises and has an after-tax cost of capital of 12%.

Required:

(a) Calculate the net present value of the proposed investment in Product FT7. Assume that it is now 1 December 20X5. **(18 marks)**

(b) Comment on the acceptability of the proposed investment in Product FT7 and discuss what additional information might improve the decision-making process.

(7 marks)

(Total: 25 marks)

25   CHARM INC
(JUNE 06)

Charm Inc, a software company, has developed a new game, 'Fingo', which it plans to launch in the near future. Sales of the new game are expected to be very strong, following a favourable review by a popular PC magazine. Charm Inc has been informed that the review will give the game a 'Best Buy' recommendation. Sales volumes, production volumes and selling prices for 'Fingo' over its four-year life are expected to be as follows:

Year	1	2	3	4
Sales and production (units)	150,000	70,000	60,000	60,000
Selling price ($ per game)	$25	$24	$23	$22

Financial information on 'Fingo' for the first year of production is as follows:

Direct material cost	$5.40 per game
Other variable production cost	$6.00 per game
Fixed costs	$4.00 per game

Advertising costs to stimulate demand are expected to be $650,000 in the first year of production and $100,000 in the second year of production. No advertising costs are expected in the third and fourth years of production. Fixed costs represent incremental cash fixed production overheads. 'Fingo' will be produced on a new production machine costing $800,000. Although this production machine is expected to have a useful life of up to ten years, government legislation allows Charm Inc to claim the capital cost of the machine against the manufacture of a single product. Capital allowances will therefore be claimed on a straight-line basis over four years.

Charm Inc pays tax on profit at a rate of 30% per year and tax liabilities are settled in the year in which they arise. Charm Inc uses an after-tax discount rate of 10% when appraising new capital investments. Ignore inflation.

Required:

(a)   Calculate the net present value of the proposed investment and comment on your findings.   **(11 marks)**

(b)   Calculate the internal rate of return of the proposed investment and comment on your findings.   **(5 marks)**

(c)   Discuss the reasons why the net present value investment appraisal method is preferred to other investment appraisal methods such as payback, return on capital employed and internal rate of return.   **(9 marks)**

(Total: 25 marks)

26   SC CO
(JUNE 08)

SC Co is evaluating the purchase of a new machine to produce product P, which has a short product life-cycle due to rapidly changing technology. The machine is expected to cost $1 million. Production and sales of product P are forecast to be as follows:

Year	1	2	3	4
Production and sales (units/year)	35,000	53,000	75,000	36,000

The selling price of product P (in current price terms) will be $20 per unit, while the variable cost of the product (in current price terms) will be $12 per unit. Selling price inflation is expected to be 4% per year and variable cost inflation is expected to be 5% per year. No increase in existing fixed costs is expected since SC Co has spare capacity in both space and labour terms.

Producing and selling product P will call for increased investment in working capital. Analysis of historical levels of working capital within SC Co indicates that at the start of each year, investment in working capital for product P will need to be 7% of sales revenue for that year.

SC Co pays tax of 30% per year in the year in which the taxable profit occurs. Liability to tax is reduced by capital allowances on machinery (tax-allowable depreciation), which SC Co can claim on a straight-line basis over the four-year life of the proposed investment. The new machine is expected to have no scrap value at the end of the four-year period.

SC Co uses a nominal (money terms) after-tax cost of capital of 12% for investment appraisal purposes.

Required:

(a)   Calculate the net present value of the proposed investment in product P. **(12 marks)**

(b)   Calculate the internal rate of return of the proposed investment in product P.
(3 marks)

(c)   Advise on the acceptability of the proposed investment in product P and discuss the limitations of the evaluations you have carried out. **(5 marks)**

(d)   Discuss how the net present value method of investment appraisal contributes towards the objective of maximising the wealth of shareholders. **(5 marks)**

(Total: 25 marks)

27   DUO CO   *Walk in the footsteps of a top tutor*

(DEC 07)

Duo Co needs to increase production capacity to meet increasing demand for an existing product, 'Quago', which is used in food processing. A new machine, with a useful life of four years and a maximum output of 600,000 kg of Quago per year, could be bought for $800,000, payable immediately. The scrap value of the machine after four years would be $30,000. Forecast demand and production of Quago over the next four years is as follows:

Year	1	2	3	4
Demand (kg)	1.4 million	1.5 million	1.6 million	1.7 million

Existing production capacity for Quago is limited to one million kilograms per year and the new machine would only be used for demand additional to this.

The current selling price of Quago is $8.00 per kilogram and the variable cost of materials is $5.00 per kilogram. Other variable costs of production are $1.90 per kilogram. Fixed costs of production associated with the new machine would be $240,000 in the first year of production, increasing by $20,000 per year in each subsequent year of operation.

Duo Co pays tax one year in arrears at an annual rate of 30% and can claim capital allowances (tax-allowable depreciation) on a 25% reducing balance basis. A balancing allowance is claimed in the final year of operation.   WDA

Duo Co uses its after-tax weighted average cost of capital when appraising investment projects. It has a cost of equity of 11% and a before-tax cost of debt of 8.6%. The long-term finance of the company, on a market-value basis, consists of 80% equity and 20% debt.

Required:

(a)   Calculate the net present value of buying the new machine and advise on the acceptability of the proposed purchase (work to the nearest $1,000).   (13 marks)

(b)   Calculate the internal rate of return of buying the new machine and advise on the acceptability of the proposed purchase (work to the nearest $1,000).   (4 marks)

(c)   Explain the difference between risk and uncertainty in the context of investment appraisal, and describe how sensitivity analysis and probability analysis can be used to incorporate risk into the investment appraisal process.   (8 marks)

(Total: 25 marks)

28   ARG CO
(JUNE 05)

ARG Co is a leisure company that is recovering from a loss-making venture into magazine publication three years ago. The company plans to launch two new products, Alpha and Beta, at the start of July 20X7, which it believes will each have a life-cycle of four years. Alpha is the deluxe version of Beta. The sales mix is assumed to be constant. Expected sales volumes for the two products are as follows:

Year	1	2	3	4
Alpha	60,000	110,000	100,000	30,000
Beta	75,000	137,500	125,000	37,500

The selling price and direct material costs for each product in the first year will be as follows:

Product	Alpha	Beta
	$/unit	$/unit
Direct material costs	12.00	9.00
Selling price	31.00	23.00

Incremental fixed production costs are expected to be $1 million in the first year of operation and are apportioned on the basis of sales value. Advertising costs will be $500,000 in the first year of operation and then $200,000 per year for the following two years. There are no incremental non-production fixed costs other than advertising costs.

In order to produce the two products, investment of $1 million in premises, $1 million in machinery and $1 million in working capital will be needed, payable at the start of July 20X7.

Selling price per unit, direct material cost per unit and incremental fixed production costs are expected to increase after the first year of operation due to inflation:

Selling price inflation	3.0% per year
Direct material cost inflation	3.0% per year
Fixed production cost inflation	5.0% per year

These inflation rates are applied to the standard selling price and direct material cost data provided above. Working capital will be recovered at the end of the fourth year of operation, at which time production will cease and ARG Co expects to be able to recover

$1.2 million from the sale of premises and machinery. All staff involved in the production and sale of Alpha and Beta will be redeployed elsewhere in the company.

ARG Co pays tax in the year in which the taxable profit occurs at an annual rate of 25%. Investment in machinery attracts a first-year capital allowance of 100%. ARG Co has sufficient profits to take the full benefit of this allowance in the first year. For the purpose of reporting accounting profit, ARG Co depreciates machinery on a straight line basis over four years. ARG Co uses an after-tax money discount rate of 13% for investment appraisal.

Required:

(a)   **Calculate the net present value of the proposed investment in products Alpha and Beta as at 30 June 20X7.** **(18 marks)**

(b)   **Identify and discuss any likely limitations in the evaluation of the proposed investment in Alpha and Beta.** **(7 marks)**

(Total: 25 marks)

29   UMUNAT INC
(DEC 04)

Umunat Inc is considering investing $50,000 in a new machine with an expected life of <u>five</u> years. The machine will have <u>no scrap value</u> at the end of five years. It is expected that <u>20,000 units</u> will be sold each year at a selling price of $3.00 per unit. Variable production costs are expected to be $1.65 per unit, while incremental fixed costs, mainly the wages of a maintenance engineer, are expected to be $10,000 per year. Umunat Inc uses a discount rate of 12% for investment appraisal purposes and expects investment projects to recover their initial investment within two years.

Required:

(a)   **Explain why risk and uncertainty should be considered in the investment appraisal process.** **(5 marks)**

(b)   **Calculate and comment on the payback period of the project.** **(4 marks)**

(c)   **Evaluate the sensitivity of the project's net present value to a change in the following project variables:**

(i)   **sales volume;**

(ii)   **sales price;**

(iii)   **variable cost;**

and discuss the use of sensitivity analysis as a way of evaluating project risk.

(10 marks)

(d)   Upon further investigation it is found that there is a significant chance that the expected sales volume of 20,000 units per year will not be achieved. The sales manager of Umunat Inc suggests that sales volumes could depend on expected economic states that could be assigned the following probabilities:

Economic state	Poor	Normal	Good
Probability	0.3	0.6	0.1
Annual sale volume (units)	17,500	20,000	22,500

Required:

Calculate and comment on the expected net present value of the project. **(6 marks)**

(Total: 25 marks)

30 TOWER RAILWAYS INC
(DEC 01)

Assume that 'now' is December 20X7.

Tower Railways Inc, which has a financial year-end of 31 December, operates a rail passenger service between the major cities in its home country. It is currently negotiating with the regulatory authorities about a five-year extension and enhancement of its existing contract. Tower Railways has forecast passenger use over the next five-year period to 31 December 20Y2 and, based on its proposed carriage capacity, has calculated the following figures:

Five year projections:

Number of carriages used on the line:	8
Maximum passengers per carriage:	55
Average occupancy rate:	60%
Average number of return journeys per day:	10
Average price per return trip:	$12
Number of days operating per year:	340

Contribution per unit (sales price less variable costs) is expected to remain at a constant 35% of price over the period. Additional fixed costs of $1m per annum will be incurred on the new project. The management accountant has suggested that, in addition, the existing fixed overhead apportionment be increased by $200,000 per annum to reflect the increased activities relating to this part of the business. If the contract is renewed, other services offered by Tower Railways will be reduced to enable capacity expansion on the new contract. This will involve the loss of a long-standing contract, which was expected to continue indefinitely, worth $250,000 in pre-tax cash inflows per annum.

One of the conditions of a successful new bid is that a minimum investment of $5m, in support equipment to enhance the existing service, is required at the start of the new contract on 31 December 20X7. This equipment will no longer be needed to support the contract after four years and will be disposed of for $0.5m on 31 December 20Y1. Capital allowances are available for these transactions. A balancing charge or allowance would arise on disposal of the asset. The investment in this asset should be treated separately from any other asset investment for tax purposes (ignore any pooling requirements). Assume all tax payments and allowances arise at the end of the year in which the taxable transactions arise (in other words, not delayed). Assume that all operating cash inflows arise at the relevant year-end.

Other relevant information:

After tax discount rate per annum:	10%
Corporation tax rate:	30%
Writing down allowance:	25% per annum, reducing balance

Required:

(a) Calculate separately the present value of the net operating cash flows (after payment of corporation tax and using annuities and perpetuities where appropriate), and the capital flows (investment, disposal and related tax flows). Assess if it is beneficial for Tower Railways to begin the new contract on 31 December 20X7.

Express all calculations in this and other parts of the question to the nearest $1,000. State any assumptions you make. **(18 marks)**

(b) The Chairman of Tower Railways is concerned about the risk of the project, particularly with respect to the average price charged.

Calculate the sensitivity of the project in relation to the average price charged.

(4 marks)

Assume, in your answer that all other factors are as per your analysis in part (a).

(c) On reviewing the initial proposal from your answer to part (a), the regulatory authorities are now insisting that further investment of $7m be made to ensure carriage availability to meet targets for the level of proposed service provision. This would not involve the purchase of additional carriages. Assume that by incorporating the additional $7m investment on top of the existing $5m, a total NPV at 31 December 20X7 of $9.220m (negative) for the capital cash flows only will arise.

Required:

Calculate the occupancy rate required to break even (that is, to produce a zero NPV).

(3 marks)

(Total: 25 marks)

31   SPRINGBANK INC
(JUNE 03)

Springbank Inc is a medium-sized manufacturing company that plans to increase capacity by purchasing new machinery at an initial cost of $3 million. The new machine will also require a further investment in working capital of $400,000. The investment is expected to increase annual sales by 5,500 units. Investment in replacement machinery would be needed after five years. Financial data on the additional units to be sold is as follows:

	$
Selling price per unit	500
Production costs per unit	200

Variable administration and distribution expenses are expected to increase by $220,000 per year as a result of the increase in capacity. The full amount of the initial investment in new machinery of $3 million will give rise to capital allowances on a 25% per year reducing balance basis. The scrap value of the machinery after five years is expected to be negligible. Tax liabilities are paid in the year in which they arise and Springbank Inc pays tax at 30% of annual profits.

The Finance Director of Springbank Inc has proposed that the $3.4 million investment should be financed by an issue of loan stock at a fixed rate of 8% per year.

Springbank Inc uses an after tax discount rate of 12% to evaluate investment proposals. In preparing its financial statements, Springbank Inc uses straight-line depreciation over the expected life of non-current assets.

Required:

(a) Calculate the net present value of the proposed investment in increased capacity of Springbank Inc, clearly stating any assumptions that you make in your calculations.

(11 marks)

(b) Calculate the increase in sales (in units) that would produce a zero net present value for the proposed investment.

(8 marks)

(c) On the basis of your previous calculations and analysis, comment on the acceptability of the proposed investment and discuss whether the proposed method of financing can be recommended. **(6 marks)**

(Total: 25 marks)

 Online question assistance

32 BREAD PRODUCTS CO
(PILOT 01)

Bread Products Co is considering the replacement policy for its industrial size ovens which are used as part of a production line that bakes bread. Given its heavy usage each oven has to be replaced frequently. The choice is between replacing every two years or every three years. Only one type of oven is used, each of which costs $24,500.

Maintenance costs and resale values are as follows:

Year	Maintenance per annum	Resale value
	$	$
1	500	
2	800	15,600
3	1,500	11,200

Original cost, maintenance costs and resale values are expressed in current prices. That is, for example, maintenance for a two year old oven would cost $800 for maintenance undertaken now. It is expected that maintenance costs will increase at 10% per annum and oven replacement cost and resale values at 5% per annum. The money discount rate is 15%.

Required:

(a) Calculate the preferred replacement policy for the ovens in a choice between a two-year or three-year replacement cycle. **(12 marks)**

(b) Identify the limitations of Net Present Value techniques when applied generally to investment appraisal. **(13 marks)**

(Total: 25 marks)

33 BASRIL
(DEC 03)

Basril Inc is reviewing investment proposals that have been submitted by divisional managers. The investment funds of the company are limited to $800,000 in the current year. Details of three possible investments, none of which can be delayed, are given below.

Project 1

An investment of $300,000 in work station assessments. Each assessment would be on an individual employee basis and would lead to savings in labour costs from increased efficiency and from reduced absenteeism due to work-related illness. Savings in labour costs from these assessments in money terms are expected to be as follows:

Year	1	2	3	4	5
Cash flows (£000)	85	90	95	100	95

Project 2

An investment of $450,000 in individual workstations for staff that is expected to reduce administration costs by $140,800 per annum in money terms for the next five years.

Project 3

An investment of $400,000 in new ticket machines. Net cash savings of $120,000 per annum are expected in current price terms and these are expected to increase by 3.6% per annum due to inflation during the five-year life of the machines.

Basril Inc has a money cost of capital of 12% and taxation should be ignored.

Required:

(a)   Determine the best way for Basril Inc to invest the available funds and calculate the resultant NPV:

(i)   on the assumption that each of the three projects is divisible;

(ii)   on the assumption that none of the projects are divisible.   **(10 marks)**

(b)   Explain how the NPV investment appraisal method is applied in situations where capital is rationed.   **(3 marks)**

(c)   Discuss the reasons why capital rationing may arise.   **(7 marks)**

(d)   Discuss the meaning of the term 'relevant cash flows' in the context of investment appraisal, giving examples to illustrate your discussion.   **(5 marks)**

(Total: 25 marks)

34   LEAMINGER INC
(DEC 02)

Leaminger Inc has decided it must replace its major turbine machine on 31 December 20X2. The machine is essential to the operations of the company. The company is, however, considering whether to purchase the machine outright or to use lease financing.

Purchasing the machine outright

The machine is expected to cost $360,000 if it is purchased outright, payable on 31 December 20X2. After four years the company expects new technology to make the machine redundant and it will be sold on 31 December 20X6 generating proceeds of $20,000. Capital allowances for tax purposes are available on the cost of the machine at the rate of 25% per annum reducing balance. A full year's allowance is given in the year of acquisition but no writing down allowance is available in the year of disposal. The difference between the proceeds and the tax written down value in the year of disposal is allowable or chargeable for tax as appropriate.

Leasing

The company has approached its bank with a view to arranging a lease to finance the machine acquisition. The bank has offered two options with respect to leasing which are as follows:

	Finance lease	Operating lease
Contract length (years)	4	1
Annual rental	$135,000	$140,000
First rent payable	31 December 20X3	31 December 20X2

General

For both the purchasing and the finance lease option, maintenance costs of $15,000 per year are payable at the end of each year. All lease rentals (for both finance and operating options) can be assumed to be allowable for tax purposes in full in the year of payment. Assume that tax is payable one year after the end of the accounting year in which the transaction occurs. For the operating lease only, contracts are renewable annually at the discretion of either party. Leaminger Inc has adequate taxable profits to relieve all its costs. The rate of corporation tax can be assumed to be 30%. The company's accounting year-end is 31 December. The company's annual after tax cost of capital is 10%.

Required:

(a)   Calculate the net present value at 31 December 20X2, using the after tax cost of capital, for:

(i)   purchasing the machine outright

(ii)   using the finance lease to acquire the machine

(iii) using the operating lease to acquire the machine.

Recommend the optimal method. **(12 marks)**

(b)   Assume now that the company is facing capital rationing up until 30 December 20X3 when it expects to make a share issue. During this time the most marginal investment project, which is perfectly divisible, requires an outlay of $500,000 and would generate a net present value of $100,000. Investment in the turbine would reduce funds available for this project. Investments cannot be delayed.

Calculate the revised net present values of the three options for the turbine given capital rationing. Advise whether your recommendation in (a) would change.

(5 marks)

(c)   As their business advisor, prepare a report for the directors of Leaminger Inc that assesses the issues that need to be considered in acquiring the turbine with respect to capital rationing. **(8 marks)**

(Total: 25 marks)

35   AGD CO
(DEC 05)

AGD Co is a profitable company which is considering the purchase of a machine costing $320,000. If purchased, AGD Co would incur annual maintenance costs of $25,000. The machine would be used for three years and at the end of this period would be sold for $50,000. Alternatively, the machine could be obtained under an operating lease for an annual lease rental of $120,000 per year, payable in advance.

AGD Co can claim capital allowances on a 25% reducing balance basis. The company pays tax on profits at an annual rate of 30% and all tax liabilities are paid one year in arrears. AGD Co has an accounting year that ends on 31 December. If the machine is purchased, payment will be made in January of the first year of operation. If leased, annual lease rentals will be paid in January of each year of operation.

Required:

(a)   Using an after-tax borrowing rate of 7%, evaluate whether AGD Co should purchase or lease the new machine. **(12 marks)**

(b) **Explain and discuss the key differences between an operating lease and a finance lease.** **(8 marks)**

(c) The after-tax borrowing rate of 7% was used in the evaluation because a bank had offered to lend AGD Co $320,000 for a period of five years at a before-tax rate of 10% per year with interest payable every six months.

Required:

(i) **Calculate the annual percentage rate (APR) implied by the bank's offer to lend at 10% per year with interest payable every six months.** **(2 marks)**

(ii) **Calculate the amount to be repaid at the end of each six-month period if the offered loan is to be repaid in equal instalments.** **(3 marks)**

(Total: 25 marks)

36 CAVIC
(DEC 06)

Cavic Co services custom cars and provides its clients with a courtesy car while servicing is taking place. It has a fleet of 10 courtesy cars which it plans to replace in the near future. Each new courtesy car will cost $15,000. The trade-in value of each new car declines over time as follows:

Age of courtesy car (years)	1	2	3
Trade-in value ($/car)	11,250	9,000	6,200

Servicing and parts will cost $1,000 per courtesy car in the first year and this cost is expected to increase by 40% per year as each vehicle grows older. Cleaning the interior and exterior of each courtesy car to keep it up to the standard required by Cavic's clients will cost $500 per car in the first year and this cost is expected to increase by 25% per year.

Cavic Co has a cost of capital of 10%. Ignore taxation and inflation.

Required:

(a) **Using the equivalent annual cost method, calculate whether Cavic Co should replace its fleet after one year, two years, or three years.** **(12 marks)**

(b) **Discuss the causes of capital rationing for investment purposes.** **(4 marks)**

(c) **Explain how an organisation can determine the best way to invest available capital under capital rationing. Your answer should refer to the following issues:**

(i) **single-period capital rationing;**

(ii) **multi-period capital rationing;**

(iii) **project divisibility;**

(iv) **the investment of surplus funds.** **(9 marks)**

(Total: 25 marks)

BUSINESS FINANCE

37 COLLINGHAM
(JUNE 95)

Collingham Inc produces electronic measuring instruments for medical research. It has recorded strong and consistent growth during the past 10 years since its present team of managers bought it out from a large multinational corporation. They are now contemplating obtaining a stock market listing.

Collingham's accounting statements for the last financial year are summarised below. Non-current assets, including freehold land and premises, are shown at historic cost net of depreciation. The loan stock is redeemable in two years although early redemption without penalty is permissible.

Income statement for the year ended 31 December 20X7

	$m
Sales revenue	80.0
Cost of sales	(70.0)
Operating profit	10.0
Interest charges	(3.0)
Pre-tax profit	7.0
Corporation tax (after capital allowances)	(1.0)
Profits attributable to ordinary shareholders	6.0
Dividends	0.5
Net change in equity (retained profit)	5.5

Statement of financial position as at 31 December 20X7

	$m	$m
Non-current assets:		
Land and premises		10.0
Machinery		20.0
		30.0
Current assets:		
Inventories	10.0	
Receivables	10.0	
Cash	3.0	
		23.0
Total assets		53.0

	$m	$m
Equity and liabilities		
Issued share capital (par value 50¢)		
Voting shares		2.0
Non-voting 'A' shares		2.0
Retained profit		24.0
Total equity		28.0
Non-current liabilities: 14% loan stock		5.0
Current liabilities:		
Trade payables	15.0	
Bank overdraft	5.0	
		20.0
Total equity and liabilities		53.0

The following information is also available regarding key financial indicators for Collingham's industry.

Return on (long-term) capital employed	22% (pre-tax)
Return on equity	14% (post-tax)
Operating profit margin	10%
Current ratio	1.8:1
Acid-test	1.1:1
Gearing (total debt equity)	18%
Interest cover	5.2
Dividend cover	2.6
P/E ratio	13:1

Required

(a) Briefly explain why companies like Collingham seek stock market listings. **(5 marks)**

(b) Discuss the performance and financial health of Collingham in relation to that of the industry as a whole. **(10 marks)**

(c) In what ways would you advise Collingham:

   (i) to restructure its balance sheet prior to floatation, **(5 marks)**

   (ii) to change its financial policy following floatation? **(5 marks)**

(Total: 25 marks)

38 JERONIMO INC
(JUNE 99)

Jeronimo Inc currently has 5 million ordinary shares in issue, which have a market value of $1.60 each. The company wishes to raise finance for a major investment project by means of a rights issue, and is proposing to issue shares on the basis of 1 for 5 at a price of $1.30 each.

James Brown currently owns 10,000 shares in Jeronimo Inc and is seeking advice on whether or not to take up the proposed rights.

Required:

(a)   Explain the difference between a rights issue and a scrip issue. Your answer should include comment on the reasons why companies make such issues and the effect of the issues on private investors.   **(7 marks)**

(b)   Calculate:

(i)   the theoretical value of James Brown's shareholding if he takes up his rights

(ii)   the theoretical value of James Brown's rights if he chooses to sell them.
                                                                            (5 marks)

(c)   Using only the information given below, and applying the dividend growth model formula, calculate the required return on equity for an investor in Jeronimo Inc.

Jeronimo Inc:

Current share price:	$1.60
Number of shares in issue:	5 million
Current earnings:	$1.5 million
Dividend paid	(Cents per share):
20X5:	8
20X6:	9
20X7:	11
20X8:	11
20X9:	12

                                                                            (5 marks)

(d)   If the stock market is believed to operate with a strong level of efficiency, what effect might this have on the behaviour of the finance directors of publicly quoted companies?   **(8 marks)**

                                                                    (Total: 25 marks)

39 **ECHO CO** *Walk in the footsteps of a top tutor*

(DEC 07)

The following financial information relates to Echo Co:

Income statement information for the last year

	$m
Profit before interest and tax	12
Interest	3
Profit before tax	9
Income tax expense	3
Profit for the period	6
Dividends	2
Retained profit for the period	4

Statement of financial position information as at the end of the last year

	$m	$m
Ordinary shares, par value 50c	5	
Retained earnings	15	
Total equity		20
8% loan notes, redeemable in three years' time		30
Total equity and non-current liabilities		50

Average data on companies similar to Echo Co:

Interest coverage ratio	8 times
Long-term debt/equity (book value basis)	80%

The board of Echo Co is considering several proposals that have been made by its finance director. Each proposal is independent of any other proposal.

Proposal A   *Increase Div.*

The current dividend per share should be increased by 20% in order to make the company more attractive to equity investors.

Proposal B   *Debt.*

A bond issue should be made in order to raise $15 million of new debt capital. Although there are no investment opportunities currently available, the cash raised would be invested on a short-term basis until a suitable investment opportunity arose. The loan notes would pay interest at a rate of 10% per year and be redeemable in eight years time at par.

Proposal C   *right issue.*

A 1 for 4 rights issue should be made at a 20% discount to the current share price of $2.30 per share in order to reduce gearing and the financial risk of the company.

Required:

(a) Analyse and discuss Proposal A. (5 marks)

(b) Evaluate and discuss Proposal B. (7 marks)

(c) Calculate the theoretical ex rights price per share and the amount of finance that would be raised under Proposal C. Evaluate and discuss the proposal to use these funds to reduce gearing and financial risk. (7 marks)

(d) Discuss the attractions of operating leasing as a source of finance. (6 marks)

(Total: 25 marks)

40 PAVLON
(JUNE 86)

(a) Pavlon Inc has recently obtained a listing on the Stock Exchange. 90% of the company's shares were previously owned by members of one family but, since the listing, approximately 60% of the issued shares have been owned by other investors.

Pavlon's earnings and dividends for the five years prior to the listing are detailed below:

Years prior to listing	Profit after tax ($)	Dividend per share (cents)
5	1,800,000	3.6
4	2,400,000	4.8
3	3,850,000	6.16
2	4,100,000	6.56
1	4,450,000	7.12
Current year	5,500,000(estimate)	

The number of issued ordinary shares was increased by 25% three years prior to the listing and by 50% at the time of the listing. The company's authorised capital is currently $25,000,000 in 25¢ ordinary shares, of which 40,000,000 shares have been issued. The market value of the company's equity is $78,000,000.

The board of directors is discussing future dividend policy. An interim dividend of 3.16 cents per share was paid immediately prior to the listing and the finance director has suggested a final dividend of 2.34 cents per share.

The company's declared objective is to maximise shareholder wealth.

Required:

(i) Comment upon the nature of the company's dividend policy prior to the listing and discuss whether such a policy is likely to be suitable for a company listed on the Stock Exchange. (6 marks)

(ii) Discuss whether the proposed final dividend of 2.34 cents is likely to be an appropriate dividend:

– If the majority of shares are owned by wealthy private individuals; and

– If the majority of shares are owned by institutional investors.(10 marks)

(b) The company's profit after tax is generally expected to increase by 15% per year for three years, and 8% per year after that. Pavlon's cost of equity capital is estimated to be 12% per year. Dividends may be assumed to grow at the same rate as profits.

Required:

(i) Use the dividend valuation model to give calculations to indicate whether Pavlon's shares are currently under- or over-valued. **(6 marks)**

(ii) Briefly outline the weaknesses of the dividend valuation model. **(3 marks)**

(Total: 25 marks)

41 **ARWIN**

(JUNE 04)

Arwin plans to raise $5m in order to expand its existing chain of retail outlets. It can raise the finance by issuing 10% loan stock redeemable in ten years' time, or by a rights issue at $4.00 per share. The current financial statements of Arwin are as follows:

Income statement for the last year

	$000
Sales revenue	50,000
Cost of sales	30,000
Gross profit	20,000
Administration costs	14,000
Profit before interest and tax	6,000
Interest	300
Profit before tax	5,700
Taxation at 30%	1,710
Profit after tax	3,990

Changes in equity

	$000
Dividends	2,394
Net change in equity (retained profits)	1,596

Statement of financial position

	$000
Net non-current assets	20,100
Net current assets	4,960
	25,060
Ordinary shares, par value 25¢	2,500
Retained profit	20,060
12% loan stock (redeemable in six years)	2,500
	25,060

The expansion of business is expected to increase sales revenue by 12% in the first year. Variable cost of sales makes up 85% of cost of sales. Administration costs will increase by 5% due to new staff appointments. Arwin has a policy of paying out 60% of profit after tax as dividends and has no overdraft.

Required:

(a)   For each financing proposal, prepare the forecast income statement after one additional year of operation.   **(5 marks)**

(b)   Evaluate and comment on the effects of each financing proposal on the following:

    (i)   Financial gearing;

    (ii)   Operational gearing;

    (iii)   Interest cover;

    (iv)   Earnings per share.   **(12 marks)**

(c)   Discuss the dangers to a company of a high level of gearing, including in your answer an explanation of the following terms:

    (i)   Business risk;

    (ii)   Financial risk.   **(8 marks)**

                                                      (Total: 25 marks)

42 SPENDER CONSTRUCTION INC
(JUNE 00)

Assume that 'now' is the end of December 20X7.

Spender Construction Inc is an expanding building company wishing to raise funds to invest in building a new headquarters and IT centre with upgraded facilities for its logistics and project management business. The total investment required is estimated to be $7 million. The financial justification for the investment is based upon estimates that the new centre will cut fixed administration costs by approximately $500,000 per annum, and reduce the cost of sales by 2%. Sales for the year to 31 December 20X8 are forecast to rise 15% above 20X7 levels (regardless of the investment decision), and so the company anticipates a need for higher working capital funding, in addition to finance for the capital expenditure.

Spender's finance director has commented that in raising funds the Board need to be conscious of the fact that the company operates in a sector which is notorious for its volatility of demand, and also that the company has relatively high levels of fixed operating costs. The industry average is for fixed operating costs to equal 7% of sales revenue. Summarised financial statements for Spender Construction Inc are shown below:

Income statement, year ending 31 December 20X7

	$000
Sales revenue	55,258
Cost of sales	41,827
Gross profit	13,431
Selling and distribution costs	348
Administration costs	8,250
Operating profit	4,833
Interest charges	327
Profit before tax	4,506
Corporation tax payable	1,352
Profit after tax	3,154
Note:	
Dividends	1,520
Net change in equity (retained profits)	1,634

Statement of financial position as at 31 December 20X7

	$000
Non-current assets	5,800
Current assets	27,928
Total assets	33,728
Equity and liabilities	
Ordinary share capital	4,000
Share premium account	800
Retained profit	7,652
Total equity	12,452
10% loan stock 20X6	1,200
Current liabilities	20,076
Total equity and liabilities	33,728

Additional information

(1) The nominal value of ordinary share capital is 50 cents per share.

(2) Costs are classified as fixed or variable as follows:

Cost of sales: 100% variable.

Selling and distribution: $100,000 per annum fixed, balance variable.

Administration costs: $7 million per annum fixed, balance variable.

(3) The current rate of corporation tax is 30%.

(4)   Current liabilities as at 31 December 20X7 includes a $2 million overdraft, and a $450,000 sales tax bill.

(5)   The current market price of ordinary shares in Spender Inc is $6.50.

(6)   Working capital needs are expected to rise in line with sales.

(7)   The dividend forecast for year ending 31 December 20X8 is 25 cents per share.

(8)   Bank interest charges for the year to 31 December 20X8 are forecast to be $280,000. Interest is charged at 12.5% per annum.

(9)   Depreciation charges on non-current assets for the year to 31 December 20X7 are $435,000.

(10) Assume that payments totalling $2.5 million were made during 20X7 in respect of trade payables outstanding at the end of the previous year.

(11) Working capital requirements for 20X7 were the same as those for the previous year.

Required:

(a)   Explain and illustrate, using the above data, each of the following terms and comment upon the implications of these two forms of gearing for the equity investors in Spender Construction Inc:

   (i)   operational gearing

   (ii)   financial gearing.   **(12 marks)**

(b)   Evaluate (by comparison of shareholder risks and returns, including EPS) the relative merits of raising the $7 million required for the capital investment via a 1 for 6 rights issue priced at $5.25, or 10% loan stock issue redeemable in 20 years time. Ignore issue costs.   **(10 marks)**

(c)   Explain the meaning of the term dividend cover and, using the forecast figures for the year ending 31 December 20X8, calculate the dividend cover for Spender Construction Inc assuming the loan stock issue is made.   **(3 marks)**

                                                                          (Total: 25 marks)

43 ASSOCIATED INTERNATIONAL SUPPLIES CO
(PILOT 01)

The following are summary financial statements for Associated International Supplies Co.

	20X4	20X9
	$000	$000
Non-current assets	115	410
Current assets	650	1,000
Total assets	765	1,410
Capital and reserves	210	270
Non-current liabilities	42	158
Current liabilities	513	982
	765	1,410

	20X4	20X9
	$000	$000
Sales revenue	1,200	3,010
Cost of sales, expenses and interest	1,102	2,860
Profit before tax	98	150
Tax and distributions	33	133
Retained earnings	65	17

Notes: Cost of sales was $530,000 for 20X4 and $1,330,000 for 20X9.

Trade receivables are 50% of current assets; trade payables 25% of current liabilities for both years.

Required:

(a) You are a consultant advising Associated International Supplies Co. Using suitable financial ratios, and paying particular attention to growth and liquidity, write a report on the significant changes faced by the company since 20X4. The report should also comment on the capacity of the company to continue trading, together with any other factors considered appropriate. An appendix to the report should be used to outline your calculations. **(17 marks)**

(b) Explain and evaluate the sources of finance available to small businesses for non-current assets. **(8 marks)**

(Total: 25 marks)

44 GTK INC *Walk in the footsteps of a top tutor*

(JUNE 07)

The finance director of GTK Inc is preparing its capital budget for the forthcoming period and is examining a number of capital investment proposals that have been received from its subsidiaries. Details of these proposals are as follows:

Proposal 1

Division A has requested that it be allowed to invest $500,000 in solar panels, which would be fitted to the roof of its production facility, in order to reduce its dependency on oil as an energy source. The solar panels would save energy costs of $700 per day but only on sunny days. The Division has estimated the following probabilities of sunny days in each year.

	Number of sunny days	Probability
Scenario 1	100	0.3
Scenario 2	125	0.6
Scenario 3	150	0.1

Each scenario is expected to persist indefinitely, i.e. if there are 100 sunny days in the first year, there will be 100 sunny days in every subsequent year. Maintenance costs for the solar panels are expected to be $2,000 per month for labour and replacement parts, irrespective of the number of sunny days per year. The solar panels are expected to be used indefinitely.

Proposal 2

Division C has requested approval and funding for a new product which it has been secretly developing, Product RPG. Product development and market research costs of $350,000 have already been incurred and are now due for payment. $300,000 is needed for new machinery, which will be a full scale version of the current pilot plant. Advertising takes place in the first year only and would cost $100,000. Annual cash inflow of $100,000, net of all production costs but before taking account of advertising costs, is expected to be generated for a five-year period. After five years Product RPG would be retired and replaced with a more technologically advanced model. The machinery used for producing Product RPG would be sold for $30,000 at that time.

Other information

GTK Inc is a profitable, listed company with several million dollars of shareholders' funds, a small overdraft and no long-term debt. For profit calculation purposes, GTK Inc depreciates assets on a straight-line basis over their useful economic life. The company can claim writing down allowances on machinery on a 25% reducing balance basis and pays tax on profit at an annual rate of 30% in the year in which the liability arises. GTK Inc has a before-tax cost of capital of 10%, an after-tax cost of capital of 8% and a target return on capital employed of 15%.

Required:

(a)   For the proposed investment in solar panels (Proposal 1), calculate:

    (i)   the net present value for each expected number of sunny days

    (ii)   the overall expected net present value of the proposal

    Comment on your findings. Ignore taxation in this part of the question.   **(9 marks)**

(b)   Calculate the before-tax return on capital employed (accounting rate of return) of the proposed investment in Product RPG (Proposal 2), using the average investment method, and advise on its acceptability.   **(6 marks)**

(c)   Assuming GTK Inc wishes to raise $1.1 million, discuss how equity finance or traded debt (bonds) might be raised, clearly indicating which source of finance you recommend and the reasons for your recommendation.   **(10 marks)**

(Total: 25 marks)

45   TFR
(JUNE 07)

TFR is a small, profitable, owner-managed company which is seeking finance for a planned expansion. A local bank has indicated that it may be prepared to offer a loan of $100,000 at a fixed annual rate of 9%. TFR would repay $25,000 of the capital each year for the next four years. Annual interest would be calculated on the opening balance at the start of each year. Current financial information on TFR is as follows:

Current turnover:	$210,000
Net profit margin:	20%
Annual taxation rate:	25%
Average overdraft:	$20,000
Average interest on overdraft:	10% per year
Dividend payout ratio:	50%
Shareholders funds:	$200,000
Market value of non-current assets	$180,000

As a result of the expansion, turnover would increase by $45,000 per year for each of the next four years, while net profit margin would remain unchanged. No capital allowances would arise from investment of the amount borrowed.

TFR currently has no other debt than the existing and continuing overdraft and has no cash or near-cash investments. The non-current assets consist largely of the building from which the company conducts its business. The current dividend payout ratio has been maintained for several years.

Required:

(a)   Assuming that TFR is granted the loan, calculate the following ratios for TFR for each of the next four years:

(i)   interest cover

(ii)   medium to long-term debt/equity ratio

(iii)   return on equity

(iv)   return on capital employed.   **(10 marks)**

(b)   Comment on the financial implications for TFR of accepting the bank loan on the terms indicated above.   **(8 marks)**

(c)   Discuss the difficulties commonly faced by small firms such as TFR when seeking additional finance.   **(7 marks)**

(Total: 25 marks)

COST OF CAPITAL

46   FLEET CO
(CHAPTER 18)

(a)   The finance team of Fleet Co is undertaking a financial review of a potential new project. The new project is in the same industry as Fleet Co and the capital structure of the enlarged company will remain unchanged. The following details are available:

The capital structure of Fleet Co as at 1st January 20X8 is as follows:

	$m
Issued ordinary shares (25p shares)	250
Bank term loan	300
8% irredeemable debenture	600

The ordinary shares have a current market price of $2 each. Dividends per share in the five preceding years were as follows:

20X3	6.9 pence
20X4	7.2 pence
20X5	8.8 pence
20X6	9.6 pence
20X7	10.5 pence

The dividend for 20X7 has just been paid.

The bank is currently charging 10% on the term loan.

The debenture stock has a market price of $75.

The company pays corporation tax at a rate of 30%.

Required:

Calculate a suitable discount rate for the new project.   **(8 marks)**

(b)   Fleet Co has a subsidiary company Foxes Co. It currently invests in two projects, one of which is in the leisure industry and the other in publishing. These represent 65% and 35% respectively of Foxes Co's total market value.

The firm is considering investing additional funds into one of these projects, so the Financial Manager has presented the following analysis as a starting point to an investment appraisal:

	Leisure industry	Publishing industry	Foxes Co
Average beta equity	1.10	????	1.20
Average gearing of firms in the industry (D:E)	30:70	40:60	20:80

Unfortunately, the Financial Manager's spreadsheet has been corrupted so that the Publishing Industry beta equity is illegible. He is now uncontactable on holiday, so the firm's Chief Executive has asked for your help in reconstructing the spreadsheet.

N.B. Corporate taxation is at the rate of 30%. Assume that debt is risk free, so the beta of debt is zero.

Required:

From the information presented, reconstruct the Financial Manager's spreadsheet by calculating the average beta equity of the Publishing Industry. **(8 marks)**

(c)   The directors of Foxes Co have decided to go ahead with a further investment in the leisure industry. They have presented you with the following further information:

- The financial gearing of the company is not expected to change as a result of any expansion.

- The IRR of Foxes Co's after tax cash flows on redeemable debt is 6.0%. The risk free rate is 5% and the estimated market return is 10%.

Required:

Calculate a suitable discount rate in order to appraise the additional investment in the leisure industry. **(5 marks)**

(d)   **Explain briefly how your approach to part (c) would have differed if Foxes Co had decided to change its gearing level by raising new debt finance to fund the new project. You are not required to produce any further calculations.** **(4 marks)**

(Total: 25 marks)

47   **KFP CO**
     (JUNE 09)

 Timed question with Online tutor debrief

KFP Co, a company listed on a major stock market, is looking at its cost of capital as it prepares to make a bid to buy a rival <u>unlisted company</u>, NGN. Both companies are <u>in the</u> <u>same business sector</u>. Financial information on KFP Co and NGN is as follows:

	KFP Co		NGN *New*	
	$m	$m	$m	$m
Non-current assets		36		25
Current assets	7		7	
Current liabilities	3		4	
Net current assets		4		3
Total assets less current liabilities		40		28

	KFP Co		NGN	
	$m	$m	$m	$m
Ordinary shares, par value 50c	15		5	
Retained earnings	10		3	
Total equity		25		8
① 7% bonds, redeemable at par in seven years' time		15		
② 9% bonds, redeemable at par in two years' time				20
Total equity and non-current liabilities		40		28

Other relevant financial information:

Risk-free rate of return	4·0%	rf
Average return on the market	10·5%	rm
Taxation rate	30%

b = 5% NGN has a cost of equity of 12% per year and has maintained a dividend payout ratio of 45% for several years. The current earnings per share of the company is 80c per share and its earnings have grown at an average rate of 4·5% per year in recent years.

Po = 4.2 The ex div share price of KFP Co is $4·20 per share and it has an equity beta of 1·2. The 7% bonds of the company are trading on an ex interest basis at $94·74 per $100 bond. The price/earnings ratio of KFP Co is eight times. PE = 8

The directors of KFP Co believe a cash offer for the shares of NGN would have the best chance of success. It has been suggested that a cash offer could be financed by debt.

Required:

(a) Calculate the weighted average cost of capital of KFP Co on a market value weighted basis. WACC
(10 marks)

(b) Calculate the total value of the target company, NGN, using the following valuation methods: TMV Business Valuation.

(i) Price/earnings ratio method, using the price/earnings ratio of KFP Co; and PE

(ii) Dividend growth model. g
(6 marks)

(c) Discuss the relationship between capital structure and weighted average cost of capital, and comment on the suggestion that debt could be used to finance a cash offer for NGN.
(9 marks)

(25 marks)

 Calculate your allowed time, allocate the time to the separate parts

48 BURSE CO *Walk in the footsteps of a top tutor*

(JUNE 08)

Burse Co wishes to calculate its weighted average cost of capital and the following information relates to the company at the current time:

① Number of ordinary shares	20 million
② Book value of 7% convertible debt	$29 million
③ Book value of 8% bank loan	$2 million

Market price of ordinary shares	$5·50 per share
Market value of convertible debt P_o	$107·11 per $100 bond

Equity beta of Burse Co β	1·2
Risk-free rate of return r_f	4·7%
Equity risk premium $r_m - r_f$	6·5%

Rate of taxation	30%

Burse Co expects share prices to rise in the future at an average rate of 6% per year. The convertible debt can be redeemed at par in eight years' time, or converted in six years' time into 15 shares of Burse Co per $100 bond.

Required:

(a) Calculate the market value weighted average cost of capital of Burse Co. State clearly any assumptions that you make. WACC **(12 marks)**

(b) Discuss the circumstances under which the weighted average cost of capital can be used in investment appraisal. Limitation **(6 marks)**

(c) Discuss whether the <u>dividend growth model</u> or the <u>capital asset pricing model</u> offers the better estimate of the cost of equity of a company. CAPM **(7 marks)**
Limitations
(Total: 25 marks)

49 CAPITAL STRUCTURE STRATEGY
(DEC 04)

(a) Prepare a briefing document for a board of directors discussing issues that might influence a company's capital structure strategy. **(15 marks)**

(b) Gadus Inc, a listed company, operates a fleet of fishing trawlers in Northern Europe.

The company has recently signed a long-term contract to supply a large supermarket chain with fresh fish. The new contract would increase profits significantly, but it requires investment in a processing and packaging warehouse costing $2 million.

There are two options being considered to finance the required investment of $2 million.

(1) A one for two rights issue at an issue price of $8

(2) An issue of 8% irredeemable loan stock at par.

Gadus Inc currently has 500,000 $1 ordinary shares in issue with a market price of $11and has no long term debt finance. The majority of the shares are owned by members of the founding Gadus family.

Required:

Write a report briefly advising the directors as to which form of finance should be used. Refer to any assumptions made by the directors or by you, and explain any wider factors that should be considered. **(10 marks)**

(Total: 25 marks)

50 GM CO

GM Co is a listed company that plans to expand its business. One project, which will be funded via floating rate finance, will see GM Co venturing into a new, much riskier area of the market. The other project, funded via equity finance, will expand their current operations. Overall, there is expected to be little change in the company's market weighted capital gearing. Financial data for the company before the expansion are shown below:

Financial extracts for the year ending 31 March 20X8

	$ million	$ million
Ordinary shares, par value $0.50	225	
Retained earnings	801	
Total equity		1,026
14% loan notes	75	
9% bank loan	250	
Total non-current liabilities		325

The 14% loan notes are redeemable at par in five years' time. They have a current ex-interest market price of $110 per $100 loan note. GM Co pays tax on profits at an annual rate of 30%. The market price of the company's ordinary shares is currently $3.76. GM Co's equity beta is estimated to be 1.2. The systematic risk of debt may be assumed to be zero. The risk free rate is 7% and the market return 13.5%.

The estimated equity beta of the main competitor in the same industry as the new venture is 1.8, and the competitor's capital gearing is 60% equity, 40% debt by market values.

Required:

(a) **Calculate the current weighted average cost of capital of GM Co** WACC **(10 marks)**

(b) **Estimate the risk adjusted cost of capital that GM Co should use as the discount rate for its proposed investment in the new venture. State any assumptions that you make.** Degear – Regear – CAPM – WACC **(9 marks)**

(c) **Outline the main advantages and disadvantages of the CAPM when being used to calculate the required return on equity.** **(6 marks)**

(Total 25 marks)

51 RUPAB CO
(DEC 08)

Rupab Co is a manufacturing company that wishes to evaluate an investment in new production machinery. The machinery would enable the company to satisfy increasing demand for existing products and the investment is not expected to lead to any change in the existing level of business risk of Rupab Co.

The machinery will cost $2.5 million, payable at the star t of the first year of operation, and is not expected to have any scrap value. Annual before-tax net cash flows of $680,000 per year would be generated by the investment in each of the five years of its expected operating life. These net cash inflows are before taking account of expected inflation of 3% per year. Initial investment of $240,000 in working capital would also be required, followed by incremental annual investment to maintain the purchasing power of working capital.

Rupab Co has in issue five million shares with a market value of $3.81 per share. The equity beta of the company is 1.2. The yield on short-term government debt is 4·5% per year and the equity risk premium is approximately 5% per year.

The debt finance of Rupab Co consists of bonds with a total book value of $2 million. These bonds pay annual interest before tax of 7%. The par value and market value of each bond is $100.

Rupab Co pays taxation one year in arrears at an annual rate of 25%. Capital allowances (tax-allowable depreciation) on machinery are on a straight-line basis over the life of the asset.

Required:

(a) Calculate the after-tax weighted average cost of capital of Rupab Co.   **(6 marks)**

(b) Prepare a forecast of the annual after-tax cash flows of the investment in nominal terms, and calculate and comment on its net present value.   **(8 marks)**

(c) Explain how the capital asset pricing model can be used to calculate a project-specific discount rate and discuss the limitations of using the capital asset pricing model in investment appraisal.   **(11 marks)**

(Total: 25 marks)

52 WEMERE
(JUNE 90)

The managing director of Wemere, a medium-sized private company, wishes to improve the company's investment decision-making process by using discounted cash flow techniques. He is disappointed to learn that estimates of a company's cost of capital usually require information on share prices which, for a private company, are not available. His deputy suggests that the cost of equity can be estimated by using data for Folten Inc, a similar sized, quoted company in the same industry, and he has produced two suggested discount rates for use in Wemere's future investment appraisal. Both of these estimates are in excess of 15% per year which the managing director believes to be very high, especially as the company has just agreed a fixed rate bank loan at 10% per year to finance a small expansion of existing operations. He has checked the calculations, which are numerically correct, but wonders if there are any errors of principle.

Estimate 1: capital asset pricing model

Data have been purchased from a leading business school:

Equity beta of Folten	1.4
Market return	14%
Treasury bill yield	6%

The cost of capital is 14% + (14% − 6%) 1.4 = 25.2%.

This rate must be adjusted to include inflation at the current level of 4%. The recommended discount rate is 29.2%.

Estimate 2: dividend valuation model

	Average share price (cents)	Dividend per share (cents)
20X3	193	9.23
20X4	109	10.06
20X5	96	10.97
20X6	116	11.95
20X7	130	13.03

The cost of capital is $\dfrac{D_1}{P - g} = \dfrac{14.20}{138 - 9} = 11.01\%$

where

D1	=	expected dividend
P	=	market price
g	=	growth rate of dividends (%)

When inflation is included the discount rate is 15.01%.

Other financial information on the two companies is presented below:

	Wemere	Folten
	$000	$000
Non-current assets	7,200	7,600
Current assets	7,600	7,800
Total assets	14,800	15,400
Ordinary shares (25 cents)	2,000	1,800
Reserves	6,500	5,500
Term loans	2,400	4,400
Current liabilities	3,900	3,700
	14,800	15,400

Notes:

(1) The current ex-div share price of Folten Inc is 138 cents.

(2) Wemere's board of directors has recently rejected a take-over bid of $10.6 million.

(3) Corporate tax is at the rate of 35%.

Required:

(a) **Explain any errors of principle that have been made in the two estimates of the cost of capital and produce revised estimates using both of the methods. State clearly any assumptions that you make.** **(14 marks)**

(b) Discuss which of your revised estimates Wemere should use as the discount rate for capital investment appraisal. **(4 marks)**

(c) Discuss whether discounted cash flow techniques including discounted payback are useful to small unlisted companies. **(7 marks)**

(Total: 25 marks)

BUSINESS VALUATIONS

53 **ZED**
(JUNE 83)

Zed Inc is considering the immediate purchase of some or all of the share capital of one of two firms – Red Co. and Yellow Co. Both Red and Yellow have 1 million ordinary shares issued and neither company has any debt capital outstanding.

Both firms are expected to pay a dividend in one year's time – Red's expected dividend amounting to 30¢ per share and Yellow's being 27¢ per share. Dividends will be paid annually and are expected to increase over time. Red's dividends are expected to display perpetual growth at a compound rate of 6% per annum. Yellow's dividend will grow at the high annual compound rate of 33.33% until a dividend of 64¢ per share is reached in year 4. Thereafter Yellow's dividend will remain constant.

If Zed is able to purchase all the equity capital of either firm then the reduced competition would enable Zed to save some advertising and administrative costs which would amount to $225,000 per annum indefinitely and in year 2, to sell some office space for $800,000. These benefits and savings will only occur if a complete take-over were to be carried out.

Zed would change some operations of any company completely taken-over – the details are:

(i) Red – No dividend would be paid until year 3. Year 3 dividend would be 25¢ per share and dividends would then grow at 10% per annum indefinitely.

(ii) Yellow – No change in total dividends in years 1 to 4, but after year 4 dividend growth would be 25% per annum compound until year 7. Thereafter annual dividends would remain constant at the year 7 amount per share.

An appropriate discount rate for the risk inherent in all cash flows mentioned is 15%.

Required:

(a) Ignoring taxation calculate

(i) The valuation per share for a minority investment in each of the firms Red and Yellow which would provide the investor with a 15% rate of return.

(8 marks)

(ii) The maximum amount per share which Zed should consider paying for each company in the event of a complete take-over. **(9 marks)**

(b) Comment on any limitations of the approach used in part (a) and specify the other major factors which would be important to consider if the proposed valuations were being undertaken as a practical exercise. **(8 marks)**

(Total: 25 marks)

54 TAGNA

(JUNE 03)

Tagna is a medium-sized company that manufactures luxury goods for several well-known chain stores. In real terms, the company has experienced only a small growth in revenue in recent years, but it has managed to maintain a constant, if low, level of reported profits by careful control of costs. It has paid a constant nominal (money terms) dividend for several years and its managing director has publicly stated that the primary objective of the company is to increase the wealth of shareholders. Tagna is financed as follows:

	$m
Overdraft	1.0
10 year fixed-interest bank loan	2.0
Share capital and reserves	4.5
	7.5

Tagna has the agreement of its existing shareholders to make a new issue of shares on the stock market but has been informed by its bank that current circumstances are unsuitable. The bank has stated that if new shares were to be issued now they would be significantly under-priced by the stock market, causing Tagna to issue many more shares than necessary in order to raise the amount of finance it requires. The bank recommends that the company waits for at least six months before issuing new shares, by which time it expects the stock market to have become strong-form efficient.

The financial press has reported that it expects the Central Bank to make a substantial increase in interest rate in the near future in response to rapidly increasing consumer demand and a sharp rise in inflation. The financial press has also reported that the rapid increase in consumer demand has been associated with an increase in consumer credit to record levels.

Required:

(a)   Discuss the meaning and significance of the different forms of market efficiency (weak, semi-strong and strong) and comment on the recommendation of the bank that Tagna waits for six months before issuing new shares on the stock market.

(9 marks)

(b)   On the assumption that the Central Bank makes a substantial interest rate increase, discuss the possible consequences for Tagna in the following areas:

(i)   sales

(ii)   operating costs, and

(iii)   earnings (profit after tax).   (10 marks)

(c)   Explain and compare the public sector objective of 'value for money' and the private sector objective of 'maximisation of shareholder wealth'.   (6 marks)

(Total: 25 marks)

55 HENDIL (PART II)
(DEC 06)

Hendil Inc, a manufacturer of electronic equipment, has prepared the following draft financial statements for the year that has just ended. These financial statements have not yet been made public.

Income statement

	$000
Sales revenue	9,600
Cost of sales	5,568
Gross profit	4,032
Operating expenses	3,408
Profit before interest and tax	624
Interest	156
Profit before tax	468
Taxation	140
Profit after tax	328
Dividends	300
Net change in equity (retained profits)	28

Statement of financial position

	$000	$000
Non-current assets		2,250
Current assets		
Inventories	1,660	
Receivables	2,110	
Cash	780	
		4,550
Total assets		6,800
Equity and liabilities		
Ordinary shares, par value 50¢		1,000
Retained profits		3,100
Total equity		4,100
10% loan stock, repayable 2015		1,200
Current liabilities		
Trade payables	750	
Dividends	300	
Overdraft	450	
		1,500
Total equity plus liabilities		6,800

Hendil Inc pays interest on its overdraft at an annual rate of 6%. The 10% loan stock is secured on the non-current assets of the company.

Average data on companies similar to Hendil Inc:

Interest cover	6 times
Long-term debt/ equity (book value basis)	50%
Long-term debt/ equity (market value basis)	25%

The ordinary shareholders of Hendil Inc require an annual return of 12%. Its ordinary shares are currently trading on the stock market at $1.80 per share. The dividend paid by the company has increased at a constant rate of 5% per year in recent years and, in the absence of further investment, the directors expect this dividend growth rate to continue for the foreseeable future.

Required:

(a) (i) Calculate the ordinary share price of Hendil Inc, predicted by the dividend growth model. **(4 marks)**

(ii) Explain the concept of market efficiency and distinguish between strong form efficiency and semi-strong form efficiency. **(6 marks)**

(iii) Discuss why the share price predicted by the dividend growth model is different from the current market price. **(4 marks)**

(b) Hendil Inc plans to invest $1 million in a new product range and it has been suggested that the proposed investment could be financed by a new issue of loan stock with an interest rate of 8%, redeemable after 15 years and secured on existing assets of Hendil Inc. The existing loan stock of the company is trading at $113 per $100 nominal value. The directors of Hendil have estimated that the NPV of the proposed investment is +$832,000.

Required:

Evaluate and discuss the suggestion to finance the proposed investment with the new loan stock issue described above. Your answer should consider, but not be limited to, the effect of the new issue on:

(i) interest cover;

(ii) gearing;

(iii) ordinary share price. **(11 marks)**

(Total: 25 marks)

56 EMH AND DVM
(JUNE 06)

(a) Explain the meaning of the term 'Efficient Market Hypothesis' and discuss the implications for a company if the stock market on which it is listed has been found to be semi-strong form efficient. **(10 marks)**

(b) Your managing director has just attended a meeting with an investment analyst who has suggested that your company's shares are overvalued by 10%. The data used by the investment analyst in her calculations is shown below. ('Now' is June 20X7).

Year	Total dividends $000	Number of shares	Total earnings $000
20X4	5,680	28,600,000	18,260
20X5	6,134	28,600,000	21,320
20X6	8,108	35,000,000	26,710
20X7	10,007	40,000,000	28,620

Your company's current share price is 645 cents and the cost of equity is estimated to be 12.5%.

Required:

Prepare a brief report for the managing director discussing whether or not your company's shares are likely to be overvalued. Relevant calculations should form part of your report. **(15 marks)**

(Total: 25 marks)

57 LACETO
(JUNE 01)

Laceto Inc, a large retail group specialising in the sale of clothing and electrical goods is currently considering a takeover bid for a competitor in the electrical goods sector, Omnigen Inc, whose share price has fallen by 205 cents during the last three months.

Summarised data for the financial year to 31 March 20X7:

	$ million	
	Laceto	Omnigen
Sales revenue	420	180
Profit before tax (after interest payments)	41	20
Taxation	12	6

	$ million	
	Laceto	Omnigen
Non-current assets (net)	110	63
Current assets	122	94
Current liabilities	86	71
Medium and long-term liabilities	40	12
Shareholders funds	106	74

The share price of Laceto is currently 380 cents, and of Omnigen 410 cents. Laceto has 80 million issued ordinary shares and Omnigen 30 million. Typical of Laceto's medium and long-term liabilities is 12% loan stock with three years to maturity, a par value of $100, and a current market price of $108.80.

The finance team of Laceto has produced the following forecasts of financial data for the activities of Omnigen if it is taken over.

	$ million			
Financial year	20X8	20X9	20Y0	20Y1
Net sales	230	261	281	298
Cost of goods sold (50%)	115	131	141	149
Selling and administrative expenses	32	34	36	38
Capital allowances (total)	40	42	42	42
Interest	18	16	14	12
Cash flow needed for asset replacement and forecast growth	50	52	55	58

Corporate taxation is at the rate of 30% per year, payable in the year that the taxable cash flow occurs.

The risk-free rate is 6% per year and market return 14% per year. Omnigen's current equity beta is 1.2. This is expected to increase by 0.1 if the company is taken over as Laceto would increase the current level of capital gearing associated with the activities of Omnigen. Laceto's gearing post acquisition is expected to be between 18% and 23% (debt to debt plus equity by market values), depending upon the final price paid for Omnigen.

Post-takeover cash flows of Omnigen (after replacement and growth expenditure) are expected to grow at between 3% and 5% per year after 20Y1.

Additional notes:

(i)   The realisable value of Omnigen's assets, net of all debt repayments, is estimated to be $82 million.

(ii)   The P/E ratios of two of Omnigen's quoted competitors in the electrical industry are 13:1 and 15.1 respectively.

Required:

Discuss and evaluate what price, or range of prices, Laceto should offer to purchase the shares of Omnigen.

State clearly any assumptions that you make.

Approximately 17 marks are for calculations and 8 for discussion.

(25 marks)

58 THP CO   *Walk in the footsteps of a top tutor*

(JUNE 08)

THP Co is planning to buy CRX Co, a company in the same business sector, and is considering paying cash for the shares of the company. The cash would be raised by THP Co through a 1 for 3 rights issue at a 20% discount to its current share price.

The purchase price of the 1 million issued shares of CRX Co would be equal to the rights issue funds raised, less issue costs of $320,000. Earnings per share of CRX Co at the time of acquisition would be 44·8c per share. As a result of acquiring CRX Co, THP Co expects to gain annual after-tax savings of $96,000.

THP Co maintains a payout ratio of 50% and earnings per share are currently 64c per share. Dividend growth of 5% per year is expected for the foreseeable future and the company has a cost of equity of 12% per year.

Information from THP Co's statement of financial position:

Equity and liabilities	$000
Shares ($1 par value)	3,000
Reserves	4,300
	7,300
Non-current liabilities	
8% loan notes	5,000
Current liabilities	2,200
Total equity and liabilities	14,500

Required:

Total MV of equity.

Po

(a) Calculate the current ex dividend share price of THP Co and the current market capitalisation of THP Co using the dividend growth model. **(4 marks)**

(b) Assuming the rights issue takes place and ignoring the proposed use of the funds raised, calculate:

(i) the rights issue price per share;

(ii) the cash raised;

(iii) the theoretical ex rights price per share; and

(iv) the market capitalisation of THP Co. **(5 marks)**

PE

(c) Using the price/earnings ratio method, calculate the share price and market capitalisation of CRX Co before the acquisition. $PE = \frac{Price}{Earning}$ **(3 marks)**

(d) Assuming a semi-strong form efficient capital market, calculate and comment on the post acquisition market capitalisation of THP Co in the following circumstances:

(i) THP Co does not announce the expected annual after-tax savings; and

(ii) the expected after-tax savings are made public. **(5 marks)**

(e) Discuss the factors that THP Co should consider, in its circumstances, in choosing between equity finance and debt finance as a source of finance from which to make a cash offer for CRX Co.

F
A
I
R
C
A
R

(8 marks)

(Total: 25 marks)

59 PHOBIS
(DEC 07)

(a) Phobis Co is considering a bid for Danoca Co. Both companies are stock-market listed and are in the same business sector. Financial information on Danoca Co, which is shortly to pay its annual dividend, is as follows:

Number of ordinary shares	5 million
Ordinary share price (ex div basis)	$3.30 Po
Earnings per share	40.0c EPS
Proposed payout ratio	60% → Div.
Dividend per share one year ago	23.3c
Dividend per share two years ago	22.0c
Equity beta	1.4 β

Other relevant financial information	
Average sector price/earnings ratio	10 PE
Risk-free rate of return	4.6% rf
Return on the market	10.6% rm

Required:

 Calculate the value of Danoca Co using the following methods:

(i) price/earnings ratio method;

(ii) dividend growth model;

and discuss the significance, to Phobis Co, of the values you have calculated, in comparison to the current market value of Danoca Co. **(11 marks)**

(b) Phobis Co has in issue 9% bonds which are redeemable at their par value of $100 in five years' time. Alternatively, each bond may be converted on that date into 20 ordinary shares of the company. The current ordinary share price of Phobis Co is $4.45 and this is expected to grow at a rate of 6.5% per year for the foreseeable future. Phobis Co has a cost of debt of 7% per year.

$Kd(1-T)$

Required:

Calculate the following current values for each $100 convertible bond:

(i) market value;

(ii) floor value;

(iii) conversion premium. **(6 marks)**

(c) Distinguish between weak form, semi-strong form and strong form stock market efficiency, and discuss the significance to a listed company if the stock market on which its shares are traded is shown to be semi-strong form efficient. **(8 marks)**

(Total: 25 marks)

 Online question assistance

RISK MANAGEMENT

60 RISKS OF FOREIGN TRADE
(JUNE 01)

(a) Excluding foreign exchange risks, discuss, with examples, how the risks of foreign trade might be managed. **(12 marks)**

(b) The managers of three small UK companies are discussing their strategies towards foreign exchange risk.

- Company one exports to several countries in Europe, Africa and the Americas.

- Company two imports from Europe.

- Company three is not engaged in any form of foreign trade.

All three companies believe themselves to be risk averse.

All three have decided that there is no need to take any action due to foreign exchange risk. Their reasons for no action are:

- Company one: Foreign exchange markets are efficient, and on balance my company is as likely to gain from foreign exchange movements as to lose from them. There is, therefore, no point in paying for hedging foreign exchange risk as overall the company will not gain by using such hedges.

- Company two: My company only trades with Europe and as it is always invoiced in £s this prevents foreign exchange losses.

- Company three: As my company is not engaged in any form of foreign trade, foreign exchange rates are irrelevant to me.

Required:

Discuss the validity of the views of each of the three managers.

Assume that exports are denominated in the foreign currency concerned, and that imports are denominated in sterling. **(13 marks)**

(Total: 25 marks)

61   **EXCHANGE RATE SYSTEMS AND ORDER FROM KUWAIT** *Walk in the footsteps*

of a top tutor
(JUNE 99)

(a)   **Describe the main types of foreign exchange rate system. Briefly discuss how such systems might affect the ability of financial managers to forecast exchange rates.**
(10 marks)

(b)   **Your managing director has received forecasts of Euro/£ exchange rates in two years time from three leading banks.**

Euro/£ two year forecasts

Lotto	1.452
Kadbank	1.514
Grossbank	1.782

The current spot mid-rate is Euro 1.667/£

A non-executive director of your company has suggested that in order to forecast future exchange rates the interest rate differential between the two countries should be used. She states that 'as short-term interest rates are currently 6% in the UK and 3.5% in the Euro bloc, the exchange rate in two years' time will be Euro 1.747/£'.

Required:

(i)   **Prepare a brief report discussing the likely validity of the non-executive directors estimate.** **(4 marks)**

(ii)   **Explain briefly whether or not forecasts of future exchange rates using current interest rate differentials are likely to be accurate.** **(3 marks)**

(c)   You have also been asked to give advice to the managing director about a tender by the company's Italian subsidiary for an order in Kuwait. The tender conditions state that payment will be made in Kuwait dinars 18 months from now. The subsidiary is unsure as to what price to tender. The marginal cost of producing the goods at that time is estimated to be €340,000 and a 25% mark up is normal for the company.

Exchange rates

Euro/Dinar

Spot 0.256

No forward market exists for 18 months' time

	Italy	Kuwait
Annual inflation rates	3%	9%

Required:

Discuss how the Italian subsidiary might protect itself against foreign exchange rate changes and recommend what tender price should be used. (8 marks)

(Total: 25 marks)

62 LAGRAG CO

The following data was published in the financial press on 1 January 20X7:

normal yield curve, going up.

Redemption Yield (%)	As at 1/1/X7	As at 1/1/X6
Treasury 20X8	5.21	5.17
Treasury 20Y0-Y2	5.58	5.49
Exchequer 20Y6	6.46	6.33

Lagrag Co is a <u>heavily indebted</u> company which is keen to protect the interest payments on <u>$10 million</u> of borrowings which will be required in <u>3 months</u> for a period of 4 months. The company has discovered that the following forward rate agreements are currently available to it:

3 - 7

    3 v 4 7.45 – 7.34
    3 v 7 7.53 – 7.43 ✓
    4 v 7 7.58 – 7.45

Additionally Lagrag Co is keen to protect itself against interest rate movements on some of its other debt. However, the Finance Director cannot distinguish between futures and options on futures, and hence is unsure what to use.

Required:

(a) **Explain what the <u>redemption yield</u> data indicate about interest rates and discuss possible reasons for the yields shown.** *Yield Curve - 3 theories* (8 marks)

(b) **Identify the appropriate forward rate agreement and show what the cash flows arising will be if the <u>interest rate</u> payable by Lagrag Co in 3 months is:**

    7.76% ·
    7.42% (6 marks)

(c) **Explain the difference between futures and options on futures and recommend which the Finance Director should choose.** (7 marks)

(d) **Explain the two major risks that are likely to arise if Lagrag Co sells to an overseas customer. For each risk identified explain a method by which the risk could be reduced.** (4 marks)

(Total 25 marks)

63 BOLUJE CO
(DEC 08)

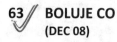

Three years ago Boluje Co built a factory in its home country costing $3.2 million. To finance the construction of the factory, Boluje Co issued peso-denominated bonds in a foreign country whose currency is the peso. Interest rates at the time in the foreign country were historically low. The foreign <u>bond issue</u> raised 16 million pesos and the exchange rate at the time was 5·00 pesos/$.

Each foreign bond has a par value of 500 pesos and pays interest in pesos at the end of each year of 6.1%. The bonds will be redeemed in five years' time at par. The current cost of debt of peso-denominated bonds of similar risk is 7%.   *Kd : Require return by debt holder*

In addition to domestic sales, Boluje Co exports goods to the foreign country and receives payment for export sales in pesos. Approximately 40% of production is exported to the foreign country.

The spot exchange rate is *So* 6.00 pesos/$ and the 12-month forward exchange rate is *F* 6.07 pesos/$. Boluje Co can borrow money on a short-term basis at 4% per year in its home currency and it can deposit money at 5% per year in the foreign country where the foreign bonds were issued. Taxation may be ignored in all calculation parts of this question.

Required:

(a)   **Briefly explain the reasons why a company may choose to finance a new investment by an issue of debt finance.**   *Same as Q58(e)*   **(7 marks)**

(b)   **Calculate the current total market value (in pesos) of the foreign bonds used to finance the building of the new factory.**   **(4 marks)**

(c)   **Assume that Boluje Co has no surplus cash at the present time:**

    (i)   **Explain and illustrate how a money market hedge could protect Boluje Co against exchange rate risk in relation to the dollar cost of the interest payment to be made in one year's time on its foreign bonds.**   **(4 marks)**

    (ii)   **Compare the relative costs of a money market hedge and a forward market hedge.**   **(2 marks)**

(d)   **Describe other methods, including derivatives, that Boluje Co could use to hedge against exchange rate risk.**   *Options & Futures*   **(8 marks)**

(Total: 25 marks)

 Online question assistance

---

64   EXPORTERS PLC *Walk in the footsteps of a top tutor*

(a)   **You are required to define a forward exchange contract and to explain the differences between fixed forward exchange contracts and option forward exchange contracts.**   **(2 marks)**

(b)   Exporters plc, a UK company, is due to receive 500,000 Northland dollars in 6 months' time for goods supplied. The company decides to hedge its currency exposure by using the forward market. The short-term interest rate in the UK is 12% per annum and the equivalent rate in Northland is 15%. The spot rate of exchange is 2.5 Northland dollars to the pound.

    Required:

    (i)   **Calculate how much Exporters plc actually gains or loses as a result of the hedging transaction if, at the end of the six months, the pound, in relation to the Northland dollar, has:**

        (1)   **gained 4%,**

        (2)   lost 2% or

        (3)   remained stable.

        You may assume that the forward rate of exchange simply reflects the interest differential in the two countries (i.e. it reflects the Interest Rate Parity analysis of forward rates); **(7 marks)**

    (ii)   **Explain the rationale behind the interest rate parity analysis of forward rates.**

        (4 marks)

    (iii)   **Compare a forward market currency hedge with:**

        (1)   **a currency futures hedge,**

        (2)   **a currency options hedge.**

        Indicate in each of the three cases how the hedging facility is actually provided, the nature of the costs and the potential outcomes of the hedge.

        (12 marks)

        (Total: 25 marks)

65   UNIPROD
(PILOT 94)

It is now 31 December 20X7. The corporate treasurer of Uniprod Inc is concerned about the level of cash flows of the company during the next six months, and how the company might be protected from the adverse effects of changing interest rates. Interest rates are widely expected to change in late April when a general election is due, but the size and direction of the change is dependent upon the result of the election which is forecast by opinion polls to be very close. Current interest rates for Uniprod are 11% per year for short-term borrowing, and 8% per year for short-term investment. Sales of the company in December 20X7 were 824,180 units at a price of $10.60 per unit. Sales have been recently increasing at the rate of 1.5% per month, and this trend is expected to continue.

There will be an opening cash balance of $800,000 at the beginning of January 20X8. However the company's treasurer is forecasting a cash deficit of approximately $2.4 million by the end of April 20X8

Apart from an overdraft facility to finance short-term cash shortages, the company has no other form of floating rate debt.

June $ three month time deposit futures are currently priced at 90.25, equivalent to an interest rate of 9.75%. The standard contract size is $500,000 and the minimum price movement is one tick (the value of one tick is 0.01% per year of the contract size).

Interest rate guarantees at 11.5% per year for a two month period from May are available to Uniprod for a premium of 0.2% of the size of the loan to be guaranteed.

Forward rate agreements are available for periods of up to four months from May at 11.88 − 11.83%.

Required:

(a)   **Prepare a report discussing the advantages and disadvantages of alternative strategies that the managers of Uniprod might adopt to protect the company from interest rate risk associated with the company's expected cash flows during the next six months.**

The company does not wish to seek speculative profits from interest rate movements.

State clearly any assumptions that you make and include relevant calculations as part of your report.   **(15 marks)**

(b)   What macro-economic factors might be expected to cause increases in interest rates?

(10 marks)

(Total: 25 marks)

Section 2

ANSWERS TO PRACTICE QUESTIONS

FINANCIAL MANAGEMENT FUNCTION

1 OBJECTIVES

Key answer tips

This is a difficult question where it would be easy to write down everything you know about objectives and still not address the requirement. It is important to decide on an appropriate structure for your answer, including the sub-headings you will use, before your start writing. Try to use as many examples as possible to make it easier to make your point. The highlighted words are key phrases that markers are looking for.

(a) Non-financial issues, ethical and environmental issues in many cases overlap, and have become of increasing significance to the achievement of primary financial objectives such as the maximisation of shareholder wealth. Most companies have a series of secondary objectives that encompass many of these issues.

Traditional **non-financial issues** affecting companies include:

(i) **Measures that increase the welfare of employees** such as the provision of housing, good and safe working conditions, social and recreational facilities. These might also relate to managers and encompass generous perquisites.

(ii) **Welfare of the local community and society as a whole**. This has become of increasing significance, with companies accepting that they have some responsibility beyond their normal stakeholders in that their actions may impact on the environment and the quality of life of third parties.

(iii) **Provision of, or fulfilment of, a service**. Many organisations, both in the public sector and private sector provide a service, for example to remote communities, which would not be provided on purely economic grounds.

(iv) **Growth of an organisation**, which might bring more power, prestige, and a larger market share, but might adversely affect shareholder wealth.

(v) **Quality**. Many engineering companies have been accused of focusing upon quality rather than cost effective solutions.

(vi)   **Survival**. Although to some extent linked to financial objectives, managers might place corporate survival (and hence retaining their jobs) ahead of wealth maximisation. An obvious effect might be to avoid undertaking risky investments.

Ethical issues of companies were brought into sharp focus by the actions of Enron and others. There is a trade-off between applying a high standard of ethics and increasing cash flow or maximisation of shareholder wealth. A company might face ethical dilemmas with respect to the amount and accuracy of information it provides to its stakeholders. An ethical issue attracting much attention is the possible payment of excessive remuneration to senior directors, including very large bonuses and 'golden parachutes'.

Environmental issues might have very direct effects on companies. If natural resources become depleted the company may not be able to sustain its activities, weather and climatic factors can influence the achievement of corporate objectives through their impact on crops, the availability of water etc. Extreme environmental disasters such as typhoons, floods, earthquakes, and volcanic eruptions will also impact on companies' cash flow, as will obvious environmental considerations such as the location of mountains, deserts, or communications facilities. Should companies develop new technologies that will improve the environment, such as cleaner petrol or alternative fuels? Such developments might not be the cheapest alternative.

Environmental legislation is a major influence in many countries. This includes limitations on where operations may be located and in what form, and regulations regarding waste products, noise and physical pollutants.

All of these issues have received considerable publicity and attention in recent years. *Environmental pressure groups* are prominent in many countries; companies are now producing social and environmental accounting reports, and/or corporate social responsibility reports. Companies increasingly have multiple objectives that address some or all of these three issues. In the short-term non-financial, ethical and environmental issues might result in a reduction in shareholder wealth; in the longer term it is argued that only companies that address these issues will succeed.

" Not-for-profit" (b)

- *Objectives*

- *VFM*
  - *Economy*
  - *Efficiency*
  - *Effectiveness*

In the case of a not-for-profit (NFP) organisation, the limit on the services that can be provided is the amount of funds that are available in a given period. A key financial objective for an NFP organisation such as a charity is therefore to raise as much funds as possible. The fund-raising efforts of a charity may be directed towards the public or to grant-making bodies. In addition, a charity may have income from investments made from surplus funds from previous periods. In any period, however, a charity is likely to know from previous experience the amount and timing of the funds available for use. The same is true for an NFP organisation funded by the government, such as a hospital, since such an organisation will operate under budget constraints or cash limits. Whether funded by the government or not, NFP organisations will therefore have the financial objective of keeping spending within budget, and budgets will play an important role in controlling spending and in specifying the level of services or programmes it is planned to provide.

Since the amount of funding available is limited, NFP organisations will seek to generate the maximum benefit from available funds. They will obtain resources for use by the organisation as economically as possible: they will employ these resources efficiently, minimising waste and cutting back on any activities that do not assist in achieving the organisation's non-financial objectives; and they will ensure that their

VFM means:
etting the best
ssible service at
we least possible cost.

operations are directed as effectively as possible towards meeting their objectives. [The goals of economy, efficiency and effectiveness are collectively referred to as value for money (VFM). Economy is concerned with minimising the input costs for a given level of output. Efficiency is concerned with maximising the outputs obtained from a given level of input resources, i.e. with the process of transforming economic resources into desires services. Effectiveness is concerned with the extent to which non-financial organisational goals are achieved.]

[Measuring the achievement of the financial objective of VFM is difficult because the non-financial goals of NFP organisations are not quantifiable and so not directly measurable. However, current performance can be compared to historic performance to ascertain the extent to which positive change has occurred.] The availability of the healthcare provided by a hospital, for example, can be measured by the time that patients have to wait for treatment or for an operation, and waiting times can be compared year on year to determine the extent to which improvements have been achieved or publicised targets have been met.

[Lacking a profit motive, NFP organisations will have financial objectives that relate to the effective use of resources, such as achieving a target return on capital employed.] In an organisation funded by the government from finance raised through taxation or public sector borrowing, this financial objective will be centrally imposed.

2   CCC

Key answer tips

Part (a) is a tricky question on objective setting that requires a reasonable depth of knowledge of NFPs to score well. Part (b) is more straightforward but needs good application to the two companies concerned. The highlighted words are key phrases that markers are looking for.

(a)   The key criteria that need to be considered when objective setting are as follows:

Stakeholder expectations

All organisations need to identify key stakeholders, examine their expectations and try to set objectives to meet them.

For CCC stakeholders include:

- Local residents want to see the provision of quality health and education services and value for money in response to paying local taxes.

- Local businesses who will be interested in local infrastructure when deciding whether to invest in the area. In particular, CCC may be keen to ensure that DDD does not close its local offices, with resulting job losses, and move to the capital city.

- Central Government committees who make funding decisions based on local population and deprivation.

For DDD stakeholders include:

- Shareholders want to see their wealth increased through a mixture of growing dividends and an increasing share price. DDD has reflected this in the objective to increase shareholder wealth by 10% per annum.

- Customers will expect a certain level of quality and value for money, depending on the nature of products sold.

- The local communities affected by DDD will expect them to be good citizens and operate at high levels of corporate social responsibility.

Stakeholder power

All organisations will find conflicts between stakeholders so they need to consider how to prioritise them.

For a company like DDD the expectations of shareholders come first for the following reasons:

- This is usually reflected in companies' legislation where directors have a duty in law to put shareholder interests first. Many governance recommendations focus on protecting shareholder interests.

- Failure to deliver shareholder expectations will result in a falling share price and difficulties raising finance. Ultimately, shareholders have the power to remove directors should they feel dissatisfied.

However, this does not mean that other stakeholders' needs are ignored. Clearly if customers are unhappy then sales will be lost with a resulting fall in profitability and shareholder wealth.

For CCC the problem is more complex:

- It is much more difficult to prioritise stakeholder expectations. For example, given limited funds, should community health care needs come before educational ones?

- Even individual stakeholder groups have multiple conflicting objectives. For example, residents want to pay less tax and have better provision of services. Thus even if some groups are satisfied, other may still vote for changes in CCC.

- With companies, customers pay directly for the products they receive, ensuring that customer needs are addressed. With CCC the bulk of its funding comes from central government, not the local community who benefit from CCC's actions. Thus the needs of the funding body may take priority over locals needs, otherwise funding may be cut (note: this is less likely here as funding is mainly driven by population size).

Measurement issues

For an organisation like DDD, once shareholders have been prioritised, all decisions can be evaluated by reference to financial measures such as profitability. While non-financial targets will be incorporated as well, the 'bottom line' will be seen as key. Thus financial targets can be set for most objectives.

For CCC it is much more difficult to measure whether it is achieving its stated aims and hence to set targets.

- For example, how do you assess whether somewhere is an 'attractive place to live and work' or whether health and education provision is 'excellent'?

Other issues

All organisations need to ensure that objectives set relate to controllable factors to ensure staff is motivated to meet them.

All organisations need to differentiate between cause and effect and have objectives for both. For example, DDD may have an objective of customer satisfaction, which will need to be translated into objectives for quality, cost, etc.

(b)   As described above, companies make decisions with the primary objective of maximising shareholder wealth.

Investment decisions

Potential investments should thus be assessed using NPV or SVA, rather than ROCE to ensure that shareholder wealth is increased.

This should be the case for both MS and DDD, though the former will have more difficulty determining a suitable discount rate, being unquoted.

Dividend decisions

Once shareholder value has been created, the firm needs to decide how to return those gains to shareholders – either as dividends or reinvested to enhance the share price further.

Modigliani and Miller argued that, given certain assumptions, dividend policy was irrelevant to shareholder wealth. If a dividend was cut, for example, shareholders could manufacture dividends by selling shares without any overall loss of wealth. Central to their theory was the idea that shareholders had perfect information and would understand why a dividend policy was changed.

In the case of MS, shareholders are also employees so will have full information regarding any change in dividend policy and will not thus perceive any information content in the dividends themselves. However, should the dividend be cut, shareholders who require income will not be able to sell shares to generate cash as the company is unquoted. MS should thus try to continue the stable dividend policy it has adopted to date, even though historical dividend cover is lower than the 'rule of thumb' of two.

In the case of DDD, major institutional shareholders will have good information from the company but may have tax preferences regarding income and capital gains so DDD should adopt a consistent dividend policy to meet their requirements. DDD will probably have attracted a certain clientele of shareholder based on previous policies.

Financing decisions

Both firms need to raise finance in order to undertake new investments to increase shareholder wealth. The issue here is whether the finance used ultimately affects shareholder wealth as well.

From a theoretical point of view, Modigliani and Miller argued that in the absence of taxation, and certain other assumptions, the choice between debt or equity finance was irrelevant. With corporation tax they concluded that debt finance was preferable, due to the benefits of the tax shield. With personal taxes the conclusions depend on the specific circumstances of the company and its shareholders. Incorporating real world factors, many analysts argue that there is an optimal gearing level for each company.

DDD is already at the typical gearing ratio for its industry so it would reasonable to assume that this is their optimal gearing level. Future financing should involve a mixture of debt and equity to maintain this ratio.

MS is all-equity financed at present so it should seek to raise at least some of the $15 million required using debt finance to take advantage of the tax relief and low costs involved.

Interrelationships

All three types of decisions are inter-related, thus the financing decision will affect the cost of capital, and as a consequence, the net benefits obtainable from a particular project, thereby influencing the investment decision, while the financing decision concerning gearing will affect both the other decisions.

The dividend decision, in determining the level of retentions, will affect the cash available for investment, and the extent to which external sources of funds need to be sought in financing to optimise operations.

3   NEIGHBOURING COUNTRIES

Key answer tips

A careful read of the specifics of all parts of the question was needed to ensure you answered the requirement in full and didn't end up discussing areas that wouldn't earn marks. The highlighted words are key phrases that markers are looking for.

(a)   The objectives of the nationalised industry in Country A are likely to be influenced by the government, rather than by financial matters. The major objectives are likely to be the provision of a service to the public, and the provision of electricity for the economic development of the country. This may mean providing electricity at considerable cost to outlying areas, or to areas which the government wishes to develop. The financial objectives will be secondary, and will probably attempt to achieve a target rate of return, although the government may be prepared to accept a negative return in order to achieve its political objectives.

The primary objectives of the private sector companies in Country B will probably be the maximisation of shareholder wealth. The companies' managements will decide the objectives, which may be merely 'satisficing', with other non-financial objectives such as good working conditions for employees, market share and provision of a good service to customers. An important industry such as the provision of electricity will, however, be subject to strong government influences and constraints.

Investment planning and appraisal techniques will differ largely as a result of the differing objectives.

In the nationalised industry, strategic investment planning will be instigated by the government, with the tactical decisions left to the management of the industry. The amount of capital investment involved will be determined by the government, which is responsible for the supply of funds.

Appraisal techniques will be designed to ensure that the government targets are met, e.g. ROCE and budgetary control.

In the private sector, investment will be influenced by market forces, with managements attempting to maximise shareholder wealth, or at least satisfy their shareholders while meeting other objectives. Managements will be responsible for both strategic and tactical decisions.

Appraisal techniques will be introduced to ensure that the objectives are met, and will almost certainly include DCF and budgetary control. Failure to meet the objectives may have serious consequences on the share price, with the risk of take-over and possible job losses.

In conclusion, it may be that both the nationalised industry and the privately-controlled industry use the same evaluation techniques. It will be the objectives that are likely to be different, with the consequences of failure being more serious in the private sector.

(b)   (i)   Responding to various stakeholder groups

If a company has a single objective in terms of maximising profitability then it is only responding to one stakeholder group, namely shareholders. However, companies can no longer fail to respond to the interests and concerns of a wider range of groups, particularly with respect to those who may have a non-financial interest in the organisation. Stakeholder groups with a non-financial interest can therefore generate for companies non-financial objectives and place constraints on their operations to the extent that the company is prepared to respond to such groups.

Various stakeholder groupings can emerge. The following represents examples of likely groups, their non-financial objectives and/or the constraints they may place on a business:

Stakeholder	Objective	Constraints
Employees	Employee welfare	Maximum hours worked
Community	Responding to community concerns	Limits on activities
Customers	Product or service levels	Minimum quality standards
Suppliers	Good trading relationships	
Government	Protecting the consumer	Minimum standards on products or services
Trade bodies	Protecting professional reputation	Minimum standards on products or services

(ii)   The difficulties associated with managing organisations with multiple objectives

To the extent that an organisation faces a range of stakeholders, then they also face multiple objectives. This would not particularly be a problem if the multiple objectives were congruent, but they normally are not. There are a number of difficulties:

- Multiple stakeholders imply multiple objectives. To the extent that they conflict then compromises must be made. This will lead potentially to opportunity costs in that maximisation of profitability will potentially be reduced.

- Responding to stakeholders other than shareholders involves costs, either in management time or in directly responding to their needs.

- Some objectives are not clearly defined, for example what is actually meant by 'protecting the consumer'? It will therefore not always be clear to the organisation that they have met the needs of all of their stakeholders.

- Some of the objectives may actually be conflicting where compromise is not possible. Prioritisation and ranking will then have to take place. Questions then arise as to who is the most important stakeholder or what ranking should be assigned?

- New stakeholder groups often emerge. This can create a problem of longer-term strategic management in that plans can be diverted if new pressures arise. For example, environmental issues were not so important 20 years ago.

- Management of the organisation becomes complex when multiple objectives have to be satisfied. Each managerial decision is likely to face many constraints.

(c)   The role of financial intermediaries include:

1   **Risk diversification** – Allowing one investor to invest in many companies.

2   **Aggregation** – Allowing one company (borrower) to borrow from many investors.

3   **Maturity transformation** – By 'borrowing short and lending long' the intermediaries allow investors the opportunity to withdraw in the short term but give companies the funds for the long term.

4   **Hedging** – The intermediary may offer an opportunity for an organisation to reduce risk and uncertainty in relation to things such as interest rates and exchange rates.

5   **Making a market** – They provide a market for the funds.

6   **Advice** – A key role of intermediaries is to advise lenders and borrowers of their options.

4   RZP CO

Key answer tips

Part (a) required a large volume of albeit, relatively straightforward calculations. You must be careful not to spend too much time on the numbers at the expense of the commentary. Parts (b) and (c) were more straightforward. The highlighted words are key phrases that markers are looking for.

(a)   **Analysis of data provided**

Year	20X4	20X3	20X2	20X1	20X0
Dividend per share	2.8¢	2.3¢	2.2¢	2.2¢	1.7¢
Annual dividend growth	21.7%	4.5%	Nil	29.4%	
Earnings per share	19.04¢	14.95¢	11.22¢	15.84¢	13.43¢
Annual earnings growth	27.3%	33.2%	-29.2%	17.9%	
Price/earnings ratio	22.0	33.5	25.5	17.2	15.2
Share price P/E x EPS	418.9¢	500.8¢	286.1¢	272.4¢	204.1¢
Annual share price growth	-16.3%	75.0%	5.0%	33.5%	
Dividend per share	2.8¢	2.3¢	2.2¢	2.2¢	1.7¢
General price index	117	113	110	105	100
Real dividend per share	2.4¢	2.0¢	2.0¢	2.1¢	1.7¢
Annual dividend growth	20.0%	Nil	-4.8%	23.5%	

Average dividend growth:

Arithmetic mean $= (21.7 + 4.5 + 0 + 29.4)/4 = 55.6/4 = 13.9\%$

Equivalent annual growth rate $= [(2.8/1.7)^{0.25} - 1] \times 100 = 13.3\%$

Average earnings per share growth:

Arithmetic mean $= (27.3 + 33.2 - 29.2 + 17.9)/4 = 49.2/4 = 12.3\%$

Equivalent annual growth rate $= [(19.04/13.43)^{0.25} - 1] \times 100 = 9.1\%$

Average share price growth:

Arithmetic mean $= (-16.3 + 75.0 + 5.0 + 33.5)/4 = 97.2/4 = 24.3\%$

Equivalent annual growth rate $= [(418.9/204.1)^{0.25} - 1] \times 100 = 19.7\%$

Average real dividend growth:

Arithmetic mean $= (20.0 + 0 - 4.8 + 23.5)/4 = 38.7/4 = 9.7\%$

Equivalent annual growth rate $= [(2.4/1.7)^{0.25} - 1] \times 100 = 9.0\%$

Discussion of analysis and views expressed by chairman

The chairman's statement claims that RZP Co has delivered growth in every year in dividends, earnings and ordinary share price, apart from 20X2. Analysis shows that the chairman is correct in excluding 20X2, when no growth occurred in dividends, earnings fell by 29.2%, and real dividends fell by 4.8%. Analysis also shows that no growth in real dividends occurred in 20X3 and that the company's share price fell by 16.3% in 20X4. It is possible the chairman may not have been referring to real dividend growth, in which case his statement could be amended. However, shareholders will be aware of the decline in share price in 20X4 or could calculate the decline from the information provided, so the chairman cannot claim that RZP Co has delivered share price growth in 20X4. In fact, the statement could explain the reasons for the decline in share price in order to reassure shareholders. It also possible for the five-year summary to be extended to include annual share price data, such as maximum, minimum and average share price, so that shareholders have this information readily available.

The chairman's statement claims that RZP Co has consistently delivered above-average performance. The company may have delivered above- or below-average performance in individual years but without further information in the form of sector averages for individual years, it is not possible to reach a conclusion on this point. The average growth rates for the sector cannot therefore be used to comment on the performance of RZP Co in individual years. If the company has consistently delivered above-average performance, however, the company's average annual growth rates should be greater than the sector averages.

The growth rates can be compared as follows:

	Arithmetic mean	Equivalent annual rate	Sector
Nominal dividends	13.9%	13.3%	10%
Real dividends	9.7%	9.0%	9%
Earnings per share	12.3%	9.1%	10%
Share price	24.3%	19.7%	20%

It can be seen that if the sector average growth rates are arithmetic mean growth rates, the chairman's statement is correct. If the sector average growth rates are equivalent annual growth rates, however, only the nominal dividend growth rate is greater than the sector average. The basis on which the sector average growth rates have been prepared should therefore be clarified in order to determine whether the chairman's statement is correct.

(b)   The dividend yield and capital growth for 20X4 must be calculated with reference to the 20X3 end-of-year share price. The dividend yield is 0.56% (100 × 2.8/500.8) and the capital growth is −16.35% (100 × (418.9 − 500.8)/500.8), so the total shareholder return is −15.79% or −15.8% (0.56 − 16.35). A negative return of 15.8% looks even worse when it is noted that annual inflation for 20X4 was 3.5% (117/113).

While the negative total shareholder return is at odds with the chairman's claim to have delivered growth in dividends and share price in 20X4, a different view might have emerged if average share prices had been used, since the return calculation ignores share price volatility. The chairman should also be aware that share prices may be affected by other factors than corporate activity, so a good performance in share price terms may not be due to managerial excellence. It also possible that the negative return may represent a good performance when compared to the sector as a whole in 20X4: further information is needed to assess this.

Note that total shareholder return can also be found as (100 × (2.8 + 418.9 − 500.8)/500.8).

(c)   The objectives of managers may conflict with the objectives of shareholders, particularly with the objective of maximisation of shareholder wealth. Management remuneration package are one way in which goal congruence between managers and shareholders may be increased. Such packages should motivate managers while supporting the achievement of shareholder wealth maximisation. The following factors should be considered when deciding on a remuneration package intended to encourage directors to act in ways that maximise shareholder wealth.

Clarity and transparency

The terms of the remuneration package should be clear and transparent so that directors and shareholders are in no doubt as to when rewards have been earned or the basis on which rewards have been calculated.

Appropriate performance measure

The managerial performance measure selected for use in the remuneration package should support the achievement of shareholder wealth maximisation. It is therefore likely that the performance measure could be linked to share price changes.

Quantitative performance measure

The managerial performance measure should be quantitative and the manner in which it is to be calculated should be specified. The managerial performance measure should ideally be linked to a benchmark comparing the company's performance with that of its peers. The managerial performance measure should not be open to manipulation by management.

Time horizon

The remuneration package should have a time horizon that is linked to that of shareholders. If shareholders desire long-term capital growth, for example, the remuneration package should discourage decisions whose objective is to maximise short-term profits at the expense of long-term growth.

Impartiality

In recent years there has been an increased emphasis on decisions about managerial remuneration packages being removed from the control of managers who benefit from them. The use of remuneration committees in listed companies is an example of this. The impartial decisions of non-executive directors, it is believed, will eliminate or reduce managerial self-interest and encourage remuneration packages that support the achievement of shareholder rather than managerial goals.

Appropriate management remuneration packages for RZP Co

Remuneration packages may be based on a performance measure linked to values in the income statement. A bonus could be awarded, for example, based on growth in sales revenue, profit before tax, or earnings (earnings per share). Such performance measures could lead to maximisation of profit in the short-term rather than in the long-term, for example by deferring capital expenditure required to reduce environmental pollution, and may encourage managers to manipulate reported financial information in order to achieve bonus targets. They could also lead to sub-optimal managerial performance if managers do enough to earn their bonus, but then reduce their efforts once their target has been achieved.

RZP Co has achieved earnings growth of more than 20% in both 20X3 and 20X4, but this is likely to reflect in part a recovery from the negative earnings growth in 20X1, since over the five-year period its earnings growth is not very different from its sector's (it may be worse). If annual earnings growth were to be part of a remuneration package for RZP Co, earnings growth could perhaps be compared to the sector and any bonus made conditional upon ongoing performance in order to discourage a short-term focus.

Remuneration packages may be based on a performance measure linked to relative stock market performance, e.g. share price growth over the year compared to average share price growth for the company's sector, or compared to growth in a stock market index, such as the FTSE 100. This would have the advantage that managers would be encouraged to make decisions that had a positive effect on the company's share price and hence are likely to be consistent with shareholder wealth maximisation. However, as noted earlier, other factors than managerial decisions can have a continuing effect on share prices and so managers may fail to be rewarded for good performance due to general economic changes or market conditions.

RZP Co recorded negative share price growth in 20X4 and the reasons for this should be investigated. In the circumstances, a remuneration package linked to benchmarked share price growth could focus the attention of RZP managers on decisions likely to increase shareholder wealth. The effect of such a remuneration package could be enhanced if the reward received by managers were partly or wholly in the form of shares or share options. Apart from emphasising the focus on share price growth, such a reward scheme would encourage goal congruence between shareholders and managers by turning managers into shareholders.

5 JJG CO

Key answer tips

This question may cause problems for some students, especially regarding the level of depth to go into on part (a).

Part (a) requires an evaluation of the performance of JJG The provision of information on industry averages gives some clear indications of the ratios which any analysis should focus on.

Part (b) is a relatively straightforward calculation of the impact of a rights issue.

Part (c) gives plenty of opportunity to gain easy marks although the final words "for the expansion" means comments must be specific to the scenario presented.

The highlighted words are key phrases that markers are looking for.

(a)　Financial Analysis

	2008	2007	2006	2005
Turnover ($m)	28.0	24.0	19.1	16.8
Turnover growth	17%	26%	14%	
Geometric average growth: 18.6%				
Profit before interest and tax ($m)	9.8	8.5	7.5	6.8
PBIT growth	15%	13%	10%	
Geometric average growth: 13·0%				
Earnings ($m)	5.5	4.7	4.1	3.6
Earnings per share (cents)	100	85	75	66
EPS growth	18%	13%	14%	
Geometric average growth: 14·9%				

	2008	**2007**	**2006**	**2005**
Dividends ($m)	2.2	1.9	1.6	1.6
Dividends per share (cents)	40	35	29	29
DPS growth	14%	21%	nil	
Geometric average growth: 11·3%				
Ordinary shares ($m)	5.5	5.5	5.5	5.5
Reserves ($m)	13.7	10.4	7.6	5.1
	———	———	———	———
Shareholders' funds ($)	19.2	15.9	13.1	10.6
8% Bonds, redeemable 2015 ($m)	20	20	20	20
	———	———	———	———
Capital employed ($m)	39.2	35.9	33.1	30.6
Profit before interest and tax ($m)	9.8	8.5	7.5	6.8
Return on capital employed	25%	24%	23%	22%
Earnings ($m)	5.5	4.7	4.1	3.6
Return on shareholders' funds	29%	30%	31%	34%
8% Bonds, redeemable 2015 ($m)	20	20	20	20
Market value of equity ($m)	47.5	31.6	18.4	14.7
Debt/equity ratio (market value)	42%	63%	109%	136%
Share price (cents)	864	574	335	267
Dividends per share (cents)	40	35	29	29
Total shareholder return	58%	82%	36%	

Achievement of corporate objectives

JJG Co has shareholder wealth maximisation as an objective. The wealth of shareholders is increased by dividends received and capital gains on shares owned. Total shareholder return compares the sum of the dividend received and the capital gain with the opening share price. The shareholders of JJG Co had a return of 58% in 2008, compared with a return predicted by the capital asset pricing model of 14%. The lowest return shareholders have received was 21% and the highest return was 82%. On this basis, the shareholders of the company have experienced a significant increase in wealth. It is debatable whether this has been as a result of the actions of the company, however. Share prices may increase irrespective of the actions and decisions of managers, or even despite them. In fact, looking at the dividend per share history of the company, there was one year (2006) where dividends were constant, even though earnings per share increased. It is also difficult to know when wealth has been maximised.

Another objective of the company was to achieve a continuous increase in earnings per share. Analysis shows that earnings per share increased every year, with an average increase of 14·9%. This objective appears to have been achieved.

Comment on financial performance

Return on capital employed (ROCE) has been growing towards the sector average of 25% on a year-by-year basis from 22% in 2005. This steady growth in the primary accounting ratio can be contrasted with irregular growth in turnover, the reasons for which are unknown.

Return on shareholders' funds has been consistently higher than the average for the sector. This may be due more to the capital structure of JJG Co than to good performance by the company, however, in the sense that shareholders' funds are smaller on a book value basis than the long-term debt capital. In every previous year but 2008 the gearing of the company was higher than the sector average.

(b) *Calculation of theoretical ex rights per share*

Current share price = $8·64 per share

Current number of shares = 5·5 million shares

Finance to be raised = $15m

Rights issue price = $7·50 per share

Number of shares issued = 15m/7·50 = 2 million shares

Theoretical ex rights price per share = ((5·5m x 8·64) + (2m x 7·50))/7·5m = $8·34 per share

The share price would fall from $8·64 to $8·34 per share However, there would be no effect on shareholder wealth

Effect of rights issue on earnings per share

Current EPS = 100 cents per share

Revised EPS = 100 x 5·5m/7·5m = 73 cents per share

The EPS would fall from 100 cents per share to 73 cents per share However, as mentioned earlier, there would be no effect on shareholder wealth

Effect of rights issue on the debt/equity ratio

Current debt/equity ratio = 100 x 20/47·5 = 42%

Revised market value of equity = 7·5m x 8·34 = $62·55 million

Revised debt/equity ratio = 100 x 20/62·55 = 32%

The debt/equity ratio would fall from 42% to 32%, which is well below the sector average value and would signal a reduction in financial risk

(c) The current debt/equity ratio of JJG Co is 42% (20/47·5). Although this is less than the sector average value of 50%, it is more useful from a financial risk perspective to look at the extent to which interest payments are covered by profits.

	2008	2007	2006	2005
Profit before interest and tax ($m)	9.8	8.5	7.5	6.8
Bond interest ($m)	1.6	1.6	1.6	1.6
Interest coverage ratio (times)	6.1	5.3	4.7	4.3

The interest on the bond issue is $1·6 million (8% of $20m), giving an interest coverage ratio of 6·1 times. If JJG Co has overdraft finance, the interest coverage ratio will be lower than this, but there is insufficient information to determine if an overdraft exists. The interest coverage ratio is not only below the sector average, it is also low enough to be a cause for concern. While the ratio shows an upward trend over the period under consideration, it still indicates that an issue of further debt would be unwise.

A placing, or any issue of new shares such as a rights issue or a public offer, would decrease gearing. If the expansion of business results in an increase in profit before interest and tax, the interest coverage ratio will increase and financial risk will fall. Given the current financial position of JJG Co, a decrease in financial risk is certainly preferable to an increase.

A placing will dilute ownership and control, providing the new equity issue is taken up by new institutional shareholders, while a rights issue will not dilute ownership and control, providing existing shareholders take up their rights. A bond issue does not have ownership and control implications, although restrictive or negative covenants in bond issue documents can limit the actions of a company and its managers.

All three financing choices are long-term sources of finance and so are appropriate for a long-term investment such as the proposed expansion of existing business.

Equity issues such as a placing and a rights issue do not require security. No information is provided on the non-current assets of JJG Co, but it is likely that the existing bond issue is secured. If a new bond issue was being considered, JJG Co would need to consider whether it had sufficient non-current assets to offer as security, although it is likely that new non-current assets would be bought as part of the business expansion.

ACCA marking scheme			Marks
(a)		Relevant financial analysis	6 - 7
		Shareholder wealth discussion	2 - 3
		Earnings per share discussion	2 - 3
		Comment on financial performance	1 - 2
		Maximum	12
(b)		Share price calculation and comment	2 - 3
		Earnings per share calculation and comment	2 - 3
		Debt / equity ratio calculation and comment	1 - 2
		Maximum	6
(c)		Financial analysis	1 - 2
		Discussion of rights issue and placing	2 - 3
		Discussion of bond issue	2 - 3
		Maximum	7
Total			25

Examiner's comments

This question provided historical information relating to a company and average values for its business sector.

In part (a), candidates were required to evaluate the financial performance of the company and to discuss the extent to which it had achieved its objectives of maximising shareholder wealth and continuous growth in earnings per share (EPS).

Many candidates had difficulty in calculating accounting ratios to compare with the sector averages provided. Accounting ratios have standard names and standard definitions and candidates should know these. Some candidates calculated profit after tax, even though the question gave annual earnings for each of four years. Some candidates averaged the four years of data provided, simply because the question provided average sector data. Some candidates calculated ratios for one year only and ignored the three other years.

Many candidates did not understand the significance of the inclusion in the question of an average sector value for the return predicted by the capital asset pricing model (CAPM). This value (14%) provided a way to assess whether the company had achieved its objective of maximising the wealth of shareholders. If the return that shareholders had received each year, in the form of capital gains and dividend, exceeded the return predicted by the CAPM, it could be argued that the objective had been achieved, since the company had outperformed the business sector as a whole. Since total shareholder return was 36%, 82% and 58%, this certainly seemed to be the case here. Some candidates argued that this objective had been achieved on the basis of inappropriate analysis, such as that the amount of reserves or the return on capital employed had increased each year.

It could be demonstrated that the objective of achieving continuous growth in EPS had been achieved by calculating the EPS figure for each year.

Part (b) asked candidates to calculate and comment on the effect of the rights issue on the company's share price, earnings per share (EPS) and debt/equity ratio. To do this, candidates had to calculate the number of shares issued by dividing the amount of cash to be raised ($15 million) by the rights issue price ($7.50 per share). Weaker answers were unable to do this and, instead, assumed a form for the rights issue (such as 1 for 2 or 1 for 4). Better answers calculated all three values and commented on the changes with respect to their historical values, noting that a rights issue has no effect on shareholder wealth and that a fall in the EPS does mean that shareholder wealth has decreased.

Part (c) asked for an analysis and discussion of the relative merits of a rights issue, a placing and an issue of bonds as ways of raising the $15 million of finance needed. Better answers started with analysis and used this as the basis for discussion. The effect of raising the $15 million of finance on gearing and interest cover, for example, had to be assessed before an informed answer could be offered.

Many answers had little or no analysis and compared the three financing methods in general terms, for example looking at ownership and control, increase or decrease in gearing and financial risk, issue costs, servicing costs and maturity.

6 DOE INC

Key answer tips

For part (a) of the question, remember to present the answer in a report format. To provide an answer, you need to make it clear that you understand what overtrading is (trying to carry on too much business with insufficient long-term finance) and what the symptoms of overtrading might be (rapid increase in sales, increases in current assets financed largely or entirely by current liabilities, growing bank overdraft, deteriorating current ratio and acid test ratio). These symptoms are evident in the figures for Doe Inc.

Parts (b) and (c) are a good test of your understanding of DCF techniques, and you should check how long it takes you to write an answer. The two parts of the question together are only worth 13 marks, and you need to work quickly to complete the question within the time allowed. The highlighted words are key phrases that markers are looking for.

(a) **REPORT**

To:	The Board of Doe Inc
From:	Accountant
Date:	xx/xx/xx
Subject:	Is the company overtrading?

1 Introduction

This report presents my findings regarding the suggestion made at the last board meeting that our company is overtrading. Overtrading is also known as under capitalisation, and occurs when the volume of trade is not supported by an adequate supply of capital. Overtrading can lead to liquidity problems that can cause serious difficulties if they are not dealt with promptly.

2 Signs of overtrading

There are a number of generally recognised signs that a company may be overtrading. These are considered, together with relevant financial data from Appendix 1, in the following paragraphs.

Rapid increase in sales revenue

The forecast financial statements for 20X8 show that our sales revenue is expected to increase by 25% during the year.

Rapid increase in current assets

Current assets are expected to rise by 27%, slightly more than the increase in sales revenue.

Increase in inventory days and receivables days

Receivables days are expected to increase from 110 to 121 days, with a 38% increase in total receivables, but inventory days are not expected to increase, but to fall from 265 days to 238 days. Nevertheless, a 19% increase in inventory is anticipated.

Increased reliance on short-term finance

Reserves are expected to increase by $100,000 whereas total assets are expected to increase by $1,400,000. The expansion of our business activity is therefore based primarily on an expansion of short-term finance (trade payables and overdraft). Payables days will increase from 177 to 190 days, while in relative terms payables will increase by 42% – more than the expected rise in sales revenue (25%) and in our overdraft (20%).

Decrease in current ratio and quick ratio

The current ratio is expected to fall very slightly from 1.04 to 1.03, but the quick ratio is not expected to fall, but to increase from 0.44 to 0.47.

However, any interpretation of these ratios should reflect the fact that different industries have different working capital needs. Sector average data can be useful here.

3 Comparison with sector averages

Any conclusion about the signs of overtrading needs to be put in the context of the normal values of accounting ratios for other companies in the industry, as indicated by the sector averages. However, it should be recognised that averages exist because no two companies are identical, even when in the same business sector, and the following discussion should be read with this in mind.

The increasing trend of receivables days away from the sector average of 100 days is clearly a cause for concern. If our level of receivables was brought into line with the sector average our financing need would fall by $477,000 ($2.75m × 21/121), which is equivalent to 17% of our forecast overdraft. The decrease in inventory days is encouraging, although forecast inventory days remain 13% higher than the sector average, indicating the possibility of further improvement.

There is clear evidence of an increased reliance on short-term finance. The trend of payables days is increasing away from the sector average of 120 days and the forecast of 190 days is a very worrying 58% more than the average. This represents $940,000 ($2.55m × 70/190) more in trade finance that our company is carrying compared to a similar company in our business sector. On this evidence, it is likely that our suppliers will begin to press for earlier settlement in the near future and this will add to the pressure already being exerted by our bank.

The quick ratio is expected to increase but will still be 15% below the sector average, while the current ratio is expected to be 25% lower than the average. The low current and quick ratios reflect the increased reliance of our company in comparative terms on short-term sources of finance.

4 Conclusion on overtrading

Most of the evidence suggests that our company is moving into an overtrading situation, although the evidence is not conclusive. Current pressure from our bank to reduce our overdraft serves to highlight the fact that our company needs to reduce its reliance on short-term finance, whether trade finance or overdraft finance. Improved working capital management could reduce the level of investment in receivables, and to a lesser extent perhaps in inventories, which would ease our financial difficulties. However, more drastic measures than this will be needed to deal with our reliance on short-term finance. Although the size of the reduction in the overdraft required by the bank is not known at present, simply reducing trade credit to an average level would need $1m of additional finance. Our company has no long-term debt and given our continuing growth, this source of finance deserves serious consideration.

Appendix 1: Financial analysis

Growth in sales revenue	=	$(8,300 - 6,638)/6,638 = 0.25$ or 25%	
Growth in current assets	=	$(5,950 - 4,700)/4,700 = 0.27$ or 27%	
Increase in overdraft	=	$(2,750 - 2,300)/2,300 = 0.20$ or 20%	
Increase in trade payables	=	$(2,550 - 1,800)/1,800 = 00.42$ or 42%	

		20X8		20X7
Inventory days	$365 \times 3,200/4,900$	238 days	$365 \times 2,700/3,720$	265 days
Receivables days	$365 \times 2,750/8,300$	121 days	$365 \times 2,000/6,638$	110 days
Payables days	$365 \times 2,550/4,900$	190 days	$365 \times 1,800/3,720$	177 days
Current ratio	5,950/5,800	1.03	4,700/4,500	1.04
Quick ratio	2,750/5,800	0.47	2,000/4,500	0.44

(b) It is appropriate to use the after-tax cost of borrowing as the discount rate since Doe Inc is clearly in a tax-paying situation and hence is in a position to claim the tax benefits of lease payments and capital allowances.

Care must be taken when determining the timing of cash flows, since financial evaluation models seek to represent the real world. As lease payments are made on the first day of Doe Inc's accounting period, it is appropriate to treat them for discounting purposes as though they occur at the end of the previous accounting period. However, the tax benefits of lease payments will occur in the accounting period following that in which payment is made. Similarly, it is appropriate to treat the purchase cost on 1 January of the first year of use as being made at year 0 for discounting purposes, even though the tax benefit from the first capital allowance will arise in year 2, i.e. in the accounting period following the one in which payment is made.

Capital allowances and associated tax benefits:

Start of Year	Written down value of asset	Capital allowance (25%)	Tax benefit (30%)	Tax benefit cash flow in year
	$	$	$	
1	365,000	91,250	27,375	2
2	273,750	68,437	20,531	3
3	205,313	51,328	15,398	4
4	153,985	38,496	11,549	5
5	115,489		34,647	6

Evaluation of borrowing to buy:

Year		Cash flow	Discount factor at 7%	Present value
		$		$
0	Capital expenditure	(365,000)	1.000	(365,000)
2	Tax savings	27,375	0.873	23,898
3	Tax savings	20,531	0.816	16,753
4	Tax savings	15,398	0.763	11,749
5	Tax savings	11,549	0.713	8,234
6	Tax savings	34,647	0.666	23,075
	Net present value			(281,291)

The cost of borrowing to buy the machine is $281,291.

Evaluation of leasing

Years		Cash flow	Discount factor at 7%	Present value
		$		$
0 – 4	Lease rentals	(77,250)	4.387	(338,896)
2 – 6	Savings in tax payments	23,175	3.832	88,807
	Net present value			(250,089)

Notes:

Discount factor, years 0 – 4 = 1.000 + 3.387 = 4.387

Discount factor, years 2 – 6 = 4.767 – 0.935 = 3.832

The cost of leasing is $250.089.

Leasing has the lower cost by $31,202 and is therefore preferred to borrowing.

(c) The optimum price will be the one that maximizes total contribution over the five-year life of the new machine. (Taxation and the time value of money are ignored, as required by the question.)

Sales price of $70 per unit

Contribution per unit = $70 – $42 = $28 per unit.

Sales growth is 20% per annum.

Year	1	2	3	4	5
Sales volume (units)	10,000	12,000	14,400	17,280	20,000
Contribution ($/unit)	28	28	28	28	28
Total contribution ($)	280,000	336,000	403,200	483,840	560,000

Year 5 sales volume is limited to the maximum capacity of the new machine.

Total contribution over the five years is $2,063,400

Sales price of $67 per unit

Contribution per unit = 67 – 42 = $25 per unit.

Sales growth is 23% per annum.

Year	1	2	3	4	5
Sales volume (units)	11,000	13,530	16,640	20,000	20,000
Contribution ($/unit)	25	25	25	25	25
Total contribution ($)	275,000	338,250	416,050	500,000	500,000

Sales volume is restricted in years 4 and 5.

Total contribution over the five years is $2,029,300.

Conclusion

The sales price of $70 per unit appears to be marginally preferable on the basis of total contribution. The incremental fixed production overheads will be the same irrespective of which sales price is selected and so may be omitted from the analysis.

7   DARTIG CO *Walk in the footsteps of a top tutor*

Key answer tips

This question has a few trickier elements that may unnerve some students.

Part (e) gives the easiest opportunity to grab marks. A straightforward explanation of the agency problem as well as how share options could be used to reduce the issue should allow most students to score highly. Being unrelated to the other parts, it should be tackled first.

The other four parts to the question all require some degree of calculations. Part (a) is also straightforward, and should result in full marks for most candidates.

Part (d) should be reasonable for most candidates. The highlighted words are key phrases that markers are looking for.

(a)   Rights issue price = 2.5 × 0.8 = $2.00 per share

Theoretical ex rights price = ((2.50 × 4) + (1 × 2.00)/5=$2.40 per share

(Alternatively, number of rights shares issued = $5m/$2.00 = 2.5m shares

Existing number of shares = 4 × 2.5m = 10m shares

Theoretical ex rights price per share = ((10m × 2.50) + (2.5m × 2.00))/12.5m = $2.40)

Tutor's top tips:

In parts (b) and (c), students may be thrown by the assertion that "the expansion of existing business will allow the average growth rate of earnings per share over the last four years to be maintained". A rights issue would normally result in a fall in EPS due to the higher number of shares in issue. In this case though, the new finance from the rights issue will be invested and will earn a sufficiently high return to avoid the usual reduction. Indeed, growth of 4% is being predicted.

Some background calculations may help to illustrate this further:

$$\frac{\$5m}{\$2.50 \times 80\%} = 2.5 \text{ million new shares to be issued.}$$

A 1 for 4 rights issue therefore implies the company must have 10 million shares in issue at present and will have 12.5 million after the rights issue.

Current EPS = 32.4 cents. Total earnings is therefore 0.324 × 10 million = $3.24 million

New total earnings will be 12.5 million × $0.324 × 1.04 = $4.21 million.

In the cold light of day it is not unreasonable to expect the finance raised to increase earnings by this amount (an annual return of just under 20%). However, such rational thought often escapes candidates within the pressure of the exam hall.

(b)   Current price/earnings ratio = 250/32.4 = 7·7 times

Average growth rate of earnings per share = $100 \times ((32.4/27.7)^{0.25} - 1) = 4.0\%$

Earnings per share following expansion = 32.4 × 1.04 = 33.7 cents per share

Share price predicted by price/earnings ratio method = 33.7 × 7.7 = $2.60

Since the price/earnings ratio of Dartig Co has remained constant in recent years and the expansion is of existing business, it seems reasonable to apply the existing price/earnings ratio to the revised earnings per share value.

(c)   The proposed business expansion will be an acceptable use of the rights issue funds if it increases the wealth of the shareholders. The share price predicted by the price/earnings ratio method is $2.60. This is greater than the current share price of $2.50, but this is not a valid comparison, since it ignores the effect of the rights issue on the share price. The rights issue has a neutral effect on shareholder wealth, but the cum rights price is changed by the increase in the number of shares and by the transformation of cash wealth into security wealth from a shareholder point of view. The correct comparison is with the theoretical ex rights price, which was found earlier to be $2.40. Dartig Co shareholders will experience a capital gain due to the business expansion of $2.60 – 2.40 = 20 cents per share. However, these share prices are one year apart and hence not directly comparable.

If the dividend yield remains at 6% per year (100 × 15.0/250), the dividend per share for 2008 will be 15.6 cents (other estimates of the 2008 dividend per share are possible). Adding this to the capital gain of 20 cents gives a total shareholder return of 35.6 cents or 14.24% (100 × 35.6/240). This is greater than the cost of equity of 10% and so shareholder wealth has increased.

Tutor's top tips:

The model answer for both parts (b) and (c) both illustrate an approach to the question set but it is doubtful that many students actually produced the results presented, especially regarding the total shareholder return. However, even if you have difficulties getting your head around the situation, it is still possible to gather many of the marks. Method marks are available for any students who demonstrate a logical approach and utilise the basic price/earnings ratio method.

(d) In order to use the dividend growth model, the expected future dividend growth rate is needed. Here, it may be assumed that the historical trend of dividend per share payments will continue into the future. The geometric average historical dividend growth rate = $100 \times ((15.0/12.8)^{0.25} - 1) = 4\%$ per year.

(Alternatively, the arithmetical average of annual dividend growth rates could be used. This will be $(5.5 + 0.0 + 7.4 + 3.5)/4 = 4.1\%$. Another possibility is to use the Gordon growth model. The average payout ratio over the last 4 years has been 47%, so the average retention ratio has been 53%. Assuming that the cost of equity represents an acceptable return on shareholders' funds, the dividend growth rate is approximately $53\% \times 10\% = 5.3\%$ per year.)

Using the formula for the dividend growth model from the formula sheet, the ex dividend share price = $(15.0 \times 1.04)/(0.1 - 0.04) = \$2.60$

This is 10 cents per share more than the current share price of Dartig Co. There are several reasons why there may be a difference between the two share prices. The future dividend growth rate for example, may differ from the average historical dividend growth rate, and the current share price may factor in a more reasonable estimate of the future dividend growth rate than the 4% used here. The cost of equity of Dartig Co may not be exactly equal to 10%. More generally, there may be a degree of inefficiency in the capital market on which the shares of Dartig Co are traded.

(e) The primary financial management objective of a company is usually taken to be the maximisation of shareholder wealth. In practice, the managers of a company acting as agents for the principals (the shareholders) may act in ways which do not lead to shareholder wealth maximisation. The failure of managers to maximise shareholder wealth is referred to as the agency problem.

Shareholder wealth increases through payment of dividends and through appreciation of share prices. Since share prices reflect the value placed by buyers on the right to receive future dividends, analysis of changes in shareholder wealth focuses on changes in share prices. The objective of maximising share prices is commonly used as a substitute objective for that of maximising shareholder wealth.

The agency problem arises because the objectives of managers differ from those of shareholders: because there is a divorce or separation of ownership from control in modern companies; and because there is an asymmetry of information between shareholders and managers which prevents shareholders being aware of most managerial decisions.

One way to encourage managers to act in ways that increase shareholder wealth is to offer them share options. These are rights to buy shares on a future date at a price which is fixed when the share options are issued. Share options will encourage managers to make decisions that are likely to lead to share price increases (such as investing in projects with positive net present values), since this will increase the rewards they receive from share options. The higher the share price in the market when the share options are exercised, the greater will be the capital gain that could be made by managers owning the options.

Share options therefore go some way towards reducing the differences between the objectives of shareholders and managers. However, it is possible that managers may be rewarded for poor performance if share prices in general are increasing. It is also possible that managers may not be rewarded for good performance if share prices in general are falling. It is difficult to decide on a share option exercise price and a share option exercise date that will encourage managers to focus on increasing shareholder wealth while still remaining challenging, rather than being easily achievable.

	ACCA marking scheme	Marks	Marks
(a)	Rights issue price	1	
	Theoretical ex rights price per share	2	
			3
(b)	Existing price/earnings ratio	1	
	Revised earnings per share	1	
	Share price using price/earnings method	1	
			3
(c)	Discussion of share price comparisons	3 - 4	
	Calculation of capital gain and comment	1 - 2	
			Max 5
(d)	Average dividend growth rate	2	
	Ex div market price per share	2	
	Discussion	2	
			6
(e)	Discussion of agency problem	4 – 5	
	Discussion of share option schemes	4 – 5	
			Max 8
	Total		25

Examiner's comments

In part (a), candidates were asked to calculate a theoretical ex rights price per share. Many candidates gained full marks for their calculations. Weaker answers made errors as regards the form of the issue (it was 1 for 4, not 4 for 1), or thought the theoretical ex rights price was the rights issue price, or calculated the value of the rights.

Part (b) required the calculation of the share price after the business expansion, using the price/earnings ratio method. The first step was to calculate the current price/earnings ratio. The second step was to calculate the earnings per share (EPS) after the proposed business expansion. The final step was to calculate the future share price by multiplying the two together.

A number of candidates were not able to calculate the price/earnings ratio by dividing the current share price by the current EPS. Calculating the EPS after the expansion by multiplying the current EPS by the average historic EPS growth rate was also a problem for some candidates, who were unable to calculate average historic growth rate, or who applied the growth rate to the average EPS rather than the current EPS.

Some students were also unfamiliar with the PER valuation method, even though this is discussed in the study texts.

Part (c) asked for a discussion of whether the business expansion was an acceptable use of the rights issue funds, and an evaluation of the effect of the expansion on the wealth of shareholders. The two parts of the question are linked, since the question of whether the use made of the finance is acceptable depends on the effect on the wealth of shareholders.

If shareholder wealth increases, the proposed use of the finance is acceptable. Better answers therefore looked to compare the theoretical rights price per share (the share price before the rights issue funds were invested) with the share price after the investment had taken place (for example the share price calculated in part (b)), or to compare the return from the investment (for example, total shareholder return, which is the sum of capital gain and divided yield) with the cost of equity.

Part (d) required candidates to calculate the share price predicted by the dividend growth model and compare it with the current share price, explaining any difference that might be found. Many candidates gained full marks for their answer to this question. Marks were lost where candidates used EPS rather than dividend per share in the dividend growth model, or were not able to calculate the dividend growth rate, or used incorrect values in the dividend growth model. A surprising number of candidates did not use the dividend growth model given in the formula sheet, but used the rearranged version of the formula that is used to calculate the cost of equity. Some candidates mistakenly thought that the cost of equity calculated by this formula was the same as the share price.

Part (e) required candidates to explain the nature of the agency problem and to discuss using share option schemes to reduce it in a stock-market listed company. The agency problem is that managers may act in ways that do not lead to the maximisation of shareholder wealth. Shareholder wealth increases through receiving dividends and through capital gains in share prices, and is usually assessed through changes in share prices. Better answers referred to these key financial management concepts.

Share option schemes, in making managers into shareholders, lead to convergence of objectives, if only on a shared focus on increased wealth through increasing share prices. Unfortunately, while share prices increases can arise from good managerial decisions, share price changes can arise for other reasons as well. There was scope here for candidates to discuss a range of issues relating to the difficulty of designing a share option scheme that rewarded managers for good performance, but not for poor performance.

FINANCIAL MANAGEMENT ENVIRONMENT

8   NEWS FOR YOU

Key answer tips

To score well on part (a), you must ensure you apply your basic knowledge of economics to the specifics of News For You's situation. In part (b) the majority of marks are available for the justifications you provide as opposed to the conclusion you reach. The highlighted words are key phrases that markers are looking for.

(a)   Economic opinion on the effect of an **interest rate change** on News For You might vary. Keynesian economists argue that if base rate (and other interest rates) fall, this will lead to an increase in consumer demand (i.e. consumer spending). Unfortunately, however, even if the recent drop in the base rate increases consumer demand, it is unlikely to have any significant impact on the particular business of News For You. Sales are likely to remain unchanged, because newspapers and small confectionery items are low cost purchases, often bought on impulse. Interest rate movements will not make such items suddenly affordable where before they were not.

News For You needs to think about other ways in which the interest rate change might affect its business, and particularly its impact on business costs. If the company has an overdraft facility, its cost of borrowing will have been reduced. At the same time, the expansion plans require the business to raise $2 million, and changes in interest rates affect the cost of all types of capital, both loans and equity. Corporate borrowing rates are generally linked to the prevailing base rate or inter-bank lending rate, with companies paying a premium above base or interbank rate for their loans. The drop in interest rates will therefore affect the required return on the finance needed to fund the proposed expansion. If News For You uses Discounted Cash Flow analysis for investment appraisals, the fall in the cost of capital resulting from the drop in the base rate will mean that a lower discount rate can be applied to the investment evaluation. A lower rate of discount will result in a higher Net Present Value for any given proposal.

Keynesian economists, however, do not agree that changes in interest rates affect corporate investment decisions. They argue that investments are more dependent on the level of business confidence. It might be possible to suggest that News For You will see the fall in the base rate as stimulating general economic confidence. If so, it will be more confident about the future of its business, and so regardless of any changes in the cost of capital, it might be more willing to undertake the expansionary investment. (On the other hand, a fall in interest rates could be a response to a deterioration in the economy, and a loss of business confidence.)

The **inflation figures** are useful to News For You because they can directly affect profit and cash flow forecasts. The impact of inflation on cash flows and profit will be dependent to a large degree on the relative rates of increase in wages, the cost of wholesale supplies for the shop, and the prices that News For You can charge its customers. The quoted rate of inflation is very low at just over 1% per year and, although the rate is not expected to fall any further, its current level is unlikely to have a dramatic effect on the ability of the business to trade profitably. The greater risk for the business might come from the problem that, because inflation is so low, customers are not prepared to tolerate any price rises at all. If so, News For You might become more vulnerable to loss of business to the large food stores which can draw away customers via price cutting campaigns.

Personal and corporation tax rates are relevant to the owners of News For You because they will affect the net gain to the business that may be generated by expansion. As with interest rates, tax rates can affect personal spending patterns and therefore affect the sales revenue of a particular business. News For You, however, is unlikely to have a business that is sensitive to tax rates, because its products are basic essentials and low cost items. Nonetheless, the information that tax rates will remain unchanged is useful because it allows the business to be certain of the amount of tax relief that may be available on loan finance, and the relief that equity investors may claim for investing in a small unquoted company. This information might be useful in deciding whether or not to go ahead with the expansion, because it may affect the relative cost and availability of capital.

The **changes in taxes on tobacco** might be expected to have had a significant effect on News For You because it is one of the relatively high value products sold by the stores. The question indicates that tobacco sales have been falling, but it is unclear whether this drop is linked to the 10% rise in tax over the last twelve months, or simply a result of the population becoming more health conscious and so buying fewer cigarettes. If customers are price-sensitive in their purchasing of tobacco, News For You might once again find itself vulnerable to competition from the food retailers that can exercise greater buying power and sell similar products at lower prices. The high cost of these items also means that inventory holding costs are high, and if inventory turnover is reduced because of tax increase, then the amount of working capital required by News For You will rise.

The **investigation into the food sector** might prove detrimental to News For You if it serves to initiate a price war amongst the retailers, all of whom will be anxious to prove that they look after their customers. The business grew very quickly between 20X2 and 20X6, but since then sales revenue has increased by just 2% per year, and the owners must be concerned that further growth potential is limited, at least within the existing outlets. Moving into the sale of basic foodstuffs has been used as a strategy to compensate for loss of sales in other products such as tobacco, but in many countries a large proportion of people do their food shopping in large retail outlets. By expanding their product range, News For You has also created for itself another set of competitors in the form of food retailers. The only way in which the business might gain from this investigation is if it also covers food wholesaling, and the result is a drop in the prices that News For You have to pay for their inventory.

(b)   **Arguments in favour of the expansion include the following:**

- The sales revenue figures suggest that there is only limited opportunity for the business to continue to grow organically. The business is seeking to replace sales of tobacco and newspapers with sales of foods, but as suggested in answer to (a), the potential of this side of the business may be limited. News For You may be advised to try to grow sales revenue by means of acquiring new outlets instead.

- If News For You is being forced into paying relatively high prices for supplies from a local wholesaler, then expansion may allow it to gain more bargaining power, and purchase at reduced rates from a national wholesale chain. Increased size will offer the opportunity to take advantage of possible economies of scale via bulk ordering. In this way, margins could be widened and the overall business made more profitable.

- With a larger number of stores covering a wider geographic area, News For You will be able to broaden the nature of their business base, so that it will be less vulnerable to regional economic trends.

Arguments against any expansion include the following:

- The potential to increase sales substantially via food sales is very limited. The majority of people purchase most of their food from larger stores, and will only use a local shop for small low cost items, for which it is not worthwhile making a special car journey to the supermarket. It is unlikely a profitable business can be created based on this type of sale.

- The widespread ownership of televisions and access to differing forms of mass media communications is likely to mean that fewer people will purchase newspapers on a daily basis. This is particularly true of those papers that are also published in electronic form. Many newsagents are dependent for the bulk of their sales on customers who come into the shop to buy a newspaper and then purchase additional items at the same time. If customers do not come in for a newspaper, then the associated sales income will also be lost. Expanding a business where there is such a risk of demand falling away may be regarded as very risky.

- The information in the question suggests that the competitive environment for News For You is becoming much tougher on a number of different fronts simultaneously, with rising excise duties, powerful food retailers and a reduction in tobacco and newspaper purchases. Expansion usually occurs because a business is very confident of the future, but in this case it is questionable whether News For You has much about which to be confident.

It would therefore seem advisable for News For You to postpone its expansion plans, and perhaps look at ways of using its existing outlets to sell very different products, thereby 're-inventing' their business, perhaps by moving completely away from confectionery and into, for example, video rental.

9 DISCOURAGING MONOPOLIES

Key answer tips

To answer part (a), a knowledge of basic economics would be helpful, but common sense and an awareness of the business environment could help you to provide a reasonable answer. Don't let part (a) put you off the question. Part (b) and part (c) are both relatively straightforward. The answer provided here discusses obtaining a listing to issue shares on a main stock market, as well as private sources of equity finance. The highlighted words are key phrases that markers are looking for.

(a) Many governments consider it necessary to prevent or control monopolies.

A **pure monopoly** exists when one organisation controls the production or supply of a good that has no close substitute. In practice, legislation may consider a monopoly situation to occur when there is limited competition in a particular market. For example, UK legislation considers a monopoly to occur if an organisation controls 25% or more of a particular market.

Governments consider it necessary to act against an existing or potential monopoly because of the economic problems that can arise through the abuse of a dominant market position. Monopoly can lead to *economic inefficiency in the use of resources*, so that output is at a higher cost than necessary. Further inefficiency can arise as a monopoly *may lack the incentive to innovate*, to research technological improvements, or to eliminate unnecessary managers, since it can always be sure of passing on the cost of its inefficiencies to its customers. Inefficiencies such as these have been seen as major problems in state-owned monopolies and have fuelled the movement towards privatisation in recent years. It has been expected that the competition arising following privatisation will lead to the elimination of these kinds of inefficiency.

Monopoly can also result in *high prices* being charged for output, so that the cost to customers is higher than would be the case if significant competition existed, allowing monopolies to generate monopoly profits.

The government can prevent monopolies occurring by *monitoring proposed takeovers and mergers*, and acting when it decides that a monopoly situation may occur. This monitoring is carried out in the UK by the Office of Fair Trading, which can refer takeovers and mergers that are potentially against the public interest to the Competition Commission for detailed investigation.

The Competition Commission has the power to prevent a proposed takeover or merger, or to allow it to proceed with conditions attached, such as disposal of a portion of the business in order to preserve competition.

Tutorial note:

Your answer might refer to legislation or regulations in a country other than the UK.

(b) In the UK, a company is required by law to offer an issue of new shares to raise cash on a pro-rata basis to its existing shareholders. This ensures that the existing pattern of ownership and control will not be affected if all shareholders take up the new shares offered. Because this right of existing shareholders to be offered new equity is a legal one, such an issue is called a **rights issue**. (However, shareholders can vote to waive their rights, such as when the company wishes to obtain a stock market quotation for the shares.)

If an unlisted company decides that it needs to raise a large amount of equity finance and provided existing shareholders have agreed, it can decide to obtain a listing for its shares, and offer ordinary shares to new investors (the public at large) via an **offer for sale**. Such an offer is usually part of the process of seeking a stock exchange quotation, and it leads to the wider spread of ownership that is needed to meet the requirements of the listing regulations and the stock exchange concerned. An offer for sale may be either at a fixed price, where the offer price is set in advance by the issuing company, or by tender, where investors are invited to submit bids for shares.

Tutorial note:

Offers for sale by tender are uncommon.

An offer for sale will result in a significant change to the shareholder structure of the company, for example by bringing in institutional investors. In order to ensure that the required amount of finance is raised, offers for sale are underwritten by institutional investors who guarantee to buy any unwanted shares.

A **placing** is cheaper than an offer for sale. In a placing, large blocks of shares are placed with institutional investors, so that the spread of new ownership is not as wide as with an offer for sale. While a placing may be part of seeking a listing and a stock exchange quotation (for example, it is very popular with companies wanting to float on markets for smaller companies such as the Alternative Investment Market in the UK), it can also provide equity finance for a company that wishes to remain unlisted.

New shares can also be sold by an unlisted company by **private negotiation,** to individual investors or a venture capital organisation. While the amount of equity finance raised by this method is small, it has been supported in the UK in recent years by government initiatives such as the Enterprise Investment Scheme and Venture Capital Trusts schemes in the UK.

(c) The factors that should be considered by a company when choosing between an issue of debt and issue of equity finance could include the following:

Risk and return

Raising debt finance will increase the gearing and the financial risk of the company, while raising equity finance will lower gearing and financial risk.

Financial risk arises since raising debt brings a commitment to meet regular interest payments, whether fixed or variable. Failure to meet these interest payments gives debt holders the right to appoint a receiver to recover their investment. In contrast, there is no right to receive dividends on ordinary shares, only a right to participate in any dividend (share of profit) declared by the directors of a company. If profits are low, then dividends can be passed, but interest must be paid regardless of the level of profits. Furthermore, increasing the level of interest payments will increase the volatility of returns to shareholders, since only returns in excess of the cost of debt accrue to shareholders.

Cost

Debt is cheaper than equity because debt is less risky from an investor point of view. This is because it is often secured by either a fixed or floating charge on company assets and ranks above equity on liquidation, and because of the statutory requirement to pay interest. Debt is also cheaper than equity because interest is an allowable deduction in calculating taxable profit. This is referred to as the tax efficiency of debt.

Ownership and control

Issuing equity can have ownership implications for a company, particularly if the finance is raised by means of a placing or offer for sale. Shareholders also have the right to appoint directors and auditors, and the right to attend general meetings of the company. While issuing debt has no such ownership implications, an issue of debt can place restrictions on the activities of a company by means of restrictive covenants included in the issue documents. For example, a restrictive covenant may specify a maximum level of gearing or a minimum level of interest cover which the borrowing company must not exceed, or a covenant may forbid the securing of further debt on particular assets.

Redemption

Equity finance is permanent capital that does not need to be redeemed, while debt finance will need to be redeemed at some future date. Redeeming a large amount of debt can place a severe strain on the cash flow of a company, although this can be addressed by refinancing or by using convertible debt.

Flexibility

Debt finance is more flexible than equity, in that various amounts can be borrowed, at a fixed or floating interest rate and for a range of maturities, to suit the financing need of a company. If debt finance is no longer required, it can more easily be repaid (depending on the issue terms).

Availability

A new issue of equity finance may not be readily available to a listed company or may be available on terms that are unacceptable with regards to issue price or issue quantity, if the stock market is depressed (a bear market). Current shareholders may be unwilling to subscribe to a rights issue, for example if they have made other investment plans or if they have urgent calls on their existing finances. A new issue of debt finance may not be available to a listed company, or available at a cost considered to be unacceptable, if it has a poor credit rating, or if it faces trading difficulties.

10   PELLAS CO

Key answer tips

Parts (a) & (c) offer an opportunity to pick up some easy marks through the application of basic knowledge and some common sense. Part (d) requires you to do some calculations so you can comment specifically on the impact of inflation on this company. Be sure to keep your comments focussed on Pellas. The highlighted words are key phrases that markers are looking for.

(a)   The causes of inflation can be summarised under three broad headings: cost-push, demand-pull and monetarist theories.

Cost-push inflation arises when autonomous increases in production and operating costs lead businesses to raise their selling prices in an attempt to maintain profitability.

- One example of a cost increase which might generate such inflation is a rise in wage demands due to workers expecting annual increases in pay. The demand for higher wages, and the resulting cost increase for companies, is not caused by a shortage of workers, but simply by their expectation of increases and the resulting demand for a pay rise. When companies pass on the extra cost via price rises, retail inflation can result.

- Changes in exchange rates can also lead to autonomous cost increases, and subsequent price inflation. If, for example, the US Dollar weakens relative to other currencies, then US companies that import components will experience a rise in the dollar price of those components, and they may decide to pass the cost increase on to their own customers.

- A rise in the rate of indirect taxation, e.g. Sales Tax, is a third possible cause of cost-push inflation.

The second major cause of inflation is demand pressures leading to price increases. When aggregate demand exceeds aggregate supply, and the economy is operating at full capacity, demand is 'rationed' via price increases. In other words, inflation becomes the means whereby demand and supply are brought back into equilibrium.

Monetarist theory explains inflation in terms of excessive growth in the money supply. If the money supply grows more quickly than the underlying economy, then inflation can result, as seen in Russia after the collapse of communism.

(b)

	20X5/6	20X6/7
CPI	2.5%	3.3%
WPI	1.8%	2.0%

The figures show that the rate of consumer price inflation has exceeded that of wholesale price inflation over the two-year period, and that the gap between the two rates is widening. The reason for the change is likely to be a move out of recession and the substantial increase in consumer spending, particularly during 20X7. Wholesale prices are clearly just one of the factors determining consumer retail prices, and even when wholesale prices are stable, there may still be consumer price inflation.

Wholesale inflation rates have remained relatively low, for a number of possible reasons. It may be that the economy concerned has been suffering from a recession. In a recession, retailing companies tend to run down their inventory levels, which lowers demand from wholesalers. They in turn become reluctant to increase prices for fear of losing what few sales opportunities remain. At the same time, more and more companies are looking overseas for new markets, but such companies are then sensitive to changes in exchange rates. When a currency becomes relatively strong, it becomes increasingly difficult to sell abroad, as price competitiveness is eroded. As the world develops, new countries begin manufacturing and wholesaling basic consumer goods, and the competition for a share of that market increases. In the face of such competition, and faced with the risk of exchange rate fluctuations, many wholesale companies have been reluctant to increase prices. Price competitiveness is seen as a means of preserving market share.

Despite the low rate of wholesale inflation, consumer price inflation has been rising. One of the reasons why this is the case is because changes in interest rates can have a significant effect on the CPI. This is one of the reasons why economists view interest rates and inflation as interdependent.

Central banks often increase interest rates to choke consumer demand. At the same time, however, a rise in interest rates will cause company borrowing costs to increase, and if companies wish to maintain their profit margins, they will need to pass on such increases to customers via price rises. Interest rates can therefore indirectly affect the price of the goods which form the CPI.

(c)   Inflation can affect a number of different areas of business including pricing decisions, investment decisions, wage settlements, cash flow and working capital management. High rates of inflation can also mean that the traditional measures of company performance need to be adjusted to take account of price changes. The rate of inflation will affect both the prices that a company has to pay for its labour and materials etc and the prices that it is able to charge its own customers. Consequently, inflation can influence the profit performance of a company.

Where inflation rates are very high, such as in Mexico or Turkey, businesses selling into such markets may find that they need very frequent price reviews. Monthly reviews are not uncommon, and weekly reviews not unknown. Inflation erodes the real return being earned on any sale, and so regular price increases are necessary to try and maintain real earnings. In contrast, when inflation rates are very low, a business make take care when contemplating price increases for fear of losing market share to competitors who hold prices stable.

Investment decisions are sensitive to the rate of inflation because interest rates and inflation rates are inter-related. Evidence suggests that business investment is lower in times of inflation, partly because of uncertainty regarding the real returns that can be expected from an investment. At the same time, companies may be tempted into investing in short term rather than longer-term projects, because they offer a faster and more predictable payback. This has the effect of distorting the pattern of industrial investment. It is also the case that specific classes of business assets are more likely to retain their real value during inflationary times, and investment patterns are thus adjusted in favour of the purchase of such assets. One such example is the UK property boom of the 2000s when rising property prices attracted many investors at the expense of manufacturing industry,- which offered comparatively poor real returns.

Wage settlements are clearly sensitive to the rate of inflation because workers do not wish to see their spending power eroded. It is therefore likely that when inflation rates are high, companies will be faced with higher wage demands, and a need to maintain profitability in the face of such rising costs. At the same time, because inflation erodes the relative value of currencies, the cost of imported components is likely to be increasing. Conversely, however, inflation can make a company's overseas sales much easier, as products become more price competitive due to the exchange rate movements. Thus inflation may be bad for importers but good for exporters.

Cash flow is sensitive to the rate of inflation because if costs are rising, and prices have not been increased, cash flow may come under severe strain. The strain may be exacerbated if higher selling prices lead to a drop in demand, as people forego new spending, in response to reductions in the levels of real income. Working capital management becomes even more important. Investment in inventories and receivables becomes increasingly expensive, and so tight control becomes important. At the same time care must be taken not to under invest in inventory only to find that replenishment is more expensive as a consequence of the inflation. Precautionary inventory holdings may well increase. Cash holdings should be kept to a minimum during inflationary times, because spending power is being eroded.

Measurements of profitability and returns to investors need to be changed under inflationary conditions, as historic cost accounts may give a misleading picture of company performance. Alternative approaches that have been suggested in the past include the use of either Current Purchasing Power, or Current Cost Accounting. Neither method is currently in widespread use in the UK, for example.

(d)   REPORT

To: Board of Directors, Pellas Co

Prepared by: A N Accountant

Subject: Management of sales and costs 20X6/20X7

Dear Sirs

Over the period 20X5-20X7 Pellas Co has been faced with the difficulty of maintaining profits in an environment of rising costs, but low levels of demand. I believe that the company has responded well to this challenge, and that both sales and cost management have been very good over the period in question.

The decision to hold selling prices fixed was done in order to maintain sales levels in a weak market. In fact, sales volumes have shown a healthy rate of growth, increasing by 20% between 20X5 and 20X6, and 8% between 20X6 and 20X7. This would suggest that demand is price sensitive, and the competitive pricing of Pellas' products has allowed us to increase sales and, possibly also, market share.

At the same time, the company was faced with the problem of maintaining margins, given that the main component supplier has insisted on significant annual price increases. Pellas has succeeded in compensating for the higher component costs by tight management and reduction of the other costs of sales. This is demonstrated in the figures shown overleaf.

Component cost   = 80% of cost of sales

                                 = $0.520 million in 20X5

In 20X6, given a 20% increase in volume, plus a 10% price rise, component costs can be estimated as: = $0. 520 x 1.2 x 1.1 million

                                 = $0.686 million

For 20X7, the component cost, adjusted for the sales volume and price rises is:

                                 = $0.686 x 1.08 x 1.1

                                 = $0.815 million

This gives a year by year breakdown of cost figures as follows:

$million

	20X5	20X6	20X7
Components	0.520	0.686	0.815
Other cost of sales	0.130	0.144	0.152
Cost of Sales	0.650	0.830	0.967

It can be seen that the rate of increase in the non-component element of the cost of sales is much slower than the rate of volume growth in the business. Whilst sales rose by 20% in 20X6, the other costs increased by just over 10.75%. The comparable figures for 20X7 were 8% and 4% respectively. This indicates greater efficiency, and a high level of internal cost control.

The reported profits (as per the accounts) show a fall in operating profit of just below 3% between 20X6 and 20X7. Clearly, any fall in profits is undesirable, but it is difficult to see how performance could have been bettered. If Pellas had chosen to increase prices in line with the CPI, as demonstrated above, profits could have been maintained and indeed increased. The calculations assume, however, that the market is insensitive to price changes, and this is unlikely to be the case in practice. Higher prices could serve to reduce demand to unprofitable levels, particularly if non-manufacturing expenses are high. No information is given on non-manufacturing costs, but it is reasonable to assume that Pellas has some scope to reduce these, and in so doing retain a fixed level of reported pre-tax profit.

WORKING CAPITAL MANAGEMENT

11   GORWA CO

Key answer tips

In part (a) students may go into more depth about how to hedge interest rate risk and miss marks for analysing the effects of an increase in interest rates on the company concerned. Although the model answer presents a number of calculations that could be performed, there are only 1 – 2 marks available for the financial analysis. This is another reminder that the F9 paper is far from wholly numerical.

In part (b), again a huge range of calculations are possible. If students only manage a selection of those presented in the model answer, they should still be able to score highly. The weighting between calculations and discussion is 50:50 and the discussion provided in the model answer demonstrates the style the examiner is hoping for.

Part (c) is a fairly straightforward appraisal of the costs and benefits involved in a factoring agreement. With a requirement of "evaluate", it is clear that this section will require a good number of calculations.

(a)   **Financial analysis**

Fixed interest debt proportion (2006) = 100 × 2,425/(2,425 + 1,600) = 60%

Fixed interest debt proportion (2007) = 100 × 2,425/(2,425 + 3,225) = 43%

Fixed interest payments = 2,425 × 0.08 = $194,000

Variable interest payments (2006) = 274 – 194 = $80,000 or 29%

Variable interest payments (2007) = 355 – 194 = $161,000 or 45%

(Alternatively, considering the overdraft amounts and the average variable overdraft interest rate of 5% per year:

Variable interest payments (2006) = 1.6m × 0·05 = $80,000 or 29%

Variable interest payments (2007) = 3.225m × 0·05 = $161,250 or 45%)

Interest coverage ratio (2006) = 2,939/ 274 = 10.7 times

Interest coverage ratio (2007) = 2,992/ 355 = 8.4 times

Debt/equity ratio (2006) = 100 × 2,425/ 11,325 = 21%

Debt/equity ratio (2007) = 100 × 2,425/ 12,432 = 20%

Total debt/equity ratio (2006) = 100 x (2,425 +1,600)/ 11,325 = 35%

Total debt/equity ratio (2007) = 100 × (2,425 +3,225)/ 12,432 = 45%

Discussion

Gorwa Co has both fixed interest debt and variable interest rate debt amongst its sources of finance. The fixed interest bonds have ten years to go before they need to be redeemed and they therefore offer Gorwa Co long term protection against an increase in interest rates.

In 2006, 60% of the company's debt was fixed interest in nature, but in 2007 this had fallen to 43%. The floating-rate proportion of the company's debt therefore increased from 40% in 2006 to 57% in 2007. The interest coverage ratio fell from 10.7 times in 2006 to 8.4 times in 2007, a decrease which will be a cause for concern to the company if it were to continue. The debt/equity ratio (including the overdraft due to its size) increased over the same period from 35% to 45% (if the overdraft is excluded, the debt/equity ratio declines slightly from 21% to 20%). From the perspective of an increase in interest rates, the financial risk of Gorwa Co has increased and may continue to increase if the company does not take action to halt the growth of its variable interest rate overdraft. The proportion of interest payments linked to floating rate debt has increased from 29% in 2006 to 45% in 2007. An increase in interest rates will further reduce profit before taxation, which is lower in 2007 than in 2006, despite a 40% increase in turnover.

One way to hedge against an increase in interest rates is to exchange some or all of the variable-rate overdraft into long-term fixed-rate debt. There is likely to be an increase in interest payments because long-term debt is usually more expensive than short-term debt. Gorwa would also be unable to benefit from falling interest rates if most of its debt paid fixed rather than floating rate interest.

Interest rate options and interest rate futures may be of use in the short term, depending on the company's plans to deal with its increasing overdraft.

For the longer term, Gorwa Co could consider raising a variable-rate bank loan, linked to a variable rate-fixed interest rate swap.

(b) **Financial analysis**

		2007	2006
Inventory days	(365 × 2,400)/23,781		37 days
	(365 × 4,600)/34,408	49 days	
Receivables days	(365 × 2,200)/26,720		30 days
	(365 × 4,600)/37,400	45 days	
Payables days	(365 × 2,000)/23,781		31 days
	(365 × 4,750)/34,408	51 days	
Current ratio	4,600/3,600		1.3 times
	9,200/7,975	1.15 times	
Quick ratio	2,200/3,600		0.61 times
	4,600/7,975	0.58 times	
Sales/net working capital	26,720/1,000		26.7 times
	37,400/1,225	30.5 times	
Turnover increase	37,400/26,720	40%	

Non-current assets increase	13,632/12,750	7%
Inventory increase	4,600/2,400	92%
Receivables increase	4,600/2,200	109%
Payables increase	4,750/2,000	138%
Overdraft increase	3,225/1,600	102%

Discussion

Overtrading or undercapitalisation arises when a company has too small a capital base to support its level of business activity. Difficulties with liquidity may arise as an overtrading company may have insufficient capital to meet its liabilities as they fall due. Overtrading is often associated with a rapid increase in turnover and Gorwa Co has experienced a 40% increase in turnover over the last year. Investment in working capital has not matched the increase in sales, however, since the sales/net working capital ratio has increased from 26.7 times to 30.5 times.

Inventory days ✓ Overtrading could be indicated by a deterioration in inventory days. Here, inventory days have increased from 37 days to 49 days, while inventory has increased by 92% compared to the 40% increase in turnover. It is possible that inventory has been stockpiled in anticipation of a further increase in turnover, leading to an increase in operating costs.

Receivables days ✓ Overtrading could also be indicated by deterioration in receivables days. In this case, receivables have increased by 109% compared to the 40% increase in turnover. The increase in turnover may have been fuelled in part by a relaxation of credit terms.

Short-term finance ↑ ✓ As the liquidity problem associated with overtrading deepens, the overtrading company increases its reliance on short-term sources of finance, including overdraft, trade payables and leasing. The overdraft of Gorwa Co has more than doubled in size to $3.225 million, while trade payables have increased by $2.74 million or 137%. Both increases are much greater than the 40% increase in turnover. There is evidence here of an increased reliance on short-term finance sources.

Current Ratio ✓
Quick Ratio ↓ Overtrading can also be indicated by decreases in the current ratio and the quick ratio. The current ratio of Gorwa Co has fallen from 1.3 times to 1.15 times, while its quick ratio has fallen from 0.61 times to 0.58 times.

There are clear indications that Gorwa Co is experiencing the kinds of symptoms usually associated with overtrading. A more complete and meaningful analysis could be undertaken if appropriate benchmarks were available, such as key ratios from comparable companies in the same industry sector, or additional financial information from prior years so as to establish trends in key ratios.

(c) Current receivables = $4,600,000

Receivables under factor = 37,400,000 × 30/365 = $3,074,000 ✓

Reduction in receivables = 4,600 – 3,074 = $1,526,000

Reduction in finance cost = 1,526,000 × 0·05 = $76,300 per year

Administration cost savings = $100,000 per year ✓

Bad debt savings = $350,000 per year ✓

Factor's annual fee = 37,400,000 × 0.03 = $1,122,000 per year

Extra interest cost on advance = 3,074,000 × 80% × (7% – 5%) = $49,184 per year

Net cost of factoring = 76,300 + 100,000 + 350,000 – 1,122,000 – 49,184 = $644,884

The factor's offer cannot be recommended, since the evaluation shows no financial benefit arising.

ACCA marking scheme			
		Marks	Marks
(a)	Discussion of effects of interest rate increase	3 – 4	
	Relevant financial analysis	1 – 2	
	Interest rate hedging	2 – 3	
		――	
			Max 7
(b)	Financial analysis	5 – 6	
	Discussion of overtrading	4 – 5	
	Conclusion as to overtrading	1	
		――	
			Max 10
(c)	Reduction in financing cost	3	
	Factor's fee	1	
	Interest on advance	2	
	Net cost of factoring	1	
	Conclusion	1	
		――	
			8
			――
	Total		25
			――

Examiner's comments

Part (a) asked for a discussion, with supporting calculations, of the possible effects on a company of an increase in interest rates, and advice on how to protect against interest rate risk.

Some candidates were not aware of the difference between interest rate and interest payment, and consequently discussed how the company's finance costs (interest payments) had increased from one year to the next. Analysis would have shown that the increase in the finance cost was due to the increase in the overdraft and that the interest rate applied to the overdraft was 5% in each year, i.e. the interest rate had not changed. The bonds were fixed-rate in nature, as they were given in the balance sheet as 8% bonds. As the question asked about hedging interest rate risk, looking at the balance between fixed rate debt (bonds) and floating rate debt (overdraft) was also relevant here, as was a consideration of gearing and interest cover.

The question was, in fact, very open in nature, and a discussion of the effects of an increase in interest rates could look at an increase in financial risk, a decrease in sales due to a fall in demand, an increase in operating costs and a cutting back of investment plans.

Many answers offered a number of ways of protecting (hedging) against interest rate risk, including matching and smoothing: using forward rate agreements, interest rate futures, interest rate options and interest rates swaps; and taking steps to decrease the dependency on variable-rate overdraft finance and hence the exposure to interest rate increases, for example by improving working capital management.

In part (b), the requirement was to discuss, with supporting calculations, whether a company was overtrading (undercapitalised). Relevant financial analysis, including ratio analysis, therefore needed to look at the level of business activity and the area of working capital management.

Better answers calculated a series of accounting ratios, perhaps adding some growth rates and changes in financial statement entries, and used this analysis to look at the increasing dependence of the company on short-term sources of finance while sales were expanding at a high rate. Some answers noted that short-term finance had been used to acquire additional non-current assets, that inventory growth exceeded sales growth, and so on. Weaker answers often did little more than repeat in words the financial ratios that had been already calculated, without explaining how or why the identified changes supported the idea that the company was overtrading.

Part (c) required the evaluation of an offer from a factor using cost-benefit analysis.

Many candidates seemed to be unfamiliar with the relationship between credit sales, the level of trade receivables in the balance sheet, trade receivables days (the trade receivables collection period), and the cost of financing trade receivables. This unfamiliarity led to applying the revised trade receivables days to the current level of receivables instead of to credit sales: calculating the factor's advance on the current level of receivables rather than on the revised level of receivables: and calculating the factor's fee on the level of receivables rather than on credit sales.

Since marks were available for each element of the cost-benefit analysis, most candidates were able to obtain reasonable marks on this part of question 3, even where answers were incomplete or contained some of the errors identified above.

12   FLG CO

Key answer tips

Parts (a) and (b) are both standard textbook material. In part (a), for six marks you should discuss at least three factors. Don't forget the requirement is to "discuss" not "state" so you must give some commentary: 'the length of the working capital cycle' will not get the full marks available.

In part (b) the requirement is again to "discuss". Given the emphasis is on how both factoring and invoice discounting can assist in the **_management_** of accounts receivable, there should be more discussion on factoring than invoice discounting (the latter being a tool for managing cash flow rather than managing accounts receivable). Don't forget to define each of the terms to collect some easy marks.

The calculation in part (c) requires some "out of the box" thinking in order to see how the brief information provided can be used to work out the size of the overdraft. Not only does it involve re-arranging the usual working capital ratios we're used to seeing, it also requires a disaggregation of the operating cycle to reveal the inventory holding period.

In contrast, part (d) is a fairly straightforward application of the EOQ model which shouldn't pose many difficulties. The highlighted words are key phrases that markers are looking for.

(a)   There are a number of factors that determine the level of investment in current assets and their relative importance varies from company to company.

Length of working capital cycle

The working capital cycle or operating cycle is the period of time between when a company settles its accounts payable and when it receives cash from its accounts receivable. Operating activities during this period need to be financed and as the operating period lengthens, the amount of finance needed increases. Companies with comparatively longer operating cycles than others in the same industry sector, will therefore require comparatively higher levels of investment in current assets.

Terms of trade

These determine the period of credit extended to customers, any discounts offered for early settlement or bulk purchases, and any penalties for late payment. A company whose terms of trade are more generous than another company in the same industry sector will therefore need a comparatively higher investment in current assets.

Policy on level of investment in current assets

Even within the same industry sector, companies will have different policies regarding the level of investment in current assets, depending on their attitude to risk. A company with a comparatively conservative approach to the level of investment in current assets would maintain higher levels of inventory, offer more generous credit terms and have higher levels of cash in reserve than a company with a comparatively aggressive approach. While the more aggressive approach would be more profitable because of the lower level of investment in current assets, it would also be more risky, for example in terms of running out of inventory in periods of fluctuating demand, of failing to have the particular goods required by a customer, of failing to retain customers who migrate to more generous credit terms elsewhere, and of being less able to meet unexpected demands for payment.

Industry in which organisation operates

Another factor that influences the level of investment in current assets is the industry within which an organisation operates. Some industries, such as aircraft construction, will have long operating cycles due to the length of time needed to manufacture finished goods and so will have comparatively higher levels of investment in current assets than industries such as supermarket chains, where goods are bought in for resale with minimal additional processing and where many goods have short shelf-lives.

(b) Factoring involves a company turning over administration of its sales ledger to a factor, which is a financial institution with expertise in this area. The factor will assess the creditworthiness of new customers, record sales, send out statements and reminders, collect payment, identify late payers and chase them for settlement, and take appropriate legal action to recover debts where necessary.

The factor will also offer finance to a company based on invoices raised for goods sold or services provided. This is usually up to 80% of the face value of invoices raised. The finance is repaid from the settled invoices, with the balance being passed to the issuing company after deduction of a fee equivalent to an interest charge on cash advanced.

If factoring is without recourse, the factor rather than the company will carry the cost of any bad debts that arise on overdue accounts. Factoring without recourse therefore offers credit protection to the selling company, although the factor's fee (a percentage of credit sales) will be comparatively higher than with non-recourse factoring to reflect the cost of the insurance offered.

Invoice discounting is a way of raising finance against the security of invoices raised, rather than employing the credit management and administration services of a factor. A number of good quality invoices may be discounted, rather than all invoices, and the service is usually only offered to companies meeting a minimum turnover criterion.

(c)   Calculation of size of overdraft

Inventory period = operating cycle + payables period − receivables period = 3 + 1 − 2 = 2 months

Inventory = 1·89m × 2/12 = $315,000

Accounts receivable = 4·2m × 2/12 = $700,000

Current assets = 315,000 + 700,000 = $1,015,000

Current liabilities = current assets/current ratio = 1,015,000/1·4 = $725,000

Accounts payable = 1·89m × 1/12 = $157,500

Overdraft = 725,000 − 157,500 = $567,500

Net working capital = current assets − current liabilities = 1,015,000 − 725,000 = $290,000

Short-term financing cost = 567,500 × 0·07 = $39,725

Long-term financing cost = 290,000 × 0·11 = $31,900

Total cost of financing current assets = 39,725 + 31,900 = $71,625

(d)   (i)   Economic order quantity = (2 × 6 × 60,000/0·5)0·5 = 1,200 units

Number of orders = 60,000/1,200 = 50 order per year

Annual ordering cost = 50 × 6 = $300 per year

Average inventory = 1,200/2 = 600 units

Annual holding cost = 600 × 0·5 = $300 per year

Inventory cost = 60,000 × 12 = $720,000

Total cost of inventory with EOQ policy = 720,000 + 300 + 300 = $720,600 per year

(ii)   Order size for bulk discounts = 10,000 units

Number of orders = 60,000/10,000 = 6 orders per year

Annual ordering cost = 6 × 6 = $36 per year

Average inventory = 10,000/2 =5,000 units

Annual holding cost = 5,000 × 2 = $10,000 per year

Discounted material cost =12 × 0·99 = $11·88 per unit

Inventory cost = 60,000 × 11·88 = $712,800

Total cost of inventory with discount = 712,800 + 36 + 10,000 = $722,836 per year

The EOQ approach results in a slightly lower total inventory cost

ACCA marking scheme			
			Marks
(a)	Discussion of key factors	Maximum	6
(b)	Discussion of factoring		4–5
	Discussion of Invoice discounting		1–2
			───
	Maximum		6
(c)	Value of inventory		1
	Accounts receivable and accounts payable		1
	Current liabilities		1
	Size of overdraft		1
	Net working capital		1
	Total cost of financing working capital		1
			───
			6
(d)	(i) Economic order quantity		1
	Ordering cost and holding cost under EOQ		1
	Inventory cost under EOQ		1
	Total cost of inventory with EOQ policy		1
			───
			4
	(ii) Ordering cost and holding cost with discount		1
	Inventory cost with discount		1
	Total cost of inventory with bulk purchase discount		1
	Conclusion		1
			───
	Maximum		3
			───
	Total		25
			───

Examiner's comments

Part (a) asked for a discussion of the factors which determine the level of investment in current assets. Although this topic is clearly identified in the F9 Study Guide (C3a), answers often referred incorrectly to working capital funding strategies (C3b). The suggested answer to this question refers to factors mentioned in the F9 Study Guide, such as length of working capital cycle, terms of trade, working capital policy and so on. Answers that discussed these or similar factors gained high marks.

Part (b) asked for a discussion of the ways in which factoring and invoice discounting could help in managing accounts receivable. Many candidates discussed relevant points in relation to factoring and received credit accordingly. Discussions of invoice discounting tended to be variable in quality, with a significant number of students believing incorrectly that invoice discounting meant early settlement discounts.

In part (c), candidates were asked to calculate the size of an overdraft, the net working capital, and the total cost of financing current assets.

The variable quality of the answers indicates a need for candidates to ensure, not only that they are familiar with accounting ratios, but also that they are familiar with the accounting items to which the ratios relate, in this case sales, cost of sales, inventory, trade receivables, trade payables and so on. Many candidates were unable to calculate the inventory turnover period, given the operating cycle, the average collection period and the average payable period. Many candidates were also unable to work backwards from the provided ratios, for example to calculate the level of receivables given the average collection period and the amount of credit sales. Some candidates omitted the overdraft when calculating net working capital, indicating unfamiliarity with the structure of the balance sheet.

Part (d) asked candidates to calculate the total cost of inventory using the economic order quantity model (EOQ) and to evaluate a discount offered by a supplier. Many candidates gained high marks here by offering a comprehensive answer. Candidates who did not gain high marks appeared to be unsure of the meaning of the variables in the EOQ, even though the units of each were clearly specified in the question.

13   PKA CO   *Walk in the footsteps of a top tutor*

Key answer tips

This question combines elements from throughout the working capital management area of the syllabus with the foreign currency risk section. It is a good reflection of the examiner's style. The highlighted words are key phrases that markers are looking for.

Tutor's top tips:

Within the 15 minutes reading time, you should have managed a detailed read of the requirement and perhaps a quick skim read of the scenario. This will have highlighted that the question is a good balance of words and calculations and that parts (a) & (c) give an opportunity to capture some easy marks. You should consider doing these sections first.

Tutor's top tips:

Part (a) covers two aspects; the objectives of working capital management and the conflicts between them. Use the requirement to help structure your answer by picking out words that can be used as sub-headings. Any discussion on working capital can be reduced to a balance between profitability and liquidity, these being the overriding objectives. You will need to give definitions for both before moving on to talk about how they might conflict. Giving examples can be an easy way to explain things and will make the topic come to life.

(a)   The objectives of working capital management are profitability and liquidity. The objective of profitability supports the primary financial management objective, which is shareholder wealth maximisation. The objective of liquidity ensures that companies are able to meet their liabilities as they fall due, and thus remain in business.

However, funds held in the form of cash do not earn a return, while near-liquid assets such as short-term investments earn only a small return. Meeting the objective of liquidity will therefore conflict with the objective of profitability, which is met by investing over the longer term in order to achieve higher returns.

Good working capital management therefore needs to achieve a balance between the objectives of profitability and liquidity if shareholder wealth is to be maximised.

Tutor's top tips:

Part (b) will require a bit more thought. This is a fairly common exam question but the complexity of it can change depending on the information given. Your starting point should be to work out the economic order quantity (EOQ). We're given the formula in the exam so it's really just a case of finding the three pieces of information required, all of which are clearly stated in the scenario. Having calculated the EOQ, you are now equipped to work out the relative costs of the current policy compared to a potential new policy based on the EOQ. You will need to calculate:

- Total order costs (using annual demand, order size and cost per order)

- Total holding costs (using the cost of holding one unit and the average level of inventory)

Four of these five things are given to us in the scenario or have already been calculated. The tricky one is the average level of inventory as we need to consider not only the size of the order but also the level of buffer stocks held. You would be forgiven for thinking the buffer stock is 35,000 units, however you would be wrong. Some of these units would in fact be used in the two weeks it takes for the order to arrive. The information provided on annual demand will enable us to calculated how many units would be used in those two weeks, from which we can work out the level of inventory just prior to the order being delivered. This is by far the trickiest part of this question and it's important to keep it in context. Had you not spotted this, you would only have lost 2 marks. Don't forget, the requirement asks for the saving – be sure that you specifically calculate this to get all the marks.

(b) **Cost of current ordering policy of PKA Co**

Ordering cost = €250 × (625,000/100,000) = €1,563 per year

Weekly demand = 625,000/50 = 12,500 units per week

Consumption during 2 weeks lead time = 12,500 × 2 = 25,000 units

Buffer stock = re-order level less usage during lead time = 35,000 − 25,000 = 10,000 units

Average stock held during the year = 10,000 + (100,000/2) = 60,000 units

Holding cost = 60,000 × €0.50 = €30,000 per year

Total cost = ordering cost plus holding cost = €1,563 + €30,000 = €31,563 per year

Economic order quantity = $((2 \times 250 \times 625{,}000)/0.5)_{1/2}$ = 25,000 units

Number of orders per year = 625,000/25,000 = 25 per year

Ordering cost = €250 × 25 = €6,250 per year

Holding cost (ignoring buffer stock) = €0.50 × (25,000/2) = €0.50 × 12,500 = €6,250 per year

Holding cost (including buffer stock) = €0.50 × (10,000 + 12,500) = €11,250 per year

Total cost of EOQ-based ordering policy = €6,250 + €11,250 = €17,500 per year

Saving for PKA Co by using EOQ-based ordering policy = €31,563 – €17,500 = €14,063 per year

Tutor's top tips:

A quick read of the scenario for accounts receivable management gives us some ideas for sub-headings to use to answer part (c); accounts receivable period and bad debts. For 7 marks you should be aiming for a couple of points under each heading.

(c) The information gathered by the Financial Manager of PKA Co indicates that two areas of concern in the management of domestic accounts receivable are the increasing level of bad debts as a percentage of credit sales and the excessive credit period being taken by credit customers.

Reducing bad debts

The incidence of bad debts, which has increased from 5% to 8% of credit sales in the last year, can be reduced by assessing the creditworthiness of new customers before offering them credit and PKA Co needs to introduce a policy detailing how this should be done, or review its existing policy, if it has one, since it is clearly not working very well. In order to do this, information about the solvency, character and credit history of new clients is needed. This information can come from a variety of sources, such as bank references, trade references and credit reports from credit reference agencies. Whether credit is offered to the new customer and the terms of the credit offered can then be based on an explicit and informed assessment of default risk.

Reduction of average accounts receivable period

Customers have taken an average of 75 days credit over the last year rather than the 30 days offered by PKA Co, i.e. more than twice the agreed credit period. As a result, PKA Co will be incurring a substantial opportunity cost, either from the additional interest cost on the short-term financing of accounts receivable or from the incremental profit lost by not investing the additional finance tied up by the longer average accounts receivable period. PKA Co needs to find ways to encourage accounts receivable to be settled closer to the agreed date.

Assuming that the credit period offered by PKA Co is in line with that of its competitors, the company should determine whether they too are suffering from similar difficulties with late payers. If they are not, PKA Co should determine in what way its own terms differ from those of its competitors and consider whether offering the same trade terms would have an impact on its accounts receivable. For example, its competitors may offer a discount for early settlement while PKA Co does not and introducing a discount may achieve the desired reduction in the average accounts receivable period. If its competitors are experiencing a similar accounts receivable problem, PKA Co could take the initiative by introducing more favourable early settlement terms and perhaps generate increased business as well as reducing the average accounts receivable period.

PKA Co should also investigate the efficiency with which accounts receivable are managed. Are statements sent regularly to customers? Is an aged accounts receivable analysis produced at the end of each month? Are outstanding accounts receivable contacted regularly to encourage payment? Is credit denied to any overdue accounts seeking further business? Is interest charged on overdue accounts?

These are all matters that could be included by PKA Co in a revised policy on accounts receivable management.

Tutor's top tips:

Finally, in part (d), you must be very clear on the scenario before your start. PKA has a foreign supplier so to settle their debts, PKA will need to buy Dollars. If PKA is buying, the bank will be selling (remember the rhyme – the bank will always sell low (sounds like hello) and buy high (sounds like bye bye)!) We therefore know the appropriate spot rate is 1.998 – 0.002 = $1.996:€ and the appropriate forward rate is 1.979 – 0.004 = $1.975:€.

Once you're happy on which rates are to be used, you can calculate the Euros payable under the forward market hedge (don't let this term confuse you – it simply means a forward exchange contract) using the forward rate. You can also start the calculation for the lead payment using the spot rate. Finish this by thinking about the interest payable on the required loan. Since this is a Euro loan, you need half of the one year Euro borrowing rate.

Lastly, you can work on the money market hedge. Start by drawing out a diagram of the process, remembering the purpose is to eliminate the exchange risk by doing the translation now but then making sure that money continues to work for us by investing it in a Dollar bank account to earn interest.

(d) **Money market hedge**

PKA Co should place sufficient dollars on deposit now so that, with accumulated interest, the six-month liability of $250,000 can be met. Since the company has no surplus cash at the present time, the cost of these dollars must be met by a short-term euro loan.

Six-month dollar deposit rate = 3.5/2 = 1.75%

Current spot selling rate = 1.998 – 0.002 = $1.996 per euro

Six-month euro borrowing rate = 6.1/2 = 3.05%

Dollars deposited now = 250,000/1.0175 = $245,700

Cost of these dollars at spot = 245,700/1.996 = 123,096 euros

Euro value of loan in six months' time = 123,096 × 1.0305 = 126,850 euros

Forward market hedge

Six months forward selling rate = 1.979 – 0.004 = $1.975 per euro

Euro cost using forward market hedge = 250,000/1.975 = 126,582 euros

Lead payment

Since the dollar is appreciating against the euro, a lead payment may be worthwhile.

Euro cost now = 250,000/1.996 = 125,251 euros

This cost must be met by a short-term loan at a six-month interest rate of 3.05%

Euro value of loan in six months' time = 125,251 × 1.0305 = 129,071 euros

Evaluation of hedges

The relative costs of the three hedges can be compared since they have been referenced to the same point in time, i.e. six months in the future. The most expensive hedge is the lead payment, while the cheapest is the forward market hedge. Using the forward market to hedge the account payable currency risk can therefore be recommended.

Tutor's top tips:

The key learning points from this question are the importance of doing the easy parts of the question first and making sure you maintain good time discipline to ensure you don't get bogged down in one part of the question at the expense of another part.

	ACCA marking scheme	Marks
(a)	Profitability and liquidity	1
	Discussion of conflict between objectives	2
		3
(b)	Cost of current ordering policy	3
	Cost of EOQ-based ordering policy	3
	Saving by using EOQ model	1
		7
(c)	Reduction of bad debts	3–4
	Reduction of average accounts receivable period	3–4
	Discussion of other improvements	1–2
		7
d)	Money market hedge	3
	Forward market hedge	2
	Lead payment	2
	Evaluation	1
		8
Total		25

Examiner's comments

Part (a) of this question asked candidates to identify the objectives of working capital management and to discuss the conflict that might arise between them. There were many good answers here and most candidates gained high marks. However, some answers tended to be somewhat general rather than focussing on the objectives of working capital management and some answers were much too long for the three marks on offer.

In part (b) candidates were asked to calculate the cost of a company's current ordering policy and to determine the saving that could be made by using the economic order quantity (EOQ) model. Many candidates gained high marks for their answers to this part of question 4, calculating correctly the ordering costs of both the current and the EOQ policies, and comparing the total costs of each policy to show the saving arising from adoption of the EOQ policy. Many of these comparisons, however, were based on incorrect calculations of the holding costs of each policy.

Some candidates failed to consider the buffer inventory in calculating holding costs. Others used the re-order inventory level as the buffer level, failing to reduce inventory by consumption during the lead time it took for orders to arrive after being placed. Others added the re-order level to order quantity before dividing by two to calculate average inventory level, when only the order quantity is averaged.

Part (c) required candidates to discuss the ways in which a company could improve the management of domestic accounts receivable and many gained full marks here. Candidates failing to gain high marks tended to offer a limited number of possible methods, for example by focussing at length on factoring to the exclusion of internal accounts receivables management methods. Despite the requirement to discuss domestic accounts receivable, some candidates discussed export factoring and exchange rate hedging.

In part (d) candidates were required to evaluate whether a money market hedge, a forward market hedge or a lead payment should be used to hedge a foreign account payable. Some candidates offered discursive answers, for which they gained little credit since the question asked for an evaluation of hedging methods.

Many candidates were unable to calculate correctly the spot and forward exchange rates from the information provided. Many candidates failed to compare all three hedges from a common time horizon perspective, i.e. either from the current time or from three months hence.

Since it was a foreign currency account payable that was being hedged (a liability), the money market hedge involved creating a foreign currency asset (a deposit). The hedging company therefore needed to borrow euros, exchange them into dollars and place these dollars on deposit. Some candidates offered the opposite hedge, i.e. borrowing dollars and exchanging them into euros.

14   VELM

Key answer tips

To answer part (a), you will need to evaluate both the costs and benefits associated with offering the discount. This is best tackled on a line by line basis and even if your answer is not 100% accurate, you will still earn marks for each element you calculate correctly.

Parts (b) – (d) offer an opportunity for some relatively easy marks but you must ensure you justify your comments to Velm's specific policy if you are to earn high marks in (c).

The highlighted words are key phrases that markers are looking for.

(a)   The benefits of the proposed policy change are as follows.

Trade terms are 40 days, but customers are taking 365 x $550,000/4 million = 50 days.

Current level of receivables = $550,000.

Cost of 1% discount = 0.01 x $4m x 2/3 = $26,667.

Proposed level of receivables = ($4,000,000 – $26,667) x (26/365) = $283,000.

Reduction in receivables = $550,000 – $283,000 = $267,000.

Receivables appear to be financed by the overdraft at an annual rate of 9%.

		$
Reduction in financing cost	$267,000 × 9%	24,030
Reduction of 0.6% in bad debts	0.6% × $4 million	24,000
Salary saving from early retirement		12,000
Total benefits		60,030
Cost of 1% discount (see above)		(26,667)
Net benefit of discount		33,363

A discount for early payment of one per cent will therefore lead to an increase in profitability for Velm Inc.

(b) **Short-term sources of debt finance** include overdrafts and short-term loans. An **overdraft** offers flexibility but it is technically repayable on demand. Consequently it is a relatively risky source of finance. A company could experience liquidity problems if an overdraft were called in, until an alternative source of finance were found. The danger with a **short-term loan** as a source of finance is that it may be renewed at maturity on less favourable terms if economic circumstances have deteriorated and short-term interest rats are higher.

Short-term finance should be cheaper than long-term finance, based on the assumption of a normal shape to the yield curve. Economic circumstances could invert the yield curve, for example if short-term interest rates have been increased in order to curb economic growth or to dampen inflationary pressures.

Long-term sources of debt finance include loan stock, debentures and long-term loans. These are relatively secure forms of finance. For example if a company meets its contractual obligations on debentures in terms of interest payments and loan covenants, it will not have to repay the finance until maturity. The risk for the company is therefore lower if it finances working capital from a long-term source.

However, long-term finance is usually more expensive than short-term finance. The shape of the normal yield curve indicates that providers of debt finance will expect compensation for deferred consumption and default risk, as well as protection against expected inflation.

The choice between short-term and long-term debt for the financing of working capital is hence a choice between cheaper but riskier short-term finance and more expensive but less risky long-term debt.

(c) Working capital policies on the method of financing working capital can be characterised as conservative, moderate and aggressive. A **conservative financing policy** would involve financing working capital needs predominantly from long-term sources of finance. If current assets are analysed into permanent and fluctuating current assets, a conservative policy would use long-term finance for permanent current assets and some of the fluctuating current assets. Such a policy would increase the amount of lower-risk finance used by the company, at the expense of increased interest payments and lower profitability.

Velm Inc is clearly not pursuing a conservative financing policy, since long-term debt only accounts for 2.75% (40/1,450) of non-cash current assets. Rather, it seems to be following an **aggressive financing policy**, characterised by short-term finance being used for all of fluctuating current assets and most of the permanent current assets as well. Such a policy will decrease interest costs and increase profitability, but at the expense of an increase in the amount of higher-risk finance used by the company.

Between these two extremes in policy terms lies a **moderate or matching approach**, where short-term finance is used for fluctuating current assets and long-term finance is used for permanent current assets. This is an expression of the matching principle, which holds that the maturity of the finance should match the maturity of the assets.

(d) The objectives of working capital management are often stated to be profitability and liquidity. These objectives are often in conflict, since liquid assets earn the lowest return and so liquidity is achieved at the expense of profitability. However, liquidity is needed in the sense that a company must meet its liabilities as they fall due if it is to remain in business. For this reason cash is often called the lifeblood of the company, since without cash a company would quickly fail. Good working capital management is therefore necessary if the company is to survive and remain profitable.

The fundamental objective of the company is to maximise the wealth of its shareholders and good working capital management helps to achieve this by **minimising the cost of investing in current assets**. **Good credit management**, for example, aims to minimise the risk of bad debts and expedite the prompt payment of money due from debtors in accordance with agreed terms of trade. Taking steps to optimise the level and age of debtors will minimise the cost of financing them, leading to an increase in the returns available to shareholders.

A similar case can be made for the **management of inventory**. It is likely that Velm Inc will need to have a good range of stationery and office supplies on its premises if customers' needs are to be quickly met and their custom retained. Good inventory management, for example using techniques such as the economic order quantity model, ABC analysis, stock rotation and buffer stock management can minimise the costs of holding and ordering stock. The application of just-in-time methods of stock procurement and manufacture can reduce the cost of investing in stock. Taking steps to improve stock management can therefore reduce costs and increase shareholder wealth.

Cash budgets can help to determine the transactions need for cash in each budget control period, although the optimum cash position will also depend on the precautionary and speculative need for cash. Cash management models such as the Baumol model and the Miller-Orr model can help to maintain cash balances close to optimum levels.

The different elements of good working capital management therefore combine to help the company to achieve its primary financial objective.

15 FRANTIC CO

Key answer tips

Part (a) is a fairly straightforward application of the economic order quantity model. Part (b) is slightly more challenging and a methodical approach, with good use of supporting workings / notes is essential to completing the question on time.

(a)   Inventory evaluation without early settlement discounting

Annual production (demand) = 800 cars = 800 engines.

Cost of ordering = cost of delivery = $1,200.

Annual inventory holding cost = 22% × $1,300 = $286.

EOQ ignoring discounts = $\sqrt{\dfrac{2C_oD}{C_H}}$ = $\sqrt{\dfrac{2 \times 1,200 \times 800}{286}}$ = 81.93 or 82 whole units.

At this batch ordering level, a quantity discount of 2% would apply. The annual holding cost would therefore be 22% × 98% x $1,300 = $280.28. Re-working the previous calculation with the quantity discount gives:

EOQ = $\sqrt{\dfrac{2C_oD}{C_H}}$ = $\sqrt{\dfrac{2 \times 1,200 \times 800}{280.28}}$ = 82.77 or 83 whole units.

Hence the choice facing Frantic Co is between ordering 83 units and getting a 2% discount, or 250 units, which is the minimum purchase quantity needed to get a 3% discount.

Evaluation for an order quantity of 83:

		$
Total purchase costs:	$1,300 × 98% × 800 =	1,019,200
Holding costs:	83/2 × $280.28 =	11,632
Order costs:	(800/83) × $1,200 =	11,566
		————
Total annual costs:		1,042,398
		————

Evaluation for an order quantity of 250:

		$
Total purchase costs:	$1,300 × 97% × 800 =	1,008,800
Holding costs:	250/2 × 22% × 97% × $1,300 =	34,678
Order costs:	(800/250) × $1,200 =	3,840
		————
Total annual costs:		1,047,318
		————

Difference in costs: Buying in quantities of 250 is more expensive by $4,920 each year. **The optimal policy** is to order in quantities that minimises total costs, which in this case is to **order in batches of 83 engines**.

Tutorial note:

An alternative answer takes an incremental cost approach, and compares the incremental costs or savings from ordering in batches of 250 compared to ordering in batches of 83. The initial assumption is that the company orders in batches of 83. This approach is shown on the next page.

	$	$
Saving in purchase price by buying 250: (800 × 1% × $1,300)		10,400
Saving in ordering costs by buying in batches of 250:		
[(800 × 1,200)/83] − [(800 × 1,200)/250]		7,726
Total cost savings		18,126
Holding costs with order quantity of 250 (above)	34,678	
Holding costs with order quantity of 83 (above)	11,632	
Additional holding costs from ordering in batches of 250		23,046
Increased costs arising from ordering 250 units		4,920

The same conclusion is reached as above. The optimal policy is to order 83 engines at a time.

(b) As stated in solution (a) the optimal policy is to order 83 engines at a time. This involves ordering 800/83 = 9.64 times per year. A production schedule can be drawn-up to assess when the orders would be made. If this is undertaken the following ordering schedule would result:

Month	1	2	3	4	5	6
Car production[1]	66.7	66.7	66.7	66.7	66.7	66.7
Engine orders placed[2]	83	83	83	83	83	
Inventory at month-end	16	32	48	64	80	13

[1] Fractional production allowed and reflected in work in progress

[2] No orders are placed in the sixth month due to the ordering policy and the resulting inventory build up. This does not have any implications for the six month cash flow since creditors will be paid with one month delay.

Cash flow for first six months:

Month	1	2	3	4	5	6
Receipts						
Cash sales (Note 1)	1,416,667	1,416,667	1,416,667	1,416,667	1,416,667	1,416,667
Credit sales (Note 1)	1,062,500	1,062,500	1,416,667	1,416,667	1,416,667	1,416,667
Total income	**2,479,167**	**2,479,167**	**2,833,334**	**2,833,334**	**2,833,334**	**2,833,334**
Payments						
Capital costs			3,200,000			
Engine costs (Note 2)	97,500	104,156	104,156	104,156	104,156	104,156
Other expenses (Note 3)	1,841,667	1,841,667	1,841,667	1,841,667	1,841,667	1,841,667
Fixed costs	18,000	18,000	18,000	22,000	22,000	22,000
Costs net of overdraft	**1,957,167**	**1,963,823**	**5,163,823**	**1,967,823**	**1,967,823**	**1,967,823**

Receipts less payments	522,000	515,344	(2,330,489)	865,511	865,511	865,511
Opening bank balance	(25,000)	496,687	1,012,031	(1,318,458)	(469,428)	390,215
Interest (Note 4)	(313)	–	–	(16,481)	(5,868)	–
Closing bank balance	**496,687**	**1,012,031**	**(1,318,458)**	**(469,428)**	**390,215**	**1,255,726**

Notes:

(1) Monthly sales = 800/12 units. Cash sales are 50% of 800/12 × $42,500 = $1,416,667. Credit sales are the same in each month, but customers take two months' credit. Receipts from credit sales in months 1 and 2 are as stated in the question.

(2) Engine cost payments. Month 1 payment is given in the question. The company will take a bulk purchase discount of 2% and an early settlement discount of 1.5%. Cash paid in subsequent months = quantity purchased in previous month × 98.5% of 98% of $1,300 = $104,156 per month.

(3) Other expenses are 65% × monthly sales = 65% × (800/12) × $42,500 = $1,841,667.

(4) Assumption = Overdraft costs are calculated as (1/12) × 15% × opening bank balance. (Other bases of calculation are acceptable such as interest calculated on average balances.)

16   HGR CO

Key answer tips

The generic requirement of part (a), to "discuss the working capital financing strategy of HGR" can result in a lack of direction and focus in your answer. This sort of question highlights the importance of good exam preparation that includes sitting as many past exam questions as possible as requirements such as this are not unusual.

Part (b) may overwhelm some students as the initial perception is that many calculations need to be made. However, this is not the case. Part (i) (for 2 marks) involves simply plugging in the numbers provided before doing a quick calculation of overdraft interest. In part (ii), (for 5 marks) you need to evaluate the impact of the finance director's proposals surrounding both accounts receivable and inventory management. Both calculations involve a manipulation of the standard working capital cycle formulae that students should be familiar, although this might not be obvious to some students. The model answer shows the most efficient way of laying out the answer. Of the 10 marks available for part (b), up to 4 are available for commenting on the forecast position and making suitable recommendations. This could easily be overlooked if you're not careful.

Finally, part (c) gives a good opportunity to pick up some easier marks. This part of the question should be attempted first. The highlighted words are key phrases that markers are looking for.

(a)   When considering the financing of working capital, it is useful to divide current assets into fluctuating current assets and permanent current assets. Fluctuating current assets represent changes in the level of current assets due to the unpredictability of business activity. Permanent current assets represent the core level of investment in current assets needed to support a given level of turnover or business activity. As turnover or level of business activity increases, the level of permanent current assets will also increase. This relationship can be measured by the ratio of turnover to net current assets.

The financing choice as far as working capital is concerned is between short-term and long-term finance. Short-term finance is more flexible than long-term finance: an overdraft, for example, is used by a business organisation as the need arises and variable interest is charged on the outstanding balance. Short-term finance is also more risky than long-term finance: an overdraft facility may be withdrawn, or a short-term loan may be renewed on less favourable terms. In terms of cost, the term structure of interest rates suggests that short-term debt finance has a lower cost than long-term debt finance.

The matching principle suggests that long-term finance should be used for long-term investment. Applying this principle to working capital financing, long-term finance should be matched with permanent current assets and non-current assets. A financing policy with this objective is called a 'matching policy'. HGR Co is not using this financing policy, since of the $16,935,000 of current assets, $14,000,000 or 83% is financed from short-term sources (overdraft and trade payables) and only $2,935,000 or 17% is financed from a long-term source, in this case equity finance (shareholders' funds) or traded bonds.

The financing policy or approach taken by HGR Co towards the financing of working capital, where short-term finance is preferred, is called an aggressive policy. Reliance on short-term finance makes this riskier than a matching approach, but also more profitable due to the lower cost of short-term finance. Following an aggressive approach to financing can lead to overtrading (undercapitalisation) and the possibility of liquidity problems.

(b) Bank balance in three months' time if no action is taken:

Month	1	2	3
	$'000	$'000	$'000
Receipts	4,220	4,350	3,808
Payments	(3,950)	(4,100)	(3,750)
Interest on bonds		(200)	
Overdraft interest	(19)	(18)	(18)
Capital investment			(2,000)
Net cash flow	251	32	(1,960)
Opening balance	(3,800)	(3,549)	(3,517)
Closing balance	(3,549)	(3,517)	(5,477)

*Overdraft.

Bank balance in three months' time if the finance director's proposals are implemented:

Month	1	2	3
	$'000	$'000	$'000
Receipts	4,220	4,350	3,808
Payments	(3,950)	(4,100)	(3,750)
Interest on bonds		(200)	
Overdraft interest	(19)	(15)	(13)
Capital investment			(2,000)
Accounts receivable	270	270	270
Inventory	204	204	204
Net cash flow	725	509	(1,481)
Opening balance	(3,800)	(3,075)	(2,566)
Closing balance	(3,075)	(2,566)	(4,047)

Workings:

Reduction in accounts receivable days

Current accounts receivable days = (8,775/49,275) x 365 = 65 days

Reduction in days over six months = 65 – 53 = 12 days

Monthly reduction = 12/6 = 2 days

Each receivables day is equivalent to 8,775,000/65 =$135,000 (Alternatively, each receivables day is equivalent to 49,275,000/365 =$135,000)

Monthly reduction in accounts receivable = 2 x 135,000 = $270,000

Reduction in inventory days

Current inventory days = (8,160/37,230) x 365 = 80 days

Each inventory day is equivalent to 8,160,000/80 = $102,000 (Alternatively, each inventory day = 37,230,000/365 = $102,000)

Monthly reduction in inventory = 102,000 x 2 = $204,000

Overdraft interest calculations

Monthly overdraft interest rate = 1.06171/12 = 1.005 or 0.5%

If no action is taken:

Period 1 interest = 3,800,000 x 0.005 = $19,000

Period 2 interest = 3,549,000 x 0.005 = $17,745 or $18,000

Period 3 interest = 3,517,000 x 0.005 = $17,585 or $18,000

If action is taken:

Period 1 interest = 3,800,000 x 0.005 = $19,000

Period 2 interest = 3,075,000 x 0.005 = $15,375 or $15,000

Period 3 interest = 2,566,000 x 0.005 = $12,830 or $13,000

Discussion

If no action is taken, the cash flow forecast shows that HGR Co will exceed its overdraft limit of $4 million by $1·48 million in three months' time. If the finance director's proposals are implemented, there is a positive effect on the bank balance, but the overdraft limit is still exceeded in three months' time, although only by $47,000 rather than by $1·47 million.

In each of the three months following that, the continuing reduction in accounts receivable days will improve the bank balance by $270,000 per month. Without further information on operating receipts and payments, it cannot be forecast whether the bank balance will return to less than the limit, or even continue to improve.

The main reason for the problem with the bank balance is the $2 million capital expenditure. Purchase of non-current assets should not be financed by an overdraft, but a long-term source of finance such as equity or bonds. If the capital expenditure were removed from the area of working capital management, the overdraft balance at the end of three months would be $3·48 million if no action were taken and $2·05 million if the finance director's proposals were implemented. Given that HGR Co has almost $50 million of non-current assets that could possibly be used as security, raising long-term debt through either a bank loan or a bond issue appears to be sensible. Assuming a bond interest rate of 10% per year, current long-term debt in the form of traded bonds is approximately ($200m x 2)/0·1 = $4m, which is much less than the amount of noncurrent assets.

A suitable course of action for HGR Co to follow would therefore be, firstly, to implement the finance director's proposals and, secondly, to finance the capital expenditure from a long-term source. Consideration could also be given to using some long-term debt finance to reduce the overdraft and to reduce the level of accounts payable, currently standing at 100 days.

(c)   When credit is granted to foreign customers, two problems may become especially significant. First, the longer distances over which trade takes place and the more complex nature of trade transactions and their elements means foreign accounts receivable need more investment than their domestic counterparts. Longer transaction times increase accounts receivable balances and hence the level of financing and financing costs. Second, the risk of bad debts is higher with foreign accounts receivable than with their domestic counterparts. In order to manage and reduce credit risks, therefore, exporters seek to reduce the risk of bad debt and to reduce the level of investment in foreign accounts receivable.

Many foreign transactions are on 'open account', which is an agreement to settle the amount outstanding on a predetermined date. Open account reflects a good business relationship between importer and exporter. It also carries the highest risk of non-payment.

One way to reduce investment in foreign accounts receivable is to agree early payment with an importer, for example by payment in advance, payment on shipment, or cash on delivery. These terms of trade are unlikely to be competitive, however, and it is more likely that an exporter will seek to receive cash in advance of payment being made by the customer.

One way to accelerate cash receipts is to use bill finance. Bills of exchange with a signed agreement to pay the exporter on an agreed future date, supported by a documentary letter of credit, can be discounted by a bank to give immediate funds.

This discounting is without recourse if bills of exchange have been countersigned by the importer's bank.

Documentary letters of credit are a payment guarantee backed by one or more banks. They carry almost no risk, provided the exporter complies with the terms and conditions contained in the letter of credit. The exporter must present the documents stated in the letter, such as bills of lading, shipping documents, bills of exchange, and so on, when seeking payment. As each supporting document relates to a key aspect of the overall transaction, letters of credit give security to the importer as well as the exporter.

Companies can also manage and reduce risk by gathering appropriate information with which to assess the creditworthiness of new customers, such as bank references and credit reports.

Insurance can also be used to cover some of the risks associated with giving credit to foreign customers. This would avoid the cost of seeking to recover cash due from foreign accounts receivable through a foreign legal system, where the exporter could be at a disadvantage due to a lack of local or specialist knowledge.

Export factoring can also be considered, where the exporter pays for the specialist expertise of the factor as a way of reducing investment in foreign accounts receivable and reducing the incidence of bad debts.

ACCA marking scheme			
		Marks	
(a)	Analysis of current assets	1 - 2	
	Short-term and long-term finance	2 - 3	
	Matching principle	1 - 2	
	Financing approach used by company	1 - 2	
		Maximum	7
(b)	Bank balance if no action is taken	2	
	Bank balance if action is taken	5	
	Working capital management implications	1 - 2	
	Advice on course of action	1 - 2	
		Maximum	10
(c)	Relevant discussion		8
Total			25

Examiner's comments

Part (a) required candidates to discuss the working capital financing strategy of a company. Some candidates ignored the word 'financing' and discussed working capital strategy in general. Other candidates took 'working capital financing strategy' to mean the proposals in the question to reduce the level of account receivables and inventory by operational improvements.

The question gave extracts from a statement of financial position which showed that the company was financing 83% of its current assets from short-term sources, namely a bank overdraft and trade receivables. This is an aggressive rather than a conservative financing strategy and better answers recognised this, discussing how current assets could be divided into fluctuating and permanent current assets, and linking this analysis of current assets via the matching principle to the use of short-term and long-term finance.

Part (b) asked candidates to calculate the bank balance in three months' time if no action were taken, and if the proposals were implemented. Many candidates had great difficulty in rolling forward the current cash balance (the overdraft of $3.8 million) using the receipts and payments given in the question, while allowing for one month's interest on the balance of the account at the start of each month. Common errors included failing to recognise that the opening balance was the overdraft and therefore having no opening balance: calculating annual interest rather than monthly interest; and including cash flows other than those given in the question (for example from the credit sales and cost of sales figures given in the question). All candidates are expected to be able to prepare cash flow forecasts and the general standard of answers to this question showed that many candidates need further preparation in this important area.

Part (c) required candidates to discuss how risks arising from granting credit to foreign customers could be managed and reduced. Many candidates gave answers of a good standard, although some answers were one-sided, concentrating on exchange rate risk rather than on credit risk. Since the question referred to foreign customers, it was inappropriate to limit answers to a discussion of domestic receivables management.

17   ANJO

Key answer tips

This is a fairly straightforward question with some easier written marks within part (c). Tackle these first to ensure you give yourself the most amount of time for the calculations. The highlighted words are key phrases that markers are looking for.

(a)   **Calculation of ratios**

Inventory days	20X6:	(3,000/9,300) x 365	= 118 days
	20X5:	(1,300/6,600) x 365	= 72 days
		Sector average: 90 days	
Receivables days	20X6:	(3,800/15,600) x 365	= 89 days
	20X5:	(1,850/11,100) x 365	= 61 days
		Sector average: 60 days	
Payables days	20X6:	(2,870/9,300 x 0.95) x 365	= 119 days
	20X5:	(1,600/6,600 x 0.95) x 365	= 93 days
		Sector average: 80 days	

In each case, the ratio in 20X6 is higher than the ratio in 20X5, indicating that deterioration has occurred in the management of inventories, receivables and payables in 20X6.

Inventory days have increased by 46 days or 64%, moving from below the sector average to 28 days – one month – more than it. Given the rapid increase in sales revenue (40%) in 20X6, Anjo Inc may be expecting a continuing increase in the future and may have built up inventories in preparation for this, i.e. inventory levels reflect future sales rather than past sales. Accounting statements from several previous years and sales forecasts for the next period would help to clarify this point.

Receivables days have increased by 28 days or 46% in 20X6 and are now 29 days above the sector average. It is possible that more generous credit terms have been offered in order to stimulate sales. The increased sales revenue does not appear to be due to offering lower prices, since both gross profit margin (40%) and net profit margin (34%) are unchanged.

In 20X5, only management of payables was a cause for concern, with Anjo Inc taking 13 more days on average to settle liabilities with trade payables than the sector. This has increased to 39 days more than the sector in 20X6. This could lead to difficulties between the company and its suppliers if it is exceeding the credit periods they have specified. Anjo Inc has no long-term debt and the balance sheet (statement of financial position) indicates an increased reliance on short-term finance, since cash has reduced by $780,000 or 87% and the overdraft has increased by $850,000 to $1 million.

Perhaps the company should investigate whether it is undercapitalised (overtrading). It is unusual for a company of this size to have no long-term debt.

(b)   Cash operating cycle (20X5) = 72 + 61 – 93 = 40 days
        Cash operating cycle (20X6) = 118 + 89 – 119 = 88 days

The cash operating cycle or working capital cycle gives the average time it takes for the company to receive payment from receivables after it has paid its trade payables. This represents the period of time for which payables require financing. The cash operating cycle of Anjo Inc has lengthened by 48 days in 20X6 compared with 20X5. This represents an increase in working capital requirement of approximately $15,600,000 x 48/365 = $2.05 million.

(c)   The objectives of working capital management are liquidity and profitability, but there is a tension between these two objectives. Liquid funds, for example cash, earn no return and so will not increase profitability. Near-liquid funds, with short investment periods, earn a lower return than funds invested for a long period. Profitability is therefore decreased to the extent that liquid funds are needed.

The main reason that companies fail, though, is because they run out of cash and so good cash management is an essential part of good working capital management. Business solvency cannot be maintained if working capital management in the form of cash management is of a poor standard.

In order to balance the twin objectives of liquidity and profitability in terms of cash management, a company needs to decide on the optimum amount of cash to hold at any given time. There are several factors that can aid in determining the optimum cash balance.

First, it is important to note that cash management is a forward-looking activity, in that the optimum cash balance must reflect the expected need for cash in the next budget period, for example in the next month. The cash budget will indicate expected cash receipts over the next period, expected payments that need to be made, and any shortfall that is expected to arise due to the difference between receipts and payments. This is the transactions need for cash, since it is based on the amount of cash needed to meet future business transactions.

However, there may be a degree of uncertainty as to the timing of expected receipts. Receivables, for example, may not all pay on time and some may take extended credit, whether authorised or not. In order to guard against a possible shortfall of cash to meet future transactions, companies may keep a 'buffer inventory' of cash by holding a cash reserve greater than called for by the transactions demand. This is the precautionary demand for cash and the optimum cash balance will reflect management's assessment of this demand.

Beyond this, a company may decide to hold additional cash in order to take advantage of any business opportunities that may arise, for example the possibility of taking over a rival company that has fallen on hard times. This is the speculative demand for cash and it may contribute to the optimum cash level for a given company, depending on that company's strategic plan.

(d)

	$000
Current receivables =	3,800
Receivables under factor = 3,800 x 0.7 =	2,660
	———
Reduction in receivables =	1,140
	———

	$000
Finance cost saving = 1,140 x 0.08 =	91.2
Administration cost saving = 1,000 x 0.02 =	20.0
Interest on advance = 2,660 x 0.8 x 0.01 =	(21.3)
Factor's annual fee = 15,600 x 0.005 =	(78.0)
	———
Net benefit of accepting factor's offer	11.9
	———

Although the terms of the factor's offer are financially acceptable, suggesting a net financial benefit of $11,900, this benefit is small compared with annual sales revenue of $15.6 million. Other benefits, such as the application of the factor's expertise to the receivables management of Anjo Inc, might also be influential in the decision on whether to accept the offer.

18   BLIN

Key answer tips

Parts (a) and (c) of this question should be fairly straightforward. For part (a), your answer should give some emphasis to the yield curve. Part (b) is probably more difficult, because it is not necessarily easy to see what the examiner had in mind with 'approaches'. Thinking about the question logically might help you to construct an answer. You are asked to comment on approaches to the mix of long-term and short-term funding to finance working capital. Logically, the approaches are (1) to have mainly long-term capital and not much short-term capital, (2) to have mainly short-term capital and not much long-term capital, and (3) to have a more balanced mixture of short-term and long-term capital. These are the approaches in the solution.

However, the distinction between 'permanent' levels of current assets and 'fluctuating' levels of current assets is a useful distinction, which the solution in part (b) uses as a basis for analysis. A company's current assets are continually changing in total amount, up and down, but there is usually a 'permanent' amount below which the total of current assets does not fall. Fluctuating current assets are current assets in excess of the minimum level. The highlighted words are key phrases that markers are looking for.

(a)   The following factors will influence the rate of interest charged on the new bank loan.

General level of interest rates

Interest rates charged on loans will depend on the general level of interest rates. Typically, interest rates on a bank loan are set at a margin above a 'base rate' or 'prime rate' or at a margin above a money market benchmark rate such as LIBOR. Similarly, longer-term fixed interest rates are at a margin above either a government bond rate or the swap rate. When the general level of interest rates goes up, rates on new lending will also rise.

Risk of default

The bank providing the loan to Blin will make an assessment of the risk that the company might default on its loan commitments and charge an interest rate that reflects this risk. Since Blin is listed on a stock exchange it will be seen as less risky than an unlisted company and will pay a lower interest rate as a result. The period of time that the company has been listed may also be an influential factor.

Since Blin has expanded sales significantly and relies heavily on overdraft finance, it may be overtrading. This could increase the risk of default and so increase the rate of interest charged on the loan. The bank would need to be convinced through financial information supporting the loan application, such as cash flow forecasts, that Blin would be able to meet future interest payments and repayments of principal.

Security offered

The rate of interest charged on the loan will be lower if the debt is secured against an asset or assets of the company. It is likely in Blin's case that the loan will carry a fixed charge on particular assets, such as land or buildings. In the event of default by the company, the bank can recover its loan by selling the secured assets.

Duration of loan

The longer the period of the loan taken out by Blin, the higher the interest rate that will be charged. This reflects the shape of the normal yield curve.

The normal yield curve shows that the yield required on debt increases in line with the term to maturity. One reason for this is that loan providers require compensation for deferring their use of the cash they have lent, and the longer the period for which they are deprived of their cash, the more compensation they require. This is described as the liquidity preference explanation for the shape of the normal yield curve.

Other explanations for the shape of the normal yield curve are expectations theory and market segmentation theory. Expectations theory suggests that interest rates rise with maturity because rates of interest are expected to rise in the future, for example due to an expected increase in inflation. Market segmentation theory suggests that the market for long-term debt differs from the market for short-term debt.

Amount borrowed

The rate of interest charged on the new loan could be lower if the amount borrowed is not a small sum. It is more convenient from an administrative point of view for a bank to lend a large sum rather than several small amounts.

(b)   The approaches that Blin could adopt regarding the relative proportions of long- and short-term finance to meet its working capital needs could be described as conservative, moderate and aggressive.

The assets of a business are categorised into current and non-current assets. Current assets are used up on a regular basis within a single accounting period and non-current assets benefit a business for several accounting periods. Current assets can be further categorised into permanent current assets and fluctuating current assets. Permanent current assets represent the core level or minimum level of investment in current assets needed for a given level of business activity, and arise from the need for businesses to carry inventory and to extend credit. Fluctuating current assets represent a variable need for investment in current assets, arising from either seasonal or unpredictable variations in business activity.

With a *conservative* approach to the financing mix, long-term finance is the main source of working capital funds. Long-term finance is used to finance non-current assets, permanent current assets and some fluctuating current assets.

Long-term debt finance is less risky to a company than short-term debt finance, since once in place it is not subjected to the dangers of renewal or immediate repayment. However, it is more expensive in that the rate of interest charged normally increases with maturity. A conservative approach would therefore increase the amount of lower-risk long-term debt finance used by the company, but would also incur higher total interest payments than an approach emphasizing the use of short-term debt. This approach will therefore lead to relatively lower profitability. A similar argument can be made when equity finance is used as long-term finance; equity requires an even higher return than long-term debt finance.

With an *aggressive* approach to the financing mix, short-term finance is the main source of working capital funds. This approach, which is currently being used by Blin, uses short-term finance for fluctuating current assets and some permanent current assets, with long-term finance being used for the balance of permanent current assets and non-current assets. This increases the relative amount of higher-risk short-term finance used by the company, but will also incur lower total interest payments than the conservative approach discussed above, leading to relatively higher profitability.

Between these two approaches lies a moderate or matching approach. This approach applies the matching principle, whereby the maturity of the funding is matched with life of the assets financed. Here, long-term finance is used for permanent current assets and non-current assets, while short-term finance is used for fluctuating current assets.

The repayment of the overdraft will result in Blin adopting a conservative approach to the mix of long- and short-term finance. This will resolve an overtrading situation, if it exists. However, it may reduce profitability more than necessary. If Blin continues to expand sales, or reintroduces overdraft finance, the conservative position will only be temporary and a moderate position may arise in the future. The speed with which this happens will depend on the size of the loan taken out, and whether a moderate position is desirable will depend on the company's attitude to risk and return. It may be preferable to reduce the overdraft to a lower level rather than repaying it completely. A clearer picture would emerge if we knew the intended use for, and the amount of, the balance of the loan not being used to repay the overdraft.

(c) The cash operating cycle is the length of time between paying trade payables and receiving cash from receivables. It can be calculated by adding together the average inventory holding period and the average time for receivables to pay, and then subtracting the average time taken to pay trade payables. The inventory holding period may be subdivided into the holding periods for raw materials, work-in-progress and finished goods. Using accounting ratios, the cash operating cycle can be approximated by adding together inventory days and receivables days and subtracting payables days.

The significance of the cash operating cycle in determining the level of investment in working capital is that the longer the cash operating cycle, the higher the investment in working capital.

The length of the cash operating cycle varies between industries: for example, a service organization may have no inventory holding period, a retail organization will have an inventory holding period based almost entirely on finished goods and a very low level of receivables, and a manufacturing organization will have an inventory holding period based on raw materials, work-in-progress and finished goods. The level of investment in working capital will therefore depend on the nature of business operations.

The cash operating cycle and the resulting level of investment in working capital does not depend only on the nature of the business, however. Companies within the same business sector may have different levels of investment in working capital, measured for example by the accounting ratio of sales/net working capital, as a result of adopting different working capital policies. A relatively aggressive policy on the level of investment in working capital is characterised by lower levels of inventory and receivables: this lower level of investment increases profitability but also increases the risk of running out of inventory, or of losing potential customers due to better credit terms being offered by competitors. A relatively conservative policy on the level of investment in working capital has higher levels of investment in inventory and receivables: profitability is therefore reduced, but the risk of inventory stock-outs is lower and new credit customers may be attracted by more generous terms.

It is also possible to reduce the level of investment in working capital by reducing the length of the cash operating cycle. This is achieved by reducing the inventory holding period (for example by using JIT methods), by reducing the average time taken by receivables to pay (for example by improving receivables management), or by increasing the length of credit period taken from suppliers (for example by settling invoices as late as possible). In this way an understanding of the cash operating cycle can assist in taking steps to improve working capital management and profitability.

19   PNP PLC

Key answer tips

Part (a) requires the usual comparison of the costs and benefits of implementing a discount. The complexity of the question means there are a large number of elements to consider and key to tackling the calculations is to recognise that the average payment period per class of receivable will equal the receivables days. Remember, each individual calculation will earn marks so you don't need to have identified all of them to score well. Both parts (a) and (b) of this question require a significant amount of workings. Laying your workings out neatly and clearly cross referencing them to your answer will ensure you have the best chance of scoring well. When laying out your answer to part (d), use plenty of sub-headings to clearly indicate to your marker the points you are making. The highlighted words are key phrases that markers are looking for.

(a)   Effect on profitability of implementing the proposal

	£	£
Benefits:		
Increased contribution (W1)	200,000	
Decrease in irrecoverable debts (W2)	6,300	
		206,300
Costs		
Increase in current Class 1 discount (W3)	12,167	
Discount from transferring Class 2 receivables (W4)	11,498	
Discount from new Class 1 receivables (W5)	3,750	
Increase in irrecoverable debts, new Class 2 receivables (W6)	2,055	
Increase in financing cost from new receivables (W7)	4,932	34,402
Net benefit of implementing the proposal		171,898

The proposed change appears to be financially acceptable and so may be recommended. Uncertainty with respect to some of the assumptions underlying the financial evaluation would be unlikely to change the favourable recommendation.

Workings

Contribution/sales ratio = $100 \times (5,242 - 3,145)/5,242 = 40\%$

Irrecoverable debts ratio for Class 2 receivables = $100 \times (12,600/252,000) = 5\%$

Increase in Class 1 receivables from new business = $250,000 \times 30/365 = £20,548$

Increase in Class 2 receivables from new business = $250,000 \times 60/365 = £41,096$

(W1) Contribution from increased business = $500,000 \times 40\% = £200,000$

(W2) Decrease in irrecoverable debts for transferring current Class 2 receivables = 12,600 × 0.5 = £6,300

(Note that other assumptions regarding irrecoverable debts are possible here)

(W3) Current sales of Class 1 receivables = 200,000 × (365/30) = £2,433,333

Rise in discount cost for current Class 1 receivables = 2,433,333 × 0.005 = £12,167

(W4) Current sales of Class 2 receivables = 252,000 × (365/60) = £1,533,000

Discount cost of transferring Class 2 receivables = 1,533,000 × 0.5 × 0.015 = £11,498

(W5) Discount cost for new Class 1 receivables = 250,000 × 0.015 = £3,750

(W6) Irrecoverable debts arising from new Class 2 receivables = 41,096 × 0.05 = £2,055

(Note that other assumptions regarding irrecoverable debts are possible here)

(W7) Increase in financing cost from new receivables = (20,548 + 41,096) × 0.08 = £4,932

(Note that it could be assumed that transferring receivables pay after 30 days rather than 60 days)

Examiner's Note: because of the various assumptions that could be made regarding irrecoverable debts and payment period, other approaches to a solution are also acceptable.

Tutorial note:

An alternative approach to this part of the question is to lay out all of the calculations regarding the current and revised position before getting into the detail. This can often allow a clearer thought process and a more time efficient approach to the question.

You know from your studies that the main costs and benefits to consider when deciding on a level of discount to offer are:

- *The cost of the discount itself (for this you will need to know the value of sales for each class)*

- *The benefit of reduced financing costs (for this you will need to know the level of receivables under the current strategy and the proposed strategy*

- *The benefit of reduced irrecoverable debts (for this you will need to know the new level of receivables by class together with the typical ratio of bad debts)*

In this particular case, we will also need to consider the contribution that will be earned on the additional sales resulting from the revised policy.

Now we know the information we will require, we can set about obtaining it

	Current level of discount		Revised level of discount	
		£'000		£'000
Class 1 sales	£200k × 365/30	2,433.3	£2,433.3k + £250k (being half of the new sales) + £766.5k (being half of the previous class 2 receivables)	3,449.8
Class 1 receivables	Per question	200	£3,449.8k × 30/365	283.5
Cost of financing class 1 receivables	£200k × 8%	16	£283.5k × 8%	22.7
Class 2 sales	£252k × 365/60	1,533	£1,533k / 2 + £250k	1,016.5
Class 2 receivables	Per question	252	£1,016.5k × 60/365	167
Cost of financing class 2 receivables	£252k × 8%	20.2	£167k × 8%	13.4

The other pieces of information required were shown at the beginning of this answer; the contribution/sales ratio of 40% and the irrecoverable debts ratio for class 2 receivables of 5%.

Having gathered all of the information, it is quite a simple job to detail out the costs and benefits.

Costs

Additional discount

Remember this will need to reflect both the additional 0.5% payable on existing class 1 sales as well as the full 1.5% payable on all new sales and the previous class 2 sales that will now pay promptly.

£2,433.3k × 0.5%	= £12.2k
(£3,449.8k - £2,433.3k) × 1.5%	= £15.2k
Total cost	**= £27.4k**

Benefits

Additional contribution

£500k × 40%	= £200k

Reduction in irrecoverable debts

(£167k - £252k) × 5%	= £4.2k

Reduction in financing costs

(£16k + £20.1k) − (£22.7k + £13.4k)	= £0.1k
Total benefit	**= £204.3k**
Net benefit	**= £176.9k**

Note: this answer differs from that presented above due to the approach taken. It would however, score in full.

(b)   Current cash operating cycle:

Inventory days = (603/3,145) × 365 = 70 days
Payables days = (574.5/3,145) × 365 = 67 days
Average receivables days = (744.5/5,242) × 365 = 52 days
Cash operating cycle = 70 + 52 − 67 = 55 days

After implementation of the proposal, it is reasonable to assume that inventory days and payables days remain unchanged. Total receivables have increased by £61,644 to £806,144 and sales revenue has increased to £5.742m. Average receivables days are now 365 × (806/5,742) = 51 days. The cash operating cycle has marginally decreased by one day to 54 days (70 + 51 – 67).

(c)   Current sterling value of overseas receivables = £182,500

Current dollar value of overseas receivables = 182,500 × 1.7348 = $316,601

A forward market hedge (i.e. a forward exchange contract) will lock the sterling value of the receivables at the three-month forward rate.

Hedged sterling value of overseas receivables in three months = 316,601/1.7367 = £182,300

This is less than the current sterling value of the overseas receivables because sterling is expected to appreciate against the dollar.

(d)   The key elements of a receivables management system may be described as establishing a credit policy, credit assessment, credit control and collection of amounts due.

Establishing credit policy

The credit policy provides the overall framework within which the receivables management system of PNP plc operates and will cover key issues such as the procedures to be followed when granting credit, the usual credit period offered, the maximum credit period that may be granted, any discounts for early settlement, whether interest is charged on overdue balances, and actions to be taken with accounts that have not been settled in the agreed credit period. These terms of trade will depend to a considerable extent on the terms offered by competitors to PNP plc, but they will also depend on the ability of the company to finance its receivables (financing costs), the need to meet the costs of administering the system (administrative costs) and the risk of irrecoverable debts.

Credit assessment

In order to minimise the risk of irrecoverable debts, PNP plc should assess potential customers as to their creditworthiness before offering them credit. The depth of the credit check depends on the amount of business being considered, the size of the client and the potential for repeat business. The credit assessment requires information about the customer, whether from a third party as in a trade reference, a bank reference or a credit report, or from PNP itself through, for example, its analysis of a client's published accounts. The benefits of granting credit must always be greater than the cost involved. There is no point, therefore, in PNP plc paying for a detailed credit report from a credit reference agency for a small credit sale.

Credit control

Once PNP plc has granted credit to a customer, it should monitor the account at regular intervals to make sure that the agreed terms are being followed. An aged receivables analysis is useful in this respect since it helps the company focus on those clients who are the most cause for concern. Customers should be reminded of their debts by prompt despatch of invoices and regular statements of account. Customers in arrears should not be allowed to take further goods on credit.

Collection of amounts due

The customers of PNP plc should ideally settle their accounts within the agreed credit period. There is no indication as to what this might be, but the company clearly feels that a segmental analysis of its clients is possible given their payment histories, their potential for irrecoverable debts and their geographical origin. Clear guidelines are needed over the action to take when customers are late in settling their accounts or become irrecoverable debts, for example indicating at what stage legal action should be initiated.

Overseas receivables

PNP plc will need to consider the ways in which overseas receivables differ from domestic receivables. For example, overseas receivables tend to take longer to pay and so will need financing for longer. Overseas receivables will also give rise to exchange rate risk, which will probably need to be managed. The credit risk associated with overseas customers can be reduced in several ways, however, for example by using advances against collection, requiring payment through bills of exchange, arranging documentary letters of credit or using export factoring.

INVESTMENT APPRAISAL

20 ARMCLIFF CO

Key answer tips

In part (a) the first part of the data in the question relates to current operations – try to think why the examiner has given you this. The requirement is to determine whether the proposed project is attractive to *Armcliff* – not the parent company. Presumably what will make a project attractive to a division's management is one that will improve their current performance measure. Thus it is useful to know what the current level of ARR being achieved. This can then be compared with the project ARR.

Remember that the ARR is a financial accounting based measure – returns are in terms of accounting profits, and investments valued at balance sheet amounts – you must try to put all 'relevant cost' principles to the back of your mind. Whilst there are various possible definitions of the ARR (a point that can be raised in (b)) here you are given precise directions, so make sure you follow them. Both average profits and average investment need to be ascertained.

Don't forget to conclude by comparison with both current and required rates of return.

In part (b) the question requires you to show both theoretical and practical knowledge about investment appraisal methods.

In part (c), even though this is a examining a general area of credit management, try wherever you can to relate your points to the business in the question – it is stated that Armcliff intends to extend its credit to improve sales. Again make sure that you explain points enough to get the marks available, whilst still offering sufficient variety. Note that it is not enough simply to say that the advantage of ARR is its simplicity. With spreadsheets, this is hardly going to be a consideration. Show instead that you appreciate that mangers are influenced by the methods used for their performance measurement – both internally and externally. The highlighted words are key phrases that markers are looking for.

(a)   **Current return on capital employed**

= Operating profit/capital employed

= $20m/($75m + $25m) = $20m/$100m = 20%.

Analysis of the project

Project capital requirements are $14 million fixed capital plus $0.5 million inventory. The annual depreciation charge (straight line) is:

($14m − expected residual value of $2m)/4 = $3 million per annum.

Profit profile ($m)

Year	1	2	3	4
Sales revenue	(5.00 × 2m) = 10.00	(4.50 × 1.8m) = 8.10	(4.00 × 1.6m) = 6.40	(3.50 × 1.6m) = 5.60
Operating costs	(2.00)	(1.80)	(1.60)	(1.60)
Fixed costs	(1.50)	(1.35)	(1.20)	(1.20)
Depreciation	(3.00)	(3.00)	(3.00)	(3.00)
Profit	3.50	1.95	0.60	(0.20)

Total profit over four years = $5.85 million.

Capital employed (start-of-year):

Non-current assets	14.00	11.00	8.00	5.00
Inventories	0.50	0.50	0.50	0.50
Profit	14.50	11.50	8.50	5.50

Average capital employed = (14.50 + 11.50 + 8.50 + 5.50)/4 = $10 million.

$$\text{Average rate of return} = \frac{\text{Average profit}}{\text{Average capital employed}} = \frac{\$5.85m / 4}{\$10.0m} = \frac{\$1.46m}{\$10.0m}$$

= 14.6%

Note: If receivables were to be included in the definition of capital employed, this would reduce the calculated rate of return, while the inclusion of payables would have an offsetting effect. However, using the ARR criterion as defined, the proposal has an expected return above the minimum stipulated by Shevin Inc. It is unlikely that the managers of Armcliff will propose projects which offer a rate of return below the present 20% even where the expected return exceeds the minimum of 10%. To undertake projects with returns in this range will depress the overall divisional return and cast managerial performance in a weaker light.

However, it is unlikely that the senior managers of the Armcliff subsidiary would want to undertake the project.

(b) (i) The **ARR can be expressed in a variety of ways**, and is therefore susceptible to manipulation. Although the question specifies average profit to average capital employed, many other variants are possible, such as average profit to initial capital, which would raise the computed rate of return.

It is also **susceptible to variation in accounting policy** by the same firm over time, or as between different firms at a point in time. For example, different methods of depreciation produce different profit figures and hence different rates of return.

Perhaps, most fundamentally, it is **based on accounting profits expressed net of deduction for depreciation provisions, rather than cash flows**. This effectively results in double-counting for the initial outlay i.e. the capital cost is allowed for twice over, both in the numerator of the ARR calculation and also in the denominator. This is likely to depress the measured profitability of a project and result in rejection of some worthwhile investment.

Finally, because it simply averages the profits, it **makes no allowance for the timing of the returns** from the project.

(ii) The continuing use of the ARR method can by explained largely by its utilisation of balance sheet (statement of financial position) and income statement magnitudes familiar to managers, namely 'profit' and 'capital employed'. In addition, the impact of the project on a company's financial statements can also be specified. Return on capital employed is still the commonest way in which business unit performance is measured and evaluated, and is certainly the most visible to shareholders. It is thus not surprising that some managers may be happiest in expressing project attractiveness in the same terms in which their performance will be reported to shareholders, and according to which they will be evaluated and rewarded.

(c) Armcliff intends to achieve a sales increase by extending its receivables collection period. This policy carries several dangers. It implies that credit will be extended to customers for whom credit is an important determinant of supplier selection, hinting at financial instability on their part. Consequently, the risk of later than expected, or even no payment, is likely to increase. Although losses due to default are limited to the incremental costs of making these sales rather than the invoiced value, Armcliff should recognise that there is an opportunity cost involved in tying up capital for lengthy periods. In addition, companies which are slow payers often attempt to claim discounts to which they are not entitled. Armcliff may then face the difficult choice between acquiescence to such demands versus rejection, in which case, it may lose repeat sales.

The creditworthiness of customers can be assessed in several ways as follows.

Analysis of accounting statements

In the case of companies that have to publish their annual accounts, key financial ratios can be examined to assess their financial stability. However, these almost certainly will be provided in arrears and may not give a true indication of the companies' current situation. Some customers may be prepared to supply more up-to-date accounts directly to the seller, although these are unlikely to have been audited.

Analysis of credit reports

It may be possible to obtain detailed assessment of the creditworthiness of customers from other sources, such as their bankers, specialist credit assessment agencies such as Dun & Bradstreet, and from trade sources such as other companies who supply them. These assessments are likely to be more up-to-date than company accounts, but will inevitably be more subjective.

Previous experience

If the firm has supplied the customer in the past, its previous payment record will be available.

Cash-only trial period

If accounting and other data is sparse, and there is no previous trading record with the customer, the seller may offer a trial period over which cash is required, but if the payment record is acceptable (e.g. if the customer's cheques always clear quickly), further transactions may be conducted on credit.

Background information

General background information on the industry in which the customer operates will generate insights into the financial health of companies in that sector, and by implication, that of the customer. Many agencies supply such information, although it should only be used as a back-up to other assessments.

21 HENDIL (PART I)

Key answer tips

This is a relatively straightforward net present value calculation. However, marks are easily lost if you didn't pick up on the fact that the project will be expected to continue beyond the original four years. Always read the scenario carefully and consider the impact of each piece of information on the calculation you're attempting.

(a) **Calculation of NPV**

Year	1	2	3	4
	$000	$000	$000	$000
Sales revenue	2,800	4,050	5,100	3,825
Variable costs	2,184	2,727	3,040	2,370
Contribution	616	1,323	2,060	1,455
Fixed costs	515	530	546	563
Taxable cash flow	101	793	1,514	892
Taxation	30	238	454	268
	71	555	1,060	624
Capital allowance tax	60	45	34	25
After-tax cash flow	131	600	1,094	649
11% discount factors	0.901	0.812	0.731	0.659
Present values	118	487	800	428

	$000
Sum of present values of future	1,833
Less Initial investment	1,000
Net present value	833

Because the investment continues in operation after the four-year period, working capital is not recovered in the above calculation. It is possible to make an assumption concerning incremental investment in working capital to accommodate inflation, but no specific inflation rate for working capital is provided. An assumption of 3–4% inflation in working capital would be reasonable given the expected inflation in variable and fixed costs.

The NPV calculation uses the company's four-year evaluation period, but the terminal value of the investment at the end of this period could sensibly be considered. The remaining capital allowance tax benefit of $76,000 (800 x 30% – 60 – 45 – 34 – 25) could be taken at the end of year 5 (other assumptions are possible) giving a present value of 76 x 0.593 = $45,100. The after-tax cash flow (before capital allowance tax benefits) of $624,000 in year 4 could be assumed to continue for another four years (other assumptions are possible) giving a present value of 624 x 3.102 x 0.659 = $1,276,000. These considerations would increase the net present value of the investment by 158% to $2,154,100.

Workings

Year	1	2	3	4
Sales revenues				
Sales volume (units)	70,000	90,000	100,000	75,000
Selling price ($/unit)	40	45	51	51
Sales revenue ($000/yr)	2,800	4,050	5,100	3,825
Variable costs				
Variable costs ($/unit)	30	28	27	27
Inflated cost ($/unit)	31.2	30.3	30.4	31.6
Sales volume (units)	70,000	90,000	100,000	75,000
Variable costs ($000/yr)	2,184	2,727	3,040	2,370
Fixed costs ($ per year)	500,000	500,000	500,000	500,000
Inflated cost ($/yr)	515,000	530,000	546,000	563,000

Capital allowance tax benefits

Year	Capital allowance	Tax benefit	
1	$800,000 x 0.25 = $200,000	$200,000 x 0.3	= $60,000
2	$600,000 x 0.25 = $150,000	$150,000 x 0.3	= $45,000
3	$450,000 x 0.25 = $112,500	$112,500 x 0.3	= $33,750
4	$337,500 x 0.25 = $84,375	$84,375 x 0.3	= $25,312

(b) **Calculation of payback**

Year	Cash flows ($000)	Cumulative cash flow ($000)
0	(1,000)	(1,000)
1	131	(869)
2	600	(269)
3	1,094	825
4	649	1,474

Payback period = 2 + (269/1,094) = 2 years 3 months

Calculation of discounted payback

Year	Discounted cash flow ($000)	Cumulative cash flow ($000)
0	(1,000)	(1,000)
1	118	(882)
2	487	(395)
3	800	405
4	428	833

Discounted payback period = 2 + (395/800) = 2 years 6 months

(c)   The proposed investment has a positive net present value of $833,000 over four years of operation compared with an initial investment of $1 million and so is financially acceptable. The company has payback and discounted payback targets, but these are not a guide to project acceptability because of the shortcomings of payback as an investment appraisal method. The proposed investment fails to meet the payback target of two years, but meets the discounted payback target of three years. While discounted payback counters the criticism that payback ignores the time value of money, it still ignores cash flows outside of the discounted payback period and so cannot be recommended to evaluate other than conventional investments.

The net present value calculation could be improved in several ways. One obvious improvement would be the consideration of project cash flows beyond the four-year evaluation period used by Hendil Inc. The company expects the new product range to sell for several years after the end of the evaluation period and if these sales are at a profit, the net present value would be higher than calculated. Another improvement would be more detailed information about the new product range, for which only average selling price and average variable cost data are provided. The basis for these averages is not stated and it is not known whether the products in the new range are substitutes or alternatives, or whether a constant product mix is being assumed. The basis for the changing annual sales volumes should also be explained.

The assumption of constant annual inflation for variable and fixed costs is questionable. The information provided implies that inflation may have been taken into account in forecasting selling prices, but the selling price growth rates are sequentially 12.5%, 13.3% and zero, and so some factor other than inflation has also been used in the selling price forecast. The net present value evaluation could be improved if the basis for the forecast was known and could be verified as reasonable.

22   INVESTMENT APPRAISAL

Key answer tips

Parts (a) & (b)(i) should present an opportunity to gain some easy marks by outlining some basic areas of the syllabus. The calculations in part (b) (ii) were relatively straightforward. Make sure you don't neglect the final part of the requirement – to identify other factors that the company should take into account when deciding of the optimal cycle.   The highlighted words are key phrases that markers are looking for.

(a)   Accounting rate of return (ARR) is a measure of the return on an investment where the annual profit before interest and tax is expressed as a percentage of the capital

$$ARR = \frac{\frac{1}{n}(\Sigma \text{ Net Revenue Cashflow} - \text{Total Depn})}{\text{Initial Investment}} \times 100\%$$

PBIT

ARR and Payback
Limitation

sum invested.] There are a number of alternative formulae which can be used to calculate ARR, which differ in the way in which they define capital cost. The more common alternative measures available are:

- average annual profit to initial capital invested, and

formular.

- average annual profit to average capital invested.

The method selected will affect the resulting ARR figure, and for this reason it is important to recognise that the measure might be subject to manipulation by managers seeking approval for their investment proposals. The value for average annual profit is calculated after allowances for depreciation, as shown in the example below:

ARR
— Advantage
• Use whole life
of project
• Use readily available
information.

Suppose ARR is defined as: $\dfrac{\text{Average profit (after depreciation)}}{\text{Initial capital invested}} \times 100\%$

A project costing $5 million, and yielding average profits of $1,250,000 per year after depreciation charges of $500,000 per year, would give an ARR of:

1,250,000/5,000,000 × 100% = 25%

If the depreciation charged were to be increased to $750,000 per year, for example as a result of technological changes reducing the expected life of an asset, the ARR becomes:

— Disadvantages
1,000,000/5,000,000 × 100% = 20%

Advantages

★ Ignores time value
of money

★ Doesn't measure
Disadvantages
gains to shareholder

★ A comparative
figure. Is required

★ Doesn't take amount
of the value of the
return.

The attraction of using ARR as a method of investment appraisal lies in its simplicity and the ease with which it can be used to specify the impact of a project on a company's income statement. The measure is easily understood and can be directly linked to the use of ROCE as a performance measure. Nonetheless, ARR has been criticised for a number of major drawbacks, perhaps the most important of which is that it uses accounting profits after depreciation rather than cash flows in order to measure return. This means that the capital cost is over-stated in the calculation, via both the numerator and the denominator. In the numerator, the capital cost is taken into account via the depreciation charges used to derive accounting profit, but capital cost is also the denominator. The practical effect of this is to reduce the ARR and thus make projects appear less profitable. This might in turn result in some worthwhile projects being rejected. Note, however, that this problem does not arise where ARR is calculated as average annual profit as a percentage of average capital invested.

The most important criticism of ARR is that it takes no account of the time value of money. A second limitation of ARR, already suggested, is that its value is dependent on accounting policies and this can make comparison of ARR figures across different investments very difficult. A further difficulty with the use of ARR is that it does not give a clear decision rule. The ARR on any particular investment needs to be compared with the current returns being earned within a business, and so unlike NPV for example, it is impossible to say 'all investments with an ARR of x or below will always be rejected.

The payback method of investment appraisal is used widely in industry – generally in addition to other measures. Like ARR, it is easily calculated and understood. The payback approach simply measures the time required for cumulative cash flows from an investment to sum to the original capital invested.]

Example

Original investment $100,000

Cash flow profile: Years 1–3 $25,000 p.a.

Years 4 – 5 $50,000 p.a.

Year 6 $5,000

The cumulative cash flows are therefore:

End Year 1	$25,000
End Year 2	$50,000
End Year 3	$75,000
End Year 4	$125,000
End Year 5	$175,000
End Year 6	$180,000

[handwritten note top right: Payback Period : How long it takes to payback the initial investment.]

[handwritten note: Advantages :
– Liquidity.
– Concentrates on earlier, less risky cash flow.

Disadvantages
** Ignores cashflow after the payback*
** Doesn't give the gain to shareholder*
** A comparative figure is required*
** Estimate CF / df / Life of project]*

The original sum invested is returned via cash flows some time during the course of Year 4. If cash flows are assumed to be even throughout the year, the cumulative cash flow of $100,000 will have been earned halfway through year 4. The payback period for the investment is thus 3 years and 6 months.

The payback approach to investment appraisal is useful for companies which are seeking to claw back cash from investments as quickly as possible. At the same time, the concept is intuitively appealing as many businessmen will be concerned about how long they may have to wait to get their money back, because they believe that rapid repayment reduces risks. This means that the payback approach is commonly used for initial screening of investment alternatives. *[handwritten: Liquidity]*

The disadvantages of the payback approach are as follows:

(i) Payback ignores the overall profitability of a project by ignoring cash flows after payback is reached. In the example above, the cash flows between 3–4 years and the end of the project total $80,000. To ignore such substantial cash flows would be naïve. As a consequence, the payback method is biased in favour of fast-return investments. This can result in rejecting investments that generate cash flows more slowly in the early years, but which are overall more profitable.

(ii) As with ARR, the payback method ignores the time value of money.

(iii) The payback method, in the same way as ARR, offers no objective measure of what is the desirable return, as measured by the length of the payback period.

(b) (i) Discounted cash flow analysis is a technique whereby the value of future cash flows is discounted back to a present value, so that the monetary values of all cash flows are equivalent, regardless of their timing. The logic for discounting is that the value of money declines over time because of individual time preferences and the impact of inflation in eroding spending power. People value money received sooner rather than later because as soon as cash is received they can increase consumption, or re-invest the capital. *[handwritten: · Risk · Inflation · Int. rate]*

[handwritten left margin: NPV and IRR Difference.]

NPV uses discounting to calculate the present value of all cash flows associated with a project. The present value of cash outflows is then compared with the present value of cash inflows, to obtain a net present value (NPV). If the present value (PV) of cash outflows exceeds the PV of cash inflows, then the NPV will be negative. If the present value (PV) of cash inflows exceeds the PV of cash outflows, then the NPV will be positive. The size of the NPV is dependent on the cash flow pattern and the rate of discount that is applied. The general rule is that a company will discount the forecast cash flows at a rate equal to its cost of capital. The reason for this is that if a company has an overall cost of capital of, for example, 12%, it is essential that the rate of return exceeds 12% or the funding costs will not be covered. Hence if the cash flows are discounted at the cost of capital and the project yields a positive NPV, this implies that the return exceeds the cost of capital. When using NPV for investment appraisal then a simple rule is applied: invest if NPV is positive, and do not invest if it is negative.

IRR uses discounting in a slightly different way to determine the profitability of an investment. The Internal Rate of Return is defined as the discount rate at which the net present value equals zero. For example, an investment may yield a forecast NPV of $15,000 when the cash flows are discounted at 10%. If the rate of discount is increased, the net present value will fall, and the IRR represents the effective, break-even discount rate for the investment. Suppose, for example, that the IRR is 15%, this figure can then be used to establish a decision rule for investments. An IRR of 15% means that if the cost of capital exceeds 15% then the investment would generate a negative NPV. If the company is currently having to pay 12% on its investment funds, then it knows that it can afford to see its cost of capital rise by 3% before the investment will become financially non-viable. As long as the IRR exceeds the cost of capital, then the company should invest and so, as a general rule, the higher the IRR the better.

NPV and IRR measures may sometimes contradict one another when used in relation to mutually exclusive investments. An example of the ambiguity which can occur when choosing between mutually exclusive decisions is when one of the investments has a higher NPV than the other, and so is preferable on that basis, but at the same time it has a lower IRR. When IRR and NPV give conflicting results, the preferred alternative is the project with the highest NPV.

In conclusion, although both NPV and IRR use discounted cash flows as a method of arriving at an investment decision, the results that they generate need to be interpreted with care, and they do not always yield the same investment decisions. NPV is the preferred criterion for selecting between two or more mutually exclusive investments, where the two approaches give differing recommendations.

(ii)   If the laptops are replaced every year:

NPV of one year replacement cycle

Year	Cash flow	DF at 14%	PV
	$		$
0	(2,400)	1.000	(2,400.0)
1	1,200	0.877	1,052.4
			(1,347.6)

Equivalent annual cost = PV of cost of one replacement cycle/Cumulative discount factor

= $1,347.6/0.877 = $1,536.6

NPV of two-year replacement cycle

Year	Cash flow	DF at 14%	PV
	$		$
0	(2,400)	1.000	(2,400.0)
1	(75)	0.877	(65.8)
2	800	0.769	615.2
			(1,850.6)

EAC = $1,850.6/1.647 = $1,123.6

NPV of three-year replacement cycle

Year	Cash flow	DF at 14%	PV
	$		$
0	(2,400)	1.000	(2,400.0)
1	(75)	0.877	(65.8)
2	(150)	0.769	(115.4)
3	300	0.675	202.5
			(2,378.7)

EAC = $2,378.7/2.322 = $1,024.4

Conclusion

The optimal cycle for replacement is every three years, because this has the lowest equivalent annual cost. Other factors which need to be taken into account are the non-financial aspects of the alternative cycle choices. For example, computer technology and the associated software is changing very rapidly and this could mean that failure to replace annually would leave the salesmen unable to utilise the most up to date systems for recording, monitoring and implementing their sales. This could have an impact on the company's competitive position. The company needs to consider also the compatibility of the software used by the laptops with that used by the in-house computers and mainframe. If system upgrades are made within the main business that render the two computers incompatible, then rapid replacement of the laptops to regain compatibility is essential.

23 PV CO

Key answer tips

Part (a) offers some relatively easy marks and should therefore be attempted first. When dealing with inflation in investment appraisal questions, it is very often easier to work with the money method, inflating the cash flows before discounting using the money cost of capital. This is particularly true here since the money cost of capital has been provided and different cash flows are expected to inflate at different rates. The highlighted words are key phrases that markers are looking for.

(a) The key stages in the capital investment decision-making process are identifying investment opportunities, screening investment proposals, analysing and evaluating investment proposals, approving investment proposals, and implementing, monitoring and reviewing investments.

Identifying investment opportunities

Investment opportunities or proposals could arise from analysis of strategic choices, analysis of the business environment, research and development, or legal requirements. The key requirement is that investment proposals should support the achievement of organisational objectives.

Screening investment proposals

In the real world, capital markets are imperfect, so it is usual for companies to be restricted in the amount of finance available for capital investment. Companies therefore need to choose between competing investment proposals and select those with the best strategic fit and the most appropriate use of economic resources.

Analysing and evaluating investment proposals

Candidate investment proposals need to be analysed in depth and evaluated to determine which offer the most attractive opportunities to achieve organisational objectives, for example to increase shareholder wealth. This is the stage where investment appraisal plays a key role, indicating for example which investment proposals have the highest net present value.

Approving investment proposals

The most suitable investment proposals are passed to the relevant level of authority for consideration and approval. Very large proposals may require approval by the board of directors, while smaller proposals may be approved at divisional level, and so on. Once approval has been given, implementation can begin.

Implementing, monitoring and reviewing investments

The time required to implement the investment proposal or project will depend on its size and complexity, and is likely to be several months. Following implementation, the investment project must be monitored to ensure that the expected results are being achieved and the performance is as expected. The whole of the investment decision-making process should also be reviewed in order to facilitate organisational learning and to improve future investment decisions.

(b) (i) Calculation of NPV

Year	0	1	2	3	4
	$	$	$	$	$
Investment	(2,000,000)				
Income		1,236,000	1,485,400	2,622,000	1,012,950
Operating costs		676,000	789.371	1,271,227	620,076
Net cash flow	(2,000,000)	560,000	696,028	1,350,773	392,874
Discount at 10%	1.000	0.909	0.826	0.751	0.683
Present values	(2,000,000)	509,040	574,919	1,014,430	268,333

Net present value $366,722

Workings

Calculation of income

Year	0	1	2	3	4
Inflated selling price ($/unit)		20.60	21.22	21.85	22.51
Demand (units/year)		60,000	70,000	120,000	45,000
Income ($/year)		1,236,000	1,485,400	2,622,000	1,012,950

Calculation of operating costs

Year	0	1	2	3	4
Inflated variable cost ($/unit)		8.32	8.65	9.00	9.36
Demand (units/year)		60,000	70,000	120,000	45,000
Variable costs ($/year)		499,200	605,500	1,080,000	421,000
Inflated fixed costs ($/year)		176,800	183,872	191,227	198,876
Operating costs ($/year		676,000	789,371	1,271,227	620,076

Alternative calculation of operating costs

Year	0	1	2	3	4
Variable cost ($/unit)		8.00	8.00	8.00	8.00
Demand (units/year)		60,000	70,000	120,000	45,000
Variable costs ($/year)		480,000	560,000	960,000	360,000
Fixed costs ($/year)		170,000	170,000	170,000	170,000
Operating costs ($ / year		650,000	730,000	1,130,000	530,000
		676,000	789,568	1,271,096	620,025

(ii)   Calculation of internal rate of return

Year	0	1	2	3	4
	$	$	$	$	$
Net cash flow	(2,000,000)	560,000	696,028	1,350,773	392,874
Discount at 20%	1.000	0.833	0.694	0.579	0.482
Present values	(2,000,000)	466,480	483,043	782,098	189,365

Net present value ($79,014)

Internal rate of return = 10 + ((20 − 10) x 366,722)/(366,722 + 79,014) = 10 + 8·2 = 18·2%

(iii)   Calculation of return on capital employed

Total cash inflow = 560,000 + 696,028 + 1,350,773 + 392,874 = $2,999,675

Total depreciation and initial investment are same, as there is no scrap value

Total accounting profit = 2,999,675 − 2,000,000 = $999,675

Average annual accounting profit = 999,675/4 = $249,919

Average investment = 2,000,000/2 = $1,000,000

Return on capital employed = 100 x 249,919/1,000,000 = 25%

(iv)   Calculation of discounted payback

Year	0	1	2	3	4
	$	$	$	$	$
Present values	(2,000,000)	509,040	574,919	1,014,430	268,333
Cumulative PV	(2,000,000)	(1,490,960)	(916,041)	98,389	366,722

Discounted payback period = 2 + (916,041/1,014,430) = 2 + 0·9 = 2·9 years

(c)   The investment proposal has a positive net present value (NPV) of $366,722 and is therefore financially acceptable. The results of the other investment appraisal methods do not alter this financial acceptability, as the NPV decision rule will always offer the correct investment advice.

The internal rate of return (IRR) method also recommends accepting the investment proposal, since the IRR of 18·2% is greater than the 10% return required by PV Co. If the advice offered by the IRR method differed from that offered by the NPV method, the advice offered by the NPV method would be preferred.

The calculated return on capital employed of 25% is less than the target return of 30%, but as indicated earlier, the investment proposal is financially acceptable as it has a positive NPV. The reason why PV Co has a target return on capital employed of 30% should be investigated. This may be an out-of-date hurdle rate that has not been updated for changed economic circumstances.

The discounted payback period of 2·9 years is a significant proportion of the forecast life of the investment proposal of four years, a time period which the information provided suggests is limited by technological change. The sensitivity of the investment proposal to changes in demand and life-cycle period should be analysed, since an earlier onset of technological obsolescence may have a significant impact on its financial acceptability.

ACCA marking scheme			
		Marks	
(a)	Identification of decision-making stages	1 - 2	
	Explanation of decision-making stages	4 - 6	
	Role of investment appraisal	1 - 2	
		Maximum	7
(b)	Inflated income	2	
	Inflated operating costs	2	
	Discount factors	1	
	Net present value	1	
	Internal rate of return	3	
	Return on capital employed	2	
	Discounted payback	2	
			13
(c)	Discussion of investment appraisal findings	4	
	Advice on acceptability of project	1	
			5
Total			25

Examiner's comments

Part (a) of this question asked for an identification and explanation of the stages of the capital investment decision-making process, and the role of investment appraisal in this process. Better answers identified and discussed identification: screening; analysis and evaluation; approving; implementation and monitoring. Poorer answers looked at different aspects of the analysis and evaluation stage, or went off track by discussing the relative merits of the investment appraisal methods required in part (b) of this question.

Part (b) required the evaluation of an investment project using net present value (NPV), internal rate of return (IRR), return on capital employed (ROCE) and discounted payback, incorporating inflation.

Some candidates introduced capital allowances and taxation into their answers, but this was not required by the question. There is no point in doing unnecessary work in the examination, as marks will be lost elsewhere due to time pressure.

Most candidates calculated correctly the NPV of the investment project, although some answers did not handle inflation correctly, or omitted the fixed costs, or calculated and used (unnecessarily) a real discount rate.

Many candidates calculated correctly the IRR of the investment project, although there was a tendency for some candidates to use a second discount rate that led to unnecessary inaccuracy. For example, if the NPV is positive at a 10% discount rate, there is little point in calculating the NPV at a 5% discount rate and extrapolating to find the IRR. A more accurate result would arise by using the NPV calculated at a higher rate than 10%, for example 20%, as in the suggested answers to the exam.

Most candidates were not able to calculate correctly the ROCE of the investment project. The most common error was using average annual net cash flow, rather than average annual accounting profit. Although a depreciation method was not given in the question, total depreciation could be subtracted from total net cash flow in order to give total accounting profit. Some candidates were unable to calculate the average investment.

Many candidates were able to calculate discounted payback, although some used an unnecessary amount of rounding, e.g. giving 3 years rather than 2.9 years.

Part (c) asked for a discussion of the findings from part (b) and a recommendation as to the acceptability of the investment project. Many candidates failed, either explicitly or implicitly, to recognise the superiority of the NPV method.

Most candidates stated correctly that the investment project was acceptable because it had a positive NPV and because the IRR was greater than the nominal discount rate used by the company. Some answers suggested that the project was acceptable because the ROCE was higher than the target ROCE, but this investment appraisal method cannot be relied upon to give correct investment advice. Better answers gave reasons why ROCE cannot be relied upon. Some candidates said the investment project was acceptable because the discounted payback period was less than the life of the project. This is almost the same as saying that the project has a positive NPV (it might not be true for a non-conventional project), but few candidates recognised this. Without a target payback period, payback cannot say whether a project is acceptable or not.

24   BFD CO

Key answer tips

Part (a) asks for a NPV calculation. The first consideration is how to set out your answer as there are cash flows for the first four years and annuities for t=5-∞ and t=1–10. These can be incorporated as separate calculations or you could have had columns for flows 0,1,2,3,4,5-10 and 11–∞. Either way you needed to be particularly careful when calculating the tax flows given the lack of a delay.

In part (b) it is vital that issues are applied to the scenario, making reference to specific figures where possible. The highlighted words are key phrases that markers are looking for.

(a)   **Net present value evaluation of proposed investment**

	20X5/6 $000	20X6/7 $000	20X7/8 $000	20X8/9 $000
Sales revenue	1,800	2,160	2,340	2,520
Variable costs	850	1,020	1,105	1,190
Contribution	950	1,140	1,235	1,330
Fixed costs	450	450	450	450
Net cash flow	500	690	785	880
Taxation @ 25%	125	173	196	220
After-tax cash flow	375	517	589	660
12% discount factors	0.893	0.797	0.712	0.636
Present values	335	412	419	419

	$
Sum of present values	1,585,000
PV of writing down allowances	423,750
PV of cash flows after Year 4 =	3,498,000
	5,506,750
Less initial investment	3,200,000
Net present value	2,306,750

Workings

	20X5/6	20X6/7	20X7/8	20X8/9
Sales volume (units)	100,000	120,000	130,000	140,000
Selling price ($/unit)	18.00	18.00	18.00	18.00
Sales revenue ($)	1,800,000	2,160,000	2,340,000	2,520,000
Variable costs ($/unit)	8.50	8.50	8.50	8.50
Variable costs ($)	850,000	1,020,000	1,105,000	1,190,000

Fixed costs = 4.50 × 100,000 = $450,000 per year

Annual writing down allowance = 3,000,000/10 = $300,000

Annual writing down allowance tax benefits = 25% × 300,000 = $75,000

Ten-year annuity factor at 12% = 5.650

Present value of writing down allowance tax benefits = 75,000 × 5.650 = $423,750

Year 4 value of year 5 after-tax cash flows in perpetuity = 660,000/0.12 = $5,500,000

Present value of these cash flows = 5,500,000 × 0.636 = $3,498,000

(b)   From a net present value perspective the proposed investment is acceptable, since the net present value (NPV) is large and positive. However, a large part of the present value of benefits (63%) derives from the assumption that cash flows will continue indefinitely after Year 4. This is very unlikely to occur in practice and excluding these cash flows will result in a negative net present value of approximately $1.2m. In fact the proposed investment will not show a positive NPV until more than seven years have passed.

Before rejecting the proposal, steps should be taken to address some of the limitations of the analysis performed.

Inflation

Forecasts of future inflation of sales prices and variable costs should be prepared, so that a nominal NPV evaluation can be undertaken. This evaluation should employ a nominal after-tax cost of capital: it is not stated whether the 12% after-tax cost of capital is in nominal or real terms. Sales price is assumed to be constant in real terms, but in practice substitute products are likely to arise, leading to downward pressure on sales price and sales volumes.

Constant fixed costs

The assumption of constant fixed costs should be verified as being acceptable. Sales volumes are forecast to increase by 40% and this increase may result in an increase in incremental fixed costs.

Constant working capital

The assumption of constant working capital should be investigated. Net working capital is likely to increase in line with sales and so additional investment in working capital may be needed in future years. Inflation will increase required incremental working capital investment.

Taxation and capital allowances

The assumptions made regarding taxation should be investigated. The tax rate has been assumed to be constant, when there may be different rates of profit tax applied to companies of different size. The method available for claiming capital allowances should be confirmed, since it is usual to find a different method being applied to buildings compared to that applied to machinery, whereas here they are the same.

Machine replacement

The purchase of replacement machinery has been ignored, which seems unreasonable. Future reinvestment in new machinery will be needed and this will reduce the net present value of the proposed investment. Technological change is also possible, bringing perhaps new manufacturing methods and improved or substitute products, and these may affect the size of future cash flows.

Changes in technology

Technological change is also possible, bringing perhaps new manufacturing methods and improved or substitute products, and these may affect the size of future cash flows.

Financing

The method of financing the proposed investment should be considered. It may be that leasing will be cheaper than borrowing to buy, increasing the net present value and making the project more attractive.

25 CHARM INC

Key answer tips

In part (a) the NPV calculation is reasonably straightforward provided you read the information carefully. In this scenario we are told two facts to do with tax that are not what we usually see in questions, firstly capital allowances are given on a straightline basis and secondly, there is no lag in the payment of tax. The calculation of fixed costs is also an easy number to get wrong if you didn't carefully read that the financial information presented on 'Fingo' was for the first year of production.

In part (c) ensure you compare with NPV with other appraisal methods rather than just stating the benefits of NPV. The highlighted words are key phrases that markers are looking for.

(a) Calculation of NPV of 'Fingo' investment project

Year	1	2	3	4
	$000	$000	$000	$000
Sales revenue	3,750	1,680	1,380	1,320
Direct materials	(810)	(378)	(324)	(324)
Variable production	(900)	(420)	(360)	(360)
Advertising	(650)	(100)		
Fixed costs	(600)	(600)	(600)	(600)
Taxable cash flow	790	182	96	36
Taxation	(237)	(55)	(29)	(11)
	553	127	67	25
CA tax benefits	60	60	60	60
Net cash flow	613	187	127	85
Discount at 10%	0.909	0.826	0.751	0.683
Present values	557.2	154.5	95.4	58.1

	$000
Present value of future benefits	865.2
Initial investment	800.0
Net present value	65.2

Workings

Fixed costs in year 1 = $150,000 × 4 = $600,000 and since these represent a one-off increase in fixed production overheads, these are the fixed costs in subsequent years as well.

Annual capital allowance (CA) tax benefits = (800,000/4) × 0.3 = $60,000 per year

Comment

The net present value of $65,200 is positive and the investment can therefore be recommended on financial grounds. However, it should be noted that the positive net present value depends heavily on sales in the first year. In fact, sensitivity analysis shows that a decrease of 5% in first year sales will result in a zero net present value. (Note: you are not expected to conduct a sensitivity analysis)

(b)   Calculation of IRR of 'Fingo' investment project

Year	1	2	3	4
	$000	$000	$000	$000
Net cash flow	613	187	127	85
Discount at 20%	0.833	0.694	0.579	0.482
Present values	510.6	129.8	73.5	41.0

	$000
Present value of future benefits	754.9
Initial investment	800.0
Net present value	(45.1)

Internal rate of return = 10 + [(920 -10) x 65.2) / (65.2 + 45.1)] = 16%

Since the internal rate of return is greater than the discount rate used to appraise new investments, the proposed investment is financially acceptable.

(c)   There are many reasons that could be discussed in support of the view that net present value (NPV) is superior to other investment appraisal methods.

NPV considers cash flows

This is the reason why NPV is preferred to return on capital employed (ROCE), since ROCE compares average annual accounting profit with initial or average capital invested. Financial management always prefers cash flows to accounting profit, since profit is seen as being open to manipulation. Furthermore, only cash flows are capable of adding to the wealth of shareholders in the form of increased dividends. Both internal rate of return (IRR) and Payback also consider cash flows.

NPV considers the whole of an investment project

In this respect NPV is superior to Payback, which measures the time it takes for an investment project to repay the initial capital invested. Payback therefore considers cash flows within the payback period and ignores cash flows outside of the payback period. If Payback is used as an investment appraisal method, projects yielding high returns outside of the payback period will be wrongly rejected. In practice, however, it is unlikely that Payback will be used alone as an investment appraisal method.

NPV considers the time value of money

NPV and IRR are both discounted cash flow (DCF) models which consider the time value of money, whereas ROCE and Payback do not. Although Discounted Payback can be used to appraise investment projects, this method still suffers from the criticism that it ignores cash flows outside of the payback period. Considering the time value of money is essential, since otherwise cash flows occurring at different times cannot be distinguished from each other in terms of value from the perspective of the present time.

NPV is an absolute measure of return

NPV is seen as being superior to investment appraisal methods that offer a relative measure of return, such as IRR and ROCE, and which therefore fail to reflect the amount of the initial investment or the absolute increase in corporate value. Defenders of IRR and ROCE respond that these methods offer a measure of return that is understandable by managers and which can be intuitively compared with economic variables such as interest rates and inflation rates.

NPV links directly to the objective of maximising shareholders' wealth

The NPV of an investment project represents the change in total market value that will occur if the investment project is accepted. The increase in wealth of each shareholder can therefore be measured by the increase in the value of their shareholding as a percentage of the overall issued share capital of the company. Other investment appraisal methods do not have this direct link with the primary financial management objective of the company.

NPV always offers the correct investment advice

With respect to mutually exclusive projects, NPV always indicates which project should be selected in order to achieve the maximum increase on corporate value. This is not true of IRR, which offers incorrect advice at discount rates which are less than the internal rate of return of the incremental cash flows. This problem can be overcome by using the incremental yield approach.

NPV can accommodate changes in the discount rate

While NPV can easily accommodate changes in the discount rate, IRR simply ignores them, since the calculated internal rate of return is independent of the cost of capital in all time periods.

NPV has a sensible re-investment assumption

NPV assumes that intermediate cash flows are re-invested at the company's cost of capital, which is a reasonable assumption as the company's cost of capital represents the average opportunity cost of the company's providers of finance, i.e. it represents a rate of return which exists in the real world. By contrast, IRR assumes that intermediate cash flows are reinvested at the internal rate of return, which is not an investment rate available in practice,

NPV can accommodate non-conventional cash flows

Non-conventional cash flows exist when negative cash flows arise during the life of the project. For each change in sign there is potentially one additional internal rate of return. With non-conventional cash flows, therefore, IRR can suffer from the technical problem of giving multiple internal rates of return.

26   SC CO

Key answer tips

As soon as the scenario refers to inflation, you should look for factors to help you decide whether to use the 'money' method or the 'real' method to perform your discounting. Here, having two different rates of inflation, the presence of capital allowances in the calculation, and the fact that you're been given the money cost of capital were all clear indicators that the 'money' method would be the most efficient.   The highlighted words are key phrases that markers are looking for.

(a)   Calculation of net present value

Year	0	1	2	3	4
	$	$	$	$	$
Sales revenue		728,000	1,146,390	1,687,500	842,400
Variable costs		(441,000)	(701,190)	(1,041,750)	(524,880)
Contribution		287,000	445,200	645,750	317,520
Capital allowances		(250,000)	(250,000)	(250,000)	(250,000)
Taxable profit		37,000	195,200	395,750	67,520
Taxation		(11,100)	(58,560)	(118,725)	(20,256)
After-tax profit		25,900	136,640	277,025	47,264
Capital allowances		250,000	250,000	250,000	250,000
After-tax cash flow		275,900	386,640	527,025	297,264

Year	0	1	2	3	4
	$	$	$	$	$
After-tax CF b/f		275,900	386,640	527,025	297,264
Initial investment	(1,000,000)				
Working capital	(50,960)	(29,287)	(37,878)	59,157	58,968
Net cash flows	(1,050,960)	246,613	348,762	586,182	356,232
Discount at 12%	1·000	0·893	0·797	0·712	0·636
Present values	(1,050,960)	220,225	277,963	417,362	226,564

NPV = $91,154

Tutorial note:

This layout of deducting the capital allowances before the calculation of taxation followed by adding the capital allowances back, is just an alternative way of calculating the tax effect of the capital allowances. It would be perfectly acceptable to calculate the tax charge on contribution and then bring in the tax effect of the capital allowances as an additional line in the calculation. This second approach is the more common method seen in the majority of NPV questions in this exam kit.

Workings

Sales revenue

Year	1	2	3	4
Selling price ($/unit)	20·80	21·63	22·50	23·40
Sales volume (units)	35,000	53,000	75,000	36,000
Sales revenue ($)	728,000	1,146,390	1,687,500	842,400

Variable costs

Year	1	2	3	4
Variable cost ($/unit)	12·60	13·23	13·89	14·58
Sales volume (units)	35,000	53,000	75,000	36,000
Variable costs ($)	441,000	701,190	1,041,750	524,880

Total investment in working capital

Year 0 investment = 728,000 × 0·07 = $50,960

Year 1 investment = 1,146,390 × 0·07 = $80,247

Year 2 investment = 1,687,500 × 0·07 = $118,125

Year 3 investment = 842,400 × 0·07 = $58,968

Incremental investment in working capital

Year 0 investment = 728,000 × 0·07 = $50,960

Year 1 investment = 80,247 – 50,960 = $29,287

Year 2 investment = 118,125 – 80,247 = $37,878

Year 3 recovery = 58,968 – 118,125 = $59,157

Year 4 recovery = $58,968

Tutorial note:

Make sure you present your workings clearly. In this working capital calculation, it is clear that the starting point is the sales revenue from the previous working. If you had made an error in the calculation of sales revenue, you could still get full marks for working capital if it is clear to your marker that you have applied the correct method.

(b) Calculation of internal rate of return

Year	0	1	2	3	4
	$	$	$	$	$
Net cash flows	(1,050,960)	246,613	348,762	586,182	356,232
Discount at 20%	1·000	0·833	0·694	0·579	0·482
Present values	(1,050,960)	205,429	242,041	339,399	171,704

NPV at 20% = ($92,387)
NPV at 12% = $91,154

IRR = 12 + [(20 – 12) × 91,154/(91,154 + 92,387)] = 12 + 4 = 16%

(c) **Acceptability of the proposed investment in Product P**

The NPV is positive and so the proposed investment can be recommended on financial grounds. The IRR is greater than the discount rate used by SC Co for investment appraisal purposes and so the proposed investment is financially acceptable. The cash flows of the proposed investment are conventional and so there is only one internal rate of return. Furthermore, only one proposed investment is being considered and so there is no conflict between the advice offered by the IRR and NPV investment appraisal methods.

Limitations of the investment evaluations

Both the NPV and IRR evaluations are heavily dependent on the production and sales volumes that have been forecast and so SC Co should investigate the key assumptions underlying these forecast volumes. It is difficult to forecast the length and features of a product's life cycle so there is likely to be a degree of uncertainty associated with the forecast sales volumes. Scenario analysis may be of assistance here in providing information on other possible outcomes to the proposed investment.

The inflation rates for selling price per unit and variable cost per unit have been assumed to be constant in future periods. In reality, interaction between a range of economic and other forces influencing selling price per unit and variable cost per unit will lead to unanticipated changes in both of these project variables. The assumption of constant inflation rates limits the accuracy of the investment evaluations and could be an important consideration if the investment were only marginally acceptable.

Since no increase in fixed costs is expected because SC Co has spare capacity in both space and labour terms, fixed costs are not relevant to the evaluation and have been omitted. No information has been offered on whether the spare capacity exists in future periods as well as in the current period. Since production of Product P is expected to more than double over three years, future capacity needs should be assessed before a decision is made to proceed, in order to determine whether any future incremental fixed costs may arise.

(d) The primary financial management objective of private sector companies is often stated to be the maximisation of the wealth of its shareholders. While other corporate objectives are also important, for example due to the existence of other corporate stakeholders than shareholders, financial management theory emphasises the importance of the objective of shareholder wealth maximisation.

Shareholder wealth increases through receiving dividends and through share prices increasing over time. Changes in share prices can therefore be used to assess whether a financial management decision is of benefit to shareholders. In fact, the objective of maximising the wealth of shareholders is usually substituted by the objective of maximising the share price of a company.

The net present value (NPV) investment appraisal method advises that an investment should be accepted if it has a positive NPV. If a company accepts an investment with a positive NPV, the market value of the company, theoretically at least, increases by the amount of the NPV. A company with a market value of $10 million investing in a project with an NPV of $1 million will have a market value of $11 million once the investment is made. Shareholder wealth is therefore increased if positive NPV projects are accepted and, again theoretically, shareholder wealth will be maximised if a company invests in all projects with a positive NPV. This is sometimes referred to as the optimum investment schedule for a company.

The NPV investment appraisal method also contributes towards the objective of maximising the wealth of shareholders by using the cost of capital of a company as a discount rate when calculating the present values of future cash flows. A positive NPV represents an investment return that is greater than that required by a company's providers of finance, offering the possibility of increased dividends being paid to shareholders from future cash flows.

	ACCA marking scheme	Marks
(a)	Inflated sales revenue	2
	Inflated variable costs	2
	Capital allowances	2
	Taxation	1
	Working capital	3
	Discount factors	1
	Net present value calculation	1
		12
(b)	Net present value calculation	1
	Internal rate of return calculation	2
		3
(c)	Net present value comment	1
	Internal rate of return comment	1–2
	Discussion of limitations	3–4
	Maximum	5
(d)	Discussion of shareholder wealth maximisation	1–2
	Link to share price maximisation	1–2
	Discussion of NPV investment appraisal method	2–3
	Maximum	5
	Total	25

Examiner's comments

Part (a) of this question asked candidates to calculate the net present value (NPV) of a proposed investment. Many answers gained high marks and dealt correctly with most of the issues involved with the calculation, for example inflation of sales and variable costs.

The treatment of working capital investment was a source of regular errors, however. The question specified clearly the timing and the level of working capital investment in relation to sales. Candidates had to calculate the initial and incremental amounts of investment. In the last two years of the investment, declining levels of working capital meant that working capital would be recovered. Many answers put the investment in working capital at the end, rather than at the start, of each year, and included total investment rather than incremental investment. Another common error was to treat investment in working capital as tax-allowable (and even to call it a fixed cost), when in fact it has no tax effect at all.

Although the question specified straight-line capital allowances, some candidates used 25% reducing balance allowances instead. Some candidates also mistakenly included capital allowances as a cash flow item, rather than (or as well as) capital allowance tax benefits.

In part (b) candidates were asked to calculate the internal rate of return cost (IRR) of the proposed investment. Many answers gained high marks and produced a result consistent with findings in part (a). Markers noted that some candidates made illogical choices of discount rates in their calculations, choosing to work for example with two negative NPV values, rather with one positive and one negative NPV value. While linear interpolation and linear extrapolation use the same mathematical approach, candidates should note that interpolation is more likely to be accurate than extrapolation in calculating IRR.

It was pleasing to note that very few candidates confused IRR with accounting rate of return (return on capital employed).

Part (c) asked for advice on the acceptability of the investment project and discussion of the limitations of the NPV and IRR evaluations performed.

Most answers correctly advised on acceptability in terms that were consistent with their earlier evaluations.

Many answers struggled to discuss the limitations of the evaluations in any depth, tending to offer one or two general criticisms of the NPV and IRR appraisal methods. Better answers discussed the limiting assumptions underlying the values selected for the project variables and the reasons why, for example, fixed costs had been omitted. Since only on investment project was being considered, the advice offered by the two investment appraisal methods was, of course, the same.

In part (d) candidates were asked to discuss how the NPV investment appraisal method contributes towards the objective of maximising shareholder wealth. Few answers were able to explain why accepting positive NPV projects will increase shareholder wealth. The important thing to remember here is that the discount rate used in investment appraisal represents the return required by the company in order to provide satisfactory returns to its sources of finance. Projects with a positive NPV offer a higher return than this and so increase the company's value. Shareholders therefore gain immediately in wealth terms through capital appreciation.

A general discussion of the advantages of the NPV investment appraisal method over other investment appraisal methods was not asked for or required.

27   **DUO CO**   *Walk in the footsteps of a top tutor*

Key answer tips

Given the generic nature of part (c) and the significant number of marks available (32% of the total), it would be sensible to tackle this part of the requirement first. You can then follow on with the calculations in part (a) and (b).

The key learning point from this question is the importance of being efficient when reading the scenario to cut down on the amount of time wasted trying to locate information. By forming an expectation of what you'll be given and considering the significance of information that you read, you can easily complete the question in the time allocated. The highlighted words are key phrases that markers are looking for.

(a)   Net present value evaluation of investment

Tutor's top tips:

An NPV calculation in part (a) followed by an IRR calculation in part (b) is a fairly common exam question. Clearly it is more logical to tackle part (a) first. One important aspect to note from the requirement is to work to the nearest $1,000. This can help to save a significant amount of time when performing the calculations and noting your workings.

Knowing that you must calculate an NPV, you should carefully read the scenario, looking for details on:

- *Relevant cash flows*

- *Tax payments (1 year time lag or not)*

- *Capital expenditure and scrap values*

- *Timescales and length of the project*

- *Working capital*

- *Inflation*

- *Discount rate*

Whenever you read any details, make a note in the margin on what that section provides you information on. This will help prevent you having to re-read the scenario several times to find the bit of information you require.

From reading this scenario, you should have noted that:

- *Relevant cash flows will be the incremental contribution and fixed costs only*

- *Incremental contribution will be calculated based on the excess of demand over current production capacity (one million kilograms)*

- *The maximum output of the new machine is 600,000 kg meaning that even with the new machine, Duo will be unable to produce more that 1.6 million kg.*

- *The tax rate is 30% and there is a one year time lag*

> - The cost of the machine is $800,000 and it will be scrapped in four years time for $30,000
>
> - The length of the project is four years
>
> - You are not given any information on working capital requirements or inflation. These can therefore be ignored.
>
> - You have not been told what discount rate to use. Instead you've been given information on the cost of equity and the cost of debt, together with the capital structure (ratio of equity to debt) in the company
>
> Having gleaned this information, you should start by setting up your proforma NPV calculation based on 5 periods (4 years of the project + 1 year time lag for tax). Next you should enter in any easy numbers that require little or no calculation. This would include the asset purchase and scrap and the incremental fixed costs.
>
> Now you can move on to calculating some of the more complex numbers. All of these calculations should be performed using workings that should be clearly cross referenced to your main NPV calculation. You should end up with workings for contribution (make sure you clearly show how many extra units will be sold), the tax effect of capital allowances and the weighted average cost of capital / discount factors. As you complete each working, transfer the numbers into your main calculation and add anything extra that you can now complete (for example, once you have calculated contribution, you can enter the tax charge at 30%). When all of your workings are complete, discount the cash flow in each year and work out the net present value. Don't forget that the requirement is to calculate and advise. There will always be marks available for reaching a conclusion and stating whether the project should be accepted or not. Note the examiner's comment (below) about explaining your decision.

After-tax weighted average cost of capital = $(11 \times 0.8) + (8.6 \times (1 - 0.3) \times 0.2) = 10\%$

Year	1	2	3	4	5
	$000	$000	$000	$000	$000
Contribution	440	550	660	660	
Fixed costs	(240)	(260)	(280)	(300)	
Taxable cash flow	200	290	380	360	
Taxation		(60)	(87)	(114)	(108)
CA tax benefits		60	45	34	92
Scrap value				30	
After-tax cash flows	200	290	338	310	(16)
Discount at 10%	0.909	0.826	0.751	0.683	0.621
Present values	182	240	254	212	(10)

	$000
Present value of benefits	878
Initial investment	800
Net present value	78

The net present value is positive and so the investment is financially acceptable. However, demand becomes greater than production capacity in the fourth year of operation and so further investment in new machinery may be needed after three years. The new machine will itself need replacing after four years if production capacity is to be maintained at an increased level. It may be necessary to include these expansion and replacement considerations for a more complete appraisal of the proposed investment.

A more complete appraisal of the investment could address issues such as the assumption of constant selling price and variable cost per kilogram and the absence of any consideration of inflation, the linear increase in fixed costs of production over time and the linear increase in demand over time. If these issues are not addressed, the appraisal of investing in the new machine is likely to possess a significant degree of uncertainty.

Workings

Annual contribution

Year	1	2	3	4
Excess demand (kg/yr)	400,000	500,000	600,000	700,000
New machine output (kg/yr)	400,000	500,000	600,000	600,000
Contribution ($/kg)	1.1	1.1	1.1	1.1
Contribution ($/yr)	440,000	550,000	660,000	660,000

Capital allowance (CA) tax benefits

Year	Capital allowance ($)		Tax benefit ($)	
1	200,000	(800,000 × 0.25)	60,000	(0.3 × 200,000)
2	150,000	(600,000 × 0.25)	45,000	(0.3 × 150,000)
3	112,500	(450,000 × 0.25)	33,750	(0.3 × 112,500)
	462,500			
	30,000	(scrap value)		
	492,500			
4	307,500	(by difference)	92,250	(0.3 × 307,500)
	800,000			

(b) Internal rate of return evaluation of investment

Tutor's top tips:

Finally, for part (b) you will need to quickly calculate a second NPV, using the cash flows you've worked out for part (a). Try to choose you second discount rate sensibly. For example, if your answer to part (a) was a positive NPV, you should select a second discount rate that is higher than the one you originally used.

If you are running out of time, a useful shortcut is to add up the undiscounted cash flows and treat that as an NPV at 0%. Your resulting answer will not be as accurate and you may not pick up all of the marks available but it will allow you to access the marks for advising on the acceptability of the proposal.

Year	1	2	3	4	5
	$000	$000	$000	$000	$000
After-tax cash flows	200	290	338	310	(16)
Discount at 20%	0.833	0.694	0.579	0.482	0.402
Present values	167	201	196	149	(6)

	$000
Present value of benefits	707
Initial investment	800
Net present value	(93)

Internal rate of return = 10 + [((20 – 10) × 78)/(78 + 93)] = 10 + 4.6 = 14.6%

The investment is financially acceptable since the internal rate of return is greater than the cost of capital used for investment appraisal purposes. However, the appraisal suffers from the limitations discussed in connection with net present value appraisal in part (a).

Tutor's top tips:

A careful read of the requirement shows that part (c) is essentially three requirements rolled into one:

(i)   Explain the difference between risk and uncertainty

(ii) Describe how sensitivity analysis can be used to incorporate risk into investment appraisal

(iii) Describe how probability analysis can be used to incorporate risk into investment appraisal

Given the verbs being used (both 'explain' and 'describe' imply much more that merely 'stating') we can expect between 2 & 3 marks for each section, with 2 or 3 relevant comments picking up those marks.

Don't forget, there are often marks available for defining terms. So in part (i), a definition should be given of both risk and uncertainty before the differences between the two are explained. Similarly, in parts (ii) & (iii), you could define both sensitivity analysis and probability analysis before describing how they incorporate risk into the appraisal process.

Finally, you could touch on the common problems with the two techniques although be careful not to spend too much time on this as it wasn't specifically mentioned in the requirement. Now you can move on to the numerical aspects of the question.

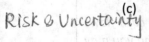

Risk & Uncertainty

(c) Risk refers to the situation where probabilities can be assigned to a range of expected outcomes arising from an investment project and the likelihood of each outcome occurring can therefore be quantified. Uncertainty refers to the situation where probabilities cannot be assigned to expected outcomes. Investment project risk therefore increases with increasing variability of returns, while uncertainty increases with increasing project life. The two terms are often used interchangeably in financial management, but the distinction between them is a useful one.

[handwritten margin notes:]

* look at how much % an estimate would have to change by to get NPV=0.

* can only change one variable at a time, whereas in reality several projects variables may change simultaneously

← Not a way to valuate project risk, but it may identify key/critical area (variables)

$E \cdot V$ (Expected Value) = $\sum$ Probabilities × x
↓
each outcome

Sensitivity analysis assesses how the net present value of an investment project is affected by changes in project variables. Considering each project variable in turn, the change in the variable required to make the net present value zero is determined, or alternatively the change in net present value arising from a fixed change in the given project variable. In this way the key or critical project variables are determined. However, sensitivity analysis does not assess the probability of changes in project variables and so is often dismissed as a way of incorporating risk into the investment appraisal process.

Probability analysis refers to the assessment of the separate probabilities of a number of specified outcomes of an investment project. For example, a range of expected market conditions could be formulated and the probability of each market condition arising in each of several future years could be assessed. The net present values arising from combinations of future economic conditions could then be assessed and linked to the joint probabilities of those combinations. The expected net present value (ENPV) could be calculated, together with the probability of the worst-case scenario and the probability of a negative net present value. In this way, the downside risk of the investment could be determined and incorporated into the investment decision.

ACCA marking scheme		
		Marks
(a)	After-tax weighted average cost of capital	2
	Annual contribution	2
	Fixed costs	1
	Taxation	1
	Capital allowance tax benefits	3
	Scrap value	1
	Discount factors	1
	Net present value	1
	Comment	1–2
		13
(b)	Net present value calculation	1
	Internal rate of return calculation	2
	Comment	1–2
		4
(c)	Risk and uncertainty	2–3
	Discussion of sensitivity analysis	2–3
	Discussion of probability analysis	2–3
		8
	Total	25

Examiner's comments

Part (a) of this question asked candidates to calculate the net present value (NPV) of buying a new machine and to advise on its acceptability. Many candidates gained very high marks here.

Common errors (where there were errors) included failing to calculate correctly the weighted average cost of capital of the investing company (for example using the before-tax rather than the after-tax cost of debt in the calculation): failing to use incremental demand as the production volume of the new machine; failing to recognise the cap on production in Year 4 compared to demand; failing to lag tax liability by one year; including scrap value or tax benefits of capital allowances with taxable income; incorrect calculation of balancing allowance; treating initial investment as a Year 1 rather than a Year 0 cash flow; and using annuity factors rather than discount factors in calculating NPV.

A number of candidates lost straightforward marks by failing to comment on the calculated NPV, or by simply saying 'accept' without referring to the NPV decision rule. The reason for accepting an investment project must be clearly explained.

In part (b) candidates were asked to calculate the internal rate of return (IRR) of buying the new machine and to advise on its acceptability. Many candidates gained full marks here. Some candidates lost marks through the incorrect application of linear interpolation in calculating IRR (for example adding instead of subtracting values, or multiplying instead of adding). Some candidates said that both a positive NPV and a negative NPV were needed in order to calculate IRR, when in fact two positive values can be used (resulting in extrapolation, but the extrapolation calculation is identical in structure to an interpolation calculation). A number of candidates lost a straightforward mark by not commenting on their calculated IRR.

Some candidates confused IRR with accounting rate of return (ARR) and as a result gained no credit.

Candidates were asked in part (c) to explain the difference between risk and uncertainty in the context of investment appraisal, and to describe how sensitivity analysis and probability analysis could be used to incorporate risk and uncertainty into investment appraisal. Answers here tended to be weaker than answers to parts (a) and (b).

Many candidates were not able to explain the difference between risk and uncertainty in investment appraisal, offering answers that were founded on interpretations of the words 'risk' and 'uncertainty', or which discussed the various kinds of risk to be found in financial management. The key point is to recognise that risk can be quantified (probabilities can be assigned and outcomes can be predicted) while uncertainty cannot be quantified. Answers that offered numerical examples of sensitivity analysis or probability analysis gained credit, although candidates should note that sensitivity analysis is not a method of measuring or predicting risk.

28 ARG CO

Key answer tips

Given the different inflation rates that apply to different cash flows, this question is best attempted using the 'money' method where all cash flows are inflated and are discounted using the money cost of capital. Well laid out workings will help to ensure the marker can see where your numbers have come from.

(a) **NPV calculation for Alpha and Beta**

Year	1	2	3	4
	$	$	$	$
Sales revenue	3,585,000	6,769,675	6,339,000	1,958,775
Material cost	(1,395,000)	(2,634,225)	(2,466,750)	(761,925)
Fixed costs	(1,000,000)	(1,050,000)	(1,102,500)	(1,157,625)
Advertising	(500,000)	(200,000)	(200,000)	
Taxable profit	690,000	2,885,450	2,569,750	39,225
Taxation	(172,500)	(721,362)	(642,438)	(9,806)
WDA tax benefit	250,000			
Fixed asset sale				1,200,000
WC recovery				1,000,000
Net cash flow	767,500	2,164,088	1,927,312	2,229,419
Discount factors	0.885	0.783	0.693	0.613
Present values	679,237	1,694,481	1,335,626	1,366,634

	$
Sum of present values	5,075,978
Initial investment	3,000,000
Net present value	2,075,978

The positive NPV indicates that the investment is financially acceptable.

Workings

Alpha sales revenue

Year	1	2	3	4
Selling price ($/unit)	31.00	31.93	32.89	33.88
Sales (units/yr)	60,000	110,000	100,000	30,000
Sales revenue ($/yr)	1,860,000	3,512,300	3,289,000	1,016,400

Beta sales revenue

Year	1	2	3	4
Selling price ($/unit)	23.00	23.69	24.40	25.13
Sales (units/yr)	75,000	137,500	125,000	37,500
Sales revenue ($/yr)	1,725,000	3,257,375	3,050,000	942,375

Total sales revenue

Year	1	2	3	4
Sales revenue ($/yr)	3,585,000	6,769,675	6,339,000	1,958,775

Alpha direct material cost

Year	1	2	3	4
Material cost ($/unit)	12.00	12.36	12.73	13.11
Sales (units/yr)	60,000	110,000	100,000	30,000
Material cost ($/yr)	720,000	1,359,600	1,273,000	393,300

Beta direct material cost

Year	1	2	3	4
Material cost ($/unit)	9.00	9.27	9.55	9.83
Sales (units/yr)	75,000	137,500	125,000	37,500
Material cost ($/yr)	675,000	1,274,625	1,193,750	368,625

Total direct material cost

Year	1	2	3	4
Material cost ($/yr)	1,395,000	2,634,225	2,466,750	761,925

(b) The evaluation assumes that several key variables will remain constant, such as the discount rate, inflation rates and the taxation rate. In practice this is unlikely. The taxation rate is a matter of government policy and so may change due to political or economic necessity.

Specific inflation rates are difficult to predict for more than a short distance into the future and in practice are found to be constantly changing. The range of inflation rates used in the evaluation is questionable, since over time one would expect the rates to converge. Given the uncertainty of future inflation rates, using a single average inflation rate might well be preferable to using specific inflation rates.

The discount rate is likely to change as the company's capital structure changes. For example, if the company was to fund this investment entirely via debt or equity finance, the gearing of the company will change.

Looking at the incremental fixed production costs, it seems odd that nominal fixed production costs continue to increase even when sales are falling. It also seems odd that incremental fixed production costs remain constant in real terms when production volumes are changing. It is possible that some of these fixed production costs are stepped, in which case they should decrease.

The forecasts of sales volume seem to be too precise, predicting as they do the growth, maturity and decline phases of the product life-cycle. In practice it is likely that improvements or redesign could extend the life of the two products beyond five years. The assumption of constant product mix seems unrealistic, as the products are substitutes and it is possible that one will be relatively more successful. The sales price has been raised in line with inflation, but a lower sales price could be used in the decline stage to encourage sales.

Net working capital is to remain constant in real terms. In practice, the level of working capital will depend on the working capital policies of the company, the value of goods, the credit offered to customers, the credit taken from suppliers and so on. It is unlikely that the constant real value will be maintained.

The net present value is heavily dependent on the terminal value derived from the sale of non-current assets after five years. It is unlikely that this value will be achieved in practice. It is also possible that the machinery can be used to produce other products, rather than be used solely to produce Alpha and Beta.

29   UMUNAT INC

Key answer tips

The calculations in this question are quite straightforward although you would not be able to pass the question if you focussed on the numbers alone. Don't neglect the discussional element of parts of the requirement that might at first appear to be numerical. Virtually half of the marks available in parts (b), (c), & (d) will be for the commentary that accompanies your calculations. The highlighted words are key phrases that markers are looking for.

(a)   The investment appraisal process is concerned with assessing the value of future cash flows compared to the cost of investment.

Risk & Uncertainty in Investment Appraisal

Since future cash flows cannot be predicted with certainty, managers must consider how much confidence can be placed in the results of the investment appraisal process. They must therefore be concerned with the risk and uncertainty of a project. Uncertainty refers to the situation where probabilities cannot be assigned to future cash flows. Uncertainty cannot therefore be quantified and increases with project life: it is usually true to say that the more distant is a cash flow, the more uncertain is its value. Risk refers to the situation where probabilities can be assigned to future cash flows, for example as a result of managerial experience and judgement or scenario analysis. Where such probabilities can be assigned, it is possible to quantify the risk associated with project variables and hence of the project as a whole.

If risk and uncertainty were not considered in the investment appraisal process, managers might make the mistake of placing too much confidence in the results of investment appraisal, or they may fail to monitor investment projects in order to ensure that expected results are in fact being achieved. Assessment of project risk can also indicate projects that might be rejected as being too risky compared with existing business operations, or projects that might be worthy of reconsideration if ways of reducing project risk could be found in order to make project outcomes more acceptable.

(b)   Contribution per unit   = 3.00 – 1.65 = $1.35 per unit

Total annual contribution   = 20,000 × 1.35 = $27,000 per year

Annual cash flow after fixed costs   = 27,000 – 10,000 = $17,000 per year

Payback period   = 50,000/17,000 = 2.9 years

(assuming that cash flows occur evenly throughout the year)

The payback period calculated is greater than the maximum payback period used by Umunat Inc of two years and on this basis should be rejected. Use of payback period as an investment appraisal method cannot be recommended, however, because payback period does not consider all the cash flows arising from an investment project, as it ignores cash flows outside of the payback period. Furthermore, payback period ignores the time value of money.

The fact that the payback period is 2.9 years should not therefore be a reason for rejecting the project. The project should be assessed using a discounted cash flow method such as net present value or internal rate of return, since the project as a whole may generate an acceptable return on investment.

(c)   **Calculation of project net present value**

Annual cash flow = ((20,000 × (3 – 1.65)) – 10,000 = $17,000 per year

Net present value = (17,000 × 3.605) – 50,000 = 61,285 – 50,000 = $11,285

Alternatively:	PV ($)
Sales revenue: 20,000 × 3.00 × 3.605 =	216,300
Variable costs: 20,000 × 1.65 × 3.605 =	(118,965)
Contribution	97,335
Initial investment	(50,000)
Fixed costs: 10,000 × 3.605 =	(36,050)
Net present value:	11,285

Sensitivity of NPV to sales volume

Sales volume giving zero NPV = ((50,000/3.605) + 10,000)/1.35 = 17,681 units.

This is a decrease of 2,319 units or 11.6%.

Alternatively, sales volume decrease = 100 × 11,285/97,335= 11.6%.

Tutorial note:

The second method presented above is probably the method most people will feel comfortable with. This uses the generic formula of:

$$\frac{NPV}{PV\ of\ affected\ cashflow} \times 100\%$$

Sensitivity of NPV to sales price

Sales price for zero NPV = (((50,000/3.605) + 10,000)/20,000) + 1.65 = $2.843.

This is a decrease of 15.7¢ or 5.2%.

Alternatively, sales price decrease = 100 × 11,285/216,300 = 5.2%.

Sensitivity of NPV to variable cost

Variable cost must increase by 15.7¢ or 9.5% to make the NPV zero.

Alternatively, variable cost increase = $100 \times 11,285/118,965 = 9.5\%$.

Sensitivity analysis evaluates the effect on project net present value of changes in project variables. The objective is to determine the key or critical project variables, which are those where the smallest change produces the biggest change in project NPV. It is limited in that only one project variable at a time may be changed, whereas in reality several project variables may change simultaneously. For example, an increase in inflation could result in increases in sales price, variable costs and fixed costs. Sensitivity analysis is not a way of evaluating project risk, since although it may identify the key or critical variables, it cannot assess the likelihood of a change in these variables. In other words, sensitivity analysis does not assign probabilities to project variables. Where sensitivity analysis is useful is in drawing the attention of management to project variables that need careful monitoring if a particular investment project is to meet expectations. Sensitivity analysis can also highlight the need to check the assumptions underlying the key or critical variables.

(d)   **Expected value of sales volume**

$(17,500 \times 0.3) + (20,000 \times 0.6) + (22,500 \times 0.1) = 19,500$ units

Expected NPV = $(((19,500 \times 1.35) - 10,000) \times 3.605) - 50,000 = \$8,852$

Since the expected net present value is positive, the project appears to be acceptable. From earlier analysis we know that the NPV is positive at 20,000 per year, and the NPV will therefore also be positive at 22,500 units per year. The NPV of the worst case is:

$(((17,500 \times 1.35) - 10,000) \times 3.605) - 50,000 = (\$882)$

The NPV of the best case is:

$(((22,500 \times 1.35) - 10,000) \times 3.605) - 50,000 = \$23,452$

There is thus a 30% chance that the project will produce a negative NPV, a fact not revealed by considering the expected net present value alone.

The expected net present value is not a value that is likely to occur in practice: it is perhaps more useful to know that there is a 30% chance that the project will produce a negative NPV (or a 70% chance of a positive NPV), since this may represent an unacceptable level of risk as far as the managers of Umunat Inc are concerned. It can therefore be argued that assigning probabilities to expected economic states or sales volumes has produced useful information that can help the managers of Umunat Inc to make better investment decisions. The difficulty with this approach is that probability estimates of project variables or future economic states are likely to carry a high degree of uncertainty and subjectivity.

30   TOWER RAILWAYS INC

Key answer tips

Although the answer to part (a) makes the question appear uncomplicated, you are presented with a lot of data which needs filtering and processing quickly to arrive at the correct answer. This is particularly true of the calculation of annual revenue. Parts (b) and (c) are both demanding and require a good understanding of sensitivity analysis to answer in the allocated time. The highlighted words are key phrases that markers are looking for.

(a)   **Data**

After-tax discount rate (%)	10
Tax rate (%)	30
Contribution/sales ratio (%)	35
Therefore variable costs as a proportion of sales (%)	65
Occupancy rate (%)	60
Number of carriages	8
Passenger numbers per carriage	55
Number of trips	10
Average price per passenger ($)	12
Annual days travelling/operating	340

Tutorial note:

The above table is a good way of pulling together all of the key numbers that you'll end up needing for the calculation. It is particularly useful in a question such as this where there is a lot of data presented within the paragraphs of the scenario.

Assumption: It is assumed that tax cash flows occur in the same year as the benefit, allowance or cost to which they relate.

Capital allowances calculations Year to:	31 Dec X7	31 Dec X8	31 Dec X9	31 Dec Y1	31 Dec Y2
	$000	$000	$000	$000	$000
Tax written down value	5,000	3,750	2,812	2,109	1,582
Writing down allowance (25%)	1,250	938	703	527	
Sale proceeds					500
					———
Balancing allowance					1,082
Tax saving (30%)	375	281	211	158	325
Capital projections					

	Year 0 $000	Year 1 $000	Year 2 $000	Year 3 $000	Year 4 $000
Initial investment and proceeds	(5,000)				500
Capital allowances	375	281	211	158	325
Net capital flows	(4,625)	281	211	158	825
Discount factor at 10%	1.000	0.909	0.826	0.751	0.683
PV of capital flows	(4,625)	256	174	119	563
NPV of capital flows	(3,513)				

Projected annual revenue = 60% occupancy × 8 carriages × 55 passengers (carriage capacity) × $12 ticket price × 10 trips per day × 340 days = $10,771,200.

Annual operating cash surplus, years 1 – 5

	$000
Expected revenue	10,771
Variable costs (65%)	(7,001)
Contribution	3,770
Additional fixed costs (cash spend)	(1,000)
Incremental net cash income, pre-tax	2,770
Tax (30%)	(831)
Post-tax annual cash flows	1,939

Loss of revenue from long-standing contract

= $250,000 each year, before tax, in perpetuity

= $175,000 each year after tax in perpetuity.

Years	Cash flow item	Cash flow $000	Discount factor at 10%	Present value $000
1 – 5	Post-tax additional profits	1,939	3.791	7,351
1 – ∞	Post-tax loss of revenue	(175)	1/0.10 = 10	(1,750)
				5,601
	PV of capital cash flows			(3,513)
	NPV of project			2,088

Decision: The contract is worthwhile

(b)   The project will cease to be viable if the NPV falls by more than $2,088,000 and becomes negative.

This would happen if the Present Value of the annual operating profits fell by more than $2,088,000. A reduction in the average price charged would affect revenue and annual contribution, but would not affect fixed costs.

On the basis of the estimates in part (a), the expected annual contribution is $3,770,000 before tax. After tax, this is (× 70%) $2,639,000.

The discount factor at 10% for years 1 – 5 is 3.791.

In the estimates in part (a), the contribution for the five years, allowing for tax, therefore has a present value of:

$2,639,000 × 3.791 = $10,004,449.

Tutorial note:

Unlike many questions where you're asked to calculate sensitivity to selling price, the affected cash flow is contribution and not sales revenue. This is because you're told that contribution will be a set percentage of revenue (implying that variable costs will also alter if selling price alters). Whilst this may seem a little unrealistic, you have to perform the calculations on the basis of what you've been told.

If this value fell by $2,088,000, it would fall in percentage terms by (2,088,000/10,004,449) × 100% = 20.87%.

To reduce the NPV to zero, given no other changes in the estimated values, would therefore require a fall in price of about 20.87% or $2.50, from $12 to $9.50.

(c)   (i)

	$000
PV of capital cash flows (given in the question)	(9,220)
PV of lost annual revenue in perpetuity	(1,750)
PV of extra operating profits, as estimated in (a)	7,351
NPV of the project for part (c)	(3,619)

A similar analysis can be made as in part (b), except that we need to calculate the occupancy rate at which the project would just break even. This requires an increase in the PV of extra operating profits in years 1-5 by at least $3,619,000.

The PV of the after-tax additional contribution was calculated, on the basis of the original estimates, as $10,004,449 (see above). For these to increase by $3,619,000 would mean an increase in percentage terms of (3,619/10,004.449) × 100% = over 36%.

Given no other changes in the estimates, this would require an increase in the occupancy rate from 60% to (60 × 1.36) 81.6%, say 82%.

31   SPRINGBANK INC

Key answer tips

Part (a) gives an opportunity to gain some easy marks provided you read the scenario carefully. Part (b) is much harder, especially for the low marks available and a thorough understanding of sensitivity analysis is needed to produce some sensible numbers. Be careful you don't spend too much time trying to answer this part of the question. For 10 marks, part (c) requires you to demonstrate your knowledge of both investment appraisal and sources of finance. The highlighted words are key phrases that markers are looking for.

(a)   Working W1

Calculation of tax benefits of capital allowances

Year	Tax written-down value of asset	Writing down allowance – WDA (25%)	Tax saving due to WDA (30%)
	$	$	$
1	3,000,000	750,000	225,000
2	2,250,000	562,500	168,750
3	1,687,500	421,875	126,563
4	1,265,625	316,406	94,922
5	949,219		284,766

(balancing allowance in Year 5)

These figures for tax savings will be rounded to the nearest $1,000.

Calculation of net present value of proposed investment

Year	0	1	2	3	4	5
	$000	$000	$000	$000	$000	$000
Sales		2,750	2,750	2,750	2,750	2,750
Production costs		(1,100)	(1,100)	(1,100)	(1,100)	(1,100)
Admin/dist'n expenses		(220)	(220)	(220)	(220)	(220)
Net revenue		1,430	1,430	1,430	1,430	1,430
Tax payable at 30%		(429)	(429)	(429)	(429)	(429)
Tax benefits from WDAs (W1)		225	169	127	95	285
Working capital	(400)					400
Machinery	(3,000)					
Project cash flows	(3,400)	1,226	1,170	1,128	1,096	1,686
Discount factor at 12%	1.000	0.893	0.797	0.712	0.636	0.567
Present value	(3,400)	1,095	932	803	697	956

The net present value is approximately $1,083,000.

This analysis makes the following assumptions:

(1)   The first tax benefit occurs in Year 1, the last tax benefit occurs in Year 5

(2)   Cash flows occur at the end of each year.

(3)   Inflation can be ignored.

(4)   The increase in capacity does not lead to any increase in fixed production overheads.

(5)   Working capital is all released at the end of Year 5

(b)   *Solution*

Some costs and benefits would be fixed amounts. These are the cost of the investment and the tax benefits from the writing down allowances. The present value of these tax benefits is as follows:

Year	Tax benefit (see (W1))	Discount factor at 12%	Present value
	$000		$000
1	225	0.893	200.9
2	169	0.797	134.7
3	127	0.712	90.4
4	95	0.636	60.4
5	285	0.567	161.6
			———
			648.0

After-tax profit from units sold

Variable administration and distribution expenses per unit = 220,000/5,500 = $40 per unit

Net revenue from additional units sold, before tax = $500 − $200 − $40 = $260 per unit.

Net revenue from additional units sold, after tax = 70% of $260 = $182.

Let the volume of annual sales be V units.

The present value of after-tax profits from selling V units each year for 5 years (years 1 – 5) = $182V × 3.605 (at a discount rate of 12%).

Working capital

Tutorial note:

The method of reaching a solution depends on whether it is assumed that the working capital investment varies with the volume of sales, or whether it is a fixed amount at $400,000. The solution here makes the assumption, preferred by the examiner, that the investment in working capital varies with the volume of sales. If you failed to take this into account you would only lose one or two marks.

It is assumed that the amount of working capital investment varies with the volume of annual sales.

Incremental working capital per unit = 400,000/5,500 = $72.73 per unit.

The net present value of the working capital investment is therefore:

Year	Cash flow	Discount factor at 12%	Present value
	$000		$000
0	(72.73V)	1.000	(72.73V)
5	72.73V	0.567	41.24V
Net PV of cost			31.49V

The NPV of the project is zero when:

(3,000,000) + 648,000 + 656.11V − 31.49V = 0

624.62V = 2,352,000

V = 3,765 units.

To achieve breakeven will therefore require an increase in annual sales of 3,765 units.

This is about 32% (1,735/5,500) less than the expected increase in sales volume.

(c)   Since the investment has a positive NPV it is acceptable in financial terms. Sensitivity analysis shows the proposed expansion is robust in terms of sales volume, since a 32% reduction below the forecast increase in sales is needed to eliminate the positive NPV. The proposed expansion is therefore acceptable, but the choice of financing is critical.

Springbank should be able to meet future interest payments if the cash flow forecasts for the increase in capacity are sound. However, no account has been taken of expected **inflation**, and both sales prices and costs will be expected to change. There is also an underlying **assumption of constant sales volumes**, when changing economic circumstances and the actions of competitors make this assumption unlikely to be true. More detailed financial forecasts are needed to give a clearer indication of whether Springbank can meet the additional interest payments arising from the new loan stock. There is also a danger that managers may focus more on the short-term need to meet the increased interest payments, or on the longer-term need to replace the machinery and redeem the loan stock, rather than on increasing the wealth of shareholders.

Financial risk will increase from a balance sheet (statement of financial position) point of view and this is likely to have a negative effect on how financial markets view the company. The cost of raising additional finance is likely to rise, while the increased financial risk may lead to downward pressure on the company's share price. The assets available for offering as security against new debt issues will decrease, and continue to decrease as non-current assets depreciate.

No information has been offered as to the **maturity of the new loan stock issue**. If the matching principle is applied, a medium term maturity of five to six years would be suggested.

On the basis of the above discussion, careful thought needs to be given to the maturity of any new issue of loan stock and it may be advisable to use debt finance to meet only part of the financing need of the proposed capacity expansion. Alternative sources of finance such as equity and leasing should be considered.

32   BREAD PRODUCTS CO

Key answer tips

Part (a) includes an unusual twist to what is otherwise a fairly simplistic replacement analysis question. The impact of inflation on the maintenance costs and resale values is not difficult to reflect provided you follow the same rules you'd follow when including inflation in a normal NPV calculation. Since the money cost of capital has been provided, the most efficient approach is to inflate the cash flows by their specific inflation rate and discount using the rate provided.

With over 50% of the marks, make sure you spend enough time on part (b). You should be aiming to identify 6 or 7 limitations of the net present value technique, explaining specifically why each one presents a problem. The highlighted words are key phrases that markers are looking for.

(a)   Two-year cycle for replacement: (Cash flows are inflated according to their individual inflation rates)

	0	1	2
Original cost	24,500		
Maintenance		550	968
Resale values			(17,199)
Net total cost	24,500	550	(16,231)
Discount factor	1.000	0.870	0.756
Present values	24,500	479	(12,271)
Net present value of costs	12,708		

Equivalent annual cost = 12,708/(annuity factor at 15% for two years) = 12,708/1.626 = 7,815.

Three-year cycle for replacement: (Cash flows are inflated according to their individual inflation rates)

	0	1	2	3
Original cost	24,500			
Maintenance		550	968	1,997
Resale values				(12,965)
Net total cost	24,500	550	968	(10,968)
Discount factor at 15%	1.000	0.870	0.756	0.658
Present values	24,500	479	732	(7,217)
Net present value of costs	18,494			

Equivalent annual cost = 18,494/(annuity factor at 15% for three years) = 18,494/2.283 = 8,101.

The conclusion is that a two-year replacement cycle is preferable.

(b)   General limitations of Net Present Value when applied to investment appraisal

NPV is a commonly used technique employed in investment appraisal, but it is subject to a number of restrictive assumptions and limitations which call into question its general relevance. Nonetheless, if the assumptions and limitations are understood then its application is less likely to be undertaken in error.

Some of the difficulties with NPV are listed below:

(i)   NPV assumes that firms pursue an objective of maximising the wealth of their shareholders. This is questionable given the wider range of stakeholders who might have conflicting interests to those of the shareholders.

(ii)   NPV is largely redundant if organisations are not wealth maximising. For example, public sector organisations may wish to invest in capital assets but will use non-profit objectives as part of their assessment.

(iii) NPV is potentially a difficult method to apply in the context of having to estimate what is the correct discount rate to use. This is particularly so when questions arise as to the incorporation of risk premia in the discount rate, since an evaluation of the riskiness of the business, or of the project in particular, will have to be made but may be difficult to discern. Alternative approaches to risk analysis, such as sensitivity and decision trees are, themselves, subject to fairly severe limitations.

(iv)   NPV assumes that cash surpluses can be reinvested at the discount rate. This is subject to other projects being available which produce at least a zero NPV at the chosen discount rate.

(v)   NPV can most easily cope with cash flows arising at period ends and is not a technique that is used easily when complicated, mid-period cash flows are present.

(vi)   NPV is not universally employed, especially in a small business environment. The available evidence suggests that businesses assess projects in a variety of ways (payback, IRR, accounting rate of return). The fact that such methods are used which are theoretically inferior to NPV calls into question the practical benefits of NPV, and therefore hints at certain practical limitations.

(vii) The conclusion from NPV analysis is the present value of the surplus cash generated from a project. If reported profits are important to businesses, then it is possible that there may be a conflict between undertaking a positive NPV project and potentially adverse consequences on reported profits. This will particularly be the case for projects with long time horizons, large initial investment and very delayed cash inflows. In such circumstances, businesses may prefer to use accounting measures of investment appraisal.

(viii) Managerial incentive schemes may not be consistent with NPV, particularly when long time horizons are involved. Thus managers may be rewarded on the basis of accounting profits in the short term and may be incentivised to act in accordance with these objectives, and thus ignore positive NPV projects. This may be a problem of the incentive schemes and not of NPV; nonetheless, a potential conflict exists and represents a difficulty for NPV.

(ix) NPV treats all time periods equally, with the exception of discounting far cash flows more than near cash flows. In other words, NPV only accounts for the time value of money. To many businesses, distant horizons are less important than near horizons, if only because that is the environment in which they work. Other factors besides applying higher discount rates may work to reduce the impact of distant years. For example, in the long term, nearly all aspects of the business may change and hence a too-narrow focus on discounting means that NPV is of limited value and more so the further the time horizon considered.

(x) NPV is of limited use in the face of non-quantifiable benefits or costs. NPV does not take account of non-financial information which may even be relevant to shareholders who want their wealth maximised. For example, issues of strategic benefit may arise against which it is difficult to immediately quantify the benefits but for which there are immediate costs. NPV would treat such a situation as an additional cost since it could not incorporate the indiscernible benefit.

33   BASRIL

Key answer tips

With 15 of the 25 marks available being for discussing various elements relating to capital rationing and relevant cashflows, this question should be a good opportunity to pick up some easy marks. Students who score badly on this question do so because they get bogged down in the numerical caluclations in part (a). The best way to avoid this trap is to tackle the wordy parts of the requirement first. The highlighted words are key phrases that markers are looking for.

(a)   (i)   Analysis of projects assuming they are divisible

	Discount factor at 12%	Project 1 Cash flow	PV	Project 3 Cash flow	PV
		$	$	$	$
Initial investment	1.000	(300,000)	(300,000)	(400,000)	(400,000)
Year 1	0.893	85,000	75,905	124,320	111,018
Year 2	0.797	90,000	71,730	128,795	102,650
Year 3	0.712	95,000	67,640	133,432	95,004
Year 4	0.636	100,000	63,600	138,236	87,918
Year 5	0.567	95,000	53,865	143,212	81,201
PV of savings			332,740		477,791
NPV			32,740		77,791

Profitability index   332,740/300,000   477,791/400,000
                                    = 1.11   = 1.19

	Discount factor at 12%	Project 2 Cash flow	PV
		$	$
Initial investment	1.000	(450,000)	(450,000)
Annual cash flows, years 1 - 5	3.605	140,800	507,584
Net present value			57,584

Profitability index   507,584/450,000   = 1.13

Order of preference (in order of profitability index) = Project 3 then Project 2 then Project 1.

Project	Profitability index	Ranking	Investment	NPV	
			$	$	
3	1.19	1st	400,000	77,791	
2	1.13	2nd	400,000	51,186	(= 57,584 × 400/450)
			800,000	128,977	

(ii) **Analysis of projects assuming they are indivisible**

If the projects are assumed to be indivisible, the total NPV of combinations of projects must be considered.

Projects	Investment	NPV	
	$	$	
1 and 2	750,000	90,324	£(32,740 + 57,584)
1 and 3	700,000	110,531	£(32,740 + 77,791)
2 and 3	850,000	not feasible, too much investment	

The optimum combination is now projects 1 and 3.

(b) The NPV decision rule requires that a company invest in all projects that have a positive net present value. This assumes that sufficient funds are available for all incremental projects, which is only true in a perfect capital market. When insufficient funds are available, that is when capital is rationed, projects cannot be selected by ranking by absolute NPV. Choosing a project with a large NPV may mean not choosing smaller projects that, in combination, give a higher NPV. Instead, if projects are divisible, they can be ranked using the profitability index in order make the optimum selection. If projects are not divisible, different combinations of available projects must be evaluated to select the combination with the highest NPV.

(c) The NPV decision rule, to accept all projects with a positive net present value, requires the existence of a perfect capital market where access to funds for capital investment is not restricted. In practice, companies are likely to find that funds available for capital investment are restricted or rationed.

Hard capital rationing is the term applied when the restrictions on raising funds are due to causes external to the company. For example, potential providers of debt finance may refuse to provide further funding because they regard a company as too risky. This may be in terms of financial risk, for example if the company's gearing is too high or its interest cover is too low, or in terms of business risk if they see the company's business prospects as poor or its operating cash flows as too variable. In practice, large established companies seeking long-term finance for capital investment are usually able to find it, but small and medium-sized enterprises will find raising such funds more difficult.

Soft capital rationing refers to restrictions on the availability of funds that arise within a company and are imposed by managers. There are several reasons why managers might restrict available funds for capital investment. Managers may prefer slower organic growth to a sudden increase in size arising from accepting several large investment projects. This reason might apply in a family-owned business that wishes to avoid hiring new managers. Managers may wish to avoid raising further equity finance if this will dilute the control of existing shareholders. Managers may wish to avoid issuing new debt if their expectations of future economic conditions are such as to suggest that an increased commitment to fixed interest payments would be unwise.

One of the main reasons suggested for soft capital rationing is that managers wish to create an internal market for investment funds. It is suggested that requiring investment projects to compete for funds means that weaker or marginal projects, with only a small chance of success, are avoided. This allows a company to focus on more robust investment projects where the chance of success is higher. This cause of soft capital rationing can be seen as a way of reducing the risk and uncertainty associated with investment projects, as it leads to accepting projects with greater margins of safety.

(d)   When undertaking the appraisal of an investment project, it is essential that **only relevant cash flows** are included in the analysis. If non-relevant cash flows are included, the result of the appraisal will be misleading and incorrect decisions will be made. A relevant cash flow is a differential (incremental) cash flow, one that changes as a direct result of an investment decision.

If current fixed production overheads are expected to increase, for example, the additional fixed production overheads are a relevant cost and should be included in the investment appraisal. Existing fixed production overheads should not be included.

A new cash flow arising as the result of an investment decision is a relevant cash flow. For example, the purchase of raw materials for a new production process and the net cash flows arising from the production process are both relevant cash flows.

The incremental tax effects arising from an investment decision are also relevant cash flows, providing that a company is in a tax-paying position. Direct labour costs, for example, are an allowable deduction in calculating taxable profit and so give rise to tax benefits: tax liabilities arising on incremental taxable profits are also a relevant cash flow.

One area where caution is required is interest payments on new debt used to finance an investment project. They are a differential cash flow and hence relevant, but the effect of the cost of the debt is incorporated into the discount rate used to determine the net present value. Interest payments should not therefore be included as a cash flow in an investment appraisal.

Market research undertaken to determine whether a new product will sell is often undertaken prior to the investment decision on whether to proceed with production of the new product. This is an example of a **sunk cost**. These are costs already incurred as a result of past decisions, and so are not relevant cash flows.

34   LEAMINGER INC

Key answer tips

Once all of the information has been extracted from the scenario, part (a) includes some simple calculations and gives the opportunity to score well. The concept of an opportunity cost on the available cash within part (b) is more complex and requires a good understanding of the impact of capital rationing. Part (c) requires you to think practically about the advantages and disadvantages of the financing methods that are not included within a financial calculation. The highlighted words are key phrases that markers are looking for.

(a)   Purchase outright

	20X2 $	20X3 $	20X4 $	20X5 $	20X6 $	20X7 $
Outlay/residual value	(360,000)				20,000	
Maintenance		(15,000)	(15,000)	(15,000)	(15,000)	
Resulting reduction in tax			4,500	4,500	4,500	4,500
Tax effect of WDAs (W1)		27,000	20,250	15,188	11,391	
Tax effect of balancing allowance (W2)						28,172
Cash flow	(360,000)	12,000	9,750	4,688	20,891	32,672
Discount factor at 10%	1.000	0.909	0.826	0.751	0.683	0.621
Present value	(360,000)	10,908	8,054	3,251	14,269	20,289

NPV of cost = $(302,959)

(W1) Writing down allowances

Year	Tax written down value b/d $	Writing down allowance (WDA) 25% $	Tax effect at 30% – tax reduction $
20X2	360,000	90,000	27,000
20X3	270,000	67,500	20,250
20X4	202,500	50,625	15,188
20X5	151,875	37,969	11,391
20X6	113,906		

The tax effect is one year in arrears, so the reduction relating to 20X2 affects cash flows in 20X3, and so on.

(W2) Balancing allowance/charge and its tax effect

	$
Tax written down value at start of year of sale	113,906
Sale proceeds	20,000
Balancing allowance	93,906
Effect on tax: reduction in tax at 30%	$28,172

The cash flow effect is one year in arrears.

Finance lease

Annuity factor (AF) at 10% for 4 years is 3.17

Thus PV outflows = (135,000 + 15,000)3.17 = (475,500)

PV of tax relief = {(150,000 × 0.3)3.17)}/1.1 = $129,682

Net present cost = $(345,818)

Operating lease

Annuity factor at 10% for 3 years is 2.487

Thus PV of outflows = (140,000)(2.487 +1) = (488,180)

PV of tax relief = (140,000 × 0.3)(2.487 +1)/1.1 = $133,140

Net present cost = $(355,040)

On the basis of net present value, purchasing outright appears to be the least cost method.

(b)   Each $1 of outlay before 31 December 20X3 would mean a loss in NPV on the alternative project of $0.20. There is thus an opportunity cost of using funds in 20X2.

Purchasing	$
Net present value of cost	(302,959)
Opportunity cost (0.2 × 360,000)	(72,000)
	———
Net PV of cost	(374,959)
	———

Finance lease

Net present cost = $(345,818)

There is no cash flow before 31 December 20X3 in this case, and thus no opportunity cost.

Operating lease	$
Net present value of cost	(355,040)
Opportunity cost (0.2 × 140,000)	(28,000)
	———
Net PV of cost	(383,040)
	———

Thus the finance lease is now the lowest cost option.

All the above assume that the alternative project cannot be delayed.

(c)   REPORT

To: The Directors of Leaminger Inc

From: A Business Advisor

Date: xx/xx/xx

Subject: Acquiring the turbine machine

Introduction

In financial terms, and without capital rationing, outright purchase is the preferred method of financing as it has the lowest NPV of cost. With capital rationing, a finance lease arrangement becomes the least-cost method. There are, however, a number of other factors to be considered before a final decision is taken.

(1)   If capital rationing persists into further periods, the value of cash used in leasing becomes more significant and so purchasing would become relatively more attractive.

(2)   Even without capital rationing, leasing has a short-term cash flow advantage over purchasing, which may be significant for liquidity.

(3)   The use of a 10% cost of capital may be inappropriate as these are financing issues and are unlikely to be subject to the average business risk. Also they may alter the capital structure and thus the financial risk of the business and thus the cost of capital itself. This may alter the optimal decision in the face of capital rationing.

(4)   The actual cash inflows generated by the turbine are constant for all options, except that under an operating lease the lessor may refuse to lease the turbine at the end of any annual contract thus making it unavailable from this particular source. On top of capital rationing, we need to consider the continuing availability of finance under the operating lease.

(5)   Conversely, however, with the operating lease Leaminger Inc can cancel if business conditions change (e.g. a technologically improved asset may become available). This is not the case with the other financing options. On the other hand, if the market is buoyant then the lessor may raise lease rentals, whereas the cost is fixed under the other options and hence capital rationing might be more severe.

(6)   On the issue of maintenance costs of $15,000 per annum, this is included in the operating lease if the machine becomes unreliable, but there is greater risk beyond any warranty period under the other two options.

(7)   It is worth investigating if some interim measure can be put in place which would assist in lengthening the turbine's life such as sub-contracting work outside or overhauling the machine.

35   AGD CO

Key answer tips

Part (a): To evaluate lease v buy the examiner's preferred approach is to perform two separate calculations. A combined approach will also gain credit but be careful of the signs of cash flows. Particular care is needed regarding the tax flows; they are delayed in this question and the asset would be bought on the first day of a new accounting period. Likewise the lease payments are in advance.

In part (b) ensure you both explain and discuss the differences. This requires you to describe the differences and look at the implications of them.

In part (c) the key is to recognise that there will be ten payments with an interest rate of 5% per six months. The highlighted words are key phrases that markers are looking for.

(a) **Borrowing to buy evaluation**

	Year 0 $000	Year 1 $000	Year 2 $000	Year 3 $000	Year 4 $000
Purchase and sale	(320)			50	
Capital allowance tax benefits			24	18	39
Maintenance costs		(25)	(25)	(25)	
Maintenance cost tax benefits			8	8	8
Net cash flow	(320)	(25)	7	51	47
Discount factors (7%)	1.000	0.935	0.873	0.816	0.763
Present values	(320)	(23)	6	42	36

PV of borrowing to buy = –$259,000

Workings: Capital allowance tax benefits

Year	Capital allowance	Tax benefit	Taken in year
1	320,000 × 0.25 =	80,000 80,000 × 0.3 = 24,000	2
2	80,000 × 0.75 =	60,000 60,000 × 0.3 = 18,000	3
3	Balancing allowance =	130,000 130,000 × 0.3 = 39,000	4

Balancing allowance = (320,000 – 50,000) – (80,000 + 60,000) = $130,000

Leasing evaluation

	Year 0 $000	Year 1 $000	Year 2 $000	Year 3 $000	Year 4 $000
Lease rentals	(120)	(120)	(120)		
Lease rental tax benefits			36	36	36
Net cash flow	(120)	(120)	(84)	36	36
Discount factors (7%)	1.000	0.935	0.873	0.816	0.763
Present values	(120)	(112)	(73)	29	27

PV of leasing = –$249,000

On financial grounds, leasing is to be preferred as it is cheaper by $10,000. Note that the first lease rental is taken as being paid at year 0 as it is paid in the first month of the first year of operation.

An alternative form of evaluation combines the cash flows of the above two evaluations. Because this evaluation is more complex, it is more likely to lead to computational errors.

Combined evaluation

	Year 0 $000	Year 1 $000	Year 2 $000	Year 3 $000	Year 4 $000
Purchase and sale	(320)			50	
Capital allowance tax benefits			24	18	39
Maintenance costs		(25)	(25)	(25)	
Maintenance cost tax benefits			8	8	8
Lease rentals saved	120	120	120		
Lease rental tax benefits lost			(36)	(36)	(36)
Net cash flow	(200)	95	91	15	11
Discount factors (7%)	1.000	0.935	0.873	0.816	0.763
Present values	(200)	89	79	12	8

The PV of −$12,000 indicates that leasing would be $12,000 cheaper than borrowing. The difference between this and the previous evaluation is due to rounding.

(b) A finance lease exists when the substance of the lease is that the lessee enjoys substantially all of the risks and rewards of ownership, even though legal title to the leased asset does not pass from lessor to lessee. A finance lease is therefore characterised by one lessee for most, if not all, of its useful economic life, with the lessee meeting maintenance and similar regular costs. A finance lease cannot be cancelled, once entered into, without incurring severe financial penalties. A finance lease therefore acts as a kind of medium- to long-term source of debt finance which, in substance, allows the lessee to purchase the desired asset. This ownership dimension is recognised in the balance sheet (statement of financial position), where a finance-leased asset must be capitalised (as a non-current asset), together with the amount of the obligations to make lease payments in future periods (as a liability).

In contrast, an operating lease is a rental agreement where several lessees are expected to use the leased asset and so the lease period is much shorter than the asset's useful economic life. Maintenance and similar costs are borne by the lessor, with this cost being reflected in the lease rentals charged. An operating lease can usually be cancelled without penalty at short notice. This allows the lessee to ensure that only up-to-date assets are leased for use in business operations, avoiding the obsolescence problem associated with the rapid pace of technological change in assets such as personal computers and photocopiers. Because the substance of an operating lease is that of a short-term rental agreement, operating leases do not require to be capitalised in the balance sheet (statement of financial position), allowing companies to take advantage of this form of 'off-balance sheet financing'.

(c) (i) The offer of 10% per year with interest payable every six months means that the bank will require 5% every six months. This is equivalent to an annual percentage rate of 10.25% ($100 \times (1.05^2 - 1)$) before tax.

OR

$1 + \text{annual rate} = (1 + \text{six monthly rate})^2 = 1.05^2 = 1.1025$

(ii) To calculate the repayment schedule use:

PV of repayments = PV of amount borrowed

Here we have a simple annuity, so

Instalment (A) × annuity factor = 320,000

where we want an annuity discount factor for ten payments and a rate of 5%.

Using annuity tables:

A = 320,000/7.722 = $41,440

36   CAVIC

Key answer tips

This question is a good balance between discussional aspects (in parts (b) & (c)) and calculations (in part (a)). The numerical aspects are uncomplicated and a basic understanding of replacement analysis should be enough to gain most of the marks available. The highlighted words are key phrases that markers are looking for.

(a)   Calculation of annual equivalent cost

Year	1	2	3
Servicing costs	10,000	14,000	19,600
Cleaning costs	5,000	6,250	7,813
Total costs	15,000	20,250	27,413
Discount factors	0.909	0.826	0.751
Present values of costs	13,635	16,727	20,587
Replacement cycle (years)	1	2	3
Cost on new vehicles	150,000	150,000	150,000
PV of Year 1 costs	13,635	13,635	13,635
PV of Year 2 costs		16,727	16,727
PV of Year 3 costs			20,587
Sum of PV of costs	163,635	180,362	200,949
Less PV of trade-in value	102,263	74,340	46,562
Net PV of cost of cycle	61,372	106,022	154,387
Annuity factor	0.909	1.736	2.487
Equivalent annual cost	67,516	61,073	62,078

Replacement after two years is recommended, since this replacement cycle has the lowest equivalent annual cost.

Tutorial note:

The above evaluation could have been carried out on a per car basis rather than on a fleet basis with the same conclusion being made.

Workings

Servicing costs

Year 1: 1,000 x 10	= $10,000
Year 2: 10,000 x 1.4	= $14,000
Year 3: 14,000 x 1.4	= $19,600

Cleaning costs

Year 1: 500 x 10	= $5,000
Year 2: 5,000 x 1.25	= $6,250
Year 3: 6,250 x 1.25	= $7,813

PV of trade-in values

Year 1: 11,250 x 10 x 0.909	= $102,263
Year 2 9,000 x 10 x 0.826	= $74,340
Year 3: 6,200 x 10 x 0.751	= $46,562

(b)   In order to invest in all projects with a positive net present value a company must be able to raise funds as and when it needs them: this is only possible in a perfect capital market. In practice capital markets are not perfect and the capital available for investment is likely to be limited or rationed. The causes of capital rationing may be external (hard capital rationing) or internal (soft capital rationing). Soft capital rationing is more common than hard capital rationing.

When a company cannot raise external finance even though it wishes to do so, this may be because providers of debt finance see the company as being too risky. In terms of financial risk, the company's gearing may be seen as too high, or its interest cover may be seen as too low. From a business risk point of view, lenders may be uncertain whether a company's future profits will be sufficient to meet increased future interest payments because its trading prospects are poor, or because they are seen as too variable.

When managers impose restrictions on the funds they are prepared to make available for capital investment, soft capital rationing is said to occur. One reason for soft capital rationing is that managers may not want to raise new external finance. For example, they may not wish to raise new debt finance because they believe it would be unwise to commit the company to meeting future interest payments given the current economic outlook. They may not wish to issue new equity because the finance needed is insufficient to justify the transaction costs of a new issue, or because they wish to avoid dilution of control. Another reason for soft capital rationing is that managers may prefer slower organic growth, where they can remain in control of the growth process, to the sudden growth arising from taking on one or more large investment projects.

A key reason for soft capital rationing is the desire by managers to make capital investments compete for funds, i.e. to create an internal market for investment funds. This competition for funds is likely to weed out weaker or marginal projects, thereby channelling funds to more robust investment projects with better chances of success and larger margins of safety, and reducing the risk and uncertainty associated with capital investment.

(c) The net present value decision rule is to invest in all projects that have a positive net present value. By following this decision rule, managers will maximise the value of a company and therefore maximise the wealth of ordinary shareholders, which is a primary objective of financial management. Even when capital is rationed, it is still essential to be able to offer advice on which capital investment projects should be selected in order to secure the maximum return for the investing company, i.e. the maximum overall net present value.

Single-period and multi-period capital rationing

Capital may be rationed in more than one period, i.e. not only in the current period at the start of an investment project (single-period rationing), but in future periods as well (multi-period capital rationing). Selecting the best projects for investment in order to maximise overall net present value when faced with multi-period capital rationing calls for the use of linear programming. Here, the available capital investments are expressed as an objective function, subject to a series of constraints. Only simple linear programming problems can be solved by hand, for example using the simplex method. More complex linear programming problems require the use of computers.

Project divisibility

The approach to solving single-period capital rationing problems depends on whether projects are divisible or not. A divisible project is one where a partial investment can be made in order to gain a pro rata net present value. For example, investing in a forest is a divisible project, since the amount of land purchased can be varied according to the funds available for investment (providing the seller agrees to a partial sale, of course). A non-divisible project is one where it is not possible to invest less than the full amount of capital. When building an oil refinery, for example, it is not possible to build only one part of the overall facility.

Where projects are divisible, the objective of maximising the net present value arising from invested funds can be achieved by ranking projects according to their profitability index and investing sequentially in order of decreasing profitability index, beginning with the highest, assuming that each project can be invested in only once, i.e. is non-repeatable. The profitability index can be defined as net present value divided by initial investment. Ranking projects by profitability index is an example of limiting factor analysis. Because projects are divisible, there will be no investment funds left over: when investment funds are insufficient to for the next ranked project, part of the project can be taken on because it is divisible.

When projects are non-divisible, the objective of maximising the net present value arising from invested funds can be achieved by calculating the net present value arising from different combinations of projects. With this approach, there will usually be some surplus funds remaining from the funds initially available.

The investment of surplus funds

When investigating combinations of non-divisible projects in order to find the combination giving rise to the highest net present value, any return from investing surplus funds is ignored. The net present value analysis has been based on the company's average cost of capital and it is unlikely that surplus funds can be invested in order to earn a return as high as this. Investment of surplus funds in, for example, the money markets would therefore be an investment project that would be rejected as having a negative net present value, or an internal rate of return less than the company's average cost of capital if using IRR to assess investments projects. However, it is good working capital management to ensure that liquid funds are invested to earn the highest available return, subject to any risk constraints, in order to increase overall profitability.

BUSINESS FINANCE

37 COLLINGHAM

Key answer tips

When comparing performance and financial health with the industry average be as specific as you can using the information provided in the scenario. It is not good enough to simply say "ROCE is better than the industry average" or "the net profit margin is higher". You must offer explanations as to why this might be the case. The highlighted words are key phrases that markers are looking for.

(a)   Seeking a quotation places many strains on a company, in particular, the need to provide more extensive information about its activities. However, the costs involved in doing this may seem worthwhile in order to pursue the following aims:

   (i)   *To obtain more capital to finance growth.* Companies which apply for a market listing are often fast-growing firms which have exhausted their usual supplies of capital. Typically, they rely on retained earnings and borrowings, often on a short-term basis. A quotation opens up access to a wider pool of investors. For example, large financial institutions are more willing to invest in quoted companies whose shares are considerably more marketable than those of unlisted enterprises. Companies with a listing are often perceived to be financially stronger and hence may enjoy better credit ratings, enabling them to borrow at more favourable interest rates.

   (ii)   *To allow owners to realise their assets.* After several years of successful operation, many company founders own considerable wealth on paper. They may wish to liquidify some of their holdings to fund other business ventures or simply for personal reasons, even at the cost of relinquishing some measure of voting power. Most flotations allow existing shareholders to release some of their equity as well as raising new capital.

   (iii) *To make the shares more marketable.* Existing owners may not wish to sell out at present, or to the degree that a flotation may require. A quotation, effected by means of a Stock Exchange introduction, is a device for establishing a market in the equity of a company, allowing owners to realise their wealth as and when they wish.

(iv)   *To enable payment of managers by stock options.* The offer to senior managers of payment partially in the form of stock options may provide powerful incentives to improve performance.

(v)   *To facilitate growth by acquisition.* Companies whose ordinary shares are traded on the stock market are more easily able to offer their own shares (or other traded securities, such as convertibles) in exchange for those of target companies whom they wish to acquire.

(vi)   *To enhance the company's image.* A quotation gives an aura of financial respectability, which may encourage new business contracts. In addition, so long as the company performs well, it will receive free publicity when the financial press reports and discusses its results in future years.

(b)   The table below compares Collingham's ratios against the industry averages:

	Industry	Collingham	
Return on (long term) capital employed	22%	10/33=	30.3%
Return on equity	14%	6/28=	21.4%
Operating profit margin	10%	10/80=	12.5%
Current ratio	1.8:1	23/20=	1.15:1
Acid-test	1.1:1	13/20=	0.65:1
Gearing (total debt/equity)	18%	10/28=	35.7%
Interest cover	5.2	10/3=	3.33 times
Dividend cover	2.6	6/0.5=	12 times

Collingham's profitability, expressed both in terms of ROCE and ROE, compares favourably with the industry average. This may be inflated by the use of a historic cost base, in so far as assets have never been revalued. Although a revaluation might depress these ratios, the company appears attractive compared to its peers. The net profit margin of 12.5% is above that of the overall industry, suggesting a cost advantage, either in production or in operating a flat administrative structure. Alternatively, it may operate in a market niche where it is still exploiting first-comer advantages. In essence, it is this aspect which is likely to appeal to investors.

Set against the apparently strong profitability is the poor level of liquidity. Both the current and the acid-test ratios are well below the industry average, and suggest that the company should be demonstrating tighter working capital management. However, the inventory turnover of $(10/70 \times 365) = 52$ days and the receivables days of $(10/80 \times 365) = 46$ days do not appear excessive, although industry averages are not given. It is possible that Collingham has recently been utilising liquid resources to finance capital investment or to repay past borrowings.

Present borrowings are split equally between short-term and long-term, although the level of gearing is well above the market average. The loan stock is due for repayment shortly which will exert further strains on liquidity, unless it can be re-financed. Should interest rates increase in the near future, Collingham is exposed to the risk of having to lock-in higher interest rates on a subsequent long-term loan or pay (perhaps temporarily) a higher interest rate on overdraft. The high gearing is reflected also in low interest cover, markedly below the industry average. In view of high gearing and poor liquidity, it is not surprising that the pay-out ratio is below 10%, although Collingham's managers would presumably prefer to link high retentions to the need to finance ongoing investment and growth rather than to protect liquidity.

(c)　It is common for companies in Collingham's position to attempt to 'strengthen' or to 'tidy up' their balance sheets (statements of financial position) in order to make the company appear more attractive to investors. Very often, this amounts to 'window dressing', and if the company were already listed, it would have little effect in an information-efficient market. However, for unlisted companies, about whom little is generally known, such devices can improve the financial profile of the company and enhance the prospects of a successful floatation.

(i)　Some changes in the balance sheet (statement of financial position) that Collingham might consider prior to floatation are:

Revalue those non-current assets that now appear in the accounts at historic cost. The freehold land and premises are likely to be worth more at market values, although the effect of time on second-hand machinery values is more uncertain. If a surplus emerges, a revaluation reserve would be created, thus increasing the book value of shareholders' funds, and hence the net asset value per share. The disadvantage of this would be to lower the ROCE and the return on equity, although these are already well above the industry averages. Asset revaluation would also reduce the gearing ratio.

Dispose of any surplus assets in order to reduce gearing and/or to increase liquidity which is presently low, both absolutely, and also in relation to the industry.

Examine other ways to improve the liquidity position, by reducing inventories, speeding up receivables collection or slowing payment to suppliers, although it already appears to be a slow payer with a trade credit period of $(15/70 \times 365)$ = 78 days.

Conduct a share split, because at the existing level of earnings per share, the shares promise to have a 'heavyweight' rating. Applying the industry P/E multiple of 13 to the current EPS of ($6m/($4m $\times$ 2)) = 75¢, yields a share price of (13 $\times$ 75¢) = $9.75. While there is little evidence that a heavyweight rating is a deterrent to trading in already listed shares, it is likely that potential investors, certainly small-scale ones, will be deterred from subscribing to a highly-priced new issue. A one-for-one share split whereby the par value is reduced to 25¢ per share and the number of shares issued correspondingly doubles, would halve the share price, although other configurations are possible.

It may have to enfranchise the non-voting 'A' shares, if, under Stock Exchange regulations, these are not permitted for companies newly entering the market. This would be the case in the UK, for example.

(ii)　Following the floatation, Collingham would probably have to accept that a higher dividend pay-out is required to attract and retain the support of institutional investors. If it wishes to persist with a high level of internal financing, a compromise may be to make scrip issues of shares, especially if the share price remains on the 'heavy' side. Scrip issues are valued by the market because they usually portend higher earnings and dividends in the future.

Finally, if the company has not already done so, it might consider progressively lowering the gearing ratio. It might begin this by using part of the proceeds of the floatation to redeem the loan stock early. However, it must avoid the impression that it requires a floatation primarily to repay past borrowings as that might cast doubts on the company's financial stability.

38   JERONIMO INC

Key answer tips

In part (a) note there are three parts to this requirement − (1) the difference between the two types of issue, (2) why companies make rights issues and scrip issues and (3) the effect on private investors of both type of issue. Marks are allocated for each part − don't throw them away by overlooking any of them.

Part (b) (i) hinges around the computation of the theoretical ex-rights price, a fairly standard formula with which you should be familiar.

Part (c) − the dividend growth model is central to equity value theory, and you must be confident in using it. Here, growth is estimated from past dividends, and applied to the current dividend to estimate next year's.

Part (d) really tests your understanding of the *implications* of market efficiency, rather than simply the ability to regurgitate definitions. The highlighted words are key phrases that markers are looking for.

(a)   A rights issue is a way of raising finance via the issue of shares to existing equity shareholders. In order to make such an issue, a company must have an authorised share capital which exceeds the share capital that would be in issue after the rights issue. (The shareholders could be asked to vote for an increase in the authorised share capital if necessary.) Companies choose to make rights issues because they need to raise long-term finance, and choose to do so by raising new equity finance. A rights issue might well be the most cost effective or desirable method of raising finance. The finance raised may be used to fund any type of long-term investment such as an acquisition, expansion of production facilities, or overseas investment.

A scrip issue (also called a bonus issue or capitalisation issue) is an issue of shares to existing shareholders, in proportion to their existing shareholdings, for which no charge is made. In other words, the shares are issued free to existing shareholders.

The advantage of a rights issue to existing shareholders, as opposed to an issue via public subscription, is that existing shareholders are assumed to have some level of commitment to the company already. As such, it may prove relatively easy to persuade them to buy new shares, and certainly easier and less costly than making a public offering. It is, however, important for the company to explain the reason behind the share issue − what it is going to do with the cash raised. If an investor is to be persuaded to pay cash for additional shares, then it must be demonstrated that their newly-invested cash will be used to earn returns at least equal to those they are currently receiving from their investment. If the return on capital is expected to decline in the company after the rights issue, then the issue is unlikely to be successful. As with any new share issue, it is common practice for a rights issue to be underwritten.

In the UK, for example, it is a legal requirement that, unless existing shareholders have voted to waive their pre-emption rights, a new issue of shares for cash must be in the form of a rights issue.

The individual investor in a company which is making a rights issue will be invited to take up or sell his/her rights. If the rights are taken up, then the investor will have to make a payment to the company equal to the price of the rights purchased. Alternatively, the investor may choose not to increase his investment, and instead can sell the rights on the open market. In an efficient market, the investor is no better nor no worse off by choosing to sell his/her rights.

Scrip issues are often justified on the basis that there is a need to increase the number of shares in issue in order to bring down the price per share. It is often argued that the market 'dislikes' shares which individually have a very high price, and by increasing the number of shares in issue, the unit share price can be diluted. This can be beneficial to shareholders, because research evidence suggests that the drop in the unit share price is not as great as the proportionate change in the number of shares in issue. For example, if 10 million shares are in issue, and the current market price is $10 each, the market value of the equity is $100 million. If 10 million shares are now distributed via a scrip issue, one would expect the share price to drop to $5, leaving the overall equity value at $100 million. In practice, the lowering of the share price may make the shares more marketable, such that the post issue price settles at, say, $6. This results in an increase in the value of individual shareholdings, together with a rise in the total value of the equity. Individual investors may therefore experience some capital gain from a scrip issue.

When making a scrip issue, a company is converting some of the reserves into share capital, and the number of shares (fully paid up) to which an investor is entitled, will be expressed in relation to the current holding, e.g. a 2 for 5 issue means that two new shares will be given to shareholders for every five shares they currently hold. As already suggested, although the private investor gains no theoretical advantage from this conversion of reserves, there may be a benefit in practice, because the shares are now likely to be more marketable.

(b) (i) Theoretical ex-rights price/value

$$\frac{(\text{No. shares in issue} \times \text{market value}) + (\text{No. rights shares} \times \text{rights share price})}{\text{Total shares in issue post rights}}$$

$$= \frac{(5m \times 1.60) + (1m \times 1.30)}{6m}$$

= $1.55 per share

After taking up the rights issue, James Brown will hold

10,000 + (0.2 × 10,000) = 12,000 shares.

The theoretical value of the holding, at $1.55 per share is thus $18,600.

Alternative method of calculation

	$
Current value of 5 existing shares (× $1.60)	8.00
Value of 1 new share in rights issue	1.30
Theoretical value of 6 shares	9.30

Theoretical ex-rights price per share = $9.30/6 = $1.55 per share.

(ii)   The value of the rights per share

= Theoretical ex-rights price – Cost of taking up the rights

The value of the rights per share = $1.55 – $1.30 = $0.25 per share

If James Brown sells all of his rights to 2,000 shares, he can expect to receive: 2,000 × $0.25 = $500.

Alternative method of calculation

	$
Current value of shares	1.60
Theoretical ex-rights price	1.55
Theoretical value of rights per existing share	0.05

Theoretical value of each new share that can be purchased = 5 × 5¢ = $0.25. The value of the rights per share is therefore $0.25.

Tutorial note:

The price at which the investor will sell the rights should be that which leaves him no worse off than if he had taken them up. Taking them up will give him a share worth $1.55, at a cost of $1.30, a net gain of $0.25. This is therefore the compensation he needs for selling the rights instead.

(c)   Rearranging the dividend growth formula $P_0 = \dfrac{D_0(1-g)}{(r_e - g)}$ gives

$$r_e = \frac{D_0(1-g)}{P_0} + g \;=\; \frac{D_1}{P_0} + g$$

It is assumed that the average growth rate in dividends between 20X5 and 20X9 will be a reliable guide to the future annual growth rate in dividends. Between 20X5 and 20X9 (4 years) dividends per share have grown by a factor of 12/8 = 1.5 times. The average annual growth rate over this period is calculated as the fourth root of 1.5, minus 1.

$$g \;=\; \sqrt[4]{\frac{12}{8}} - 1$$

= 0.1067 or 11%

D_1 = 1.11 × 12 cents

= 13.32 cents, say 13 cents.

$$r_e \;=\; \left(\frac{13}{160} + 0.11\right) = 0.19125 \text{ or } 19.125\%$$

(d)   In a strongly efficient market, finance directors will be alert to the fact that market prices are an accurate reflection of their company's financial prospects, and that if

---

they behave in a manner which results in bad financial decisions, the share price will quickly fall to compensate for the worsening prospects.

This means that the effect of an efficient market on financial management is that it keeps managers alert to the consequences of their decisions. In an inefficient world, prices may take a while to adjust to reflect poor planning or control, but in a semi-strong or strong market environment this will not be true. It can thus be said that a strong-form efficient market encourages higher quality financial management. In a similar vein, it also serves to discourage the artificial manipulation of accounting information, as the truth will quickly be realised, and prices adjusted accordingly.

39   ECHO CO *Walk in the footsteps of a top tutor*

Key answer tips

The key learning points from this question are the benefits of answering requirements in an order that best suits you as well as the need to take guidance from the specific words used in both the scenario and the requirement itself. The highlighted words are key phrases that markers are looking for.

Tutor's top tips:

Start by reading the requirement. Having a good understanding of what is expected from you will allow you to read the scenario more effectively, processing the information as you go. Scribble you thoughts in the margins on what each piece of information could be used for in relation to the requirements.

The first thing that should strike you is this question has 4, very independent requirements. This means you can pick the order in which to tackle them to suit your strengths. For the majority, part (d) should be attempted first. The question is very generic and requires little more than regurgitation of knowledge from the syllabus.

Of the remaining three parts, part (c) has the most guidance on the structure and content of your answer. These therefore represent the easiest of the remaining marks. The layout of the scenario means you can immediately re-read the information on proposal C and then consider what additional information you will need.

Tutor's top tips:

The slightly different requirements in part (a) and part (b) is reflected in the mark allocation. In part (a) the requirement is to 'analyse' and 'discuss' compared to 'evaluate' and 'discuss' in part (b). Part (b) will therefore require some further calculations.

> *In part (a) you need to link back to the scenario where we're told the aim of proposal A is to make the company more attractive to equity investors. A sensible approach is to consider what makes a share attractive. You should immediately highlight the dividend payment, discussion of which would lead on to Modigliani & Miller's theories on dividend policy and efficient markets hypothesis.*

(a) Echo Co paid a total dividend of $2 million or 20c per share according to the income statement information. An increase of 20% would make this $2.4 million or 24c per share and would reduce dividend cover from 3 times to 2.5 times. It is debatable whether this increase in the current dividend would make the company more attractive to equity investors, who use a variety of factors to inform their investment decisions, not expected dividends alone. For example, they will consider the business and financial risk associated with a company when deciding on their required rate of return.

It is also unclear what objective the finance director had in mind when suggesting a dividend increase. The primary financial management objective is the maximisation of shareholder wealth and if Echo Co is following this objective, the dividend will already be set at an optimal level. From this perspective, a dividend increase should arise from increased maintainable profitability, not from a desire to 'make the company more attractive'. Increasing the dividend will not generate any additional capital for Echo Co, since existing shares are traded on the secondary market.

Furthermore, Miller and Modigliani have shown that, in a perfect capital market, share prices are independent of the level of dividend paid. The value of the company depends upon its income from operations and not on the amount of this income which is paid out as dividends. Increasing the dividend would not make the company more attractive to equity investors, but would attract equity investors who desired the new level of dividend being offered. Current shareholders who were satisfied by the current dividend policy could transfer their investment to a different company if their utility had been decreased.   *M&M*

The proposal to increase the dividend should therefore be rejected, perhaps in favour of a dividend increase in line with current dividend policy.

Tutor's top tips:

In part (b), the scenario directs us towards the differences between short term and long term interest rates. As in part (c) the impact on gearing and interest cover can be highlighted and the lack of any investment opportunity should by highlighted as a problem.

(b) The proposal to raise $15 million of additional debt finance does not appear to be a sensible one, given the current financial position of Echo Co. The company is very highly geared if financial gearing measured on a book value basis is considered. The debt/equity ratio of 150% is almost twice the average of companies similar to Echo Co. This negative view of the financial risk of the company is reinforced by the interest coverage ratio, which at only four times is half that of companies similar to Echo Co.

Raising additional debt would only worsen these indicators of financial risk. The debt/equity ratio would rise to 225% on a book value basis and the interest coverage ratio would fall to 2.7 times, suggesting that Echo Co would experience difficulty in making interest payments.   *The decrease in Int. coverage rato*

The proposed use to which the newly-raised funds would be put merits further investigation. Additional finance should be raised when it is needed, rather than being held for speculative purposes. Until a suitable investment opportunity comes along, Echo Co will be paying an opportunity cost on the new finance equal to the difference between the interest rate on the new debt (10%) and the interest paid on short-term investments. This opportunity cost would decrease shareholder wealth. Even if an investment opportunity arises, it is very unlikely that the funds needed would be exactly equal to $15m.

The interest charge in the income statement information is $3m while the interest payable on the 8% loan notes is $2.4m (30 × 0.08). It is reasonable to assume that $0.6m of interest is due to an overdraft. Assuming a short-term interest rate lower than the 8% loan note rate – say 6% – implies an overdraft of approximately $10m (0.6/0.06), which is one-third of the amount of the long-term debt. The debt/equity ratio calculated did not include this significant amount of short-term debt and therefore underestimates the financial risk of Echo Co.

The bond issue would be repayable in eight years' time, which is five years after the redemption date of the current loan note issue. The need to redeem the current $30m loan note issue cannot be ignored in the financial planning of the company. The proposal to raise £15m of long-term debt finance should arise from a considered strategic review of the long-term and short-term financing needs of Echo Co, which must also consider redemption or refinancing of the current loan note issue and, perhaps, reduction of the sizeable overdraft, which may be close to, or in excess of, its agreed limit.

In light of the concerns and considerations discussed, the proposal to raise additional debt finance cannot be recommended.

Analysis

Current gearing (debt/equity ratio using book values) = 30/20 = 150%

Revised gearing (debt/equity ratio using book values) = (30 + 15)/20 = 225%

Current interest coverage ratio = 12/3 = 4 times

Additional interest following debt issue = 14m × 0.1 = $1.5m

Revised interest coverage ratio = 12/(3 + 1.5) = 2.7 times

Tutorial note:

The industry gearing has been calculated as debt / equity. You must ensure your calculation is consistent with this otherwise an effective comparison could not be made.

Tutor's top tips:

To calculate the theoretical ex-rights price (TERP), you will need the current share price, the subscription price and the basis of the issue. All are contained in the paragraph labelled 'Proposal C'. To calculate the amount of finance that would be raised, you also need to

know the number of shares to be issued. This can be worked out based on the current number of shares in issue given in the Statement of financial position information. Be careful to read this carefully. There is $5m of share capital but as the nominal value of each share is 50c, this means there are 10m in issue.

Both of these are simple calculations and will most likely attract 1 mark each. This therefore leaves 5 marks for your evaluation and discussion of the proposal.

A requirement to 'evaluate' implies some further calculations will be needed, this time relating to gearing and financial risk. Start by reviewing the information given in the scenario and consider what calculations would be both possible and useful. You should identify:

— *Gearing calculations. Whilst you have market values for equity, you only have the book value of debt. To be consistent you should therefore use book values of both to calculate gearing. In order to discuss the proposal, you will need to know the existing gearing and the new gearing under the proposal. Both can be usefully compared to the industry average.*

— *You have also been provided with average data on interest cover. This signals that calculation of current and projected interest cover will be a source of further marks. Some further calculations need to be done by assuming the proceeds from the rights issue are able to earn the same rate of return as existing funds. This will therefore give an estimate of the new level of profitability. These calculations might not seem obvious and are not essential to passing the question.*

When discussing the impact of the proposal on gearing and financial risk it is essential to highlight that there doesn't appear to be a need to raise this finance as there is no plan on how it will be spent.

(c)   **Analysis**

Rights issue price = 2.30 × 0.8 = $1.84

Theoretical ex rights price = (1.84 + (2.30 × 4))/5 = $2.21 per share

Number of new shares issued = (5/0.5)/4 = 2.5 million

Cash raised = 1.84 × 2.5m = $4.6 million

Number of shares in issue after rights issue = 10 + 2.5 = 12.5 million

Current gearing (debt/equity ratio using book values) = 30/20 = 150%

Revised gearing (debt/equity ratio using book values) = 30/24.6 = 122%

Current interest coverage ratio = 12/3 = 4 times

Current return on equity (ROE) = 6/20 = 30%

In the absence of any indication as to the return expected on the new funds, we can assume the rate of return will be the same as on existing equity, an assumption consistent with the calculated theoretical ex rights price. After-tax return on the new funds = 4.6m × 0.3 = $1.38 million Before-tax return on new funds = 1.38m × (9/6) = $2.07 million Revised interest coverage ratio = (12 + 2.07)/3 = 4.7 times

The current debt/equity and interest coverage ratios suggest that there is a need to reduce the financial risk of Echo Co. A rights issue would reduce the debt/equity ratio of the company from 150% to 122% on a book value basis, which is 50% higher than the average debt/equity ratio of similar companies. After the rights issue, financial gearing is still therefore high enough to be a cause for concern.

The interest coverage ratio would increase from 4 times to 4.7 times, again assuming that the new funds will earn the same return as existing equity funds. This is still much lower than the average interest coverage ratio of similar companies, which is 8 times. While 4.7 times is a safer level of interest coverage, it is still somewhat on the low side.

No explanation has been offered for the amount to be raised by the rights issue. Why has the Finance Director proposed that $4.6m be raised? If the proposal is to reduce financial risk, what level of financial gearing and interest coverage would be seen as safe by shareholders and other stakeholders? What use would be made of the funds raised? If they are used to redeem debt they will not have a great impact on the financial position of the company, in fact it appears likely that the overdraft is twice as big as the amount proposed to be raised by the rights issue. The refinancing need therefore appears to be much greater than $4.6m. If the funds are to be used for investment purposes, further details of the investment project, its expected return and its level of risk should be considered.

There seems to be no convincing rationale for the proposed rights issue and it cannot therefore be recommended, at least on financial grounds.

(d)   Operating leasing is a popular source of finance for companies of all sizes and many reasons have been advanced to explain this popularity. For example, an operating lease is seen as protection against obsolescence, since it can be cancelled at short notice without financial penalty. The lessor will replace the leased asset with a more up-to-date model in exchange for continuing leasing business. This flexibility is seen as valuable in the current era of rapid technological change, and can also extend to contract terms and servicing cover.

Operating leasing is often compared to borrowing as a source of finance and offers several attractive features in this area. There is no need to arrange a loan in order to acquire an asset and so the commitment to interest payments can be avoided, existing assets need not be tied up as security and negative effects on return on capital employed can be avoided. Since legal title does not pass from lessor to lessee, the leased asset can be recovered by the lessor in the event of default on lease rentals. Operating leasing can therefore be attractive to small companies or to companies who may find it difficult to raise debt.

Operating leasing can also be cheaper than borrowing to buy. There are several reasons why the lessor may be able to acquire the leased asset more cheaply than the lessee, for example by taking advantage of bulk buying, or by having access to lower cost finance by virtue of being a much larger company. The lessor may also be able use tax benefits more effectively than the lessee. A portion of these benefits can be made available to the lessee in the form of lower lease rentals, making operating leasing a more attractive proposition that borrowing. Operating leases also have the attraction of being off-balance sheet financing, in that the finance used to acquire use of the leased asset does not appear in the balance sheet.

ACCA marking scheme		
		Marks
(a)	Discussion of proposal to increase dividend	
		5
(b)	Evaluation of debt finance proposal	3–4
	Discussion of debt finance proposal	4–5
		7
(c)	Theoretical ex rights price per share	1
	Amount of finance raised	1
	Evaluation of rights issue proposal	2–3
	Discussion of rights issue proposal	3–4
		7
(d)	Discussion of attractions of leasing	6
Total		25

Examiner's comments

Part (a) asked candidates to analyse and discuss a proposal to increase dividend per share. Many candidates calculated correctly the increased dividend per share and then offered very little by way of discussion in order to gain any further marks.

There were a number of points that could have been discussed, including the finance director's view that the dividend per share 'should be increased by 20% in order to make the company more attractive to equity investors'. Increases in dividends usually lag behind increases in earnings and depend on the dividend policy of a company. It is debatable whether increasing the dividend per share makes a company more attractive to investors. It could be argued, for example, that its existing dividend clientele are satisfied by its current dividend policy. It could also be argued that making a dividend decision without also considering investment and financing needs is foolish: paying an increased dividend and then borrowing to meet investment plans is not advisable for a company as highly geared as the one under consideration here. Other points are discussed in the suggested answer to this question.

Part (b) asked for evaluation and discussion of a proposal to make a $15m bond issue and to invest the funds raised on a short-term basis until a suitable investment opportunity arose.

Candidates were expected to be aware that finance should be raised in order to meet a specific need and that investing long-term funds on a short-term basis would incur an unnecessary net interest cost. In this case, a highly-geared company would be choosing to increase its gearing and financial risk, without the prospect of investing the funds in a project offering returns greater than the increased financing cost.

The sector average debt/equity ratio (D/E) was provided, but many candidates chose to calculate capital gearing (D/(D + E)) in the mistaken belief that this was the debt to equity ratio. Comparison with the sector average gearing was therefore pointless, since the gearing ratios were on a different basis. Some candidates also calculated incorrectly the interest coverage, dividing interest into profit before tax or profit after tax, rather than into profit before interest and tax.

There were some lucid discussions of the dangers attached to the proposal to make a bond issue and these gained high marks.

It was surprising to see many candidates attempting to calculate the cost of debt (internal rate of return) of the bond issue. The bonds were to be issued and redeemed at par and so their cost of debt was the same as their interest rate, as these unnecessary calculations confirmed (where they were made correctly).

In part (c), candidates were asked to calculate the theoretical ex rights price per share and the amount of finance to be raised by a proposed rights issue, which was intended to reduce gearing and financial risk.

Many candidates were able to calculate the theoretical ex rights price and the finance raised, and went on to calculate the effect of the rights issue on the gearing of the company. Some candidates mistakenly assumed that the proceeds of the right issue would be used to redeem some of the existing debt, but the question did not specify this and in practice this might not be possible. Very few candidates recognised that, just as with the proposal to make a bond issue, there had been no evaluation of the funding needs of the company. Why raise $4.6m? Why not $10m? What were the rights issue funds going to be used for? A more concrete plan than raising cash to reduce gearing was needed if shareholder wealth was going to be maximised.

Part (d) asked candidates to discuss the attractions of operating leasing as a source of finance. Many answers offered an explanation of operating leasing, but very little discussion of its attractions as a source of finance to a company. Common points made included the tax deductibility of lease rental payments (although interest payments on debt are also tax-deductible), the flexibility of operating leases, and the way in which operating leases helped to overcome the obsolescence problem. Many answers did not compare leasing as a source of finance with borrowing to buy.

40 PAVLON

Key answer tips

This is a difficult question that requires some imaginative thinking in order to tackle efficiently. The idea of calculating the dividend payout ratio for part (a) is one which seems logical when you review the answer but might not necessarily have occurred to you when attempting the question under timed conditions.

Part (b) is a more clear cut application of the dividend valuation model with the change in growth rate being the only complication. The highlighted words are key phrases that markers are looking for.

(a)   (i)   The first step is to try to determine exactly what is Pavlon's current dividend policy.

Year prior to listing	Number of shares	EPS	Growth over previous year	Dividend per share	Payout ratio
5	21,333,333	8.44¢	–	3.6¢	42.7%
4	21,333,333 (Note 2)	11.25¢	33%	4.8¢	42.7%
3	26,666,667	14.44¢	28%	6.16¢	42.7%
2	26,666,667	15.38¢	6%	6.56¢	42.7%
1	26,666,667 (Note 1)	16.69¢	8.5%	7.12¢	42.7%
Current	40,000,000	13.75¢ (est)	-18%	5.5¢ (proposed)	40%

Note 1 $\dfrac{40,000,000}{1.5} = 26,666,667$

Note 2 $\dfrac{26,666,667}{1.25} = 21,333,333$

Pavlon appears to be adopting a policy of a fixed payout ratio of 42.7% pa over the five year period. In general such a policy can lead to wide variations in dividends per share. In Pavlon's case over the last five years earnings have been rising and a continual (though declining) growth in dividend has resulted.

If it is believed that share price is affected by dividend policy then these fluctuations in dividends and the decline in growth could depress equity value.

Most listed companies attempt to adopt a stable or rising level of dividend per share even in the face of fluctuating earnings. This approach is taken in order to maintain investor confidence. If Pavlon were to continue with its present policy and earnings were to decline the resultant dividend could have serious repercussions for share price.

(ii)   The proposed final dividend gives a total for the year of 5.5¢. This is a significant fall in dividend per share and a small decline in the dividend payout ratio. In the absence of market imperfections such as taxation and transaction costs, it could be argued that dividend policy has no impact on shareholder wealth. It is the firm's future earnings stream that is of importance, not the way in which it is split between dividend and retentions.

However, once market imperfections are introduced dividend policy can be shown to have an impact on investor wealth.

Private individuals may pay income tax at a higher rate than capital gains tax due to available CGT annual exemptions. They would therefore prefer retentions to distributions. Any income required could be generated by selling shares to manufacture 'home made' dividends (note however the problem of transaction costs).

If the reduction in dividend payout were carefully explained it might therefore be acceptable to wealthy individuals.

The tax position of institutional shareholders varies and so therefore will their attitude to dividend policy. Most, however, require a steady flow of income to meet their day-to-day obligations (pensions, insurance claims etc) and may not wish (or be able) to generate home made dividends.

It could be argued that new investors have bought shares in Pavlon with full knowledge of its dividend policy and should therefore not be surprised if it sticks to a policy of a 40% payout. However, many shareholders might expect it to change its policy now that it has obtained a listing.

A further factor to consider is the informational content of dividends. The proposed dividend cut might be seen as a signal of poor earnings in the future and lead to investors of either group selling shares.

Overall there is no conclusive evidence on what makes for an optimal dividend policy. Pavlon should however consider the tax position of its investors and the potential reaction of the market to a cut in dividend.

(b) If the company's profits and dividends are expected to increase initially by 15% pa then investors will expect this year's dividend to be 7.12¢ × 1.15 = 8.188¢

(i) **Value of first three years' dividend**

Year	Dividend			PV factor 12%	Present value
Current	7.12 × 1.15	=	8.188	0.893	7.312
2	8.188 × 1.15	=	9.416	0.797	7.505
3	9.416 × 1.15	=	10.829	0.712	7.710
					22.527

Note for simplicity we assume that the current dividend is one year hence.

Value of dividends years 4 – ∞

$$= \frac{d(1+g)}{i-g} = \frac{10.829(1.08)}{0.12 - 0.08} = 292.383$$

This gives the value of the perpetuity as at year 3. To obtain year 0 values we must discount back.

292.383 x 0.712 = 208.2

Value of share at time 0 = 22.527 + 208.2 = 231¢

Since the current market value of Pavlon's shares is $78m/40m = $1.95 the share appears to be under valued.

(ii) **Weaknesses of the dividend valuation model**

In principle there is little wrong with the dividend valuation model. Its basic premise that the value of a share is the present value of all future dividends is difficult to challenge. Its major weakness is the volume of data it requires.

Specifically:

(a) the need to forecast all future dividends is a major obstacle to its use. Simplifying assumptions of constant growth make it easy to work with but their practical validity can be questioned.

(b)   if it is to be used in share valuation the problem of determining the correct discount rate is substantial.

(c)   if it is to be used to determine the cost of equity the selection of the appropriate share price free from short-term influences is difficult.

(d)   it assumes that investors are indifferent between tax and capital gains.

41   ARWIN

Key answer tips

Part (a) should be straightforward, except that you need to be careful with the calculation of the fixed costs in the cost of sales. These are not expected to rise next year, and so should be calculated using the current year figures. For part (b), the question does not state how financial gearing or operational gearing should be measured: there are different methods of calculation. Make clear the method of calculation you are using. (The solution here gives two methods of measuring financial gearing and three methods of measuring operational gearing, but your answer only needs one of each.) For part (c), you need to discuss the problems of high gearing, and you need to spot that 'gearing' in this question refers to both financial gearing and operational gearing. The question hints at this strongly, by referring to both business risk and financial risk. Unfortunately, an unwary student will overlook operational gearing and business risk entirely. The highlighted words are key phrases that markers are looking for.

(a)   The forecast income statements are as follows:

	Debt finance	Equity finance
	$000	$000
Sales revenue (50,000 × 1.12)	56,000	56,000
Variable cost of sales (85% × sales)	28,560	28,560
Fixed cost of sales (15% × 30,000)	4,500	4,500
Gross profit	22,940	22,940
Administration costs (14,000 × 1.05)	14,700	14,700
Profit before interest and tax	8,240	8,240
Interest (see working)	800	300
Profit before tax	7,440	7,940
Taxation at 30%	2,232	2,382
Profit after tax	5,208	5,558
Note: Dividends paid (60%)	3,125	3,335
Net change in equity (retained profit)	2,083	2,223

Working

Interest under debt financing = $300,000 + ($5,000,000 × 0.10) = $800,000.

(b) Financial gearing

If financial gearing is measured as the debt: equity ratio:

Using debt/equity ratio:	Current	Debt finance	Equity finance
Debt	2,500	7,500	2,500
Share capital and reserves	22,560	24,643	29,783
Debt/equity ratio (%)	11.1	30.4	8.4

Workings:

Share capital and reserves (debt finance) = 22,560 + 2,083 = $24,643

Share capital and reserves (equity finance) = 22,560 + 5,000 + 2,223 = $29,783.

If financial gearing is measured as the ratio of debt capital to total capital:

Using capital (total) gearing:	Current	Debt finance	Equity finance
Debt	2,500	7,500	2,500
Total long-term capital	25,060	32,143	32,283
Capital (total) gearing (%)	10.0	23.3	7.7

Operational gearing:

If operational gearing is measured as the ratio of fixed costs to total costs:

Using fixed costs/total costs:	Current	Debt finance	Equity finance
Fixed costs	18,500	19,200	19,200
Total costs	44,000	47,760	47,760
Operational gearing (%)	42.0%	40.2%	40.2%

Total costs are assumed to consist of cost of sales plus administration costs.

If operational gearing is measured as the ratio of fixed costs to variable costs:

Using fixed costs/variable costs:	Current	Debt finance	Equity finance
Fixed costs	18,500	19,200	19,200
Variable costs	25,500	29,560	28,560
Operational gearing (%)	0.73	3.3	3.3

If operational gearing is measured as the ratio of contribution to profit before interest and tax (PBIT):

Using contribution/PBIT	Current	Debt finance	Equity finance
Contribution	24,500	27,440	27,440
PBIT	6,000	8,240	8,240
Operational gearing	4.1	3.3	3.3

Contribution is sales revenue minus the variable cost of sales.

Interest cover:

	Current	Debt finance	Equity finance
Profit before interest and tax	6,000	8,240	8,240
Debt interest	300	800	300
Interest cover	20	10.3	27.5

Earnings per share:

	Current	Debt finance	Equity finance
Profit after tax	3,990	5,208	5,558
Number of shares	10,000	10,000	11,250
Earnings per share (cents)	39.9	52.1	49.4

Comment:

The debt finance proposal leads to the largest increase in earnings per share, but results in an increase in financial gearing and a decrease in interest cover. Whether these changes in financial gearing and interest cover are acceptable depends on the attitude of both investors and managers to the new level of financial risk; a comparison with sector averages would be helpful in this context. The equity finance proposal leads to a decrease in financial gearing and an increase in interest cover. The expansion leads to a decrease in operational gearing, whichever measure of operational gearing is used, indicating that fixed costs have decreased as a proportion of total costs.

(c)   Business risk could be described as the possibility of a company experiencing changes in the level of its profit before interest as a result of changes in sales revenue or operating costs. For this reason it is also referred to as operating risk. Business risk relates to the nature of the business operations undertaken by a company. For example, we would expect profit before interest to be more volatile for a luxury goods manufacturer than for a food retailer, since sales of luxury goods will be more closely linked to varying economic activity than sales of a necessity good such as food.

The nature of business operations influences the proportion of fixed costs to total costs. Capital intensive business operations, for example, will have a high proportion of fixed costs to total costs. From this perspective, operational gearing is a measure of business risk. As operational gearing increases, a business becomes more sensitive to changes in sales revenue and the general level of economic activity, and profit before interest becomes more volatile. A rise in operational gearing may therefore lead to a business experiencing difficulty in meeting interest payments. Managers of businesses with high operational risk will therefore be keen to keep fixed costs under control.

Financial risk in the context of this question can be described as the possibility of a company experiencing changes in the level of its distributable earnings as a result of the need to make interest payments on debt finance. The earnings volatility of companies in the same business will therefore depend not only on business risk, but also on the proportion of debt finance each company has in its capital structure. Since the relative amount of debt finance employed by a company is measured by gearing, financial risk is also referred to as gearing risk.

As financial gearing increases, the burden of interest payments increases and earnings become more volatile. Since interest payments must be met, shareholders may be faced with a reduction in dividends; at very high levels of gearing, a company may cease to pay dividends altogether as it struggles to find the cash to meet interest payments.

The pressure to meet interest payments at high levels of gearing can lead to a liquidity crisis, where the company experiences difficulty in meeting operating liabilities as they fall due. In severe cases, liquidation may occur.

The focus on meeting interest payments at high levels of financial gearing can cause managers to lose sight of the primary objective of maximizing shareholder wealth. Their main objective becomes survival and their decisions become focused on this, rather than on the longer-term prosperity of the company. Necessary investment in fixed asset renewal may be deferred or neglected.

A further danger of high financial gearing is that a company may move into a loss-making position as a result of high interest payments. It will therefore become difficult to raise additional finance, whether debt or equity, and the company may need to undertake a capital reconstruction.

It is likely that a business with high operational gearing will have low financial gearing, and a business with high financial gearing will have low operational gearing. This is because managers will be concerned to avoid excessive levels of total risk, i.e. the sum of business risk and financial risk. A business with a combination of high operational gearing and high financial gearing clearly runs an increased risk of experiencing liquidity problems, making losses and becoming insolvent.

42   SPENDER CONSTUCTION

Key answer tips

In part (a) you will need to apply your knowledge to the specifics of the scenario. Do the calculations and comment on the implications for equity investors. A good approach is to illustrate your answer with some numerical examples.

In part (b) you are specifically told to look at EPS. You will therefore need to forecast this under both scenarios. Link this part of your answer to what you've written in part (a) and financial risk to score highly. Finally, part (c) builds on part (b) and should be an opportunity to score some easy marks. The highlighted words are key phrases that markers are looking for.

(a)   (i)   **Operational gearing** may be defined as a measure of the impact of a change in sales on Earnings Before Interest and Taxation (EBIT). For any given level of output:

Operational gearing = Contribution/EBIT

(*Note:* **Other definitions of operational gearing such as fixed costs as a percentage of total costs are also acceptable**)

A company's level of operational gearing is dependent on the ratio of fixed to variable costs and the current level of profit. If a company has a high level of fixed costs, then beyond the break-even point, an increase in the volume of sales will lead to a high percentage increase in profit. However, the percentage increase declines as the size of the profit continues to grow. Applying the formula shown above to the 20X7 financial statements for Spender Construction Inc, we can compute the current level of operational gearing within the company:

Operational gearing = Contribution/EBIT

For 20X7:

Variable selling and distribution costs = $348,000 − $100,000= $0.248 million.

Variable administration costs = $8.250m − $7m (fixed) = $1.250 million

Contribution = Sales − Variable costs

= $55.258m − (41.827m + 0.248m + 1.250m)

= $11.933m

EBIT = $4.833m

Operational gearing = 11,933/4.833= 2.47

(ii) **Financial gearing** is measured by comparing a company's use of long-term debt finance relative to equity. The higher the proportion of debt finance, the higher the level of gearing. Financial gearing affects the sensitivity of the profit attributable to equity (profit after interest and tax) to changes in EBIT. Using debt as a source of finance commits a company to the payment of debt interest which, for any given level of operating profit, erodes the amount of profit attributable to equity investors. However, once operating profits are sufficient to cover the interest payments due, all additions to operating profit will be fully attributable to equity investors.

Textbooks contain a number of different formulae for financial gearing. They include the following alternatives:

$$(1) \quad \frac{\text{Long - term interest bearing debt + preference share capital}}{\text{Equity plus reserves}}$$

$$(2) \quad \frac{\text{Long - term interest bearing debt + preference share capital}}{\text{Total long - term capital}}$$

$$(3) \quad \frac{\text{Profit before interest}}{\text{Profit after interest}}$$

A further variation on the formula might be applied which includes short-term interest bearing debt in the numerator. In this way financial gearing is then measuring the proportion of total borrowing relative to total capital, rather than just the proportion of long-term loans in the total capital base.

It is useful to note the differences between the formulae. The first two differ only in relation to the denominator, but this has the effect of altering the resulting figure for financial gearing. This can be illustrated by reference to Spender Construction Inc.

Using formula (1) in respect of the 20X7 financial statements.

$$\text{Financial gearing} = \frac{1,200}{12,452} = 0.0964 \text{ or } 9.64\%$$

Using formula (2):

$$\text{Financial gearing} = \frac{1,200}{13,652} = 0.0879 \text{ or } 8.799\%$$

The second figure is lower because the denominator is larger. This means that care must be taken in interpreting figures for financial gearing to ensure that there is consistency in the formula chosen for the calculation. Finally, applying formula (3), which uses figures from the income statement (as opposed to the balance sheet (statement of financial position)), and so is more consistent with the operational gearing calculation done earlier, we get:

$$\text{Financial gearing} = \frac{\text{Profit before interest}}{\text{Profit after interest}} = \frac{4{,}833}{4{,}506} = 1.07$$

Formula (3) yields a very different result to the other two, and so serves to underline further the need for caution in interpretation of gearing figures.

Financial gearing is sometimes referred to as 'second tier' gearing because it affects the profit going to equity but not until the impact of operational gearing has already affected the level of EBIT. This means that if a company trades with a high level of operational gearing, EBIT is already highly sensitive to changes in sales revenue. If this is then combined with the potential for further erosion of the returns to equity as a result of large debt interest payments (caused by high financial gearing) then the overall risk to equity investors is high. This overall effect is most important to investors, and means that attention needs to be given to a company's level of operational and financial gearing in combination.

Spender's fixed costs (which are $7,100,000 excluding interest payments) equal over 12.5 % of sales, compared with the industry average of just 7%. The potential risk of this high operational gearing level lies in the sales volatility that is often associated with construction firms. The industry is very sensitive to the state of the economy, and an economic downturn can hit sales quite dramatically. Under such circumstances, and with an operational gearing level of 2.47, Spender Construction Inc could find that a 10% fall in sales from current levels would cause a drop of almost 25% in operating profit. It is worth noting, however, that this gearing level will come down next year as a result of increased sales and reduced fixed costs. It is probably in recognition of this sensitivity of profits to changes in sales that the company has chosen to keep its level of financial gearing relatively low at 1.07.

Spender's financial gearing cannot be compared with that of the industry because the relevant information is not available. The lower level helps to limit the potential impact of sales changes on the profit available to equity, and so limits the overall risk to equity investors. Nonetheless, Spender Construction Inc must be regarded as a somewhat risky choice for equity investors and the example clearly demonstrates how a company needs to think about how it mixes its levels of financial and operating gearing in such a way as to limit the risk to equity shareholders.

(b) Number of shares currently in issue = 8 million (i.e. $4m/$0.50).

EPS in 20X7 = 39.4 cents (i.e. $3.154m/8m).

Dividend per share in 20X7 = 19 cents (i.e. $1.520 million/8 million).

In comparing a rights issue and a loan stock issue as alternative funding sources, it is important to take account of the effect of each alternative on the returns to ordinary shareholders, and the level of risk to those shareholders. It is reasonable to assume that if we are asking shareholders to accept a higher level of risk (operational or financial) then they will expect to receive an increase in their returns in compensation. The two alternative methods of funding affect only the level of financial risk in the company. The loan stock issue will increase the level of financial gearing whilst the rights issue will reduce the level of financial gearing. As at December 20X7 the financial gearing of Spender Construction Inc was 1.07. In selecting the most appropriate source of funding, therefore, consideration must be given as to whether such changes would be acceptable to the equity shareholders. A comparison of the forecast EPS under both types of funding is useful in assessing the likely shareholder response. Care must be taken, however, in interpreting the forecast, because only one year's data is available.

Forecast income statement, Spender Construction,
Year ending 31 December 20X8

		With loan stock issue	*With rights issue*
		$000	$000
Sales revenue	($55,258 × 1.15)	63,547	63,547
Cost of sales	0.98 × ($41,827 × 1.15)	47,139	47,139
		———	———
Gross profit		16,408	16,408
Selling and dist'n costs	($248 × 1.15) + 100	385	385
Administration costs	(1,250 × 1.15) + (7,000 − 500)	7,938	7,938
		———	———
Operating profit		8,085	8,085
Interest charges	(10% of 1,200) + 280 + (10% of 7,000)	1,100	400
		———	———
Profit before tax		6,985	7,685
Corporation tax (30%)		2,096	2,306
		———	———
Profit after tax		4,889	5,379
Dividend		2,000	2,333
		———	———
Retained profit		2,889	3,046
		———	———

Assuming loan stock is issued:
Forecast EPS,
Year ending 31 December 20X8
EPS = 4,889/8,000 = 61.1 cents
Change in EPS = 55.1% growth

Assuming rights issue
Forecast EPS,
Year ending 31 December 20X8
EPS = 5,379/9,333 = 57.6 cents
Change in EPS = 46.2% growth

The figures show that if the sales targets are achieved, the **EPS will grow faster if loan stock financing is selected**, but in both instances the growth is substantial. This is largely because profits are already sufficiently high to meet the interest payments required and so, helped substantially by other changes, such as the fixed cost savings, all increases in profit (net of tax) can accrue to equity investors. The rights issue generates a smaller EPS because the number of shares in issue has been increased by 1.33 million, and so the equity earnings are shared more widely. In either case the shareholders benefit from a growth of EPS which exceeds the rate of growth of sales. However, if sales were to fall, then EPS would fall at a rate greater than the drop in sales, again because of the leverage effect. This risk from additional borrowing must be acknowledged and explained to shareholders.

If shareholders are looking for rapid growth of earnings, it is marginally preferable to fund the investment with the loan stock issue. However the **effect** of this choice **on shareholder risk** needs to be taken into account, because Spender's financial gearing will be increased by the loan stock issue. Whether shareholders will accept the higher risk or not depends to some extent on industry and economic forecasts. If the outlook for the construction industry is good, then shareholders are likely to accept such a proposal; conversely if the future prospects look poor then the rights issue is the safer choice. The attractiveness of the higher returns from using loan stock finance needs to compensate for the marginal additional risk created by the issue, and given that the use of loan stock yields an EPS 6% greater than if the rights issue is made then it is likely that this is the case.

In addition to financial considerations, Spender Construction Inc should also take into account the **organisational aspects of the two financing alternatives**, including the speed of issue, issue costs, and prevailing stock market conditions. Rights issues will tend to be slower to arrange and complete than a loan stock issue, but rights do offer the advantage that the issue costs may be kept low as it is not a requirement (though it is usual practice) for them to be underwritten. At the same time, loan stock may be easier to sell if the stock market is volatile or on a bear run.

In conclusion, the loan stock issue should be the chosen source of funding if market forecasts indicate rising future sales and earnings. The rights issue should be the chosen source of finance if the directors believe that shareholders are highly risk averse, and would prefer to avoid any additional financial gearing, and that stock market conditions are favourable to such an issue.

(c)   **Dividend cover** is calculated by dividing the profit available to equity by the total dividend payable, and it measures the extent to which equity investors can view their dividend as being 'secure'. As the level of cover rises, so does the security of the dividend, inasmuch as equity investors can still expect there to be sufficient profit available to pay the dividend. A high dividend cover offers a reasonable certainty that dividend levels can be maintained, but it should also lead investors to question how the retained profits are being utilised. By definition, a high dividend cover implies that a large proportion of profits are being retained within the business, and unless these funds are being invested wisely, the equity investor may be better off if the cash is paid out to shareholders, who can then re-invest it elsewhere to earn a better rate of return.

For Spender Construction Inc, the forecast profit available to equity (from (d)) if the loan stock issued equals $4.889m and the dividend forecast for the year is $2m. This gives a dividend cover of:

4.889/2 = 2.44 times.

This means that over half of the profit is being retained for re-investment. If the re-investment can be expected to maintain the profit growth achieved between 20X7 and 20X8, then investors have little to worry about. If, however, Spender Construction Inc gives little indication of how it intends to use this money, then shareholders should be concerned that dividend cover is perhaps a little high.

43   ASSOCIATED INTERNATIONAL SUPPLIES CO

Key answer tips

The best starting point for part (a) is to prepare the appendix to your report. You will need to calculate all the main groups of ratios; be led by the scenario and consider why each piece of information has been provided. You can use the requirement to help structure your report. In this instance you have been asked to comment on growth, liquidity and the capacity to continue trading. These would therefore make excellent sub-headings.

Part (b) is very generic and should have been tackled before part (a). The requirement is to 'explain' and 'evaluate' so make sure you draw out the advantages and disadvantages of each source of finance as well as just identifying them should. For 8 marks you have aimed for at least four sources of finance. The highlighted words are key phrases that markers are looking for.

(a)   Analysis of company position

Associated International Supplies Co

Circulation: Associated International Supplies Co (AIS Co)

Author:

Date: xx/xx/xx

General appraisal

The first point to note is that, by most standards, the company would be regarded as small, and is therefore likely to exhibit many of the problems typical of the small company sector. Generally, small companies which are characterised by strong growth also usually exhibit substantial borrowings in relation to equity funds. It is likely, therefore, that the appropriate mix of financing for the business becomes a critical issue in the appraisal of AIS Co.

Growth and liquidity

In the five year period from 20X4 to 20X9 sales for AIS have grown by 151%. In terms of supporting the business with adequate working capital, the pressures of such growth can be substantial. Thus, in the same period we see that current assets have expanded by 54% and current liabilities by 91%. Whilst this aspect of the business will be dealt-with in more detail below, it is worthwhile questioning at this stage whether sufficient funding for working capital is available to support the growth in sales.

Whilst there has been significant growth in sales during the period, profit before tax (PBT) as a percentage of sales has actually declined from 8% to about 5%. This must call into question either the management of costs (operational or financial) or whether the company is unable to force price increases on to customers. Given the information available, the most likely source of this problem appears to relate to interest costs. Both current and non-current liabilities have increased substantially (91% and 276%, respectively) against a background of barely increased equity funding. Debt funding (both long and short term) looks to have increased (see detail below) and this will have an associated interest burden. This has an importance in relation to the sustainability of the business.

Earnings retentions do not appear sufficient to fund business growth, and hence it is clear that borrowings have been increased to deal with this problem. However, a balance must be kept in the business between its earnings capability and its capacity to service its debt commitments. Whilst PBT has increased by 53% over the period, retentions have declined by about 74%. This may be partly explained by an increased tax burden, but is obviously due mainly to excessive distributions. In other words, not enough funds are being retained in the business to support its growth or funded from increased equity issues.

The impact of excessive growth in relation to its funding base might have a severe impact on liquidity. Net current assets are not seriously out of line if a ratio of current assets to current liabilities of 1.0 (unity) is considered acceptable. However, when current assets are looked at in relation to sales a different picture emerges. The ratio was 54% in 20X4 and only 33% in 20X9. This suggests, in combination with the other information, that inventories, receivables and cash resources might be insufficient to support the volume of sales. It might be argued that this reflects greater efficiency in current asset management. This is indeed the case when receivables days are compared over the period (they declined from 99 to 61), but it is not in relation to payables days which also declined (from 88 to 67 during the period). When working capital is measured as a proportion of sales, we observe a decline from 11.4% in 20X4 to 0.5% in 20X9. This appears to be a reflection of reduced current asset investment and overdraft increases.

Because it is debt rather than equity funding that has grown, the business faces a potentially critical situation. We know that current assets consist mainly of inventory and receivables (because the business has substantial borrowings, it is unlikely to simultaneously have large cash balances) and that this is being funded by borrowing rather than retained earnings. The reason why this is the case is because the business is not generating adequate profits and it is distributing too much of post tax earnings. The outlook is for greater borrowing. The poor profit figures suggest that a critical point has been reached in terms of liquidity and solvency. This is reflected in debt/equity ratios which have increased from 2.19 in 20X4 to 4.22 in 20X9 (current and non-current liabilities used as debt and capital and reserves used as equity). Unless a capital reorganisation can take place quickly, either through injected funds or conversion of debt into equity, the business is likely to become insolvent.

Company capacity to continue trading

Given the points made above, it is unlikely that the business can continue in its current form. The trading performance is obviously very strong when measured in terms of its sales capacity and growth. This indicates a good customer base and the ability to service customer needs. The markets the company serves suggest a long-term future for its product or service.

However, it is likely that the company's cost base will be overwhelmed by interest charges, which is resulting in reduced PBT/Sales ratios over the period in spite of significant sales growth. If that is the case, it may well be that the underlying trading profitability is good. If it is not found to be good after further investigation then additional action may need to be taken. For example if low profitability is due to aggressive pricing, an investigation into alternative marketing strategies may be appropriate. In addition, given the significant growth, it may now be an appropriate time to look at the customer base and withdraw service from those customers who are either unprofitable or otherwise difficult (late payers, for example). Product mix might be usefully assessed to focus on higher-margin sales activities and to decrease effort on lower-margin activities. A business plan describing the customer base and the strategy for greater profitability will underpin any bid for a reorganisation of AIS Co's finances.

Bank support is crucial to long term survival if the debt is in the form of bank related lending. Alternative sources of finance should also be considered, particularly in the form of equity which is required to re-balance the business.

Other factors

(i)   Venture capitalists might be interested in the business because of its significant growth but poorly structured finance. An equity injection would stabilise the business' finances.

(ii)   Future projections of growth might provide a clearer picture of how to respond to the situation the business is now in.

(iii)   The maturity of the debt obligations would indicate any critical repayments that may be due.

(iv)   Comparisons with other businesses in the sector may provide some assurance as to the debt levels if high debt is a characteristic of the sector.

(v)   Investigation of possible renegotiation of the debt to ease the interest burden.

(vi)   Investigation of potential sale of the business or merger with a large partner with a view to securing a realistic equity base.

(vii)   Information on detailed trading results would enable an accurate assessment of the profitability of AIS Co.

(viii) Working capital management needs to be investigated to assess if it is being efficiently organised.

Appendix to report: Ratio calculations

Sales growth:	(3,010 – 1,200)/1,200 = 151%
Current asset growth:	(1,000 – 650)/650 = 54%
Current liability growth:	(982 – 513)/513 = 91%
Non-current liabilities growth:	(158 – 42)/42 = 276%
PBT growth:	(150 – 98)/98 = 53%
Retained earnings decline:	(65 – 17)/65 = 74%

	20X4	20X9
PBT/Sales	98/1,200 = 8%	150/3,010 = 5%
Current assets/Current liabilities	650/513 = 1.3	1,000/982 = 1.0
Current assets/Sales	650/1,200 = 54%	1,000/3,010 = 33%
Working capital/Sales	(650–513)/1,200 = 11.4%	(1,000–982)/3,010 = 0.5%
Debt/Equity	(513 + 42)/210 = 2.64	(982 + 158)/270 = 4.22
Receivables at 50% of current assets	$325,000	$500,000
Sales per day (365 days)	$3,288	$8,247
Receivables days	325,000/3,288 = 99	500,000/8,247 = 61
Payables at 25% of current liabilities	$128,000	$245,500
Cost of sales per day (365 days)	$1,452	$3,643
Payables days	128,000/1,452 = 88	245,500/3,643 = 67

(b) **General**

Funds for non-current assets would normally be long term in nature in order to match asset use with funding maturity. Moreover, if the asset is a building or other major asset which has a secondary market value, then secured lending may be arranged where lower rates of interest are accessible. In particular, specific asset financing may be available (such as for fleet cars) which may represent an efficient source of funds. In general, the finance leasing option is available and represents a significant source of flexibility to the business. Non-current assets with secondary market values may also be subject to sale and leaseback arrangements.

Long-term sources of finance would typically be either equity funds (either injections or dividend retentions), bank debt or possibly venture capital equity interests for small businesses. What would not be appropriate are loan stock, convertibles, warrants, equity public issues, and listings (with the potential exception of a small company stock market like AIM in the UK).

The most significant barrier to secure external equity funding for small firms is the lack of liquidity, or the inability to either find a market or buyer for the shares when the time arrives when the investor wishes to sell. There is evidence that small companies tend to have low gearing ratios when long-term debt finance to long-term finance plus equity is used as the measure of gearing. Moreover, a large proportion of the debt finance, in general, comes from overdrafts and short-term loans.

Sources of finance

No details are given concerning the nature of a business to comment on, and hence only general recommendations can be made. Given that non-current asset finance is required, long-term finance that is likely to be the most appropriate. Below are listed some ideas of what might be most suitable:

(i) If the non-current asset is substantial, such as a new building, or tooling for a new product, then a smaller stock market, such as the Alternative Investment Market in the UK, may be suitable. AIM is directed largely at small and growing companies who do not qualify for the main stock market. The restrictions for admission are not that binding and may suit a company such as AIS Co. In particular, there are no eligibility criteria for new entrants in terms of size, profitability or existence. By listing on AIM, a company would address the market liquidity issue of equity investments for small firms.

(ii) Venture capital may also be suitable. This would be desirable from the point of view that, whilst venture capitalists may take an equity participation, they are likely to liquidate their shareholders to the owners of the business and hence ownership dilution would not occur.

(iii) Cash or dividend retentions. This would clearly take time for major asset purchases and may not be suitable for companies that face a funding shortfall in any case (the costs required in asset purchase may simply be too big for any realistic retention timescale).

(iv) Entering a merger or partnership, or accessing 'Business Angel' funding.

(v) Leasing the asset or arranging secured loans at lower interest rates.

(vi) Possible mortgages for buildings, or specialist financing for cars (for example hire purchase, leasing).

(vii) Availability of government grants, European funding or other agency assistance.

44   GTK INC   *Walk in the footsteps of a top tutor*

Key answer tip

Both parts (a) & (b) are relatively straightforward investment appraisal calculations which shouldn't pose many problems. In part (c) it is essential that you read the requirement carefully. As you have to make a recommendation you must ensure any advantages or disadvantages you note are relevant to the scenario given. The highlighted words are key phrases that markers are looking for.

(a) Expected net present value of Proposed 1

Tutor's top tips:

It's worthwhile giving some quick consideration to the best way to layout your answer to this part of the requirement. A columnar format, like that presented here, will often be the most efficient and will reduce the amount of information you need to write more than once. This is particularly important here since your answer to part (i) will naturally lead into your answer to part (ii).

Don't forget the requirement to comment on your findings. In situation involving expected values, your comments should generally focus on the reliability of the probability estimates and the risk involved (look at the variability between the best result and the worst).

	Scenario 1	*Scenario 2*	*Scenario 3*
Number of sunny days	100	125	150
Saving ($/day)	700	700	700
Annual saving ($)	70,000	87,500	105,000
Costs	(24,000)	(24,000)	(24,000)
Net annual savings	46,000	63,500	81,000
Present value of net savings at 10%	460,000	635,000	810,000
Investment	500,000	500,000	500,000
Net present value	(40,000)	135,000	310,000
Probability	30%	60%	10%

Expected net present value = (−40,000 × 0.3) + (135,000 × 0.6) + (310,000 × 0.1) = $100,000

The ENPV is $100,000 so if the investment is evaluated on this basis, it is financially acceptable. In reaching a decision, however, the company should consider that there is a 30% chance of making a loss. This may be seen as an unacceptably high risk. Furthermore, the number of sunny days each year will not be constant, as assumed here, and may or may not be exactly 100, 125 or 150 days. It is possible the net present values of Scenarios 1 and 3 represent extremes in terms of expectations, and that the net present value of Scenario 2 may be most useful as representing the most likely outcome, even on a joint probability basis. It is also worth noting that inflation has not been taken into account and that the ever-increasing cost of energy may make the proposed investment much more financially attractive if it were factored into the analysis.

Workings

Present values must be calculated with the before-tax cost of capital of 10%, since before-tax cash flows are being evaluated here. The present value of a perpetuity is found by dividing the constant annual cash flow by the cost of capital.

Present value of net savings, Scenario 1 = 46,000/0.10 = $460,000

Present value of net savings, Scenario 2 = 63,500/0.10 = $635,000

Present value of net savings, Scenario 3 = 81,000/0.10 = $810,000

(b)   Before-tax return on capital employed of Project 2

Tutor's top tips:

The key to this part is remembering that ROCE is the only investment appraisal method that links back to profits rather than cash flows.

To do the caluclation you will need to work out both the average annual profits as the average investment. You should work out each of these in turn, being careful to adjust for things like depreciation and sunk costs.

Total cash flow over five years before advertising and depreciation = $500,000

Total depreciation over five years = 300,000 – 30,000 = $270,000

Total accounting profit over five years = 500,000 – 100,000 – 270,000 = $130,000

Average annual accounting profit = 130,000/5 = $26,000 per year

Average investment = (initial investment + scrap value)/2 = (300,000 + 30,000)/2 = $165,000

ROCE = 100 × (26,000/165,000) = 15.8%

The ROCE of Proposal 3 is marginally greater than the target level of 15%. ROCE cannot be recommended as an investment appraisal method, however, and the NPV of Proposal 3 should be calculated in order to determine whether it is financially acceptable.

Tutor's top tips:

You are asked how equity finance or traded debt might be raised and will therefore need to discuss the different methods of issuing shares (rights issue, and placing being the most suitable here) and different things to consider when issuing debt.

(c)   GTK Inc is a company with a small overdraft and no long-term debt. The $1.1 million could be raised as follows:

Equity finance

The equity financing choices available to GTK Inc are a rights issue or a placing.

Rights issue

In this method of raising new equity finance, new shares are offered to existing shareholders pro rata to their existing shareholdings, meeting the requirements of company law in terms of shareholders' pre-emptive rights. Since GTK Inc has several million dollars of shareholders' funds, it may be able to raise $1.1 million through a rights issue, but further investigation will be needed to determine if this is possible. Factors to consider in reaching a decision will include

*   the number of shareholders, the type of shareholders (institutional shareholders may be more willing to subscribe than small shareholders),

*   whether a recent rights issue has been made,

*   the recent and expected financial performance of GTK Inc, and

*   the effect of a rights issue on the company's cost of capital.

A rights issue would not necessarily disturb the existing balance of ownership and control between shareholders. Approximately half of the finance needed is for a permanent investment and the permanent nature of equity finance would match this.

Placing

This way of raising equity finance involves allocating large amounts of ordinary shares with a small number of institutional investors. Existing shareholders will need to agree to waive their pre-emptive rights for a placing to occur, as it entails issuing new shares to new shareholders. The existing balance of ownership and control will therefore be changed by a placing. Since GTK Inc is a listed company, it is likely that a significant percentage of its issued ordinary share capital will be in public hands and the effect of a placing on this fraction will need to be considered. There may be a change in shareholder expectations after the placing, depending on the extent to which institutional investors are currently represented among existing shareholders, but since the company is listed there is likely to be a significant institutional representation.

Traded debt

A new issue of traded debt could be redeemable or irredeemable, secured or unsecured, fixed rate or floating rate, and may perhaps be convertible. Deep discount bonds and zero coupon bond are also a possibility, but much rarer. The effect of an issue of debt on the company's cost of capital should also be considered.

Security

Bonds may be secured on assets in order to reduce the risk of the bond from an investor point of view. Fixed charge debt is secured on specified non-current assets, such as land or buildings, while floating charge debt is secured on all assets or on a particular class of assets. In the event of default, holders of secured debt can take action to recover their investment, for example by appointing a receiver or by enforcing the sale of particular assets.

Redemption

Irredeemable corporate debt is very rare and a new issue of traded debt by GTK Inc would be redeemable, i.e. repayable on a specified future date. The project life of two of the proposed capital investments suggests that medium-term debt would be appropriate.

Fixed rate and floating rate

Fixed rate debt gives a predictable annual interest payment and, in terms of financial risk, makes the company immune to changes in the general level of interest rates. If interest rates are currently low, GTK Inc could lock into these low rates until its new debt issue needs to be redeemed. Conversely, if interest rates are currently high and expected to fall in the future, GTK Inc could issue floating rate debt rather than fixed rate debt, in the expectation that its interest payments would decrease as interest rates fell.

Cost of capital

GTK Inc has no long-term debt and only a small overdraft. Since debt is cheaper than equity in cost of capital terms, the company could reduce its overall cost of capital by issuing traded debt. A decrease in the overall cost of capital could benefit the company and its shareholders in terms of an increase in the market value of the company, and an increase in the number of financially acceptable investment projects.

45   TFR

Key answer tips

Provided you have carefully read the details of the scenario, the calculations in part (a) should be relatively uncomplicated. Parts (b) & (c) require you to be more practical. The key element in part (b) is the implications for cash flow. An estimate of this would therefore be useful. In part (c) you must ensure you draw out the difficulties of raising additional finance rather than just going through the different sources. The highlighted words are key phrases that markers are looking for.

(a)   Income statements for TFR for the four-year period

Year	Current	Year 1	Year 2	Year 3	Year 4
	$	$	$	$	$
Sales revenue	210,000	255,000	300,000	345,000	390,000
Expenses	168,000	204,000	240,000	276,000	312,000
Net profit	42,000	51,000	60,000	69,000	78,000
Interest	2,000	11,000	8,750	6,500	4,250
Profit before tax	40,000	40,000	51,250	62,500	73,750
Tax	10,000	10,000	12,813	15,625	18,438
Profit after tax	30,000	30,000	38,438	46,875	55,313
Finance					
Dividend	15,000	15,000	19,219	23,438	27,656
Retained profit	15,000	15,000	19,219	23,438	27,656
Equity finance	200,000	215,000	234,219	257,656	285,313
Debt finance	Nil	75,000	50,000	25,000	Nil
Ratios					
Interest cover (times)	21.0	4.6	6.9	10.6	18.4
Debt/equity (%)	Nil	35	21	10	Nil
Return on equity (%)	15	14	16	18	19
ROCE (%)	21	18	21	24	27
ROCE (%)*	19	16	20	23	26

*Including the existing and continuing overdraft in capital employed.

Workings

Annual interest (assuming the continuing overdraft is maintained at the current level)

Year 1 interest payment = $100,000 \times 0.09 = 9,000 + 2,000 = \$11,000$

Year 2 interest payment = $75,000 \times 0.09 = 6,750 + 2,000 = \$8,750$

Year 3 interest payment = $50,000 \times 0.09 = 4,500 + 2,000 = \$5,500$

Year 4 interest payment = $25,000 \times 0.09 = 2,250 + 2,000 = \$4,250$

(b)   Financial implications for TFR of accepting bank loan

A key consideration is whether TFR will be able to meet the annual payments of interest and capital. It is assumed, in preparing a cash flow forecast, that there is no difference between profit and cash, and that inflation can be ignored. The annual cash surplus after meeting interest and tax payments is therefore assumed to be equal to retained profit.

Year	1	2	3	4
Net change in equity (retained profit)	15,000	19,219	23,438	27,656
Capital repayment	25,000	25,000	25,000	25,000
Net cash flow	(10,000)	(5,781)	(1,563)	2,656

TFR is clearly not able to meet the annual capital repayments. In order to do so, it will need to change the dividend policy it appears to have maintained for several years of paying out a constant proportion of profit after tax as dividends. One possible course of action is to cut its dividend now and then increase it in the future as profitability allows. Since TFR is owner-managed, a change in dividend policy may be possible, depending of course on the extent to which the owner or owners rely on dividend income. The annual cash flow shortfall is less than the annual dividend payment, so a change in dividend policy would probably allow the loan to be accepted.

Year	1	2	3	4
Profit after tax	30,000	38,438	46,875	55,313
Capital repayment	25,000	25,000	25,000	25,000
Available funds	5,000	13,438	21,875	30,313

It is useful to consider key financial information after the loan has been paid off, i.e. in year 5, assuming that no further growth in sales revenue occurs after the fourth year:

Year	Year 5
Sales revenue	390,000
Expenses	312,000
Net profit	78,000
Interest	2,000
Profit before tax	76,000
Tax	19,000
Profit after tax	57,000
Dividend	28,500
Retained profit	28,500
Equity finance	313,813
Debt finance	Nil
Interest cover (times)	39
Debt/equity (%)	Nil
Return on equity (%)	18
ROCE (%)	25
ROCE (%)*	23

*Including the existing and continuing overdraft in capital employed.

The effect on financial risk of taking on the loan can be examined. If the interest and capital payments are kept up, financial risk will be lower than its current level at the end of four years, all things being equal. Interest cover increases from its current level after five years, from 21 times to 39 times, but is on the low side at the end of the first year (4.6 times), although an improved level is reached at the end of the second year (6.9 times), with further increases in subsequent years. The debt/equity ratio peaks at 35% at the end of the first year and falls rapidly thereafter, at no time looking dangerous, and TFR returns to its current ungeared position after five years. The bank, as provider of debt finance, would be interested in the trend in these ratios, as well as in the ongoing cash flow position.

Both return on equity (ROE) and return on capital employed (ROCE) improve with growth in sales revenue, but are lower than current levels in the first and second years following taking on the loan. At the end of five years ROE has improved to 18% from 15% and ROCE from 19% to 23%. Interest and capital payments would not increase with inflation.

Provided TFR can meet the interest and capital repayments, business expansion using debt finance may be financially feasible. However, this analysis has ignored any potential pressure for reduction or repayment of the overdraft. An average overdraft of $20,000 is quite large for a company with an annual sales revenue of $210,000 and therefore cannot be ignored in any assessment of financial risk. TFR may therefore consider asking for a longer repayment period, with lower annual capital repayments, if it plans to reduce the size of the overdraft or if it is concerned about future cash flow problems.

(c)   TFR is owner-managed and profitable, and financed by equity apart from its large overdraft. It is currently seeking a bank loan in order to finance an expansion of business.

Equity finance

The owner could inject new equity finance himself but his personal financial situation may make this impossible. There are unlikely to be any wealthy individuals willing to invest in his company because there are likely to be more attractive investments elsewhere. Investing in a UK pension fund, for example, carries a tax incentive in that the UK government increases any contributions by the amount of income tax paid. There is therefore a disincentive to invest in the shares of a small company which may be difficult to sell in the future unless another investor can be found who wishes to buy the shares.

However, there is in the UK a Business Angel network which can bring potential investors and small companies together, with the added bonus that the Business Angel may have expertise and experience to offer that could be useful in a small company situation. The owner of TFR may wish to look into this possibility.

There is also a UK government initiative called the Enterprise Investment Scheme, which is of potential benefit to trading companies rather than service companies. The government offers tax advantages in terms of income tax and capital gains tax in order to encourage investment by individuals in the ordinary shares of small companies.

A further UK government scheme offers tax advantages to Venture Capital Trusts, who are required to invest a large part of their funds in the ordinary shares of small companies.

Other government assistance schemes

A range of other UK and EU government assistance schemes exist but almost all of these are targeted towards companies in particular geographic locations, or within particular ranges in terms of number of employees, or with particular funding requirements, for example training.

Debt finance

Small companies are faced with a risk-averse attitude from banks when they seek to raise debt finance. Banks tend to ask for personal guarantees from owners and will set interest rates at higher levels than those charged to larger companies. TFR has non-current assets which are much greater in terms of value than the amount of its overdraft and so the company may be able to offer these as security for a loan. In fact, it is almost certain that the loan under consideration would be secured in some way. Many small companies, particularly service companies, may not be in a position to offer other than personal guarantees.

Examiner's note: Candidates will be given credit for providing local examples of financial assistance available to small firms seeking additional finance.

COST OF CAPITAL

46   FLEET CO

Key answer tips

A solid understanding of the basics of calculating the weighted average cost of capital will be sufficient to answer part (a). Parts (b) & (c) represent more of a challenge and require you to be competent in gearing and ungearing betas. Part (d) could have been attempted first as it gave an opportunity to gain some easy marks.

(a) (1) K_e – DVM with growth

$$K_e = \frac{Do \times (1+g)}{Po} + g$$

$$K_e = \frac{10.50(1.11)}{200} + 0.11 = 16.83\%$$

Calculation of growth in dividends: $\left(\frac{10.5}{6.9}\right)^{\left(\frac{1}{4}\right)} - 1 = 0.11$

(2) $K_d(1-t)$ –irredeemable debt

$K_d(1-t) = 8 \times (1-0.3)/75 = 7.47\%$

(3) $K_d(1-t)$ – bank term loan

10% (1- 0.3) = 7%

(4)   Market values

		£m	£m
Equity	250 ÷ 0.25 × £2 =		2,000
Debt			
Fixed	600m × 75/100 =	450	
Term loan	300m =	300	750
		―	―
E + D			2,750

(4)   WACC

$$\text{WACC} = 16.83\% \times \frac{2{,}000}{2{,}750} + 7.47\% \times \frac{450}{2{,}750} + 7\% \times \frac{300}{2{,}750} = 14.23\%$$

(b)   Foxes plc

The current beta equity of Foxes plc is 1.20.

Hence its beta asset is (assuming debt is risk free):

$$\text{Beta asset} = \text{beta equity} \times \frac{V_E}{V_E + V_D(1-t)}$$

$$= 1.20 \times \frac{80}{80 + 20(1 - 0.30)}$$

$$= 1.02$$

Given that Foxes has 65% of its business in the leisure sector and 35% in publishing, this total beta asset will be the weighted average of the individual beta assets of the individual industries.

i.e. Foxes $ß_a$ = (0.65 × Leisure $ß_a$) + (0.35 × Publishing $ß_a$)

Therefore it is first necessary to calculate the beta asset of the leisure industry, then use the formula to find the balancing figure for the publishing industry.

Leisure industry

$$\text{Beta asset} = \text{beta equity} \times \frac{V_E}{V_E + V_D(1-t)}$$

$$= 1.1 \times \frac{70}{70 + 30(1 - 0.30)} = 0.85$$

Thus,

Foxes $ß_a$ = (0.65 × Leisure $ß_a$) + (0.35 × Publishing $ß_a$)

1.02   = (0.65 × 0.85) + (0.35 × Publishing $ß_a$)

So, Publishing $ßa$ = 1.34

Publishing industry

Given that this is a beta asset (ungeared) we now need to gear it up to reflect the industry average D:E gearing of 40:60

$$\text{Beta asset} = \text{beta equity} \times \frac{V_E}{V_E + V_D(1-t)}$$

$$1.34 = \text{beta equity} \times \frac{60}{60 + 40(1 - 0.30)}$$

So, beta equity = 1.97 for the publishing industry.

(c)   Leisure project

Assuming the systematic risk of the leisure industry is accurately reflected by the beta equity of other leisure providers, this risk may be estimated by ungearing the equity beta of the other leisure providers and regearing it to take into account the different financial risk of Foxes plc.

In part (b) above we found that the ungeared beta asset of the leisure industry was 0.85.

Regearing this to reflect the gearing of Foxes plc gives:

$$\beta \text{ asset} = \beta \text{ equity} \times \frac{V_E}{V_E + V_D(1-t)}$$

$$0.85 = \beta \text{ equity} \times \frac{80}{80 + 20(1 - 0.30)}$$

$$0.85 = \beta \text{ equity} \times 0.85$$

$$\beta \text{ equity} = \frac{0.85}{0.85} = 1.00$$

So, using CAPM, $K_e = 10\%$ (= R_m as the beta is 1)

$K_d(1 - t) = 6\%$

WACC = $10\% \times 0.8 + 6\% \times 0.2 = 9.20\%$

(d)   If Foxes plc had changed its gearing when taking on the new project, the Adjusted Present Value ("APV") method should have been used to appraise whether the project, and the associated financing, were acceptable.

The APV of a project is found by taking the sum of the following two elements:

(1)   Base case NPV – the project cash flows are discounted at a cost of equity which reflects the business risk of the project. In this part of the APV calculation we ignore the firm's financing completely.

(2)   Present Value of financing side effects – raising new debt finance would have enabled Foxes plc to claim extra tax relief on debt interest, and may have incurred issue costs. The present value of these costs and benefits is computed using a risk free discount rate (to reflect the low risk associated with these cashflows).

47 KFP CO

Key answer tips

This is an excellent example of the examiner's style and in particular the way he combines two or more areas of the syllabus into one question. Part (c) should be fairly straightforward, just drawing on the basic theories of gearing. Don't forget to address the final sentence though – what will these theories mean if KFP were to issue further debt finance.

(a) Weighted average cost of capital (WACC) calculation

Cost of equity of KFP Co = 4·0 + (1·2 x (10·5 − 4·0)) = 4·0 + 7·8 = 11·8% using the capital asset pricing model

To calculate the after-tax cost of debt, linear interpolation is needed

After-tax interest payment = 100 x 0·07 x (1 − 0·3) = $4·90

Year	Cash flow	$	10% discount	PV ($)	5% discount	PV ($)
0	Market value	(94·74)	1·000	(94·74)	1·000	(94·74)
1 to 7	Interest	4·9	4·868	23·85	5·786	28·35
7	Redemption	100	0·513	51·30	0·711	71·10
				(19·59)		4·71

After-tax cost of debt = 5 + ((10 − 5) x 4·71)/(4·71 + 19·59) = 5 + 1·0 = 6·0%

Number of shares issued by KFP Co = $15m/0·5 = 30 million shares

Market value of equity = 30m x 4·2 = $126 million

Market value of bonds issued by KFP Co = 15m x 94·74/100 = $14·211 million

Total value of company = 126 + 14·211 = $140·211 million

WACC = ((11·8 x 126) + (6·0 x 14·211))/140·211 = 11·2%

(b) (i) Price/earnings ratio method

Earnings per share of NGN = 80c per share

Price/earnings ratio of KFP Co = 8

Share price of NGN = 80 x 8 = 640c or $6·40

Number of ordinary shares of NGN = 5/0·5 = 10 million shares

Value of NGN = 6·40 x 10m = $64 million

However, it can be argued that a reduction in the applied price/earnings ratio is needed as NGN is unlisted and therefore its shares are more difficult to buy and sell than those of a listed company such as KFP Co. If we reduce the applied price/earnings ratio by 10% (other similar percentage reductions would be acceptable), it becomes 7·2 times and the value of NGN would be (80/100) x 7·2 x 10m = $57·6 million

(ii)   Dividend growth model

Dividend per share of NGN = 80c x 0·45 = 36c per share

Since the payout ratio has been maintained for several years, recent earnings growth is the same as recent dividend growth, i.e. 4·5%. Assuming that this dividend growth continues in the future, the future dividend growth rate will be 4·5%.

Share price from dividend growth model = (36 x 1·045)/ (0·12 – 0·045) = 502c or $5·02 Value of NGN = 5·02 x 10m = $50·2 million

(c)   A discussion of capital structure could start from recognising that equity is more expensive than debt because of the relative risk of the two sources of finance. Equity is riskier than debt and so equity is more expensive than debt. This does not depend on the tax efficiency of debt, since we can assume that no taxes exist. We can also assume that as a company gears up, it replaces equity with debt. This means that the company's capital base remains constant and its weighted average cost of capital (WACC) is not affected by increasing investment.

The traditional view of capital structure assumes a non-linear relationship between the cost of equity and financial risk. As a company gears up, there is initially very little increase in the cost of equity and the WACC decreases because the cost of debt is less than the cost of equity. A point is reached, however, where the cost of equity rises at a rate that exceeds the reduction effect of cheaper debt and the WACC starts to increase. In the traditional view, therefore, a minimum WACC exists and, as a result, a maximum value of the company arises.

Modigliani and Miller assumed a perfect capital market and a linear relationship between the cost of equity and financial risk. They argued that, as a company geared up, the cost of equity increased at a rate that exactly cancelled out the reduction effect of cheaper debt. WACC was therefore constant at all levels of gearing and no optimal capital structure, where the value of the company was at a maximum, could be found.

It was argued that the no-tax assumption made by Modigliani and Miller was unrealistic, since in the real world interest payments were an allowable expense in calculating taxable profit and so the effective cost of debt was reduced by its tax efficiency. They revised their model to include this tax effect and showed that, as a result, the WACC decreased in a linear fashion as a company geared up. The value of the company increased by the value of the 'tax shield' and an optimal capital structure would result by gearing up as much as possible.

It was pointed out that market imperfections associated with high levels of gearing, such as bankruptcy risk and agency costs, would limit the extent to which a company could gear up. In practice, therefore, it appears that companies can reduce their WACC by increasing gearing, while avoiding the financial distress that can arise at high levels of gearing.

It has further been suggested that companies choose the source of finance which, for one reason or another, is easiest for them to access (pecking order theory). This results in an initial preference for retained earnings, followed by a preference for debt before turning to equity. The view suggests that companies may not in practice seek to minimise their WACC (and consequently maximise company value and shareholder wealth).

Turning to the suggestion that debt could be used to finance a cash bid for NGN, the current and post acquisition capital structures and their relative gearing levels should be considered, as well as the amount of debt finance that would be needed. Earlier calculations suggest that at least $58m would be needed, ignoring any premium paid to persuade target company shareholders to sell their shares. The current debt/equity ratio of KFP Co is 60% (15m/25m). The debt of the company would increase by $58m in order to finance the bid and by a further $20m after the acquisition, due to taking on the existing debt of NGN, giving a total of $93m. Ignoring other factors, the gearing would increase to 372% (93m/25m). KFP Co would need to consider how it could service this dangerously high level of gearing and deal with the significant risk of bankruptcy that it might create. It would also need to consider whether the benefits arising from the acquisition of NGN would compensate for the significant increase in financial risk and bankruptcy risk resulting from using debt finance.

64m — Debt

$$\frac{D'}{E} = \frac{15 + 20 + 64}{25}$$

= 396%

Current KFP

$$\frac{D}{E} = \frac{15}{25} = 60\%$$

ACCA marking scheme		Marks	
(a)	Cost of equity calculation	2	
	Correct use of taxation rate	1	
	Cost of debt calculation	3	
	Market value of equity	1	
	Market value of debt	1	
	WACC calculation	2	
			10 *10.*
(b)	Price/earnings value of company	2	
	Current dividend per share	1	
	Dividend growth model value of company	3	
			6 *4*
(c)	Traditional view of capital structure	1 - 2	
	Miller & Modigliani and capital structure	2 - 3	
	Market imperfections	1 - 2	
	Other relevant discussion	1 - 2	
	Comment on debt finance for cash offer	2 - 3	
		Maximum	9
Total			25

Examiner's comments

In part (a), candidates were asked to calculate the weighted average cost of capital (WACC) of a company. Many candidates gained full marks for their calculations. Some answers lost marks because they included the debt of the target company in their calculation. The WACC of one company is clearly independent of the debt of another company.

Information provided in the question enabled the cost of equity to be found using the CAPM formula. Some candidates ignored this information and attempted to use the dividend growth model instead. Other candidates ungeared and regeared the equity beta of the company, even though this was unnecessary since the equity beta was not from a proxy company. Most candidates calculated the cost of equity correctly.

The cost of debt had to be calculated using linear interpolation and most answers did this more or less successfully. Where errors arose, these involved using a shorter bond maturity than that in the question (7 years), exchanging the market value and the par value in the interpolation calculation, omitting to make the interest payment after-tax, and mixing total values and per share values in the same calculation.

Most candidates correctly used market values as weights.

Part (b) called for the calculation of the value of the target company using the PER (price/earnings ratio) method and the dividend growth model (DGM). These were not complicated calculations, although it was necessary to assume with the DGM that the dividend growth rate was the same as the earnings per share growth rate given in the question. This was a reasonable assumption, as the earnings per share growth rate and the dividend payout ratio had both been constant for several years.

Even though the question gave both the earnings per share (EPS) of the target company and an instruction to use the PER provided, some candidates made life difficult for themselves by doing something other than multiplying the earnings per share by the PER. The most common error was using the retained earnings of the target company instead of the EPS provided. Another common error was trying to calculate a PER value, rather than using the one given.

Many candidates had difficulty in calculating the dividend per share for using in the DGM. Since the target company EPS and payout ratio were provided in the question, this can only be explained by a lack of understanding of the payout ratio.

Part (c) called for a discussion of the relationship between WACC and the capital structure of a company. Some candidates incorrectly discussed the circumstances under which WACC could be used in investment appraisal, when in fact the question was asking for a discussion of optimal capital structure theory. Better answers looked at the traditional view, the views of Miller and Modigliani, and the effect on their views of market imperfections such as bankruptcy risk and the costs of financial distress. An optimal capital structure is one that gives a minimum WACC.

This part of the question asked candidates to comment on the use of debt to finance the acquisition. Some answers were very general in nature, discussing the attractions of debt as a source of finance. Better answers calculated the current gearing of the bidding company and then considered the effect on that gearing of adding debt equal to the value of the target company calculated earlier.

48   BURSE CO *Walk in the footsteps of a top tutor*

Key answer tips

This question is a good example of the typical style of the current F9 examiner. The layout is very straightforward with all facts being clearly presented. Parts (b) & (c) are both discussional and between them, account for 52% of the available marks. As they do not rely on the calculations in part (a), they should be attempted first.

The key learning point from this question is the importance of being organised. By utilising a summary table and noting assumptions as you go along, you save precious time not having to search for information or rack your brain for something when it just won't come to you. The highlighted words are key phrases that markers are looking for.

Tutor's top tips:

In part (a) you are required to calculated the weighted average cost of capital and state any assumptions you make, don't forget to do the latter. It's easiest if you jot down any thoughts you have as you go along.

You should start by drawing out a table listing all the different sources of finance down the left hand side. Your table should have two further columns for you to enter the cost and market value of each type of finance as you calculate it. A quick read of the scenario should therefore give you a table as follows:

	Cost (%)	Market value
Equity		
7% convertible debt		
8% bank loan		
Total		

Now you must work through each source of finance in turn, working out both the cost and market value in order to populate your table.

The bank loan is probably the easiest to start with. The cost is simply the bank's interest rate adjusted for tax. Since the bank loan is not traded, the market value is the same as the book value. Fill these results into your table.

Now move on to equity. To work out the cost of equity you will either need to apply the dividend valuation model or alternatively, use CAPM. Given the information supplied in the question, it is clear that CAPM is the appropriate method here. The scenario informs you of an equity risk premium of 6.5%. This is a term that you may not have seen before but don't let that throw you. Think about the different elements of a CAPM calculation and consider what information you have and what you don't have. This should reveal that you don't have the average market return and will therefore need to use the information on the risk premium to calculate it. When you have an answer for cost and market value, fill in your table.

The convertible loan stock is slightly trickier although don't let this worry you. The key is to remember that the cost of convertible debt is calculated just like the cost of redeemable debt but with an extra step. Before you can work out the cost, you must first calculate whether the debt is likely to be converted or not.

When you've looked at all of the different sources, your table should be fully populated. You now have all the information you need to be able to calculate the overall WACC.

Hopefully, you've remembered to jot down any ideas on assumptions implicit in your work. Note these down underneath, and add a few more by considering the general assumptions of both WACC calculations and the CAPM. Make sure you don't overlap with the points you've made in parts (b) or (c).

(a)   Calculation of weighted average cost of capital (WACC)

Cost of equity

Cost of equity using capital asset pricing model = $4.7 + (1.2 \times 6.5) = 12.5\%$

Cost of convertible debt

Annual after-tax interest payment = $7 \times (1 - 0.3) = \$4.90$ per bond
Share price in six years' time = $5.50 \times 1.066 = \$7.80$
Conversion value = $7.80 \times 15 = \$117.00$ per bond
Conversion appears likely, since the conversion value is much greater than par value.

The future cash flows to be discounted are therefore six years of after-tax interest payments and the conversion value received in year 6:

Year	Cash flow	$	10% DF	PV ($)	5% DF	PV ($)
0	market value	(107·11)	1·000	(107·11)	1·000	(107·11)
1–6	interest	4·9	4·355	21·34	5·076	24·87
6	conversion	117·00	0·564	66·00	0·746	87·28
				(19·77)		5·04

Using linear interpolation, after-tax cost of debt = $5 + [(5 \times 5.04)/(5.04 + 19.77)] = 6.0\%$.

(Note that other after-tax costs of debt will arise if different discount rates are used in the linear interpolation calculation.)

We can confirm that conversion is likely and implied by the current market price of $107·11 by noting that the floor value of the convertible debt at an after-tax cost of debt of 6% is $93·13 ($4.9 \times 6.210 + 100 \times 0.627$).

Cost of bank loan

After-tax interest rate = $8 \times (1 - 0.3) = 5.6\%$

This can be used as the cost of debt for the bank loan.

An alternative would be to use the after-tax cost of debt of ordinary (e.g. not convertible) traded debt, but that is not available here.

Market values

Market value of equity = $20m \times 5.50 = \$110$ million
Market value of convertible debt = $29m \times 107.11/100 = \$31.06$ million
Book value of bank loan = $2m
Total market value = $110 + 31.06 + 2 = \$143.06$ million

WACC = $[(12.5 \times 110) + (6.0 \times 31.06) + (5.6 \times 2)]/143.06 = 11.0\%$

Tutor's top tips:

The specific requirement in both parts (b) & (c) is to 'discuss'. This would imply a mark allocation of around 2 marks per relevant point discussed. You should therefore aim for between 3 or 4 points in each part.

Discuss the circumstance in which WACC can be used in investment appraisal.

(b) The weighted average cost of capital (WACC) can be used as a discount rate in investment appraisal provided that the risks of the investment project being evaluated are similar to the current risks of the investing company. The WACC would then reflect these risks and represent the average return required as compensation for these risks.

WACC can be used in investment appraisal provided that the business risk of the proposed investment is similar to the business risk of existing operations. Essentially this means that WACC can be used to evaluate an expansion of existing business. If the business risk of the investment project is different from the business risk of existing operations, a project specific discount rate that reflects the business risk of the investment project should be considered. The capital asset pricing model (CAPM) can be used to derive such a project-specific discount rate.

WACC can be used in investment appraisal provided that the financial risk of the proposed investment is similar to the financial risk of existing operations. This means that financing for the project should be raised in proportions that broadly preserve the capital structure of the investing company. If this is not the case, an investment appraisal method called adjusted present value (APV) should be used. Alternatively, the CAPM-derived project-specific cost of capital can be adjusted to reflect the financial risk of the project financing.

A third constraint on using WACC in investment appraisal is that the proposed investment should be small in comparison with the size of the company. If this were not the case, the scale of the investment project could cause a change to occur in the perceived risk of the investing company, making the existing WACC an inappropriate discount rate.

(c) The dividend growth model has several difficulties attendant on its use as a way of estimating the cost of equity. For example, the model assumes that the future dividend growth rate is constant in perpetuity, an assumption that is not supported by the way that dividends change in practice. Each dividend paid by a company is the result of a dividend decision by managers, who will consider, but not be bound by, the dividends paid in previous periods. Estimating the future dividend growth rate is also very difficult. Historical dividend trends are usually analysed and on the somewhat risky assumption that the future will repeat the past, the historic dividend growth rate is used as a substitute for the future dividend growth rate. The model also assumes that business risk, and hence business operations and the cost of equity, are constant in future periods, but reality shows us that companies, their business operations and their economic environment are subject to constant change. Perhaps the one certain thing about the future is its uncertainty.

It is sometimes said that the dividend growth model does not consider risk, but risk is implicit in the share price used by the model to calculate the cost of equity. A moment's thought will indicate that share prices fall as risk increases, indicating that increasing risk will lead to an increasing cost of equity. What is certainly true is that the dividend growth model does not consider risk explicitly in the same way as the capital asset pricing model (CAPM). Here, all investors are assumed to hold diversified portfolios and as a result only seek compensation (return) for the systematic risk of an investment. The CAPM represent the required rate of return (i.e. the cost of equity) as the sum of the risk-free rate of return and a risk premium reflecting the systematic risk of an individual company relative to the systematic risk of the stock market as a whole. This risk premium is the product of the company's equity beta and the equity risk premium. The CAPM therefore tells us what the cost of equity should be, given an individual company's level of systematic risk.

The individual components of the CAPM (the risk-free rate of return, the equity risk premium and the equity beta) are found by empirical research and so the CAPM gives rise to a much smaller degree of uncertainty than that attached to the future dividend growth rate in the dividend growth model. For this reason, it is usually suggested that the CAPM offers a better estimate of the cost of equity than the dividend growth model.

ACCA marking scheme		Marks
(a)	Calculation of cost of equity	2
	Calculation of cost of convertible debt	5
	Calculation of cost of bank loan	1
	Calculation of market values	2
	Calculation of WACC	2
		12
(b)	Discussion of business risk	2–3
	Discussion of financial risk	1–2
	Discussion of other relevant factors	1–2
	Maximum	6
(c)	Discussion of dividend growth model	2–3
	Discussion of capital asset pricing model	2–3
	Conclusion	1–2
	Maximum	7
	Total	25

Examiner's comments

In part (a), candidates were asked to calculate the weighted average cost of capital (WACC) of a company which was financed by equity (ordinary shares), a bank loan and convertible bonds. Answers to this part of the question were of variable quality.

The cost of equity had to be calculated using the capital asset pricing model (CAPM) because there was insufficient data in the question to use the dividend growth model. The risk-free rate of return, the equity beta and the equity risk premium were given, and so the cost of equity could be calculated from the CAPM formula (provided in the formulae sheet). A common error was to confuse the equity risk premium with the return on the market, resulting in a cost of equity less than the cost of debt. Such a result is inconsistent with the risk-return hierarchy.

Many candidates ignored the bank loan, or assumed that it was not relevant, and lost credit as a result.

Finding the cost of debt of the convertible bonds proved to be a challenge for many candidates. Some candidates stated simply that they assumed the bonds were to be redeemed rather than converted and lost marks as a result, even if they calculated correctly the cost of debt of the bond with redemption after eight years. The correct approach was to calculate that conversion was likely to occur, and then calculate the cost of debt using the current market value, the after-tax interest rate, the conversion value after six years and linear interpolation. Students gained credit for any parts of this evaluation that were carried out correctly

The costs of the individual sources of finance were then weighted on a market value basis and added to give the WACC. Many candidates were able to calculate market weights correctly, although some chose to ignore the current bond market price and calculate a market price based on the present value of the conversion value. The WACC is, of course, a percentage value and not a monetary amount.

Credit was given where method was correct but calculation errors were made.

Part (b) asked candidates to discuss the circumstances under which WACC can be used in investment appraisal. Some candidates discussed correctly the dependence of the WACC on the current capital structure and business operations, and therefore on the current financial risk and business risk, of the company, linking this with using the WACC as a discount rate in appraisal of investments that did not affect materially the current financial risk and business risk.

Candidates who were not aware of these restrictions on the use of the WACC in investment appraisal tended to discuss how the WACC is calculated, or to suggest that WACC could be used if a company had debt in its capital structure. Credit could also have been gained here through discussing risk-adjusted discount rates and the link between project-specific discount rates and the WACC.

Part (c) required candidates to discuss whether the CAPM or the dividend growth model (DGM) offered the better estimate of cost of equity. In order to answer this question, candidates had to have an understanding of the assumptions underlying the two models and the extent to which these assumptions could be challenged as being unrealistic or inappropriate. Weaker answers simply outlined the two models and their constituent variables. Better answers compared and contrasted the two models, and argued for the superiority of the CAPM.

49 CAPITAL STRUCTURE STRATEGY

Key answer tips

This is a broad question and a number of different approaches are possible. While it is important that the answer is underpinned by appropriate theoretical knowledge the approach should be practical and in a format which is appropriate for a briefing document for a Board of Directors. The highlighted words are key phrases that markers are looking for.

(a)   Briefing document on capital structure strategy

From a corporate perspective there are two vital questions:

- Can the value of a company, and hence shareholder wealth, be increased by varying the capital structure?

- What effect will capital structure have on risk?

    If value can be created by a sensible choice of capital structure then companies should try to achieve an optimal, or almost optimal, capital mix, as long as this mix does not have detrimental effects on other aspects of the company's activities.

    Evidence on the importance of capital structure to a company's value is not conclusive. There is general agreement that, as long as a company is in a tax paying position, the use of debt can reduce the overall cost of capital due to the interest on debt being a tax allowable expense in almost all countries. This was suggested by two Nobel prize winning economists, Miller and Modigliani. However, high levels of debt also bring problems, and companies with very high gearing are susceptible to various forms of risk, sometimes known as the costs of financial distress. This might include the loss of cash flows because customers and suppliers are worried about the financial stability and viability of the company and move business elsewhere or impose less favourable trading terms, or even extra costs that would exist (payments to receivers etc.) if the company was to go out of business.

A common perception about capital structure is that as capital gearing is increased the weighted average cost of capital falls at first. However, beyond a certain level of gearing the risk to both providers of debt and equity finance increases, and the return demanded by them to compensate for this risk also increases, leading to an increase in the weighted average cost of capital. There is a trade-off between the value created by additional tax relief on debt and the costs of financial distress. Overall, there is therefore an optimal capital structure, which will vary between companies and will depend upon factors such as the nature of the company's activities, realisable value of assets, business risk etc. According to the theory, companies with many tangible assets should have relatively high gearing, companies with high growth, or that are heavily dependant on R&D or advertising would have relatively low gearing.

The impact of personal taxation on the capital structure decision is less clear, although investors are undoubtedly interested in after tax returns. If personal tax treatment differs on different types of capital, then investors may have a preference for the most tax efficient type of capital.

Not all companies behave as if there is an optimal capital structure, and on average, in countries such as the UK and USA, the average capital gearing is lower than might be expected if companies were trying to achieve an optimal structure. It must however be remembered that moving from one capital structure to another cannot take place overnight. The cost of debt, via interest rates, and the cost of equity, can change quite quickly. It is therefore not surprising that companies do not appear to be at an optimal level.

Where no optimal level appears to be sought by a company, there are several suggested strategies with respect to capital structure. Among the most popular is the pecking order theory, which is based upon information asymmetry, the fact that managers have better information about their company than the company's shareholders. This leads to a company preferring internal finance to external finance, and only using external finance in order to undertake wealth creating (positive NPV) investments. Companies use the safest sources of finance first.

(1)   Internal funds (including selling marketable securities)
(2)   Debt
(3)   Equity

The amount of external finance used depends upon the amount of investment compared with the amount of internal funds, and the resultant capital structure reflects the relative balance of investment and available internal funds.

Another view is that capital structure is strongly influenced by managerial behaviour. There are potential conflicts of objectives between owners and managers (agency problems). Capital structure will be influenced by senior managers' personal objectives, attitudes to risk, compensation schemes and availability of alternative employment. A risk averse manager seeking security may use relatively little debt.

Free cash flow (cash flow available after replacement investment) is sometimes perceived to be used by managers for unwise acquisitions/investments which satisfy their personal objectives, rather than returning it to shareholders. Many such managerial/agency aspects may influence capital structure, and this does not give clear guidance as to capital structure strategy.

No matter what the conclusion about the impact of capital structure on cash flows it is likely that some financing packages may be more highly regarded by investors than others. For example, securities designed to meet the needs of certain types of investor (zero coupon bonds etc), securities that are more liquid, securities with lower transactions costs, and securities which reduce conflict between parties concerned with the company, especially shareholders, managers and the providers of debt.

Conclusion

It is likely that the choice of capital structure can directly affect cash flows and shareholder wealth, but too high a level of gearing will increase risk. The impact on cash flows and corporate value of the capital structure decision is far less than the impact of capital investment decisions.

(b)

Tutorial note:

Whenever you are given a scenario to work with, try to relate as many of your points as possible to the circumstances given.

REPORT

To: The directors of Gadus Inc

From: A Consultant

Date: Today

Subject: Future financing options

Introduction

This report has been prepared to advise on future financing options.

Factors to consider

In considering whether a rights issue or loan stock should be used, the following factors need to be taken into account.

- *Cost of capital* – the theoretical cost of the loan stock is lower than for the shares. This is because loan stock is a lower risk to investors and also because the company receives tax relief on loan stock interest.

- *Gearing* – as mentioned above, debt is cheaper than equity, so the introduction of debt (i.e. increasing gearing) should reduce the overall cost of finance to the firm. However, the introduction of debt will increase the risks faced by shareholders and so will increase their required return. The net effect has been subject to debate (see answer to part (a)) but it is generally agreed that remaining all-equity financed is unlikely to be optimal.

- *Issue costs* – it will probably cost less to issue the loan stock than the rights issue.

- *Cash flow* – equity has the advantage of greater flexibility with respect to cash payments as dividends can be cut if project cash inflows fall. In this case the new long-term contract should give fairly certain cash inflows, so flexibility is not a problem.

- *Duration* – the project is a long-term investment. Both methods of finance are also long-term, so both give a good match.

- *Control* – the loan stock will not affect the control of the Gadus family. Nor will the rights issue, provided that they can afford to take up their rights. This could be a problem, given that for every two shares worth $11 each they have to subscribe another $8. This is a significant amount; many family members may prefer to sell their rights.

- *Security* – security will have to be offered for the loan stock to avoid having to offer high interest rates. The new warehouse could comprise part of the security but other buildings and fishing vessels may also have to be included. Lenders are unlikely to consider fishing vessels as good security.

- *Marketability* – given that the loan stock is irredeemable, the only way investors can get their money back is to sell them. The likely marketability of the debt needs to be investigated to see if investors will be deterred by this.

Conclusion

The loan stock appears the more attractive option as they should reduce the company's financing costs and will not compromise Gadus family control. The long-term contract should ensure that repayment schedules can be met. The only main concern is over the adequacy of assets for security.

50 GM CO

Key answer tips

Both parts (a) & (c) should be relatively straightforward. Part (b) is slightly more challenging although a basic knowledge of gearing and ungearing betas, together with the formula provided in the exam, will be sufficient to gain most of the marks available. The highlighted words are key phrases that markers are looking for.

(a)   Calculation of weighted average cost of capital

Market values

Market value of equity = $\dfrac{\$225m}{\$0.50}$ × $3.76 = $1,692 million

Market value of 14% loan notes = 75m (110/100) = $82.5 million

Market value of 9% bank loan = book value = $250 million

Total market value = 1,692m + 82.5 + 250 = $2,024.5 million

Cost of equity

Using CAPM = 0.07 + 1.2(0.135 – 0.07) = 0.148 (14.8%)

Cost of loan notes

Annual after tax interest payments = 14 × (1 – 0.3) = 9.80

Time	Description	Cash flow	DF 5%	PV	DF 10%	PV
T0	Market value	(110)	1	(110)	1	(110)
T1-5	Interest (1-T)	9.80	4.329	42.42	3.791	37.15
T5	Redemption	100	0.784	78.40	0.621	62.10
				10.82		(10.75)

$$IRR = 5\% + \frac{10.82}{10.82 + 10.75}(10\% - 5\%) = 7.5\%$$

Cost of bank loan

$$9\%(1 - 0.3) = 6.3\%$$

$$WACC = \frac{1{,}692}{2{,}024.5}\ 14.8\% + \frac{82.5}{2{,}024.5}\ 7.5\% + \frac{250}{2{,}024.5}\ 6.3\% = 13.5\%$$

(b) The cost of capital should take account of the systematic risk of the new investment, and therefore it is not appropriate to us GM Co's existing equity beta. Since the systematic risk of debt can be assumed to be zero, the competitor's equity beta can be ungeared using the following formula:

$$\beta a = \beta e \times \frac{E}{E + D(1 - T)}$$

Where: β_a = asset beta

β_e = equity beta

E = proportion of equity in capital structure

D = proportion of debt in capital structure

T = tax rate

For the competitors:

$$\beta a = 1.8 \times \frac{60}{60 + 40(1 - 0.3)} = 1.23$$

We can now apply GM Co's gearing level (using the market values calculated in part (a) to the asset beta to calculate the relevant equity beta.   *Not BV!*

$$\beta e = \beta a \times \frac{E + D(1 - T)}{E}$$

$$\beta e = 1.23 \times \frac{1{,}692 + 332.5(1 - 0.3)}{1{,}692} = 1.4$$

Using this risk adjusted equity beta, we can calculate a new, risk adjusted cost of equity:

Using CAPM = 0.07 + 1.4(0.135 − 0.07) = 0.161 (16.1%)

Finally, we can calculate a new risk adjusted cost of capital:

$$WACC = \frac{1{,}692}{2{,}024.5}\ 16.1\% + \frac{82.5}{2{,}024.5}\ 7.5\% + \frac{250}{2{,}024.5}\ 6.3\% = 14.5\%$$

(c)   The main advantages of the CAPM are:

–   It only considers systematic risk as it assumes that investors have a diversified portfolio meaning all unsystematic risk has been eliminated. This reflects what is often seen in reality

–   The relationship between required return and systematic risk has been supported by empirical research and testing

–   It is seen as a better method of calculating the cost of equity than the dividend growth model and it takes into account a company's level of systematic risk relative to the stock market as a whole.

The main disadvantages are:

–   In order to use CAPM, it is necessary to assign values to the risk free rate of return, the average return on the market and the equity beta. In reality, it can be difficult to assign these values since:

•   The risk free rate is often taken as the yield on short term government debt. This is not a fixed rate and can change on a daily basis

•   In the short term, falling share prices could mean the stock market provides a negative return rather than a positive one. It is therefore usual to use long term average values but even these are not stable over time.

•   In a similar way, the value of the beta also changes over time

–   When using CAPM to calculate a project-specific discount rate, it is necessary to find a suitable proxy beta. This can be difficult since it is rare to find another company that only operates in the one market sector you are looking to evaluate. There is also an added difficulty in ungearing proxy betas as the calculation uses capital structure information that may not be readily available.

–   Finally, the assumption within CAPM of a single period time horizon is at odds with the multi-period nature of investment appraisal.

51   RUPAB CO

Key answer tips

Despite being an "all-in" question where you have to calculate the WACC and then use it within an NPV assessment, the numbers are all relatively simplistic.

In part (a), students may miss the short-cut available on the bonds (since market value = par, pre-tax cost = coupon rate) although working it out the long way won't take much longer. All numbers in the WACC calculation are straightforward.

The NPV in part (b) is a little more complex although there are much worse questions out there. Despite having both tax and inflation in the scenario, neither prove over-complicated. On the inflation front, students need to recognise that what they have calculated in part (a) is a money cost of capital and therefore, they should inflate their cash flows accordingly. The tax calculations are simplified by keeping the capital allowances on a straight-line basis.

The discussion on the use of CAPM to calculate a project specific discount rate should flow easily.

(a) **Calculation of weighted average cost of capital**

Cost of equity = $4.5 + (1.2 \times 5) = 10.5\%$

The company's bonds are trading at par and therefore the before-tax cost of debt is the same as the interest rate on the bonds, which is 7%.

After-tax cost of debt = $7 \times (1 - 0.25) = 5.25\%$

Market value of equity = 5m × 3.81 = $19.05 million

Market value of debt is equal to its par value of $2 million

Sum of market values of equity and debt = 19.05 + 2 = $21.05 million

WACC = $(10.5 \times 19.05/21.05) + (5.25 \times 2/21.05) = 10.0\%$

(b) **Cash flow forecast**

Year	0 $000	1 $000	2 $000	3 $000	4 $000	5 $000	6 $000
Cash inflows		700.4	721.4	743.1	765.3	788.3	
Tax on cash inflows			(175.1)	(180.4)	(185.8)	(191.4)	(197.1)
		700.4	546.3	562.7	579.6	596.9	(197.1)
CA tax benefits			125.0	125.0	125.0	125.0	125.0
After-tax cash flows		700.4	671.3	687.7	704.6	721.9	(72.1)
Initial investment	(2,500)						
Working capital	(240)	(7.2)	(7.4)	(7.6)	(7.9)	270.1	
Net cash flows	(2,740)	693.2	663.9	680.1	696.7	992.0	(72.1)
Discount factors	1.000	0.909	0.826	0.751	0.683	0.621	0.564
Present values	(2,740)	630.1	548.4	510.8	475.9	616.0	(40.7)

NPV = $500

The investment is financially acceptable, since the net present value is positive. The investment might become financially unacceptable, however, if the assumptions underlying the forecast financial data were reconsidered. For example, the sales forecast appears to assume constant annual demand, which is unlikely in reality.

Workings

Capital allowance tax benefits

Annual capital allowance (straight-line basis) = $2.5m/5 = $500,000

Annual tax benefit = $500,000 × 0.25 = $125,000 per year

Working capital investment

Year	0	1	2	3	4	5
Working capital ($000)	240	247.2	254.6	262.2	270.1	
Incremental investment ($000)		(7.2)	(7.4)	(7.6)	(7.9)	270.1

(c) The capital asset pricing model (CAPM) can be used to calculate a project-specific discount rate in circumstances where the business risk of an investment project is different from the business risk of the existing operations of the investing company. In these circumstances, it is not appropriate to use the weighted average cost of capital as the discount rate in investment appraisal.

The first step in using the CAPM to calculate a project-specific discount rate is to find a proxy company (or companies) that undertake operations whose business risk is similar to that of the proposed investment. The equity beta of the proxy company will represent both the business risk and the financial risk of the proxy company. The effect of the financial risk of the proxy company must be removed to give a proxy beta representing the business risk alone of the proposed investment. This beta is called an asset beta and the calculation that removes the effect of the financial risk of the proxy company is called 'ungearing'.

The asset beta representing the business risk of a proposed investment must be adjusted to reflect the financial risk of the investing company, a process called 'regearing'. This process produces an equity beta that can be placed in the CAPM in order to calculate a required rate of return (a cost of equity). This can be used as the project-specific discount rate for the proposed investment if it is financed entirely by equity. If debt finance forms part of the financing for the proposed investment, a project-specific weighted average cost of capital can be calculated.

The limitations of using the CAPM in investment appraisal are both practical and theoretical in nature. From a practical point of view, there are difficulties associated with finding the information needed. This applies not only to the equity risk premium and the risk-free rate of return, but also to locating appropriate proxy companies with business operations similar to the proposed investment project. Most companies have a range of business operations they undertake and so their equity betas do not reflect only the desired level and type of business risk.

From a theoretical point of view, the assumptions underlying the CAPM can be criticised as unrealistic in the real world. For example, the CAPM assumes a perfect capital market, when in reality capital markets are only semi-strong form efficient at best. The CAPM assumes that all investors have diversified portfolios, so that rewards are only required for accepting systematic risk, when in fact this may not be true. There is no practical replacement for the CAPM at the present time, however.

		Marks	Marks
	ACCA marking scheme		
(a)	Cost of equity	2	
	Cost of debt	1	
	Market value of equity	1	
	Market value of debt	1	
	WACC calculation	1	
			6
(b)	Inflated cash flows	1	
	Tax on cash flows	1	
	Capital allowance tax benefits	1	
	Working capital – initial investment	1	
	Working capital – incremental investment	1	
	Working capital - recovery	1	
	Net present value calculation	1	
	Comment	1	
			8
(c)	Explanation of use of CAPM	5 – 6	
	Discussion of limitations	6 – 7	
	Maximum		11
	Total		25

Examiner's comments

Part (a) required candidates to calculate the weighted average cost of capital of a company and many students scored full marks. There were a number of areas where marks were lost. Some candidates mistook the equity risk premium for the return on the market. Another error was to calculate the cost of debt by linear interpolation when, since the market value and the par value of the bond were the same, the cost of debt was equal to the bond interest rate. Some answers were unable to calculate the market values of equity and debt.

Part (b) asked candidates to calculate the net present value of an investment after preparing a forecast of its nominal after-tax cash flows.

Many candidates were not able to deal correctly with initial investment, incremental investment and recovery of working capital. The initial investment was frequently mistimed, being placed in year one rather than at the start of the investment. The recovery of working capital was often omitted. Working capital was sometimes invested every year at its initial amount, or the inflated total investment in working capital was invested in full every year. Better candidates including in their cash flow forecast only the incremental annual investment.

Although the question specified straight-line capital allowances or tax-allowable depreciation, some candidates used the 25% reducing balance method. Credit cannot be given where the requirements of the question are ignored. Common errors with the treatment of tax included ignoring the fact that tax liabilities were one year in arrears: treating working capital investment as a tax-allowable deduction (it is not); giving tax benefits on the initial investment in addition to the benefit received through capital allowances; including capital allowances as a cash flow; and treating capital allowance tax benefits as a cost rather than a benefit.

Although the weighted average cost of capital from part (a) was already in nominal terms, some candidates treated as a real discount rate and used the Fisher equation to calculate a nominal discount rate. A clear understanding of the distinction between real and nominal terms approaches is required in investment appraisal.

In part (c), candidates were asked to explain how the capital asset pricing model (CAPM) could be used to calculate a project-specific discount rate, and to discuss the weaknesses of using the CAPM in investment appraisal. This topic was covered in a series of articles in the student accountant.

Although many candidates were able to identify and discuss some limitation of the CAPM, these discussion often were very general in nature, rather than focussing on using the CAPM in investment appraisal. This reflected the inability of a number of candidates to explain correctly how the CAPM could be used to calculate a project-specific discount rate. Better answers referred to proxy companies, ungearing equity betas to give proxy asset betas, averaging asset betas, regearing, and calculating a project-specific discount rate using the CAPM formula. Some discussion of business risk and financial risk was also relevant here. Weaker answers often did little more than identify and describe the variables in the CAPM formula, before stating that these variables were subjective and hard to calculate, or that the CAPM was better than the dividend growth model, which was not relevant to the question asked. Some answers were very brief for the number of marks available.

52 WEMERE

Key answer tips

You will need to read the scenario carefully to ensure you pick up on all the errors of principle required in part (a).

Parts (b) and (c) offer an opportunity to gain some easier marks. The highlighted words are key phrases that markers are looking for.

(a) The first error made is to suggest using the cost of equity, whether estimated via the dividend valuation model or the capital asset pricing model (CAPM) as the discount rate. The company should use its overall cost of capital, which would normally be a weighted average of the cost of equity and the cost of debt.

Errors specific to CAPM

(i) The formula is wrong. It wrongly includes the market return twice. It should be:

$$E(r_i) = R_f = \beta_i (E(r_m) - R_f)$$

(ii) The equity beta of Folten reflects the financial risk resulting from the level of gearing in Folten. It must be adjusted to reflect the level of gearing specific to Wemere. It is also likely that the beta of an unlisted company is higher than the beta of an equivalent listed company.

(iii) The return required by equity holders i.e., the cost of equity, is inclusive of a return to allow for inflation.

Errors specific to the dividend valuation model

(i) The formula is wrong. It should be: $\dfrac{D_1}{P_0}+g$

(ii) Treatment of inflation – as for CAPM.

(iii) Again the impact of the difference in the level of gearing of Wemere and Folten on the cost of equity has not been taken into account.

Revised estimates of cost of capital

CAPM: required return $= E(r_i) = R_f = \beta_i\,(E(r_m) - R_f)$

For Folten

$$\beta_{\text{Equity ungeared}} = \beta_a = \left[\frac{V_e}{(V_e + V_d\,(1-T))}\beta_e\right] + \left[\frac{V_d(1-T)}{(V_e + V_d(1-T))}\beta_d\right]$$

Assume $\beta_d = 0$, $V_d = 4{,}400$

$E\;=\quad 1.38 \times 1{,}800 \times 4 \qquad$ (= share price $\times$ no. of equity shares) = \$9,936,000

$\therefore \beta_{\text{Equity ungeared}} \quad = \quad 1.4 \times \dfrac{9{,}936}{9{,}936 + 4{,}400(1-0.35)} \quad = \quad 1.087$

For Wemere

Assume $\beta_d = 0$, $V_d = 2{,}400$, Equity value of \$10.6 million, debt costs of 10%.

$\therefore\; 1.087 \quad = \quad \beta_{\text{Equity geared}} \times \dfrac{10{,}600}{10{,}600 + 2{,}400\,(1-0.35)}$

$1.087 \quad = \quad 0.872\,\beta_{\text{Equity geared}}$

$\beta_{\text{Equity geared}} \quad = \quad 1.25$

$\therefore$ Cost of equity $= \quad 6 + (14 - 6) \times 1.25 \;=\; 16.0\%$

$\therefore$ WACC $\;=\; 16.0\% \times \dfrac{10{,}600}{10{,}600 + 2{,}400} + 10(1-0.35) \times \dfrac{2{,}400}{10{,}600 + 2{,}400} = 4.2\%$

Dividend valuation model

Folten

$i = \dfrac{D_1}{P} + g$

We calculate dividend growth rate:

$9.23\,(1+g)^4 \quad = \quad 13.03$

$\therefore \quad (1+g)^4 \quad = \quad 1.412$

$\quad 1+g \quad = \quad 1.09$

$\quad g \quad = \quad 9\%$

$D_1 \quad = \quad 13.03\,(1 + 0.09) = 14.20¢$

$K_e \quad = \quad \dfrac{14.20}{138} + 0.09 \quad = \quad 0.193$ i.e. 19.3%

$\therefore$ WACC $\quad = \quad 19.3 \times \dfrac{10{,}600}{13{,}000} + 10(1-0.35) \times \dfrac{2{,}400}{13{,}000} = 16.9\%$

(b) The estimates of the WACC are significantly different. Using the CAPM to estimate the cost of equity results in a WACC of 14.2%. The use of the dividend valuation model results in a WACC of 16.9%. They are both based on estimates from another company which has, for example, a different level of gearing. The cost of equity derived using the dividend valuation model is based on Folten's dividend policy and share price and not that of Wemere. The dividend policy of Wemere (e.g. the dividend growth rate) is likely to be different.

CAPM involves estimating the systematic risk of Wemere using Folten. The beta of Folten is likely to be a reasonable estimate, subject to gearing, of the beta of Wemere.

CAPM is therefore likely to produce the better estimate of the discount rate to use. However, this will be incorrect if the projects being appraised have a different level of systematic risk to the average systematic risk of Folten's existing projects or if the finance used for the project significantly changes the capital structure of Wemere.

(c) Discounted cash flow techniques allow for the time value of money and should therefore be used for all investment appraisal including that carried out by small unlisted companies. It is important for all managers to recognise that money received now is worth more than money received in the future. Discounting enables future cash flows to be expressed in terms of present value and for net present value to be calculated. A positive net present value indicates that the return provided by the project is greater than the discount rate.

One non-discounting method – accounting rate of return – is used because it employs data consistent with financial accounts, but it is not theoretically sound and is not recommended as a final decision arbiter. Nevertheless it registers appreciation of the impact of a new project on the financial statements and thus likely impact on users of these statements.

Discounted payback measures how long it takes to recover the initial investment after taking account of the time value of money. It is a useful initial screening method but should not be used alone since it ignores cash flows outside the payback period. A problem for all companies, not only small unlisted companies, is estimation of the discount rate. This can be partly overcome by calculating the internal rate of return (IRR) i.e., the discount rate at which the NPV is zero. This provides a 'break-even' cost of capital – i.e., a yield which is then acceptable provided the capital cost of the business 'could not be lower'.

BUSINESS VALUATIONS

53   ZED

Key answer tips

Given the information provided in the scenario it is fairly easy to spot that the dividend valuation model is the technique being examined. The tricky part is distinguishing between part (a)(i) where you'll be using the existing expectations of dividends and part (a)(ii) where you'll be concerned with the policy Zed would propose as well as the other benefits and savings that would arise from the acquisition. The key to realising this is to put yourself in the position of the stakeholder concerned; the minority interest in part (a)(i) and Zed as a 100% owner in part (a)(ii).

Part (b) requires consideration of the practicalities of business valuation and can include inherent limitations of the DVM model. The highlighted words are key phrases that markers are looking for.

(a)   (i)   *Red* – Using the model

$$P_0 = \frac{D_0\,(1+g)}{(r_e - g)} = \$0.30/(0.15 - 0.06) = \$3.33$$

Yellow – Expected dividends and their present value for years 1-4 are:

Timing	Dividend	DF@15%	Present value
	¢		$
Year 1	27	0.870	0.235
2	36	0.756	0.272
3	48	0.658	0.316
4	64	0.572	0.366
			———
			1.189

Value, at year 4, of future dividends is $0.64 / 0.15 = $4.267

Value, at present, of year 5 and on dividends is $4.267 x 0.572 = $2.441

Total value = 1.189 + 2.411 = $3.630

(ii)   Value of savings and benefits achieved by Zed

Timing	Narrative	Cash flow $000s	DF@15%	Present value $000s
1 – ∞	Annual savings	225	1/0.15	1,500
2	Sale of property	800	0.756	604.8
				———
				2,104.8
				———

Value of Red

Total dividend = $250,000 commencing in year 3, growth rate 10% per annum

Value at year 2 = $250,000 / (0.15 − 0.10) = $5 million

Present value = $5,000,000 x 0.756 = $3,780,000

Value of Yellow

Dividends and their present value for years 1 − 7 are:

Timing	Total dividend	DF@15%	Present value
	($000)	($000)	($000)
Year 1	270	0.870	234.9
2	360	0.756	272.16
3	480	0.658	315.84
4	640	0.572	366.08
5	800	0.497	397.60
6	1,000	0.432	432.00
7	1,250	0.376	470.00
			————
			2,488.58
			————

Value at year 7 of future dividends beyond year 7 = $1,250,000/0.15 = $8,333,333

Present value of future dividends beyond year 7 = $8,333,333, × 0.376 = $3,133,333

Total value = 2,488,580 + 3,133,333 = $5,621,913

Total incremental effect of a take-over

(i) Red

	($000)
Value of Red	3,780.0
Incremental value of Zed	2,104.8
	————
Total value	5,884.8
Maximum value per share $5.88	

(ii) Yellow

	($000)
Value of Yellow	5,624.91
Incremental value of Zed	2,104.8
	————
Total value	7,726.71
Maximum value per share $7.73	

(b) The approach used in part (a) was to base equity valuation only on future dividends and no consideration was given to underlying asset values which maybe important in a take-over (see below). The dividend valuation model is a valid model capable of producing accurate results providing the date is accurate. The major limitations of the use of the model in part (a) stem not from the model itself but from the assumptions concerning the input data – the major limitations included the assumptions of:

(i)   Smooth dividend growth. In reality dividends may display some volatility from year to year.

(ii)   Perpetual growth and infinite life. It is unrealistic to expect infinite life of the firm but due to discounting this assumption may produce a good working approximation to valuation.

(iii)   Constant discount rate or expected rate of return.

Further limitations concern the lack of consideration given to taxation and to the possibly differing tax treatment of dividends and capital gains.

Other factors which should be considered include:

(i)   Risk. Are all alternatives equally risky and is risk constant over the whole life? There *may* be greater risk during periods of expected high growth (years 1–4 of Yellow) than during periods of low or zero growth. An adjustment to the required return may be necessary during periods of abnormal risk.

(ii)   Asset values may be an important aspect of risk in a take-over and should be considered. Generally the higher the asset values of the firm taken-over and the better their market then the lower is the potential risk inherent in that take-over.

(iii)   Management and competition. Will the existing management team continue and/or will competition increase/ the cash flow estimates should consider the actions of existing management and competition etc?

(iv)   Financing of take-over. The method of financing the take-over – loans, own equity etc – must be considered carefully.

(v)   Taxation. Full consideration of all tax consequences should be made.

54   TAGNA

Key answer tips

Parts (a) & (c) give an opportunity for some easy marks although don't forget in part (a) to relate your comments to the details of this scenario. Part (b) is an excellent example of a 'application' style answer – remember, all of the information provided in the question is there for a reason. Make sure you use every piece. The highlighted words are key phrases that markers are looking for.

(a)   Market efficiency is commonly discussed in terms of pricing efficiency.

A stock market is described as efficient when share prices fully and fairly reflect relevant information.

Weak form efficiency occurs when share prices fully and fairly reflect all past information, such as share price movements in preceding periods. If a stock market is weak-form efficient, investors cannot make abnormal gains by studying and acting upon past information.

Semi-strong form efficiency occurs when share prices fully and fairly reflect not only past information, but all publicly available information as well, such as the information provided by the published financial statements of companies or by reports in the financial press. If a stock market is semi-strong-form efficient, investors cannot make abnormal gains by studying and acting upon publicly available information.

Strong form efficiency occurs when share prices fully and fairly reflect not only all past and publicly available information, but all relevant private information as well, such as confidential minutes of board meetings. If a stock market is strong-form efficient, investors cannot make abnormal gains by acting upon any information, whether publicly available or not. There is no empirical evidence supporting the proposition that stock markets are strong form efficient and so the bank is incorrect in suggesting that in six months the stock market will be strong-form efficient. However, there is a great deal of evidence suggesting that stock markets are semi-strong-form efficient and so Tagna's shares are unlikely to be under-priced.

(b) A substantial interest rate increase may have several consequences for Tagna in the areas indicated.

(i) As a manufacturer and supplier of luxury goods, it is likely that Tagna will experience a **sharp decrease in sales** as a result of the increase in interest rates. One reason for this is that sales of luxury goods will be more sensitive to changes in disposable income than sales of basic necessities, and disposable income is likely to fall as a result of the interest rate increase. Another reason is the likely effect of the interest rate increase on consumer demand. If the increase in demand has been supported, even in part, by the increase in consumer credit, the substantial interest rate increase will have a negative effect on demand as the cost of consumer credit increases. It is also likely that many chain store customers will buy Tagna's goods by using credit.

(ii) Tagna may experience an **increase in operating costs** as a result of the substantial interest rate increase, although this is likely to be a smaller effect and one that occurs more slowly than a decrease in sales. As the higher cost of borrowing moves through the various supply chains in the economy, producer prices may increase and the cost of materials and other inputs Tagna may rise by more than the current rate of inflation. Labour costs may also increase sharply if the recent sharp rise in inflation leads to high inflationary expectations being built into wage demands. Acting against this will be the deflationary effect on consumer demand of the interest rate increase. If the Central Bank has made an accurate assessment of the economic situation when determining the interest rate increase, both the growth in consumer demand and the rate of inflation may fall to more acceptable levels, leading to a lower increase in operating costs.

(iii) The **earnings (profit after tax)** of Tagna are likely to fall as a result of the interest rate increase. In addition to the decrease in sales and the possible increase in operating costs discussed above, Tagna will experience an increase in interest costs arising from its overdraft. The combination of these effects is likely to result in a sharp fall in earnings. The level of reported profits has been low in recent years and so Tagna may be faced with insufficient profits to maintain its dividend, or even a reported loss.

(c) The objectives of public sector organisations are often difficult to define. Even though the cost of resources used can be measured, the benefits gained from the consumption of those resources can be difficult, if not impossible, to quantify. Because of this difficulty, public sector organisations often have financial targets imposed on them, such as a target rate of return on capital employed. Furthermore, they will tend to focus on maximising the return on resources consumed by producing the best possible combination of services for the lowest possible cost. This is the meaning of **'value for money'**, often referred to as the pursuit of economy, efficiency and effectiveness.

Economy refers to seeking the lowest level of input costs for a given level of output. **Efficiency** refers to seeking the highest level of output for a given level of input resources. **Effectiveness** refers to the extent to which output produced meets the specified objectives, for example in terms of provision of a required range of services.

In contrast, private sector organisations have to compete for funds in the capital markets and must offer an adequate return to investors. The objective of **maximisation of shareholder wealth** equates to the view that the primary financial objective of companies is to reward their owners. If this objective is not followed, the directors may be replaced or a company may find it difficult to obtain funds in the market, since investors will prefer companies that increase their wealth. However, shareholder wealth cannot be maximised if companies do not seek both economy and efficiency in their business operations.

55 HENDIL (PART II)

Key answer tips

This is a reasonable straightforward question that is more about application of models than detailed calculations. You will need to think of practical implications to score highly on the discussional aspects. The highlighted words are key phrases that markers are looking for.

(a) (i) Number of ordinary shares = 1,000,000/0.5 = 2 million

Current dividend per share = 100 × (300,000/2,000,000) = 15¢

Share price predicted by dividend growth model = (15 × 1.05)/(0.12 − 0.05) = 225¢

(ii) Market efficiency is usually taken to refer to the way in which ordinary share prices reflect information. Fama defined an efficient market as one in which share prices fully and fairly reflect all available information.

A semi-strong form efficient market is one where share prices reflect all publicly available information, such as past share price movements, published company annual reports and analysts' reports in the financial press.

A strong form market is one where share prices reflect all information, whether publicly available or not. Share prices would reflect, for example, takeover decisions made at private board meetings.

(iii) The share price predicted by the dividend growth model is 45¢ greater than the current share price of the company. However, the dividend growth model has used the proposed dividend of the company (15¢), which may not yet have been made public. If the stock market is semi-strong form efficient and therefore unaware of the proposed dividend, the company's ordinary share price could be different to that predicted by the dividend growth model because the market expects a dividend which is different from the proposed dividend used in the model. Working backwards using the dividend growth model suggests that the market expects a dividend of 12¢ per share (180 x (0.12 – 0.05)/1.05).

In a strong form efficient market, the information about the proposed dividend will already be reflected in the share price. The difference between the share price predicted by the dividend growth model and the current share price of the company may therefore be explained by different views of the expected dividend growth rate or the return required by ordinary shareholders. The market might expect a lower growth rate than the 5% expected by the directors, for example, or the return required by ordinary shareholders might have increased due to economic expectations or changing perceptions of risk. An increase in the required return to 13.75% would give a share price of $1.80 (15 x 1.05/(0.1375 – 0.05)). Another explanation is that the market may not be fully efficient.

(b) **Interest cover**

Average interest cover of similar companies = 6 times

Current interest cover = 624/156 = 4 times

Annual interest on new loan stock = $1m × 0.08 = $80,000

Assuming no change to existing interest, increased annual interest = 80 + 156 = $236,000

Interest cover after new loan stock issue = 624/236 = 2.6 times

This would not change significantly if profit before interest and tax were increased by the profit (after accounting depreciation) from the first year's sales of the proposed investment.

The current interest cover of Hendil Inc (four times) is less than the average interest cover of similar companies (six times), suggesting that the financial risk of the company is higher than that of similar companies even before the new debt is issued. After the new issue, interest cover would fall to 2.6 times, a level that would be regarded with concern by both lenders and investors. Although the interest on the new debt might be overstated in our interest cover calculation (debt in the balance sheet accounts for only part of the interest in the income statement, implying that the overdraft may have decreased substantially in the last year), it is likely that a new debt issue might be unwise.

Gearing (long-term debt/equity)

Average gearing (book value basis) of similar companies = 50%

Current gearing (book value basis) = 29%

Revised gearing (book value basis) = 54%

Average gearing (market value basis) of similar companies = 25%

Current gearing (market value basis) = 38%

Revised gearing (market value basis) = 65%

Two conclusions can be drawn from these gearing values. Firstly, the current gearing of Hendil Inc is below the average gearing of similar companies on a book value basis, but higher than the average gearing of similar companies on a market value basis. Secondly, the revised gearing of Hendil Inc after the new issue is slightly above the average gearing of similar companies on a book value basis, and more than double the average gearing of similar companies on a market value basis. Gearing based on market values is preferred in financial management.

Workings

Current gearing (book value basis) = 100 × (1,200/4,100) = 29%

Revised book value of long-term debt = 1.2m + 1m = $2.2 million

Revised gearing (book value basis) = 100 × (2,200/4,100) = 54%

Market value of debt = $1.2m × 113/ 100 = $1,356,000

Number of ordinary shares = 1,000,000/0.5 = 2 million

Market value of ordinary shares = 2m × 1.80 = $3.6 million

Current gearing (market value basis) = 100 × (1,356/3,600) =38%

Market value of new debt issue = $1 million

Total market value of debt = 1,356 + 1,000 = $2,356,000

Market value of ordinary shares = 2m × 1.80 = $3.6 million

Revised gearing (market value basis) = 100 × (2,356/3,600) = 65%

The calculation of the revised gearing (market value basis) assumes that the ordinary share price and the market value of existing debt are unchanged. An alternative calculation could use a revised share price, for example $2.22 per share (see below), giving a lower gearing on a market value basis of 100 × (2,356/(2m × 2.22)) = 53%.

Ordinary share price

Current ordinary share price = $1.80 per share

Current market value of company = 1.80 × 2m = $3.6 million

Net present value of investment = $832,000

If the market is efficient, the value of the company will increase by the NPV of the investment, although this assumes that the current average cost of capital of Hendil Inc, which was used as the discount rate in the NPV analysis, would remain unchanged by the new loan stock issue. This may not be true.

Revised market value = 3,600 + 832 = $4,432 million

Revised ordinary share price = 4,432,000/2,000,000 = $2.22 per share

Maturity

The proposed loan stock has a maturity of 15 years but the life of the proposed investment is not clear. We know that it is more than four years, but we do not know how much more. We also do not know whether the new machinery can be used to produce other products, whether at the same time as the new product range or when the new product range is in the decline phase of its product life-cycle. The matching principle holds that maturity of finance should match the expected life of the assets financed.

Security

It has been suggested that the new loan stock could be secured on existing assets of

Hendil Inc. This would be on non-current rather than current assets. Since the existing $1.2 million loan stock is already secured on non-current assets of the company, the most that might be available is $1.05 million of non-current assets. However, since loan stock is usually secured on particular assets rather than on a given value of assets, there may be insufficient existing assets to offer as security for the new loan stock issue. The new machinery may be suitable to offer as security in order to make up the deficit.

56   EMH AND DVM

Key answer tips

This question covers an area of the syllabus that all students must be competent discussing prior to sitting the exam. To gain the 'higher skills' marks you need to discuss the validity of the dividend valuation model together with implications of market efficiency. The highlighted words are key phrases that markers are looking for.

(a)   The term 'Efficient Market Hypothesis' (EMH) refers to the view that share prices fully and fairly reflect all relevant available information. There are other kinds of capital market efficiency, such as operational efficiency (meaning that transaction costs are low enough not to discourage investors from buying and selling shares), but it is pricing efficiency that is especially important in financial management.

Research has been carried out to discover whether capital markets are weak form efficient (share prices reflect all past or historic information), semi-strong form efficient (share prices reflect all publicly available information, including past information), or strong form efficient (share prices reflect all information, whether publicly available or not). This research has shown that well-developed capital markets are weak form efficient, so that it is not possible to generate abnormal profits by studying and analysing past information, such as historic share price movements. This research has also shown that well-developed capital markets are semi-strong form efficient, so that it is not possible to generate abnormal profits by studying publicly available information such as company financial statements or press releases. Capital markets are not strong form efficient, since it is possible to use insider information to buy and sell shares for profit.

If a stock market has been found to be semi-strong form efficient, it means that research has shown that share prices on the market respond quickly and accurately to new information as it arrives on the market. The share price of a company quickly responds if new information relating to that company is released. The share prices quoted on a stock exchange are therefore always fair prices, reflecting all information about a company that is relevant to buying and selling. The share price will factor in past company performance, expected company performance, the quality of the management team, the way the company might respond to changes in the economic environment such as a rise in interest rate, and so on.

There are a number of implications for a company of its stock market being semi-strong form efficient. If it is thinking about acquiring another company, the market value of the potential target company will be a fair one, since there are no bargains to be found in an efficient market as a result of shares being undervalued. The managers of the company should focus on making decisions that increase shareholder wealth, since the market will recognise the good decisions they are making and the share price will increase accordingly. Manipulating accounting information, such as 'window dressing' annual financial statements, will not be effective, as the share price will reflect the underlying 'fundamentals' of the company's business operations and will be unresponsive to cosmetic changes. It has also been argued that, if a stock market is efficient, the timing of new issues of equity will be immaterial, as the price paid for the new equity will always be a fair one.

(b) **Report on the valuation of the company's shares**

From the data provided, the analyst appears to have used the dividend growth model in the valuation process.

According to the dividend growth model the intrinsic value of the company's shares should be 600 cents, as illustrated below. The actual value is 645 cents, suggesting that the shares are overvalued by approximately 7.5%.

	Dividend per share (cents)	Growth (%)
20X4	19.86	
20X5	21.45	8
20X6	23.17	8
20X7	25.02	8

OR Solving $19.86 \times (1 + g)^3 = 25.02$ gives average growth g = 8%

Using the dividend growth model and assuming dividend growth of 8% every year in perpetuity:

$$\text{Price} = \frac{D_1}{K_e - g} = \frac{25.02(1.08)}{0.125 - 0.08} = 600 \text{ cents}$$

The belief that a share is undervalued or over-valued, based on the use of only externally available information, implies that the stock market is not semi-strong form efficient. Although markets are not efficient at all times, there is substantial evidence to suggest that semi-strong form efficiency normally exists in most well-developed markets.

Even if market efficiency is expected, the dividend growth model is by no means the only technique that might be used to estimate share value. The discounted value of expected future cash flows is a theoretically superior technique. The dividend growth model makes a number of assumptions including:

(i) Dividend growth will be constant which is very unlikely. Dividend growth is assumed to result from earnings growth which itself results from new, constant return investments financed only by retained earnings.

(ii) The company will retain a constant fraction of earnings.

In this example, the growth in earnings per share is much more volatile than the growth in dividend per share, and the company might not be able to sustain a constant 8% growth in dividends.

Estimates of share value based upon the dividend growth model are therefore themselves suspect, and the analyst is probably not justified in suggesting that the share is overvalued based on this evidence only.

57 LACETO

Key answer tips

Don't let the lack of detail in this requirement put you off. After considering the different methods of valuing a business, a brief review of the information provided in the scenario will help to guide you on the best method in this situation. Don't forget you are advising Laceto so you will want to think about the valuation from the perspective of both Laceto and Omnigen shareholders in order to offer complete advise.

The guidance on the weighting of marks between calculations and discussion should be noted. You would benefit from doing a quick answer plan to help structure your thoughts and prevent you producing a long, rambling script. The highlighted words are key phrases that markers are looking for.

Laceto will wish to pay the minimum price that will attract the majority of Omnigen's shareholders to sell. The current market price of 410 cents per share, or a total market value of $123 million, is likely to be the lowest that shareholders of Omnigen would accept, and unless there is an expectation that Omnigen's shares will fall further in value in the near future, a premium over the current market price will normally be payable.

If industry P/E ratios are used to value Omnigen, the range of values would be $182 million to $210 million. (Omnigen's total earnings after tax of $14 million, multiplied by the P/Es of 13:1 and 15:1). However, Omnigen's current PE ratio is 8.78:1, given a value of $123 million. Even if the share price had not fallen it would only have been just over 13:1, or a value of $184 million. Unless there is an expectation that Omnigen's share price will soon return to a higher level the use of a forecast P/E or comparative P/Es of companies which might have very different characteristics to Omnigen is not recommended.

The realisable value of assets, $82 million, is substantially below the estimates based upon P/E ratios, probably because Omnigen is a profitable company which is planned to continue trading after the potential acquisition. The realisable value of assets is not the recommended valuation method unless it produces a value higher than the value as a going concern.

A better method of estimating the value of Omnigen is to use the cash flow projections to find the present value of Omnigen to Laceto. This will be based upon the free cash flow after replacement expenditure and expenditure required to achieve the forecast growth levels.

$ million

Financial year	20X8	20X9	20Y0	20Y1
Net sales	230	261	281	298
Cost of goods sold (50%)	115	131	141	149
Selling and administrative expenses	32	34	36	38
Capital allowances	40	42	42	42
	187	207	219	229
Taxable	43	54	62	69

Taxation (30%)	12.9	16.2	18.6	20.7
	30.1	37.8	43.4	48.3
Add back capital allowances	40	42	42	42
Less cash flow needed for asset replacement and forecast growth	(50)	(52)	(55)	(58)
Net cash flow	20.1	27.8	30.4	32.3
Discount factors (14%) 1	0.877	0.769	0.675	0.592
Present values	17.6	21.4	20.5	19.1

Total PV 20X8 – 20Y1 = 78.6

Assuming 3% growth per annum beyond 20Y1 in perpetuity the value of the post 20Y1 cash flows in terms of 20Y1 values will be:

$$\frac{32.3(1.03)}{0.14 - 0.03} = \$302.4m$$

This gives a present value of 302.4 × 0.592 (DF at 14%) = $179.0 million

Total present value is $257.4 million (the sum of the present values for each year). This value is the value of the entire entity, i.e. equity plus debt. The value of debt will depend upon the final gearing, and will vary between approximately $46 million and $59 million (18%-23% gearing), giving a value of equity between $199.4 million and $212.4 million. If growth is 5% the present value of the entity would be $297.2 million, and the value of equity between $228.8 million and $243.7 million. These estimates use a present value to infinity estimate beyond 20Y1. If a shorter time horizon was used e.g. 10 years, the estimates would be considerably reduced. For example a ten year time horizon with growth at 3% per year would result in a present value of equity plus debt of approximately $192 million.

Assuming these cash flow projections are reasonably accurate (which itself must be subject to serious doubt, e.g. can the imbalance after year five between capital allowances and replacement capital expenditure continue indefinitely), it is clearly worth Laceto offering a premium over the current market price for the shares of Omnigen. In theory, using present values to infinity, it could afford to offer a premium of more than 50% above the current market price, but in order to increase its own value it would offer the lowest price that would attract more than 50% of the shareholders of Omnigen. It is not possible to know what this price would be. An initial bid might offer a 25 to 30% premium above the current price, or between $154 million and $160 million pounds. If that bid was refused then there is scope for increasing it up to a maximum of the estimated equity present values discussed above.

It must be stressed that all of the above estimates are subject to significant margins of error, and that valuation for takeovers is not a precise science.

Notes:

1   *Discount rate:*

Using the capital asset pricing model

k_e = 6% + (14% – 6%)1.3 = 16.4%

Omnigen's cost of equity after the acquisition is used as this is likely to reflect the systematic risk of the activities of Omnigen within Laceto. As the range of expected gearing levels is quite small (18-23%), and gearing is relatively low, it is assumed that the cost of equity will not significantly change over this range of gearing, other than the change already reflected in the increase in the equity beta by 0.1.

The cost of debt is not given but may be estimated from the data regarding Laceto's loan stock.

As Omnigen currently has a lower gearing than Laceto, it is assumed increasing Omnigen's gearing should not have a significant effect on Laceto's cost of debt, even if the overall gearing increases to 23%.

The cost of debt, by trial and error is:

At 6% interest

$12(1 - 0.3) \times 2.673 =$	22.45
$100 \times 0.840 =$	84.00
	106.45

At 5% interest

$12(1 - 0.3) \times 2.723 =$	22.87
$100 \times 0.864 =$	86.40
	109.27

By interpolation $5\% + \dfrac{0.47}{0.47 + 2.35} \times 1\% = 5.17\%$

The weighted average cost of capital may be estimated for the full range of expected gearing:

At 18% gearing:

The weighted average cost of capital is $16.4 \times 0.82 + 5.17\% \times 0.18 = 14.38\%$

At 23% gearing:

The weighted average cost of capital is $16.4 \times 0.77 + 5.17\% \times 0.23 = 13.82\%$

The estimated WACC does not change dramatically over the possible range in gearing.

14% will be used as the discount rate.

58 THP CO *Walk in the footsteps of a top tutor*

Key answer tips

The key learning point from this question is the importance of making sure your marker can follow your answer. This will often involve explaining your thought process, including commenting on why the calculation you've performed is the right approach. The highlighted words are key phrases that markers are looking for.

Tutor's top tips:

In the 15 minutes reading time you should aim to have skim read the scenario, getting a feeling for the information you've been provided with and paying particular attention to names and dates. You should also have skim read the requirement, underlining the models referred to and noted the calculations that are being asked for. Look for any part of the question that relies purely on knowledge of the syllabus (i.e. no calculations) and flag these as a good place to start. Part (e) of this question falls into this category.

Once you've completed part (e) you should look at the other requirements. Is there a specific order you will need to do them in or can you choose your strongest area to do first. Here we'll need to tackle the requirements in order as you need the output of part (a) to answer part (b).

Tutor's top tips:

Part (a) specifically asks for you to use the dividend growth (or valuation) model. Start by writing down the formula and then search the scenario for the information you need. For this calculation you need the dividend, dividend growth and the cost of equity. 2 of the 3 are clearly stated. The dividend is a bit harder to find but as you're told THP has a payout ratio of 50% and you know EPS is currently 64c, the dividend per share can be quickly worked out. Don't forget to read the requirement carefully. You are not just asked for the share price but also the current market capitalisation. You would have lost a very easy mark if you didn't spot this.

(a) Calculation of share price

THP Co dividend per share = 64 × 0·5 = 32c per share

Share price of THP Co = (32 × 1·05)/(0·12 − 0·05) = $4·80

Market capitalisation of THP Co = 4·80 × 3m = $14·4m

Tutor's top tips:

In part (b) you should follow the order presented in the requirement. It is leading you through the process. All the information is stated in the scenario or can be calculated without many complications. Part (iv) is the area most likely to cause problems (although you might not realise it at the time). The majority of situations the market capitalisation after an issue would be the TERP × new number of shares in issue. However, in this scenario, we've been told of some issue costs which must be deducted. Don't worry if you didn't spot this, it will only have been worth 2 marks (maximum). However, this does show the benefits of querying every piece of information provided by the examiner and asking "why has he told me that?"

(b)   Rights issue price

This is at a 20% discount to the current share price = 4·80 × 0·8 = $3·84 per share

New shares issued = 3m/3 = 1m

Cash raised = 1m × 3·84 = $3,840,000

Theoretical ex rights price = [(3 × 4·80) + 3·84]/4 = $4·56 per share

Market capitalisation after rights issue = 14·4m + 3·84m = $18·24 − 0·32m = $17·92m

This is equivalent to a share price of 17·92/4 = $4·48 per share

The issue costs result in a decrease in the market value of the company and therefore a decrease in the wealth of shareholders equivalent to 8c per share.

Tutor's top tips:

The key to part (c) is recognising that since CRX is in the same business sector as THP, you can use THP's P/E ratio as a proxy for CRX. Whilst you're not specifically told this, you do have the information to work it out. Make sure your answer explains what you're doing and why this is an acceptable approach.

(c)   Price/earnings ratio valuation
Price/earnings ratio of THP Co = 480/64 = 7·5

Earnings per share of CRX Co = 44·8c per share

Using the price earnings ratio method, share price of CRX Co = (44·8 × 7·5)/100 = $3·36

Market capitalisation of CRX Co = 3·36 × 1m = $3,360,000

(Alternatively, earnings of CRX Co = 1m × 0·448 = $448,000 × 7·5 = $3,360,000)

Tutor's top tips:

Part (d) starts by asking you to assume a semi-strong form efficient market. Your first thought should be to consider the implications of this, which is that only publicly available information will be reflected in the share price. Again, you should note down your thought process. Next you will need to identify what will affect the market capitalisation post acquisition. You should conclude this will be the market capitalisation of THP plus the market capitalisation of CRX less the price paid for CRX (since this cash has left the business). All of this information is available, either as a result of your previous calculations or given in the scenario. Only in part (ii) will we need to factor in the additional savings since this information has now been made public.

(d)   In a semi-strong form efficient capital market, share prices reflect past and public information. If the expected annual after-tax savings are not announced, this information will not therefore be reflected in the share price of THP Co. In this case, the post acquisition market capitalisation of THP Co will be the market capitalisation after the rights issue, plus the market capitalisation of the acquired company (CRX Co), less the price paid for the shares of CRX Co, since this cash has left the company in exchange for purchased shares. It is assumed that the market capitalisations calculated in earlier parts of this question are fair values, including the value of CRX Co calculated by the price/earnings ratio method.

Price paid for CRX Co = 3·84m – 0·32m = $3·52m

Market capitalisation = 17·92m + 3·36m – 3·52m = $17·76m

This is equivalent to a share price of 17·76/4 = $4·44 per share

The market capitalisation has decreased from the value following the rights issue because THP Co has paid $3·52m for a company apparently worth $3·36m. This is a further decrease in the wealth of shareholders, following on from the issue costs of the rights issue.

If the annual after-tax savings are announced, this information will be reflected quickly and accurately in the share price of THP Co since the capital market is semi-strong form efficient. The savings can be valued using the price/earnings ratio method as having a present value of $720,000 (7·5 × 96,000). The revised market capitalisation of THP Co is therefore $18·48m (17·76m + 0·72m), equivalent to a share price of $4·62 per share (18·48/4). This makes the acquisition of CRX Co attractive to the shareholders of THP Co, since it offers a higher market capitalisation than the one following the rights issue. Each shareholder of THP Co would experience a capital gain of 14c per share (4·62 – 4·48).

In practice, the capital market is likely to anticipate the annual after-tax savings before they are announced by THP Co.

Tutor's top tips:

Part (e) is an opportunity to score an easy 8 marks by discussing the relative things to consider when deciding between debt and equity. Be careful though, the requirement does specify that your points should be relevant to THP. So for example, don't just talk about the impact on gearing, work it out using the information provided. To ensure you don't spend too much time on this part of the question, you should think about the mark allocation. For 8 marks where you are being asked to 'discuss' you should be spend no more than 14 minutes (8 × 1.8 mins per mark) talking about 4 factors THP should consider. Contrast this with a requirement to 'state' or 'list' which is more likely to attract only 1 mark per relevant point.

(e)   There are a number of factors that should be considered by THP Co, including the following:

Gearing and financial risk

Equity finance will decrease gearing and financial risk, while debt finance will increase them. Gearing for THP Co is currently 68·5% and this will decrease to 45% if equity finance is used, or rise to 121% if debt finance is used. There may also be some acquired debt finance in the capital structure of CRX Co. THP Co needs to consider what level of financial risk is desirable, from both a corporate and a stakeholder perspective.

Target capital structure

THP Co needs to compare its capital structure after the acquisition with its target capital structure. If its primary financial objective is to maximise the wealth of shareholders, it should seek to minimise its weighted average cost of capital (WACC). In practical terms this can be achieved by having some debt in its capital structure, since debt is relatively cheaper than equity, while avoiding the extremes of too little gearing (WACC can be decreased further) or too much gearing (the company suffers from the costs of financial distress).

Availability of security

Debt will usually need to be secured on assets by either a fixed charge (on specific assets) or a floating charge (on a specified class of assets). The amount of finance needed to buy CRX CO would need to be secured by a fixed charge to specific fixed assets of THP Co. Information on these fixed assets and on the secured status of the existing 8% loan notes has not been provided.

Economic expectations

If THP Co expects buoyant economic conditions and increasing profitability in the future, it will be more prepared to take on fixed interest debt commitments than if it believes difficult trading conditions lie ahead.

Control issues

A rights issue will not dilute existing patterns of ownership and control, unlike an issue of shares to new investors. The choice between offering new shares to existing shareholders and to new shareholders will depend in part on the amount of finance that is needed, with rights issues being used for medium-sized issues and issues to new shareholders being used for large issues. Issuing traded debt also has control implications however, since restrictive or negative covenants are usually written into the bond issue documents.

Workings

Current gearing (debt/equity, book value basis) = $100 \times 5{,}000/7{,}300 = 68{\cdot}5\%$

Gearing if equity finance is used = $100 \times 5{,}000/(7{,}300 + 3{,}840) = 45\%$

Gearing if debt finance is used = $100 \times (5{,}000 + 3{,}840)/7{,}300 = 121\%$

ACCA marking scheme			
			Marks
(a)	Dividend per share		1
	Ex dividend share price		2
	Market capitalisation		1
			—
			4
(b)	Rights issue price		1
	Cash raised		1
	Theoretical ex rights price per share		1
	Market capitalisation		2
			—
			5
(c)	Calculation of price/earnings ratio		1
	Price/earnings ratio valuation		2
			—
			3
(d)	Calculations of market capitalisation		2–3
	Comment		3–4
			—
	Maximum		5
(e)	Relevant discussion		6–7
	Links to scenario in question		2–3
			—
	Maximum		8
			—
	Total		25
			—

Examiner's comments

Part (a) asked candidates to calculate the current ex dividend share price and the current market capitalisation of a company using the dividend growth model (DGM).

The first step was to calculate the current dividend per share, which surprisingly many candidates found difficult. Only one calculation, multiplying the earnings per share of the company by its payout ratio, was needed, but some candidates used half a page of calculations to produce the same answer. This highlights the importance of being familiar with the accounting ratios included in the F9 syllabus.

The formula for the DGM is given in the formula sheet, and the cost of equity and dividend growth rate were given in the question. Calculating the current ex dividend share price by inserting these values in the formula should therefore have posed no problem. Candidates who ignored or rearranged this formula created unnecessary difficulties for themselves and wasted valuable time. For example, some candidates rearranged the DGM formula into a cost of equity calculation and then called the cost of equity the current share price. This emphasises that candidates must be familiar with the formulae provided in the examination paper.

Finally, the current ex div share price had to be multiplied by the number of shares issued by the company to give its market capitalisation, or total value on the capital market. Surprisingly, some candidates did not understand 'market capitalisation' and offered no answer here for what was a straightforward calculation.

In part (b) candidates were asked to calculate the rights issue price per share, the cash raised by the rights issue, the theoretical ex rights price per share and the market capitalisation after the rights issue.

A significant number of candidates showed that they were unfamiliar with this part of the syllabus and gave answers that gained little credit. Some answers ignored the share price they had calculated in part (a) and assumed a different market price prior to the rights issue, frequently the company's ordinary share par value. Candidates should be aware that rights issues will not be made at a discount to par value. Many 'own error' marks were awarded in marking this part of question 2, following on from an assumed share price. In calculating market capitalisation after the rights issue, many answers neglected to subtract the issue costs.

Part (c) required the use of the price/earnings ratio method to calculate a share price and market capitalisation. Answers to this part of question 2 were often incomplete or adopted an incorrect methodology, for example calculating the price/earnings ratio of the target company when the question did not give the information needed for this. The correct approach is to multiply an earnings per share figure (or total earnings) by a suitable price/earnings ratio (in this case that of the acquirer).

Part (d) asked candidates to calculate and comment on market capitalisation before and after an announcement of expected annual after-tax cost savings, assuming a semi-strong form efficient market. The key thing to remember here is that in such a market, share prices fully and fairly reflect all relevant past and public information. The market capitalisation after the announcement would include the present value of the expected savings, calculated for example by the price/earnings method or by the dividend growth model. Before the announcement, the market capitalisation would not include this information and would be the market capitalisation immediately after the rights issue had taken place, adjusted for issue costs and the market value of the company acquired. Many candidates did not offer any calculations to support their discussion here, or offered calculations that did not relate to the question asked. Please refer to the suggested answer to this question for more detailed information on appropriate discussion and calculations.

Part (e) asked for a discussion of the factors that should be considered in choosing between equity and debt, with the answer being related to the circumstances of the acquirer and its proposed cash offer. Good answers focused on the circumstances of the company, considered its current capital structure, and discussed such factors as financial risk, current and expected interest rates, security and servicing costs, while weak answers offered a brief list of points with no discussion.

59   PHOBIS

Key answer tips

This question has three discreet requirements which are of varying difficulty. To score well you must ensure you capture the easy marks quickly and don't get bogged down on one particular area meaning you run out of time, or worse still, run over time and limit your ability to get all marks on later questions.   Part (b) is the most difficult of the three requirements. This should have been tackled last. The highlighted words are key phrases that markers are looking for.

(a)   (i)   Price/earnings ratio method valuation

Earnings per share of Danoca Co = 40c

Average sector price/earnings ratio = 10

Implied value of ordinary share of Danoca Co = 40 × 10 = $4.00

Number of ordinary shares = 5 million

Value of Danoca Co = 4.00 × 5m = $20 million

(ii)   Dividend growth model

Earnings per share of Danoca Co = 40c

Proposed payout ratio = 60%

Proposed dividend of Danoca Co is therefore = 40 × 0.6 = 24c

If the future dividend growth rate is expected to continue the historical trend in dividends per share, the historic dividend growth rate can be used as a substitute for the expected future dividend growth rate in the dividend growth model. Average geometric dividend growth rate over the last two years = (24/22)1/2 = 1.045 or 4.5% (Alternatively, dividend growth rates over the last two years were 3% (24/23.3) and 6% (23.3/22), with an arithmetic average of (6 + 3)/2 = 4.5%)

Cost of equity of Danoca Co using the capital asset pricing model (CAPM)

= 4.6 + 1.4 × (10.6 − 4.6) = 4.6 + (1.4 × 6) = 13%

Value of ordinary share from dividend growth model = (24 × 1.045)/(0.13 − 0.045) = $2.95

Value of Danoca Co = 2.95 × 5m = $14.75 million

The current market capitalisation of Danoca Co is $16.5m ($3.30 × 5m).The price/earnings ratio value of Danoca Co is higher than this at $20m, using the average price/earnings ratio used for the sector. Danoca's own price/earnings ratio is 8.25. The difference between the two price/earnings ratios may indicate that there is scope for improving the financial performance of Danoca Co following the acquisition. If Phobis Co has the managerial skills to effect this improvement, the company and its shareholders may be able to benefit as a result of the acquisition.

The dividend growth model value is lower than the current market capitalisation at $14.75m. This represents a minimum value that Danoca shareholders will accept if Phobis Co makes an offer to buy their shares. In reality they would want more than this as an inducement to sell. The current market capitalisation of Danoca Co of $16m may reflect the belief of the stock market that a takeover bid for the company is imminent and, depending on its efficiency, may indicate a fair price for Danoca's shares, at least on a marginal trading basis. Alternatively, either the cost of equity or the expected dividend growth rate used in the dividend growth model calculation could be inaccurate, or the difference between the two values may be due to a degree of inefficiency in the stock market.

(b) **Calculation of market value of each convertible bond**

Expected share price in five years' time = 4.45 × 1.0655 = $6.10

Conversion value = 6.10 × 20 = $122

Compared with redemption at par value of $100, conversion will be preferred

The current market value will be the present value of future interest payments, plus the present value of the conversion value, discounted at the cost of debt of 7% per year.

Market value of each convertible bond = (9 × 4.100) + (122 × 0.713) = $123.89

Calculation of floor value of each convertible bond

The current floor value will be the present value of future interest payments, plus the present value of the redemption value, discounted at the cost of debt of 7% per year.

Floor value of each convertible bond = (9 × 4.100) + (100 × 0.713) = $108.20

Calculation of conversion premium of each convertible bond

Current conversion value = 4.45 × 20 = $89.00

Conversion premium = $123.89 − 89.00 = $34.89

This is often expressed on a per share basis, i.e. 34.89/20 = $1.75 per share

(c) Stock market efficiency usually refers to the way in which the prices of traded financial securities reflect relevant information. When research indicates that share prices fully and fairly reflect past information, a stock market is described as weak-form efficient. Investors cannot generate abnormal returns by analysing past information, such as share price movements in previous time periods, in such a market, since research shows that there is no correlation between share price movements in successive periods of time. Share prices appear to follow a 'random walk' by responding to new information as it becomes available.

When research indicates that share prices fully and fairly reflect public information as well as past information, a stock market is described as semi-strong form efficient. Investors cannot generate abnormal returns by analysing either public information, such as published company reports, or past information, since research shows that share prices respond quickly and accurately to new information as it becomes publicly available.

If research indicates that share prices fully and fairly reflect not only public information and past information, but private information as well, a stock market is described as strong form efficient. Even investors with access to insider information cannot generate abnormal returns in such a market. Testing for strong form efficiency is indirect in nature, examining for example the performance of expert analysts such as fund managers. Stock markets are not held to be strong form efficient.

The significance to a listed company of its shares being traded on a stock market which is found to be semi-strong form efficient is that any information relating to the company is quickly and accurately reflected in its share price. Managers will not be able to deceive the market by the timing or presentation of new information, such as annual reports or analysts' briefings, since the market processes the information quickly and accurately to produce fair prices. Managers should therefore simply concentrate on making financial decisions which increase the wealth of shareholders.

ACCA marking scheme		Marks
(a)	Price/earnings ratio value of company	2
	Proposed dividend per share	1
	Average dividend growth rate	1
	Cost of equity using CAPM	1
	Dividend growth model value of company	
		2
	Discussion	4
		——
		11
		——
(b)	Conversion value	1
	Market value	2
	Floor value	2
	Conversion premium	1
		——
		6
		——
(c)	Weak form efficiency	1–2
	Semi-strong form efficiency	1–2
	Strong form efficiency	1–2
	Significance of semi-strong form efficiency	
		2–3
		——
		8
		——
	Total	25
		——

Examiner's comments

In part (a), candidates were asked to calculate the value of a company using the price/earnings ratio method and the dividend growth model, and to discuss the significance of calculated values, in comparison to the current market value of the company, to a potential buyer. Answers to this part of question 1 often failed to gain many marks, mainly because candidates did not calculate company values.

The prices/earnings ratio method calculates the value of a company by multiplying an earnings per share figure by a price/earnings ratio, and then multiplying by the number of issued shares. Alternatively, total earnings can be multiplied by a price/earnings ratio. Although the question provided an average sector price/earnings ratio to use in this context, many candidates simply calculated the current price/earnings ratio of the company and compared this with the sector value. Calculating a price/earnings ratio is not the same as calculating the value of a company. Candidates should also note that the price/earnings ratio is a multiple and neither a percentage nor a monetary amount.

The dividend growth model (DGM) formula is given in the formulae sheet in the examination paper. Many candidates rearranged the DGM formula in order to calculate a cost of equity, even though what was needed was to calculate a share price by inserting values for the current dividend, the cost of equity and the dividend growth rate into the DGM formula provided. The cost of equity could be calculated from the capital asset pricing model, using the formula given in the formulae sheet. The current dividend could be calculated using the dividend payout ratio and the current earnings per share value provided in the question. The future dividend growth rate could be calculated on an historical average basis, although there were many errors in its calculation. A number of candidates were unable to distinguish between some of the variables given in the question, for example confusing dividend per share with earnings per share, return on the market with cost of equity, and equity beta with retention ratio.

Even though the current market value of the company (number of shares multiplied by share price) was needed, a number of candidates failed to calculate it. The level of discussion was often limited, although some candidates demonstrated that they were aware of the weaknesses of the valuation models used.

Part (b) asked candidates to calculate the market value, floor value and conversion value of a $100 convertible bond. Many candidates either failed to answer this part of question 1, or showed in their answers that they did not understand how to calculate the present value of a stream of future cash flows (which is what the market value of a bond is equivalent to).

Candidates needed to calculate the present value of future interest payments plus the present value of the future conversion value (the market value, since conversion was financially preferable to redemption), and the present value of future interest payments plus the present value of the future redemption at par value (the floor value, since this stream of future cash flows is guaranteed). Some candidates were able to calculate the floor value, but called it the market value. Some candidates were able to calculate the current conversion value, but were not aware that this was used in calculating the conversion premium.

A number of candidates were not aware of the difference between interest rate, cost of debt and share price growth rate and used their values interchangeably. Some candidates introduced an assumed tax rate, when the question made no reference to taxation at all. There were indications of candidates learning a computation method, without acquiring an understanding of the concepts underlying it. Candidates must understand the importance, in financial management, of discounting future values in order to obtain present values, since this is used in investment appraisal, bond valuation, share valuation and company valuation.

Part (c) required candidates to distinguish between weak form, semi-strong form and strong form stock market efficiency, and to discuss the significance to a listed company of its shares being traded on a semi-strong form efficient stock market.

A number of candidates did not understand and could not discuss market efficiency, and very few correctly discussed the significance of semi-strong market efficiency to a company. Some candidates simply picked up on the terms weak, semi-strong and strong and discussed a range of stock market trading conditions, including bull and bear markets and depressed markets. Some candidates were aware of the link between market efficiency and information, but in a very tenuous way, for example saying that only past information was available, rather than saying that share prices fully and fairly reflected past information (weak form efficiency), or saying that investors were aware of current information, rather than saying that share prices fully and fairly reflected all past and public information (semi-strong-form efficiency). Overall, many answers were not of a pass standard.

RISK MANAGEMENT

60 RISKS OF FOREIGN TRADE

Key answer tips

As a purely discussional question on foreign exchange risk, care must be taken to consider the marks available and therefore the number of relevant points you should be looking to make. This is particularly so in part (b) where two of the three companies we're told about are not directly impacted by the most common of forex risks, translation risk. The highlighted words are key phrases that markers are looking for.

(a) The management of risk associated with foreign trade will depend upon the nature of the risk:

Commercial risk is risk that the client will not pay or will only pay after the due date. It may be managed by:

   (i) Credit screening prior to the contract being signed. This might include formal credit evaluation through a credit agency, use of information from trade associations, government databases (e.g. the DTI in the UK), bank references or trade references.

   (ii) The terms of sale. Some terms of sale involve much less risk than others. Most secure (but not common) is cash in advance. Others, in order of increasing risk include cash on delivery, documentary letters of credit, bills of exchange and open account.

   (iii) The method of payment. The quicker and more secure the method of payment, the lower the risk. Extremes range from secure electronic funds transfer to sending a cheque in the post.

   (iv) Insurance against non-payment or late payment. In many countries this is offered through government agencies. In the UK short-term insurance providers include NCM and Trade Indemnity.

Physical risk, the risk of damage or theft in transit is best managed through insurance cover.

Political risk is risk of non-payment or late payment as a result of the actions of a foreign government, e.g. through the introduction of exchange controls, tariffs or quotas. Political risk protection is often offered by the same insurers as commercial risk. Political risk might also be avoided by using different forms of international activity, e.g. tariffs and quotas might be avoided by direct investment in the country concerned, exchange controls might be avoided by engaging in countertrade rather than cash trade.

Cultural risk is risk associated with different cultures, ways of doing business, attitude to religion, colours (e.g. in the UK red indicates danger whereas in China it is good luck), gender, food and drink etc. In order to reduce such risk thorough research of the local market, culture, and business practices should be undertaken prior to trading.

(b)   There is some evidence that foreign exchange markets are efficient (in the context of the efficient markets hypothesis) when foreign exchange rates are allowed to float freely. However, there are very few examples of currencies that are allowed to float freely in response to economic forces; where a floating exchange rate exists it is normally in the form of a managed float (or dirty float) where a government intervenes in the foreign exchange market to influence the price of its currency. Even if an efficient foreign exchange market exists the manager of company one would be engaging in a risky strategy. The effect of changes in the exchange rate on the company's export transactions depends upon the strength of sterling relative to the currencies in the countries to which company one exports. It is possible that sterling could rise in value against all of these currencies simultaneously, and losses be made on the export sales due to exchange rate changes. The company might not be able to sustain such losses until more favourable exchange rate movements occur. Hedging, although it involves costs, can limit foreign exchange losses (if any) to a known amount.

Company two only trades within Europe. It might be thought that, as imports are contracted to be paid for in sterling, there is no foreign exchange risk with such transactions. Risk, however, does still exist, as is explained for company three.

Although company three is not engaged in foreign trade, exchange rate changes are still likely to be relevant to the company. One form of foreign exchange risk is economic exposure, which relates to the effects of unexpected changes in exchange rate on future cash flows. Changes in exchange rates might affect the company's competitive position. If exchange rate movements make foreign competitors' products cheaper, company three could lose sales to such foreign competitors. Additionally, although the company is not directly engaged in foreign trade, if it purchases components from other UK companies such components might contain imported materials. If exchange rates change, this could directly affect the price company three has to pay for components, even though these are purchased from UK suppliers. There are several other ways in which exchange rate change could affect company three. Exchange rate changes are not irrelevant to this company.

61   EXCHANGE RATE SYSTEMS AND ORDER FROM KUWAIT *Walk in the footsteps of a top tutor*

Key answer tips

This question is an excellent test of your knowledge of both foreign exchange risk management and the partity theorems.

The highlighted words are key phrases that markers are looking for.

Tutor's top tips:

All three parts are independent of each other and so you should tackle the section you feel most comfortable with first.

Tutor's top tips:

Part (a) is a generic question that relies purely on knowledge gained from the syllabus. It should therefore represent some fairly easy marks. Withe a requirement to describe, there will more than likely be 2 marks available for each type of exchange rate system you cover. With 10 marks on offer, and given that some will be available for your brief discussion on how such systems might affect the ability of financial managers to forecast exchange rates, you should aim to cover no more than 5 types of system.

(a) A wide range of exchange rate mechanisms exist. There include:

(i) Fixed or pegged exchange rates where a country fixes its exchange rate against the currency of another single country. More than 50 countries fix their exchange rates this way, mostly against the US dollar. Fixed rates are not permanently fixed and periodic revaluations and devaluations occur when the economic fundamentals of the countries concerned strongly diverge (e.g. inflation rates).

(ii) Fixed exchange rates against a basket of currencies, the basket often devised to reflect the major trading links of the country concerned. Using a basket of currencies is aimed at fixing the exchange rate against a more stable currency base than would occur with a single currency fix.

(iii) Flexible exchange rates against a single currency within a limited range of flexibility.

(iv) A joint float of a group currencies. Prior to monetary union the currencies within the exchange rate mechanism (ERM) of the European Union participated in a joint float against external currencies, whilst maintaining a flexible exchange rate within agreed ranges against other ERM members.

(v) Automatic exchange rate adjustments against a set of economic indicators.

(vi) A managed float (or dirty float). The central bank of countries using a managed float will attempt to keep currency relationships within a predetermined range of values (not usually publicly announced), and will often intervene in the exchange markets by buying or selling their currency to remain within the range.

(vii) Independent float. Almost 50 countries, including the USA and the UK use what is known as an independent float whereby exchange rates are determined primarily by market forces. In reality purely independent floats are rare, as the central banks of many of these countries will periodically intervene in the foreign exchange markets, especially when there is speculative pressure against a currency.

Forecasting exchange rates is a difficult task for financial managers, as future rates are influenced by economic and other events that are presently unknown and cannot be predicted.

Forecasting is more difficult when exchange rates are independently floating. The greater the government intervention in exchange rates the easier it is to forecast exchange rates, or at least the direction of movement of exchange rates. The further a currency is from efficient market conditions, the greater the possibility that fundamental or technical analysts will be able to produce a 'better than chance' forecast. 'Fixed' rates offer the best forecasting opportunity. With fixed exchange systems rates will either remain unchanged in the near future, or if a devaluation or revaluation occurs the direction of exchange rate movement will be obvious from inflation and interest rate differentials between the two countries. The timing and size of a devaluation will, however, be less obvious.

Tutor's top tips:

An understanding of what influences exchange rates, focussing in interest rate parity theory is needed to answer part (b). You should explain the concept and do calculations using the information given to score highly.

Remember, the formulas for both purchasing power parity and interest rate parity are given in the formula sheet. Start by writing down the formula and then identify the information you require from the question.

If you can't remember what the terms stand for in the formula, a useful solution is to work out a simple scenario. Imagine you have £100 which you could either earn 6% interest on in the UK (i.e. you'd have £106 in one year's time) or you could convert into € and earn 3.5%. With a current exchange rate of €1.667/£, this means you'd have €166.7 × 1.035 = €172.53 in one years time.

Now we can compare these two figures to calculate an expected future exchange rate of (€172.53 / £106) €1.628/£.

(b)   (i)   According to Interest Rate Parity Theory (IRPT) interest rate differentials between any two countries provide an unbiased predictor of future changes in the spot rate of exchange.

If interest rates are 6% in the UK and 3.5% in the Euro bloc, the expected exchange rate in one year's time is:

$$F_0 = S_0 \times \frac{(1+i_c)}{(1+i_b)} = 1.667 \times \frac{1.035}{1.06} = 1.628$$

Repeating this calculation, the exchange rate in two years' time will be:

$$1.628 \times \frac{1.035}{1.06} = 1.590$$

The non-executive director has incorrectly used the relationships between the interest rates and exchange rates. It would appear that she has got the interest rates the wrong way round, implying that sterling is expected to strengthen rather than weaken against the Euro. $(1.667 \times (1.06/1.035)^2 = €1.749/£)$.

(ii)   Forecasts of exchange rates using interest rate differentials are not likely to be accurate. Reasons for this include:

- The interest rate differential may change during the next two years.

- Even if the interest differential remains constant the IRPT is an unbiased not accurate predictor of future exchange rates.

- Exchange rates may not be in equilibrium at the current time. The IRPT predicts movements from an equilibrium position.

- Factors other than interest rates influences exchange rates, including government intervention in foreign exchange markets.

Tutor's top tips:

Part (c) tests your understanding of common hedging techniques as well as drawing on your understanding of the purchasing power parity theory. Read the question carefully as you don't want to waste time talking about forward exchange contracts when you're clearly told that no forward market exists.

(c)   The order is not yet definite. If the subsidiary wishes to protect against foreign exchange risk at the tender stage an over-the-counter option from a commercial bank is suggested. If the tender is not successful the option would not be exercised and the total cost would be the option premium. An option to sell Kuwait Dinar (buy a put option on dinar) could be taken for either:

(i)   the full 18 month period until payment is due

(ii)   the period until the result of the tender is known and then a further hedge taken for the remainder of the period if the tender is successful.

For a short maturity option during the tender period the premium would be relatively low. The further hedge could be another option contract, or a money market hedge involving borrowing Kuwait dinar and converting to Euro at the current spot rate. The sum to be borrowed plus interest would total the amount of the Dinar receipts in 18 months' time. The funds converted to Euro at spot would be immediately available in Italy.

Estimates of future exchange rates may be made here using the purchasing power parity theorem (PPPT). Adapting the PPPT formula gives:

$$\text{Future spot (€/Dinar) in 18 months} = S_0 \times \frac{(1+h_c)^{1.5}}{(1+h_b)^{1.5}} = 0.256 \times \frac{(1.03)^{1.5}}{(1.09)^{1.5}} = 0.235$$

(This assumes that exchange rates are currently in equilibrium).

The normal price would be Euro $340,000 \times 1.25 =$ Euro 425,000

At spot (using the purchase price of the Euro) this is: $\dfrac{425,000}{0.256} = 1,660,156$ dinars

However, in 18 months time the dinar is expected to have weakened. Using the forecast spot rate in 18 months time as the basis for the tender gives:

$\dfrac{425,000}{0.235} = 1,808,511$ dinars

If an option hedge is used the tender price could be increased by the amount of the option premium.

The recommended tender price in not less than 1,660,556 dinars plus the premium cost of an option to buy euro in 18 months time at the present spot rate, or 1,808,511 dinars if no foreign hedge is undertaken.

62 LAGRAG CO

Key answer tips

To ensure you capture all of the easy marks available in this question, you must read the requirement carefully and focus on the number of marks allocated to each part. Many students could write a lot to answer part (d) but it is only worth 4 marks. You must restrict your answer here and focus more on the earlier parts to the question. The highlighted words are key phrases that markers are looking for.

Gross Redemption Yield %

normal yield curve Term.

(a) The term structure of interest rates is revealed by the redemption yield data. As the term to maturity increases, the redemption yield also increases, producing what is known as the normal upward sloping yield curve. The shape of the yield curve can be explained as follows:

   (i) Liquidity preference theory states that as investors have a natural preference for more liquid investments, they will need to receive extra compensation in the form of an enhanced yield if they are to invest for the longer term

   (ii) Expectations theory suggests that the shape of the yield curve reflects the expectation of future interest rates. Hence if the yield curve becomes steeper, this indicates that interest rates are likely to rise, whereas if the yield curve becomes less steep, this indicates that interest rates are likely to decline.

   (iii) Market segmentation theory suggests that the market for borrowing and lending is split into segments. For instance, some lenders specialise in shorter term lending. Supply and demand variations, the fact that the different segments will have different information and the operators in the different segments will have different views means that the yield curve may not be completely smooth.

   Given the change in the redemption yields between the two years, it appears that the yield curve is becoming steeper and hence there is probably an expectation of a rise in interest rates.

(b) The appropriate forward rate agreement is the 3 v 7 agreement and as a borrower the rate agreed will be 7.53%.

   (i) If the actual interest rate payable is 7.76% in three months, then the cash flows will be as follows:

Actual interest paid	$10m × 4/12 × 7.76%	($258,667)
Compensation received	$10m × 4/12 × (7.76% - 7.53%)	$7,667
Net cost		($251,000)

(ii)   If the actual interest rate payable is 7.42% in three months, then the cash flows will be as follows:

Actual interest paid	$10m × 4/12 × 7.42%	($247,333)
Compensation paid	$10m × 4/12 × (7.53% – 7.42%)	($3,667)
Net cost		($251,000)

Whatever the actual interest rate, the net cost remains the same.

(c)   **Futures**

As a borrower, a hedge with interest rate futures will protect Lagrag plc from higher borrowing costs. Should borrowing costs rise and our borrowings incur additional interest cost, then a compensating gain will be made as a result of the movement in the futures price. Unfortunately though, if our borrowing cost was to fall and we were to make a saving on our interest cost, an offsetting loss would be made as a result of the movement in the futures price.

Hence, the impact of a futures hedge would be to effectively fix our interest cost. The cost may not be completely fixed as the hedge may be imperfect due to basis risk.

Options on futures

As a borrower, a hedge with interest rate options on futures will protect Lagrag plc from higher borrowing costs. Should borrowing costs rise and our borrowings incur additional interest cost, then a compensating gain will be possible due to the movement in the futures price. To realise this gain the option would have to be exercised. If our borrowing costs were to fall and we were to make a saving on our interest cost, there would be no compensating loss as the option would not be exercised. Hence, a hedge using options on futures provides protection against a rise in interest rates, but will allow Lagrag plc to benefit if interest rates were to fall. Unfortunately though, as options are more flexible, they are more costly and there will be a premium to pay. This premium represents a sunk cost as is cannot be reclaimed in the option is not exercised.

Recommendation

As the yield curve is indicating that interest rates will rise, it is recommended that futures are used as it is unlikely to be worth paying for the flexibility of options on futures.

(d)   If Lagrag plc were to sell to an overseas customer, the two major risks that are likely to arise would be the risk of non-collection and the transaction risk which arises as a result of potential exchange rate movements between the invoice date and the date the payment is received.

The risk of non-collection could be reduced by using, for instance, a factor who is willing to assist with collection and provide protection against bad debts.

Transaction risk could be hedged in a number of ways. The simplest of these would be the use of a forward contract if one is available. This is simple and cheap and fixes the exchange rate to be used.

[Handwritten margin note: Interest rate Futures: standardised amounts. A Bet: the amount is charged/received at the market int. rate, and Future's mkt creates a gain/loss to offset the change in int. rate]

63   BOLUJE CO

Key answer tips

Part (a) is a standard discussion on the benefits of debt finance. Part (b) may look complicated, dealing in foreign bonds denominated in pesos, but requires a straightforward application of the dividend valuation model using the base premise of the market value of an investment equalling the present value of the future cash flows.

Part (c) gives plenty of opportunity for students to cover familiar areas. The trick with the calculations (an illustration was requested) is to recognise that Boluje is hedging its interest payments only (and not the full amount of the foreign bonds).

Finally, for 8 marks part (d) should be a relatively easy discussion of other hedging methods primarily focussing on futures and options. The highlighted words are key phrases that markers are looking for.

(a)   Pecking order theory suggests that companies have a preferred order in which they seek to raise finance, beginning with retained earnings. The advantages of using retained earnings are that issue costs are avoided by using them, the decision to use them can be made without reference to a third party, and using them does not bring additional obligations to consider the needs of finance providers.

Once available retained earnings have been allocated to appropriate uses within a company, its next preference will be for debt. One reason for choosing to finance a new investment by an issue of debt finance, therefore, is that insufficient retained earnings are available and the investing company prefers issuing debt finance to issuing equity finance.

Debt finance may also be preferred when a company has not yet reached its optimal capital structure and it is mainly financed by equity, which is expensive compared to debt. Issuing debt here will lead to a reduction in the WACC and hence an increase in the market value of the company. One reason why debt is cheaper than equity is that debt is higher in the creditor hierarchy than equity, since ordinary shareholders are paid out last in the event of liquidation. Debt is even cheaper if it is secured on assets of the company. The cost of debt is reduced even further by the tax efficiency of debt, since interest payments are an allowable deduction in arriving at taxable profit.

Debt finance may be preferred where the maturity of the debt can be matched to the expected life of the investment project. Equity finance is permanent finance and so may be preferred for investment projects with long lives.

(b)   Annual interest paid per foreign bond = 500 × 0.061 = 30.5 pesos

Redemption value of each foreign bond = 500 pesos

Cost of debt of peso-denominated bonds = 7% per year

Market value of each foreign bond = (30.5 × 4.100) + (500 × 0.713) = 481.55 pesos

Current total market value of foreign bonds = 16m × (481.55/500) = 15,409,600 pesos

(c)   (i)   Interest payment in one year's time = 16m × 0.061 = 976,000 pesos

A money market hedge would involve placing on deposit an amount of pesos that, with added interest, would be sufficient to pay the peso-denominated interest in one year. Because the interest on the peso-denominated deposit is guaranteed, Boluje Co would be protected against any unexpected or adverse exchange rate movements prior to the interest payment being made.

Peso deposit required = 976,000/ 1.05 = 929,524 pesos

Dollar equivalent at spot = 929,524/ 6 = $154,921

Dollar cost in one year's time = 154,921 × 1.04 = $161,118

(ii)   Cost of forward market hedge = 976,000/6.07 = $160,790

The forward market hedge is slightly cheaper

(d)   Boluje receives peso income from its export sales and makes annual peso-denominated interest payments to bond-holders. It could consider opening a peso *foreign* account in the overseas country and using this as a natural hedge against peso exchange rate risk.

Boluje Co could consider using lead payments to settle foreign currency liabilities. This would not be beneficial as far as peso-denominated liabilities are concerned, as the peso is depreciating against the dollar. It is inadvisable to lag payments to foreign suppliers, since this would breach sales agreements and lead to loss of goodwill.

Foreign currency derivatives available to Boluje Co could include currency futures, currency options and currency swaps.

Currency futures are standardised contracts for the purchase or sale of a specified quantity of a foreign currency. These contracts are settled on a quarterly cycle, but a futures position can be closed out any time by undertaking the opposite transaction to the one that opened the futures position. Currency futures provide a hedge that theoretically eliminates both upside and downside risk by effectively locking the holder into a given exchange rate, since any gains in the currency futures market are offset by exchange rate losses in the cash market, and vice versa. In practice however, movements in the two markets are not perfectly correlated and basis risk exists if maturities are not perfectly matched. Imperfect hedges can also arise if the standardised size of currency futures does not match the exchange rate exposure of the hedging company. Initial margin must be provided when a currency futures position is opened and variation margin may also be subsequently required. Boluje Co could use currency futures to hedge both its regular foreign currency receipts and its annual interest payment.

available in standardized amounts which can be traded on currency exchanges in months cycles.

Currency options give holders the right, but not the obligation, to buy or sell foreign currency. Over-the-counter (OTC) currency options are tailored to individual client needs, while exchange-traded currency options are standardised in the same way as currency futures in terms of exchange rate, amount of currency, exercise date and settlement cycle. An advantage of currency options over currency futures is that currency options do not need to be exercised if it is disadvantageous for the holder to do so. Holders of currency options can take advantage of favourable exchange rate movements in the cash market and allow their options to lapse. The initial fee paid for the options will still have been incurred, however.

Currency swaps are appropriate for hedging exchange rate risk over a longer period of time than currency futures or currency options. A currency swap is an interest rate swap where the debt positions of the counterparties and the associated interest payments are in different currencies. A currency swap begins with an exchange of principal, although this may be a notional exchange rather than a physical exchange. During the life of the swap agreement, the counterparties undertake to service each others' foreign currency interest payments. At the end of the swap, the initial exchange of principal is reversed.

ACCA marking scheme				
			Marks	Marks
(a)		Relevant discussion		7
(b)		Market value of each foreign bond	3	
		Total market value of foreign bonds	1	
			——	
				4
(c)	(i)	Explanation of money market hedge	2	
		Illustration of money market hedge	2	
			——	
				4
	(ii)	Comparison with forward market hedge		2
(d)		Discussion of natural hedge	1 – 2	
		Description of other hedging methods	6 – 7	
				Max 8
		Total		25

Examiner's comment

In part (a) of this question, candidates were asked to explain the reasons why a company might choose to finance a new investment by an issue of debt. Answers were of variable quality, with some candidates writing very little while others gained full marks.

Weaker answers discussed other sources of finance, such as leasing or preference shares, or focussed on the disadvantages of equity finance, indicating perhaps that candidates had prepared for a question about equity, but were unprepared for a question about debt. Better answers covered such reasons as the lower cost of debt compared with other sources of finance, due to lower risk of debt finance and its tax efficiency: the relative ease with which debt finance could be raised; the potentially positive effect of the lower cost of debt on the weighted average cost of capital and the market value of the company; the place of debt finance in pecking order theory; and the matching of debt and asset maturity.

Part (b) required candidates to calculate the total market value (in pesos) of a foreign bond (denominated in pesos). The market value of a bond is the present value of future interest payments added to the present value of the future redemption value. Good answers calculated the interest payable in pesos on each bond, the market value of each bond as just described, and then the total market value by multiplying the market value per bond by the number of bonds issued. Weaker answers sought to calculate the internal rate of return of the bond, which was unnecessary as the cost of debt was given in the question. Internal rate of return is not equal to market value.

Part (c) asked for an explanation and an illustration of a money market hedge, and a comparison of the relative costs of a money market hedge and a forward market hedge. Answers were again of very variable quality.

Many candidates were unable to calculate the annual peso interest required by the illustration of the money market hedge. Both the interest rate and the par value of the bond issue were given in the question, and multiplying one by the other gives the amount of interest to be paid. Some candidates invented a cash flow to illustrate the money market hedge: candidates who invented a future peso receipt failed to notice that the interest rates given in the question could not then be used, since the peso rate was a deposit rate and the dollar rate was a borrowing rate. Weaker answers tried to hedge a future dollar payment, when the question stated that the dollar was the home currency.

Many candidates were able to calculate correctly the dollar value of a forward market hedge and indicate whether this hedge would be preferred to a money market hedge.

Many candidates gave good answers to part (d), even if some answers tended to be a list rather a description. The question was open-ended, asking for a description of methods (including derivatives) that could be used to hedge exchange rate risk. Many methods could be and were described, including netting, matching, invoicing in the home currency, leading and lagging, forward exchange contracts, futures, option and swaps.

64   EXPORTERS PLC   *Walk in the footsteps of a top tutor*

Key answer tips

Another fairly standard question that combines knowledge with application. The highlighted words are key phrases that markers are looking for.

Tutor's top tips:

Don't feel you have to tackle the different parts of the requirement in order. Part (a) and part (b) (iii) give the best opportunities for some easy marks so are the best places to start.

(a)   Forward exchange contract

- A firm and binding agreement for the future trading of a particular amount of currency at a given price.

- A fixed contract is one where the date on which the trade will take place has been specified. An option contract is one where the trade can take place within a specified period.

(b)   Exporters plc

Tutor's top tips:

This first thing to appreciate about this part of the requirement is that it's asking a question that rarely gets asked in reality – what if we hadn't entered into that hedge? Remember, the purpose of hedging a transaction is to elimate risk, and so it isn't often someone would bother looking back to calculate what would have happened if they hadn't bothered!

That said, to perform the calculation you need to keep in mind the following things:

1. *Forward rates will be determined by interest differentials (the question doesn't specify the forward rate the company is locking in to. It does however, give you the interest differentials that will allow you to work the forward rate out.*

2. *What does happen to interest rates in the future will be determined by many different factors – the rate that does occur in the future is unlikely to be the same as the future rate that was contacted. This will give rise to a gain or loss on the transaction.*

3. *If the £ gains in value (appreciates), you will get more Northland dollars for each £. Equally, if it losses value (depreciates or weakens) it will buy less Northland dollars.*

(i)   UK interest rates over 6 months are $\frac{1}{2} \times 12\% = 6\%$.

Northland interest rates over 6 months are $\frac{1}{2} \times 15\% = 7.5\%$

Implied forward rate for the £ after 6 months $= \dfrac{1.075}{1.06} \times 2.5 = 2.5354.$

Tutorial note:

If you calculated your forward rate using the annual interest rates, you would only lose one mark. All further calculations will be based on the 'own figure rule' which means that, provided you used the right technique, your answer would be marked as correct, even though you have a different answer to that shown here.

(1)   If the £ has gained 4%, N's actual rate is $2.5 \times 1.04 = 2.6$ to the £.

Hedged receipt $= \dfrac{\$500,000}{2.5354} =$ £197,208

Unhedged receipt $= \dfrac{\$500,000}{2.6} =$ £192,308

∴ Gain from hedging = £197,208 − £192,308 = £4,900.

(2)   If the £ has lost 2%, N's actual rate is $2.5 \times 0.98 = 2.45$ to the £

Unhedged receipt $= \dfrac{\$500,000}{2.45} = £204,082$

∴ Loss from hedging = £204,082 − £197,208 = £6,874.

(3)   If the £ has remained stable, N's actual rate is still 2.5 to the £.

$$\text{Unhedged receipt} = \frac{\$500,000}{2.5} = £200,000$$

$$\therefore \text{Loss from hedging} = £200,000 - £197,208 = £2,792.$$

(ii) The interest rate parity analysis of forward rates suggests that an equilibrium is reached when:

$$F_0 = S_0 \times \frac{(1 + i_c)}{(1 + i_b)}$$

If the above equation were not an equality, it would be possible to make riskless profits by buying a foreign currency and holding a deposit in that currency on which interest was earned before returning to sterling. The opportunity cost of holding the foreign currency must equal the real interest rate of that currency relative to sterling. Arbitrageurs would quickly move in to drive the relation back to equality if they identified the possibility of riskless profits.

The analysis holds true only in an efficient market, since it excludes practical factors such as transaction costs and illiquidity. However in markets such as the major currency Eurocurrency markets in the UK, there is sufficient efficiency for the analysis to hold very nearly true.

(iii) *Forward market currency hedge*

A company can use the foreign exchange markets to hedge exactly as shown in the question. A company due to receive foreign currency in 6 months time can sell that currency forward, i.e. agree an exchange rate now at which that amount of foreign currency will be exchanged into sterling. The cost involved will be paid to the bank arranging the transaction and will usually be built into the contract's exchange rate so that the foreign currency is quoted net. The benefits are peace of mind to the company that they have laid off the risks of exchange rate movements between the contract date and the date when the foreign currency will be paid or received. Part (a) illustrates a range of possible gains and losses on a forward market currency hedge depending on the actual currency movements before the contract matures.

Currency futures hedge

Currency futures contracts are traded on separate exchanges such as the London International Financial Futures and Options Exchange (LIFFE). Each contract provides a simultaneous right and obligation to buy or sell on a specific future date a standard amount of a particular currency at a price that is known at the time of entering the contract. Since the contracts are sold in standard amounts and have a limited number of maturity dates each year, they are highly standardised and a liquid market has developed to trade them.

A UK exporting company due to receive 500,000 Northland dollars in six months' time could only hedge its currency exposure by means of currency futures if contracts are available between Northland dollars and sterling, and then only could it create an exact hedge if 500,000 dollars happened to be a multiple of the standard contract size. But assuming that both these conditions are fulfilled, the company can buy contracts to sell Northland dollars into sterling at the required future time.

Currency options hedge

A call/put option gives the buyer of that option the right, but not the obligation, to buy/sell currency in the future at a particular exchange rate. A UK company which uses a forward or futures position avoids losing from adverse movements on currencies but also fails to gain from favourable movements. A currency option is suitable for a UK company which believes it knows the direction of future exchange rate movements, but is not sure and wishes to minimise the loss arising in the event of being proved incorrect.

The company in the question anticipates dollars receivable in six months' time. It can pay an option premium to buy sterling call options. These enable the company to benefit from the anticipated appreciating dollar while providing protection against the opposite movement.

65   UNIPROD

Key answer tips

To score well in part (a) you must ensure that you apply your knowledge to the specifics of the scenario you've been given. Also, take note of the need for calculations. The highlighted words are key phrases that markers are looking for.

(a)   **REPORT**

To:	The Managers of Uniprod Inc
From:	The Chief Accountant
Subject:	Alternative protective interest rate risk strategies

Introduction

The general level of interest rates is widely expected to change around the time of next April's general election. This report discusses the advantages and disadvantages of alternative strategies that you might adopt to protect the company against the risk of adverse interest rate movements during the next six months. The company is forecasting a cash deficit of approximately $2.4 million to arise by the end of April 20X8.

Four strategies that the company could adopt are as follows:

(i)   Enter into FRAs with a bank.

(ii)   Use interest rate futures.

(iii)   Use interest rate options.

(iv)   Adopt no protective strategy on the basis that the company's exposure to adverse rate movements is small.

Each of these strategies is considered in turn.

(i)   **Forward rate agreements**

A forward rate agreement (FRA) is a contract by which two parties agree on the interest rate to be paid/received during a future period. The principal amount is agreed, but not exchanged, and the contract is settled in cash. Risk exposure to differences in interest rates can therefore be eliminated for the principal amount.

In the case of Uniprod, the company might wish to borrow $2.4m from a bank during next May and June and also enter into an FRA, say at 11% pa. Note that the FRA does not include the borrowing of the principal amount; this must be arranged as a separate contract. The FRA is purely a contract based on interest rates during a future period. Uniprod's FRA would involve the bank paying the company if interest rates rose above 11% during the period, while the company would pay the bank if interest rates were below 11% during the period. Either way, the interest cost payable by Uniprod over the two months period would become a net 11%, whatever the actual rate during the period happened to be.

(ii)   **Interest rate futures**

An interest rate futures contract gives the holder the right to buy or sell a specific financial instrument at a specific price at a given future date. The idea is to establish a hedge between the futures position and the underlying cash instrument so that if, for example, the company finds itself paying more interest on its cash borrowings then it should be compensated by its future becoming more valuable.

Uniprod is particularly worried about interest rates rising in April or May around the time of the general election just as the company is entering a phase of requiring cash borrowings. Uniprod's hedge strategy using futures would be to sell $2.4m cover of dollar future contracts now, in the expectation of buying them back (i.e., closing the position) later at a cheaper price once rates have risen. If in fact interest rates fall over the holding period then a loss on the futures position will be suffered; however this will be offset by the lower interest payments payable on the underlying borrowings.

Uniprod should be able to construct a good hedge using exchange-traded futures, though a perfect hedge is unlikely to be achieved. This is unimportant however, since the risk exposure is not large anyway.

(iii)   **Interest rate options**

An interest rate options contract gives the right, but not the obligation, to buy/sell a specified financial instrument paying a fixed rate of interest at a specified price and future date. Futures exchanges, such as LIFFE, deal in option contracts in standard amounts of a selection of financial instruments, at standard strike prices and expiry dates. Alternatively over-the-counter (OTC) options can be specifically arranged by a bank.

The advantage of interest rate options over FRAs and futures is that, if there are favourable movements in the underlying market, the option need not be exercised and the company is free to enjoy the upside potential of the situation. For example, if interest rates fell between the date the option was taken out and May/June, when the borrowings are planned, the company would abandon the option and enjoy the lower interest payments on the necessary borrowings.

The disadvantage of interest rate options is the significant premium payable to buy the contract. This cost should be compared with the expected benefits of the cover provided.

(iv) **No protective strategy**

The maximum overdraft requirement over the period is $2.4m. The maximum change in interest rates over the six months period will probably not exceed 3%. So the largest changes in monthly interest received and paid will be:

Interest paid $2.42m \times 3\% \times \frac{1}{12} = \$6,050$

In the context of monthly sales of approximately $9m the risk exposure from interest rates is fairly small. Given that rates might move favourably as well as unfavourably, it might well be argued that no complicated hedging strategy should be adopted. The cost of the strategy can be avoided since the risk of adverse movements is acceptable.

(b) There are a number of economic reasons why interest rates change. Possible reasons for an increase in interest rates include:

(i) increased borrowing by the government; interest rates rise so as to increase the funds available for gilt purchase by taking funds away from other investments;

(ii) an increase in the funds demanded by the private sector; again interest rates rise to encourage such investors;

(iii) a rise in actual price inflation; causing notional interest rates to rise so that real interest rates remain constant;

(iv) a rise in the expected rate of inflation; so that investors, especially in respect of fixed rate investments, raise their interest rate demands so as to maintain a constant level of real income;

(v) government legislation to reduce the funds available for lending (e.g., by banks); so that interest rates rise to reduce the demand for funds;

(vi) government action to strengthen the value of currency on the world currency markets.

ACCA PILOT PAPER

Financial Management

Question paper

Paper F9

Time allowed
Reading and planning: 15 minutes;
Writing: 3 hours

ALL FOUR questions are compulsory and MUST be attempted
Formulae Sheet, Present Value and Annuity Tables are on pages 3, 4 and 5.
Do NOT open this paper until instructed by the supervisor.
During reading and planning time only the question paper may be annotated. You must NOT write in your answer booklet until instructed by the supervisor.
This question paper must not be removed from the examination hall.

KAPLAN

PUBLISHING

Kaplan Publishing/Kaplan Financial

---

1 DROXFOL

Droxfol Co is a listed company that plans to spend $10m on expanding its existing business. It has been suggested that the money could be raised by issuing 9% loan notes redeemable in ten years' time. Current financial information on Droxfol Co is as follows.

Income statement information for the last year

	$000
Profit before interest and tax	7,000
Interest	(500)
Profit before tax	6,500
Tax	(1,950)
Profit for the period	4,550

Statement of Financial Position for the last year

	$000	$000
Non-current assets		20,000
Current assets		20,000
Total assets		40,000
Equity and liabilities		
Ordinary shares, par value $1	5,000	
Retained earnings	22,500	
Total equity		27,500
10% loan notes	5,000	
9% preference shares, par value $1	2,500	
Total non-current liabilities		7,500
Current liabilities		5,000
Total equity and liabilities		40,000

The current ex div ordinary share price is $4.50 per share. An ordinary dividend of 35 cents per share has just been paid and dividends are expected to increase by 4% per year for the foreseeable future. The current ex div preference share price is 76.2 cents. The loan notes are secured on the existing non-current assets of Droxfol Co and are redeemable at par in eight years' time. They have a current ex interest market price of $105 per $100 loan note. Droxfol Co pays tax on profits at an annual rate of 30%.

The expansion of business is expected to increase profit before interest and tax by 12% in the first year. Droxfol Co has no overdraft.

Average sector ratios:

Financial gearing: 45% (prior charge capital divided by equity share capital on a book value basis)

Interest coverage ratio: 12 times

Required:

WACC

(a) Calculate the current weighted average cost of capital of Droxfol Co. **(9 marks)**

(b) Discuss whether financial management theory suggests that Droxfol Co can reduce its weighted average cost of capital to a minimum level. *WACC ↓* **(8 marks)** *3 theories*

Traditional

(c) Evaluate and comment on the effects, <u>after one year</u>, of the loan note issue and the *M&M—Tax* expansion of business on the following ratios:

—no Tax

(i) interest coverage ratio; *Pecking Order*

(ii) financial gearing;

(iii) earnings per share. *g*

Assume that the dividend growth rate of <u>4%</u> is unchanged. **(8 marks)**

(Total: 25 marks)

Ratio. Discussion

— why has it changed ?

— Is it better or worse ?

— How much % has it changed by ?

— What does it mean for the company ?

2 NEDWEN

Nedwen Co is a UK-based company which has the following expected transactions..

One month:	Expected receipt of $240,000
One month:	Expected payment of $140,000
Three months:	Expected receipts of $300,000

The finance manager has collected the following information:

Spot rate ($ per £):	1.7820 ± 0.0002	1.7819 – 1.7822
One month forward rate ($ per £):	1.7829 ± 0.0003	1.7826 – 1.7832
Three months forward rate ($ per £):	1.7846 ± 0.0004	1.7842 – 1.7850

Money market rates for Nedwen Co:

	Borrowing	Deposit
One year sterling interest rate:	4.9%	4.6
One year dollar interest rate:	5.4%	5.1

Assume that it is now 1 April.

Required:

(a) Discuss the differences between transaction risk, translation risk and economic risk.
(6 marks)

(b) Explain how inflation rates can be used to forecast exchange rates. (6 marks)

(c) Calculate the expected sterling receipts in one month and in three months using the forward market. (3 marks)

(d) Calculate the expected sterling receipts in three months using a money-market hedge and recommend whether a forward market hedge or a money market hedge should be used. (5 marks)

(e) Discuss how sterling currency futures contracts could be used to hedge the three-month dollar receipt. (5 marks)

(Total: 25 marks)

3/ ULNAD

Ulnad Co has annual sales revenue of $6 million and all sales are on 30 days' credit, although customers on average take ten days more than this to pay. Contribution represents 60% of sales and the company currently has no bad debts. Accounts receivable are financed by an overdraft at an annual interest rate of 7%.

Ulnad Co plans to offer an early settlement discount of 1.5% for payment within 15 days and to extend the maximum credit offered to 60 days. The company expects that these changes will increase annual credit sales by 5%, while also leading to additional incremental costs equal to 0.5% of sales revenue. The discount is expected to be taken by 30% of customers, with the remaining customers taking an average of 60 days to pay.

Required:

(a) Evaluate whether the proposed changes in credit policy will increase the profitability of Ulnad Co. **(6 marks)**

(b) Renpec Co, a subsidiary of Ulnad Co, has set a minimum cash account balance of $7,500. The average cost to the company of making deposits or selling investments is $18 per transaction and the standard deviation of its cash flows was $1,000 per day during the last year. The average interest rate on investments is 5.11%.

Determine the spread, the upper limit and the return point for the cash account of Renpec Co using the Miller-Orr model and explain the relevance of these values for the cash management of the company. **(6 marks)**

(c) Identify and explain the key areas of accounts receivable management. **(6 marks)**

(d) Discuss the key factors to be considered when formulating a working capital funding policy. **(7 marks)**

(Total: 25 marks)

4   TRECOR

Trecor Co plans to buy a new machine to meet expected demand for a new product, Product T. This machine will cost $250,000 and last for four years, at the end of which time it will be sold for $5,000. Trecor Co expects demand for Product T to be as follows:

Year	1	2	3	4
Demand (units)	35,000	40,000	50,000	25,000

The selling price for Product T is expected to be $12.00 per unit and the variable cost of production is expected to be $7.80 per unit.   Incremental annual fixed production overheads of $25,000 per year will be incurred. Selling price and costs are all in current price terms.

Selling price and costs are expected to increase as follows:

	Increase
Increase selling price of Product T:	3% per year
Variable cost of production:	4% per year
Fixed production overheads:	6% per year

Other information

Trecor Co has a real cost of capital of 5.7% and pays tax at an annual rate of 30% one year in arrears. It can claim capital allowances on a 25% reducing balance basis. General inflation is expected to be 5% per year.

Trecor Co has a target return on capital employed of 20%. Depreciation is charged on a straight-line basis over the life of an asset.

Required:

(a)   Calculate the net present value of buying the new machine and comment on your findings (work to the nearest $1,000).   **(13 marks)**

(b)   Calculate the before-tax return on capital employed (accounting rate of return) based on the average investment and comment on your findings.   **(5 marks)**

(c)   Discuss the strengths and weaknesses of internal rate of return in appraising capital investments.   **(7 marks)**

(Total: 25 marks)

Section 4

ANSWERS TO PILOT PAPER EXAM QUESTIONS

1 DROXFOL

(a) **Calculation of weighted average cost of capital (WACC)**

Market values

Market value of equity = 5m × 4.50 = $22.5 million

Market value of preference shares = 2.5m × 0.762 = $1.905 million

Market value of 10% loan notes = 5m × (105/100) = $5.25 million

Total market value = 22.5m + 1.905m + 5.25m = $29.655 million

Cost of equity using dividend growth model = [(35 × 1.04)/ 450] + 0.04 = 12.08%

Cost of preference shares = 100 × 9/ 76.2 = 11.81%

Annual after-tax interest payment = 10 × 0.7 = $7

Year	Cash flow	$	10% DF	PV ($)	5% DF	PV ($)
0	Market value	(105)	1.000	(105)	1.000	(105)
1–8	Interest	7	5.335	37.34	6.463	45.24
8	Redemption	100	0.467	46.70	0.677	67.70
				(20.96)		7.94

Using interpolation, after-tax cost of loan notes = 5 + [(5 × 7.94)/ (7.94 + 20.96)] = 6.37%

WACC = [(12.08 × 22.5) + (11.81 × 1.905) + (6.37 × 5.25)]/29.655 = 11.05%

(b) Droxfol Co has long-term finance provided by ordinary shares, preference shares and loan notes. The rate of return required by each source of finance depends on its risk from an investor point of view, with equity (ordinary shares) being seen as the most risky and debt (in this case loan notes) seen as the least risky. Ignoring taxation, the weighted average cost of capital (WACC) would therefore be expected to decrease as equity is replaced by debt, since debt is cheaper than equity, i.e. the cost of debt is less than the cost of equity.

However, financial risk increases as equity is replaced by debt and so the cost of equity will increase as a company gears up, offsetting the effect of cheaper debt. At low and moderate levels of gearing, the before-tax cost of debt will be constant, but it will increase at high levels of gearing due to the possibility of bankruptcy. At high levels of gearing, the cost of equity will increase to reflect bankruptcy risk in addition to financial risk.

In the traditional view of capital structure, ordinary shareholders are relatively indifferent to the addition of small amounts of debt in terms of increasing financial risk and so the WACC falls as a company gears up. As gearing up continues, the cost of equity increases to include a financial risk premium and the WACC reaches a minimum value. Beyond this minimum point, the WACC increases due to the effect of increasing financial risk on the cost of equity and, at higher levels of gearing, due to the effect of increasing bankruptcy risk on both the cost of equity and the cost of debt. On this traditional view, therefore, Droxfol Co can gear up using debt and reduce its WACC to a minimum, at which point its market value (the present value of future corporate cash flows) will be maximised.

In contrast to the traditional view, continuing to ignore taxation but assuming a perfect capital market, Miller and Modigliani demonstrated that the WACC remained constant as a company geared up, with the increase in the cost of equity due to financial risk exactly balancing the decrease in the WACC caused by the lower before-tax cost of debt. Since in a prefect capital market the possibility of bankruptcy risk does not arise, the WACC is constant at all gearing levels and the market value of the company is also constant. Miller and Modigliani showed, therefore, that the market value of a company depends on its business risk alone, and not on its financial risk. On this view, therefore, Droxfol Co cannot reduce its WACC to a minimum.

When corporate tax was admitted into the analysis of Miller and Modigliani, a different picture emerged. The interest payments on debt reduced tax liability, which meant that the WACC fell as gearing increased, due to the tax shield given to profits. On this view, Droxfol Co could reduce its WACC to a minimum by taking on as much debt as possible.

However, a perfect capital market is not available in the real world and at high levels of gearing the tax shield offered by interest payments is more than offset by the effects of bankruptcy risk and other costs associated with the need to service large amounts of debt. Droxfol Co should therefore be able to reduce its WACC by gearing up, although it may be difficult to determine whether it has reached a capital structure giving a minimum WACC.

(c) (i) Interest coverage ratio

Current interest coverage ratio = 7,000/500 = 14 times

Increased profit before interest and tax = 7,000 × 1.12 = $7.84m

Increased interest payment = (10m × 0.09) + 0.5m = $1.4m

Interest coverage ratio after one year = 7.84/1.4 = 5.6 times

The current interest coverage of Droxfol Co is higher than the sector average and can be regarded as quiet safe. Following the new loan note issue, however, interest coverage is less than half of the sector average, perhaps indicating that Droxfol Co may not find it easy to meet its interest payments.

(ii) Financial gearing

This ratio is defined here as prior charge capital/equity share capital on a book value basis

Current financial gearing = 100 × (5,000 + 2,500)/(5,000 + 22,500) = 27%

Ordinary dividend after one year = 0.35 × 5m × 1.04 = $1.82 million

Total preference dividend = 2,500 × 0.09 = $225,000

Income statement after one year:

	$000	$000
Profit before interest and tax		7,840
Interest		(1,400)
Profit before tax		6,440
Income tax expense		(1,932)
Profit for the period		4,508
Preference dividends	225	
Ordinary dividends	1,820	
		(2,045)
Retained earnings		2,463

Financial gearing after one year = 100 × (15,000 + 2,500)/ (5,000 + 22,500 + 2,463) = 58%

The current financial gearing of Droxfol Co is 40% less (in relative terms) than the sector average and after the new loan note issue it is 29% more (in relative terms). This level of financial gearing may be a cause of concern for investors and the stock market. Continued annual growth of 12%, however, will reduce financial gearing over time.

(iii) Earnings per share

Current earnings per share = 100 × (4,550 – 225)/5,000 = 86.5 cents

Earnings per share after one year = 100 × (4,508 – 225)/5,000 = 85.7 cents

Earnings per share is seen as a key accounting ratio by investors and the stock market, and the decrease will not be welcomed. However, the decrease is quiet small and future growth in earnings should quickly eliminate it.

The analysis indicates that an issue of new debt has a negative effect on the company's financial position, at least initially. There are further difficulties in considering a new issue of debt. The existing non-current assets are security for the existing 10% loan notes and may not available for securing new debt, which would then need to be secured on any new non-current assets purchased. These are likely to be lower in value than the new debt and so there may be insufficient security for a new loan note issue. Redemption or refinancing would also pose a problem, with Droxfol Co needing to redeem or refinance $10 million of debt after both eight years and ten years. Ten years may therefore be too short a maturity for the new debt issue.

An equity issue should be considered and compared to an issue of debt. This could be in the form of a rights issue or an issue to new equity investors.

ACCA marking scheme			
			Marks
(a)	Calculation of market values	2 marks	
	Calculation of cost of equity	2 marks	
	Calculation of cost of preference shares	1 mark	
	Calculation of cost of debt	2 marks	
	Calculation of WACC	2 marks	
			9
(b)	Relative costs of equity and debt	1 mark	
	Discussion of theories of capital structure	7–8 marks	
	Conclusion	1 mark	
	Maximum		8
(c)	Analysis of interest coverage ratio	2–3 marks	
	Analysis of financial gearing	2–3 marks	
	Analysis of earnings per share	2–3 marks	
	Comment	2–3 marks	
	Maximum		8
	Total		25

2 NEDWEN

(a) Transaction risk

This is the risk arising on short-term foreign currency transactions that the actual income or cost may be different from the income or cost expected when the transaction was agreed. For example, a sale worth $10,000 when the exchange rate is $1.79 per £ has an expected sterling value is $5,587. If the dollar has depreciated against sterling to $1.84 per £ when the transaction is settled, the sterling receipt will have fallen to $5,435. Transaction risk therefore affects cash flows and for this reason most companies choose to hedge or protect themselves against transaction risk.

Translation risk

This risk arises on consolidation of financial statements prior to reporting financial results and for this reason is also known as accounting exposure. Consider an asset worth €14 million, acquired when the exchange rate was €1.4 per $. One year later, when financial statements are being prepared, the exchange rate has moved to €1.5 per $ and the balance sheet value of the asset has changed from $10 million to $9.3 million, resulting an unrealised (paper) loss of $0.7 million. Translation risk does not involve cash flows and so does not directly affect shareholder wealth. However, investor perception may be affected by the changing values of assets and liabilities, and so a company may choose to hedge translation risk through, for example, matching the currency of assets and liabilities (e.g. a euro-denominated asset financed by a euro-denominated loan).

Economic risk

Transaction risk is seen as the short-term manifestation of economic risk, which could be defined as the risk of the present value of a company's expected future cash flows being affected by exchange rate movements over time. It is difficult to measure economic risk, although its effects can be described, and it is also difficult to hedge against it.

(b) The law of one price suggests that identical goods selling in different countries should sell at the same price, and that exchange rates relate these identical values. This leads on to purchasing power parity theory, which suggests that changes in exchange rates over time must reflect relative changes in inflation between two countries. If purchasing power parity holds true, the expected spot rate (Sf) can be forecast from the current spot rate (S0) by multiplying by the ratio of expected inflation rates ((1 + if)/ (1 + iUK)) in the two counties being considered. In formula form: Sf = S0 (1 + if)/ (1 + iUK).

This relationship has been found to hold in the longer-term rather than the shorter-term and so tends to be used for forecasting exchange rates several years in the future, rather than for periods of less than one year. For shorter periods, forward rates can be calculated using interest rate parity theory, which suggests that changes in exchange rates reflect differences between interest rates between countries.

(c) **Forward market evaluation**

Net receipt in 1 month = 240,000 – 140,000 = $100,000

Nedwen Co needs to sell dollars at an exchange rate of 1.7829 + 0.003 = $1.7832 per £

Sterling value of net receipt = 100,000/1.7832 = $56,079

Receipt in 3 months = $300,000

Nedwen Co needs to sell dollars at an exchange rate of 1.7846 + 0.004 = $1.7850 per £

Sterling value of receipt in 3 months = 300,000/1.7850 = $168,067

(d) **Evaluation of money-market hedge**

Expected receipt after 3 months = $300,000

Dollar interest rate over three months = 5.4/4 = 1.35%

Dollars to borrow now to have $300,000 liability after 3 months = 300,000/1.0135 = $296,004

Spot rate for selling dollars = 1.7820 + 0.0002 = $1.7822 per £

Sterling deposit from borrowed dollars at spot = 296,004/1.7822 = $166,089

Sterling interest rate over three months = 4.6/ 4 = 1.15%

Value in 3 months of sterling deposit = 166,089 × 1.0115 = $167,999

The forward market is marginally preferable to the money market hedge for the dollar receipt expected after 3 months.

(e) A currency futures contract is a standardised contract for the buying or selling of a specified quantity of foreign currency. It is traded on a futures exchange and settlement takes place in three-monthly cycles ending in March, June, September and December, i.e. a company can buy or sell September futures, December futures and so on. The price of a currency futures contract is the exchange rate for the currencies specified in the contract.

When a currency futures contract is bought or sold, the buyer or seller is required to deposit a sum of money with the exchange, called initial margin. If losses are incurred as exchange rates and hence the prices of currency futures contracts change, the buyer or seller may be called on to deposit additional funds (variation margin) with the exchange. Equally, profits are credited to the margin account on a daily basis as the contract is 'marked to market'.

Most currency futures contracts are closed out before their settlement dates by undertaking the opposite transaction to the initial futures transaction, i.e. if buying currency futures was the initial transaction, it is closed out by selling currency futures. A gain made on the futures transactions will offset a loss made on the currency markets and vice versa.

Nedwen Co expects to receive $300,000 in three months' time and so is concerned that sterling may appreciate (strengthen) against the dollar, since this would result in a lower sterling receipt. The company can hedge the receipt by selling sterling futures contracts and since it is 1 April, would sell June futures contracts. In June, Nedwen Co would buy the same number of futures it sold in April and sell the $300,000 it received on the currency market.

ACCA marking scheme		
		Marks
(a)	Transaction risk	2 marks
	Translation risk	2 marks
	Economic risk	2 marks
		6
(b)	Discussion of purchasing power parity	4–5 marks
	Discussion of interest rate parity	1–2 marks
	Maximum	6
(c)	Netting	1 mark
	Sterling value of 3-month receipt	1 mark
	Sterling value of 1-year receipt	1 mark
		3
(d)	Evaluation of money market hedge	4 marks
	Comment	1 mark
		5
(e)	Definition of currency futures contract	1–2 marks
	Initial margin and variation margin	1–2 marks
	Buying and selling of contracts	1–2 marks
	Hedging the three-month receipt	1–2 marks
	Maximum	5
	Total	25

3 ULNAD

(a) **Evaluation of change in credit policy**

Current average collection period = 30 + 10 = 40 days

Current accounts receivable = 6m × 40/365 = $657,534

Average collection period under new policy = (0.3 × 15) + (0.7 × 60) = 46.5 days

New level of credit sales = $6.3 million

Accounts receivable after policy change = 6.3 × 46.5/ 365 = $802,603

Increase in financing cost = (802,603 – 657,534) × 0.07 = $10,155

	$
Increase in financing cost	10,155 ✓
Incremental costs = 6.3m × 0.005 =	31,500 ✓
Cost of discount = 6.3m × 0.015 × 0.3 =	28,350 ✓
Increase in costs	70,005
Contribution from increased sales = 6m × 0.05 × 0.6 =	180,000
Net benefit of policy change	109,995

The proposed policy change will increase the profitability of Ulnad Co

(b)   Determination of spread:

Daily interest rate = 5.11/ 365 = 0.014% per day

Variance of cash flows = 1,000 × 1,000 = $1,000,000 per day

Transaction cost = $18 per transaction

Spread $= 3 \times ((0.75 \times \text{transaction cost} \times \text{variance})/\text{interest rate})^{1/3}$

$= 3 \times ((0.75 \times 18 \times 1,000,000)/0.00014)^{1/3} = 3 \times 4,585.7 = \$13,757$

Lower limit (set by Renpec Co) = $7,500

Upper limit = 7,500 + 13,757 =$21,257

Return point = 7,500 + (13,757/3) = $12,086

The Miller-Orr model takes account of uncertainty in relation to receipts and payment. The cash balance of Renpec Co is allowed to vary between the lower and upper limits calculated by the model. If the lower limit is reached, an amount of cash equal to the difference between the return point and the lower limit is raised by selling short-term investments. If the upper limit is reached an amount of cash equal to the difference between the upper limit and the return point is used to buy short-term investments. The model therefore helps Renpec Co to decrease the risk of running out of cash, while avoiding the loss of profit caused by having unnecessarily high cash balances.

(c)   There are four key areas of accounts receivable management: policy formulation, credit analysis, credit control and collection of amounts due.

Policy formulation

This is concerned with establishing the framework within which management of accounts receivable in an individual company takes place. The elements to be considered include establishing terms of trade, such as period of credit offered and early settlement discounts: deciding whether to charge interest on overdue accounts; determining procedures to be followed when granting credit to new customers; establishing procedures to be followed when accounts become overdue, and so on.

Credit analysis

Assessment of creditworthiness depends on the analysis of information relating to the new customer. This information is often generated by a third party and includes bank references, trade references and credit reference agency reports. The depth of credit analysis depends on the amount of credit being granted, as well as the possibility of repeat business.

Credit control

Once credit has been granted, it is important to review outstanding accounts on a regular basis so overdue accounts can be identified. This can be done, for example, by an aged receivables analysis. It is also important to ensure that administrative procedures are timely and robust, for example sending out invoices and statements of account, communicating with customers by telephone or e-mail, and maintaining account records.

Collection of amounts due

Ideally, all customers will settle within the agreed terms of trade. If this does not happen, a company needs to have in place agreed procedures for dealing with overdue accounts. These could cover logged telephone calls, personal visits, charging interest on outstanding amounts, refusing to grant further credit and, as a last resort, legal action. With any action, potential benefit should always exceed expected cost.

(d) When considering how working capital is financed, it is useful to divide assets into non-current assets, permanent current assets and fluctuating current assets. Permanent current assets represent the core level of working capital investment needed to support a given level of sales. As sales increase, this core level of working capital also increases. Fluctuating current assets represent the changes in working capital that arise in the normal course of business operations, for example when some accounts receivable are settled later than expected, or when inventory moves more slowly than planned.

The matching principle suggests that long-term finance should be used for long-term assets. Under a matching working capital funding policy, therefore, long-term finance is used for both permanent current assets and non-current assets. Short-term finance is used to cover the short-term changes in current assets represented by fluctuating current assets.

Long-term debt has a higher cost than short-term debt in normal circumstances, for example because lenders require higher compensation for lending for longer periods, or because the risk of default increases with longer lending periods. However, long-term debt is more secure from a company point of view than short-term debt since, provided interest payments are made when due and the requirements of restrictive covenants are met, terms are fixed to maturity. Short-term debt is riskier than long-term debt because, for example, an overdraft is repayable on demand and short-term debt may be renewed on less favourable terms.

A conservative working capital funding policy will use a higher proportion of long-term finance than a matching policy, thereby financing some of the fluctuating current assets from a long-term source. This will be less risky and less profitable than a matching policy, and will give rise to occasional short-term cash surpluses.

An aggressive working capital funding policy will use a lower proportion of long-term finance than a matching policy, financing some of the permanent current assets from a short-term source such as an overdraft. This will be more risky and more profitable than a matching policy.

Other factors that influence a working capital funding policy include management attitudes to risk, previous funding decisions, and organisation size. Management attitudes to risk will determine whether there is a preference for a conservative, an aggressive or a matching approach. Previous funding decisions will determine the current position being considered in policy formulation. The size of the organisation will influence its ability to access different sources of finance. A small company, for example, may be forced to adopt an aggressive working capital funding policy because it is unable to raise additional long-term finance, whether equity of debt.

ACCA marking scheme		Marks
(a) Increase in financing cost	2 marks	
Incremental costs	1 mark	
Cost of discount	1 mark	
Contribution from increased sales	1 mark	
Conclusion	1 mark	
		6
(b) Calculation of spread	2 marks	
Calculation of upper limit	1 mark	
Calculation of return point	1 mark	
Explanation of findings	2 marks	
		6
(c) Policy formulation	1–2 marks	
Credit analysis	1–2 marks	
Credit control	1–2 marks	
Collection of amounts due	1–2 marks	
Maximum		6
(d) Analysis of assets	1–2 marks	
Short-term and long-term debt	2–3 marks	
Discussion of policies	2–3 marks	
Other factors	1–2 marks	
Maximum		7
Total		25

4   TRECOR

(a)   Calculation of NPV

Nominal discount rate using Fisher effect: $1.057 \times 1.05 = 1.1098$ i.e. 11%

	1	2	3	4	5
	$000	$000	$000	$000	$000
Sales revenue(W1)	433	509	656	338	
Variable cost (W2)	284	338	439	228	
Contribution	149	171	217	110	
Fixed production overheads	27	28	30	32	
Net cash flow	122	143	187	78	
Tax		(37)	(43)	(56)	(23)
CA tax benefits (W3)		19	14	11	30
After-tax cash flow	122	125	158	33	7
Disposal				5	
After-tax cash flow	122	125	158	38	7
Discount factors	0.901	0.812	0.731	0.659	0.593
Present values	110	102	115	25	4

	$
PV of benefits	356,000
Investment	250,000
NPV	106,000

Since the NPV is positive, the purchase of the machine is acceptable on financial grounds.

Workings

(W1)

Year	1	2	3	4
Demand (units)	35,000	40,000	50,000	25,000
Selling price ($/unit)	12.36	12.73	13.11	13.51
Sales revenue ($/year)	432,600	509,200	655,500	337,750

(W2)

Year	1	2	3	4
Demand (units)	35,000	40,000	50,000	25,000
Variable cost ($/unit)	8.11	8.44	8.77	9.12
Variable cost ($/year)	283,850	337,600	438,500	228,000

(W3)

Year	Capital allowances		Tax benefits	
1	250,000 x 0.25 =	62,500	62,500 x 0.3 =	18,750
2	62,500 x 0.75 =	46,875	46,875 x 0.3 =	14,063
3	46,875 x 0.75 =	35,156	25,156 x 0.3 =	10,547
4	By difference	100,469	100,469 x 0.3 =	30,141
	250,000 – 5.000 =	245,000		73,501

(b)   Calculation of before-tax return on capital employed

Total net before-tax cash flow = 122 + 143 + 187 + 78 = $530,000

Total depreciation = 250,000 – 5,000 = $245,000

Average annual accounting profit = (530 – 245)/ 4 = $71,250

Average investment = (250,000 + 5,000)/ 2 = $127,500

Return on capital employed = $100 \times 71,250/ 127,500 = 56\%$

Given the target return on capital employed of Trecor Co is 20% and the ROCE of the investment is 56%, the purchase of the machine is recommended.

(c)   One of the strengths of internal rate of return (IRR) as a method of appraising capital investments is that it is a discounted cash flow (DCF) method and so takes account of the time value of money. It also considers cash flows over the whole of the project life and is sensitive to both the amount and the timing of cash flows. It is preferred by some as it offers a relative measure of the value of a proposed investment, i.e. the method calculates a percentage that can be compared with the company's cost of capital, and with economic variables such as inflation rates and interest rates.

IRR has several weaknesses as a method of appraising capital investments. Since it is a relative measurement of investment worth, it does not measure the absolute increase in company value (and therefore shareholder wealth), which can be found using the net present value (NPV) method. A further problem arises when evaluating non-conventional projects (where cash flows change from positive to negative during the life of the project). IRR may offer as many IRR values as there are changes in the value of cash flows, giving rise to evaluation difficulties. There is a potential conflict between IRR and NPV in the evaluation of mutually exclusive projects, where the two methods can offer conflicting advice as which of two projects is preferable. Where there is conflict, NPV always offers the correct investment advice: IRR does not, although the advice offered can be amended by considering the IRR of the incremental project. There are therefore a number of reasons why IRR can be seen as an inferior investment appraisal method compared to its DCF alternative, NPV.

ACCA marking scheme			
			Marks
(a)	Discount rate		1 mark
	Inflated sales revenue		2 marks
	Inflated variable cost		1 mark
	Inflated fixed production overheads		1 mark
	Taxation		2 marks
	Capital allowance tax benefits		3 marks
	Discount factors		1 mark
	Net present value		1 mark
	Comment		1 mark
			13
(b)	Calculation of average annual accounting profit		2 marks
	Calculation of average investment		2 marks
	Calculation of return on capital employed		1 mark
			5
(c)	Strengths of IRR		2–3 marks
	Weaknesses of IRR		5–6 marks
	Maximum		7
	Total		25